CIVIL WAR
FIELD
ARTILLERY

CIVIL WAR FIELD ARTILLERY

PROMISE AND PERFORMANCE
ON THE BATTLEFIELD

EARL J. HESS

LOUISIANA STATE UNIVERSITY PRESS

BATON ROUGE

Published by Louisiana State University Press
lsupress.org

Manufactured in the United States of America
First printing

Designer: Mandy McDonald Scallan
Typeface: Sentnel
Printer and binder: Sherdian Books, Inc.

Jacket illustration: *Reconnaissance by Bufords Cavalry towards the
Rapidan River,* September 1863, by Alfred R. Waud. Prints and Photographs Division, Library of Congress.

Library of Congress Cataloging-in-Publication Data are available at
the Library of Congress.
ISBN 978-0-8071-7800-3 (cloth) | ISBN 978-0-8071-7866-9 (epub) |
ISBN 978-0-8071-7867-6 (pdf)

For Julie and Pratibha,
as always

CONTENTS

TABLES

PREFACE

The Civil War witnessed the creation of the largest, most powerful force of field artillery yet to appear in the Western Hemisphere. Combining the Union and Confederate artillery arms, the total force amounted to 752 batteries, manned by about 209,000 men, and powered by at least 260,000 horses. This was a force comparable to the great wars seen in Europe during the previous sixty years. Like all other elements of Civil War armies, the artillery arm was largely improvised, consisted of amateur soldiers, and learned what it needed to know by studying tactical manuals derived from European precedents and through hard experience in the field. Artillerists, their weapons, and their animals played important roles on campaign and in battle, supporting friendly infantry and cavalry.

Despite the size and significance of field artillery in the Civil War, sound studies of the topic are relatively few in number, especially when compared with the history of infantry and cavalry forces in the war. This book seeks to fill in much of that historiographical omission. It is a general history of field artillery in the Civil War, but with a special emphasis on gauging its effectiveness in the field. This study is based on thorough research in battle reports, unit histories, published personal accounts, and archival collections. The battle reports filed by artillery officers are especially helpful because they tended to include statistics on the number of rounds fired, details on the type of projectiles used, and the observed effect of fire. Service records of artillery officers also contain a great deal of useful information in the form of requisitions, invoices, and receipts for artillery equipment and supplies.

How effective was artillery? Why did it achieve its particular level of effectiveness and why did it not become even more effective are relevant questions. This study therefore surveys a number of subtopics, including the hardware (guns, accoutrements, projectiles, and fuzes), the process of firing, the organizational structure and the management of artillery in the field, the experience of soldiering, and the story of artillery horses. Actual combat, the ultimate test of field artillery, is covered in the defensive role of the guns as well as their offensive role. How Civil War field artillery fits into the larger trends of Western military history in Europe and North America, both before 1861 and after 1865, rounds out our understanding of its history.

Serving in the most highly professional, technical arm, field artillerists strove for effectiveness more overtly and successfully than their colleagues in the infantry or cavalry. But, as the reader will gather from the following chapters, they failed to achieve the highest levels of efficiency. Field artillery did not come to dominate the battlefield in any clear or consistent way largely due to technical limitations, especially among the fuzes that ignited long-distance explosive ordnance. The projectiles themselves were of limited power and splintering capacity, indirect firing (aiming at an unseen target) was at best primitive, and working the guns was a laborious process in the era before recoilless mechanisms. Although the Civil War saw the first large-scale use of rifled artillery in world history, the new weapon failed to live up to expectations. Northern and southern artillerists wisely sought a mixed armament of about half smoothbores and half rifles to combine the long-distance capacities of the latter with the short-distance effectiveness of the former.

The Civil War represented, in short, a very small step forward in the global development of field artillery. Only twenty years later, that development accelerated rapidly with the introduction of many new technologies that would revolutionize field artillery. That era came too late for the fervent artillerists of the 1860s, who wanted to do more to support their comrades in the other two arms.

There is a natural urge on the part of historians and students to see the Civil War as a major episode in world history, as the dawn of modern ways of war. But all the evidence works against that view of the conflict. It was largely an old-fashioned war, with some exceptions to be sure, and at best can be seen as one step in a long and complicated transition toward war as practiced in the twentieth century.

DEFINING TERMS

The Civil War era saw some confusion in using the terms associated with artillery due to the similarity of those terms and what they described. Most people used the phrases "light artillery" and "field artillery" interchangeably to refer to any batteries operating with infantry or cavalry in the field. This was in distinction to "heavy" or "foot" artillery, which served guns mounted in permanent fortifications. There appears to have been little need to worry about whether "light" or "field" should be the term associated with guns that cooperated with the other two arms, but Henry J. Hunt, when he served as an aide-de-camp to George B. McClellan early in the war, thought the "proper name" for it was field artillery.[1]

More confusing than the difference between "light" and "field" was the difference between "mounted" and "horse" artillery. The term "mounted artillery" referred to batteries cooperating with the infantry wherein the men walked most of the time or, in cases of need, rode on the carriages for short distances. In other words, the cannoneers were not mounted, but horses did pull the carriages. In contrast, the term "horse artillery" referred to batteries cooperating with the cavalry because every man in those units was issued a horse to ride.[2]

According to William E. Birkhimer, a post–Civil War artillery officer and historian of the American artillery arm, this nagging confusion of terms began in 1838, when the War Department created a horse artillery unit to accompany cavalry regiments. The department failed to come up with a better term for it than one that mimicked the already commonly used "mounted artillery," which itself did not accurately reflect the reality of its deployment. The term "mounted artillery" really referred to the fact that horses rather than oxen pulled the carriages. Drivers did not ride the oxen, which had previously been used to draw the guns. Thus, when horses came into vogue drivers rode them, and that is the rationale for calling a unit a mounted battery. The term "horse artillery" referred to all the men being horsed so the battery could keep up with fast-moving cavalry units. Anyone reading the primary literature will find themselves scratching their head now and then over the use of these somewhat confusing terms.[3]

Yet another nagging issue relates to how to spell the term used for the device that ignited an explosive projectile. It has been spelled "fuze" as well as "fuse" over the centuries. Historian Oliver F. G. Hogg has made a convincing argument that the former word is best applied to artillery. Fuze derives from the word "fuzee," a tube filled with combustibles. Fuse, which derives from "fusus," to melt, is better applied to electrical devices. All the contemporary manuals and handbooks of the Civil War era spelled it "fuze," while officers and enlisted men of that era consistently spelled it "fuse." Modern historians mostly follow the lead of the officers and men, although at least one of them more correctly spells it "fuze." I have followed Hogg's lead and also spell it as did the manuals and handbooks.[4]

The last confusing term to be discussed is range. *Instruction for Field Artillery,* the army's official artillery manual, noted that the term "range" was "commonly" used to define the distance between the piece and its target. Joseph Roberts, author of an artillery handbook, also used range in that way, calling it the direction of pointing. But he also used the term "distance" to denote the elevation necessary to attain that distance firing. But the term "range" technically refers to lateral aiming rather than to distance. In other words, traversing the tube of the piece to right or left was establishing the "range" of fire rather than the "distance" of fire. Throughout this book, I will use the term "distance" to refer to how far the target was located from the cannon and "range" to refer to lateral aiming.[5]

PURPOSE OF ARTILLERY

While some terms concerning field artillery are confusing, the purpose of the big guns was clear. Whether attached to infantry or cavalry, field artillery acted in concert with the other arms of the service, supporting them in defensive or offensive action on the battlefield. They were "auxiliaries," as the artillery manual put it. The purpose of field artillery was "to act upon the field of battle; to break an enemy's line or prevent him from forming; to crush his masses; to dismount his batteries; to follow and support in a pursuit, and to cover and protect a retreat."[6]

The artillery manual strongly stated a point that many officers took as their own. "The *effect* of field artillery is generally in proportion to the *concentration of its fire.* It has therefore for its object, not to strike down a few isolated men, and here and there to dismount a gun, but by a combined and concentrated fire to destroy an enemy's cover; to break up his squares and columns; to open his ranks; to arrest his attacks, and to support those which may be directed against him."[7]

To accomplish these tasks, as Hunt, longtime chief of artillery in the Army of the Potomac, warned, the artillery officer had to make a "special study" to understand "exactly the power of his guns." The men serving those guns had "to produce the best results in the shortest time" under fire. A combination of study and experience, in Hunt's estimation, was the key to this learning curve.[8]

Hunt expressed a point strongly felt by most artillery officers and even a good proportion of the enlisted men. It related to the image of themselves as serving in a technical arm of the army, consisting of crew-served weapons.

How those weapons and their attendant devices worked was the most fundamental lesson they had to learn. Then they had to apply that knowledge to a variety of factors on the battlefield in order to achieve the purpose set out for them in the manual. Infantry and cavalry power was based on the individual soldier who operated an individual weapon and, in the case of cavalry, a horse. Each foot soldier and cavalryman had to coordinate his actions with his neighbors in line or column; such cooperation was essential to a certain degree within the infantry and cavalry arms, but it was much more important in the artillery. The seven men who loaded and fired a piece had to work as a team to keep it operating at peak efficiency.

As members of a support arm, artillerists were encouraged to fire their piece to the last possible moment in the face of a threatening attack or to stand and take their punishment while trying to silence an opposing battery. By modern standards, relatively few artillery pieces were allotted to each infantry or cavalry unit; they were expensive and precious items on the military inventory, and artillerists took much greater care of them on and off the battlefield than most soldiers cared for their individual weapons. The subculture of the artillery within the more general military culture of mid-nineteenth-century America was unique.

THE HISTORIANS

The historical literature on Civil War field artillery is relatively sparse compared to that on infantry and cavalry, and it tends to be weighted toward books on hardware. Studies of the weapons and their accoutrements, conducted by nonacademic historians, in some ways constitute the foundation of artillery literature. These ordnance studies are mostly well done, constructed by ardent students who know how to conduct research and to analyze the results. Among the better such studies are James C. Hazlett, Edwin Olmstead, and M. Hume Parks, *Field Artillery Weapons of the Civil War* (revised edition, 2004); W. Reid McKee and M. E. Mason Jr., *Civil War Projectiles: Small Arms and Field Artillery* (1971); Dean S. Thomas, *Cannons: An Introduction to Civil War Artillery* (1985); Jack W. Melton and Lawrence E. Pawl, *Guide to Civil War Artillery Projectiles* (1996); and Jack Coggins, *Arms and Equipment of the Civil War* (1962). Edward B. McCaul Jr., *The Mechanical Fuze and the Advance of Artillery in the Civil War* (2010), focuses on the fuzes used in long-distance explosive ordnance, as does Charles H. Jones, *Artillery Fuses of the Civil War* (2001).

The hardware studies are just that; there tends to be little if any discussion of the actual use of these weapons in the field, and thus the operational aspect is missing. That is an important point because understanding how artillery worked in actual practice goes directly to the topic of effectiveness. But one must start with an understanding of the technical aspects, and these hardware books do that well.

There are a handful of artillery unit histories put together by modern historians, but the number pales in comparison with modern unit histories of infantry and cavalry regiments. Civil War artillery unit studies include Nathaniel Cheairs Hughes Jr., *The Pride of the Confederate Artillery: The Washington Artillery in the Army of Tennessee* (1997); Robert K. Krick, *Parker's Virginia Battery, C.S.A.* (1989); John D. Perkins, *Daniel's Battery: The 9th Texas Field Battery* (1998); Lawrence R. Laboda, *From Selma to Appomattox: The History of the Jeff Davis Artillery* (1996); and Robert Grandchamp, *The Boys of Adams' Battery G: The Civil War through the Eyes of a Union Light Artillery Unit* (2009).

The number of histories covering the story of artillery on the level of the field army is even smaller. Jennings Cropper Wise began this limited trend with *The Long Arm of Lee, or, The History of the Artillery of the Army of Northern Virginia* (two volumes, 1915). L. Van Loan Naisawald continued it with *Grape and Canister: The Story of the Field Artillery of the Army of the Potomac, 1861–1865* (1960). Larry J. Daniel's *Cannoneers in Gray: The Field Artillery of the Army of Tennessee* (1984) is the best of the lot and the only one covering a field army in the western theater.

Very few books deal with artillery in a particular battle. Among them, Curt Johnson and Richard C. Anderson Jr., *Artillery Hell: The Employment of Artillery at Antietam* (1995), covers the major engagement of the Maryland Campaign. David Shultz, *"Double Canister at Ten Yards": The Federal Artillery and the Repulse of Pickett's Charge* (1995), deals with one day's action by one side in the Battle of Gettysburg.

What is truly missing in the artillery literature is a general history of the arm during the Civil War. No one has yet attempted it. For that matter, there are few general studies of artillery in any other wars besides the Civil War. Stephen Bull's *"The Furie of the Ordnance": Artillery in the English Civil Wars* (2008) is a shining exception to the rule when it comes to the global history of artillery. For the American scene, Justin G. Prince's recently published

Million-Dollar Barrage: American Field Artillery in the Great War (2021) fills an important need, with detail and analysis of the subject.

There are several studies of artillery history in general, covering nearly if not entirely the full scope of its existence from the fifteenth century to the present. Among them are Boyd L. Dastrup, *The Field Artillery: History and Sourcebook* (1994); Bruce I. Gudmundsson, *On Artillery* (1993); O. F. G. Hogg, *Artillery: Its Origin, Heyday, and Decline* (1970); J. B. A. Bailey, *Field Artillery and Firepower* (2004); and H. C. B. Rogers, *A History of Artillery* (1975). To a greater or lesser extent, these general histories not only cover the technical aspects of artillery history but also the operational aspects. They tend to blend studies of hardware with examinations of how the weapons were used over time to produce a balance that allows the historian to understand change.

Paddy Griffith, in *Battle Tactics of the Civil War* (1989), focused on evaluation of not only artillery but also infantry and cavalry in the internecine conflict, much as he has done for other wars in Western history. While I do not necessarily agree with all of his conclusions, it is important to think outside of the box, as Griffith does so well, and ponder new perspectives rather than blindly accept prior historical interpretations. Bull's study of artillery in the English Civil War also strives to offer fresh conclusions based on deep research. It admirably sets the story within the larger context of what was happening in artillery worldwide before the onset of that conflict and what took place after it ended as well.

DISPERSAL VERSUS CONCENTRATION

When historians evaluate Civil War field artillery, they tend to focus on three topics. First, they agree with Civil War artillery officers that management of the guns was faulty. During the early part of the war, 1861 to late 1862, northern and southern armies dispersed batteries by attaching them to infantry units. Typically, one battery was assigned to one brigade, although a reserve often was held back by higher authorities. These assigned batteries fell under the administrative control of the infantry brigade commander, whose staff was responsible for their daily supply. This brigade leader also held command authority over the battery in combat. Artillery officers complained about this arrangement, and historians support them; both groups of critics often exaggerated the dire effect of this management structure. Historians especially argue that this arrangement inhibited the ability to mass the guns for saturating a given target on the battlefield in the way that Napoleon had sometimes done in his wars half a century before.[9]

To some extent, I agree with this criticism but see it in a very different light. After looking through the numerous documents concerning this issue, it becomes clear that it is far more complicated than previous historians have guessed. The worst consequence of the dispersal system was not in command and control on the battlefield but in day-to-day supply. The quartermaster, commissary, and ordnance officers on the brigade commander's staff simply did not do a good job of providing for the attached battery, and its level of effectiveness consequently suffered.

A careful search of Civil War reports and personal accounts reveals a wide range of answers to the question, did infantry officers know how to manage artillery on the battlefield? Some of them certainly failed in this important task, having no idea where to place the battery or when it was advantageous for it to open fire. The infantry officers who were ignorant and stubborn caused the most trouble for the battery commander, sometimes leading to serious losses among the gunners for no purpose. Those officers who were ignorant and admitted it, however, generally allowed the battery commander to do as he pleased. In other words, they gave the artillerist carte blanche to work his guns on his own judgment, which was very advantageous for the battery commander. Then there was a class of infantry officers who fully understood how to manage artillery and did an excellent job of it.

There is another important way to look at this issue. The most salient examples of gathering guns to pound an enemy target with effect are the Confederate concentration on the first day at Shiloh, the Union concentration at Malvern Hill, and the Federal concentration on the second day at Stones River. All three instances took place during the period of dispersal in the first half of the war. Thus, it should be obvious that the dispersal system did not prevent concentration. It was a flexible system and, as long as higher-ranking infantry officers on the division, corps, and army level supported an ad hoc concentration, it could easily happen.

Despite these points, historians have strongly criticized the dispersal system of the early war months based almost entirely on the idea that it inhibited concentration in battle. They have not picked up on the problems it caused in terms of day-to-day supply. These historians just as strongly praise the consolidated system that generally replaced dispersal by 1863. The idea of taking batteries away from infantry brigades and grouping them into larger units more firmly under the control of artillery officers was initiated in the Army of the Potomac early in 1862, but resistance to it meant the proposal was not put into practice until the next year. Meanwhile, the same idea cropped up among artillery officers in the Army of Northern Virginia. Here it met no opposition and was put into effect very soon after its initiation in late 1862 and early 1863. In the Army of the Potomac, these larger units were called artillery brigades, with one for each corps. In the Army of Northern Virginia, they were called artillery battalions. The concept spread slowly and uncertainly to Union and Confederate armies in the West in 1863 and 1864.

Historians have praised this development as an improvement in artillery management, and to a degree it was. The most important area of improvement was in supply. The artillery officer in charge of the brigade/battalion was fully responsible for the supply and inspection of his batteries. He knew what they needed and whether they met standards of readiness far better than the staff of the infantry brigade commander.

But historians have often overlooked or shortchanged a very important point: the new artillery brigade/battalion commander had no command authority over his guns in combat. When the shooting started, infantry officers still exercised command and control over how the guns were used. This resulted because infantry officers jealously guarded their right to be in charge of all resources on the battlefield, and that was not an unreasonable point. In other words, the new consolidated system failed to enhance concentration of artillery power on the battlefield. In fact, historians rarely point to any large concentration of guns taking place during this phase of the war except perhaps on the third day at Gettysburg. But it remains true that concentration of guns took place far less often during the consolidation phase of the late war than during the dispersal phase of the early war.

THE RIFLE MUSKET

The second issue often discussed by historians has been the effect of the widespread use of a rifled small arm by Civil War infantry forces. The standard interpretation has been that it revolutionized combat because of its capability for long-distance firing, about 500 yards compared to the smoothbore's 100 yards. The assumption had been that this increased distance made the battlefield far more deadly, leading to higher losses, indecisive battles, and stalemate on the tactical level. The impact of the rifle musket on artillery was to render the big guns ineffective while confronting infantry. No longer could artillery be moved close to the enemy to soften up targets for friendly troops to attack. In the standard interpretation, Civil War battlefields became slaughter pens, and field guns had no opportunity to be effective.

More recent studies have rejected this standard interpretation and replaced it with a new view of the rifle musket. The evidence is overwhelming that officers and men alike did not use the weapon for long-distance firing. They much preferred to open fire at shorter distances consistent with the capability of the previously used smoothbore musket. The most effective firing took place within 50 yards, while long-distance firing beyond 100 yards was comparatively rare in the conflict. A study of casualty rates proves that eighteenth-century battles fought with smoothbore muskets were just as bloody as any that took place during the Civil War.

It cannot be said that the rifle musket negated the ability of field artillery to perform on the battlefields of the Civil War. There are examples of batteries planting themselves close to enemy infantry and firing away without losing too many men to make the tactic prohibitive. For that matter, some historians have tended to overemphasize Napoleon's use of artillery on the battlefield to prepare the way for infantry attacks, while others have pointed out that even the great French general only rarely could manage to concentrate and use a large assortment of guns to soften up an infantry target. In another bit of irony, the same historians who bemoan the use of the rifle musket as negating the ability of fieldpieces to soften up targets will also praise the effectiveness of the artillery concentrations at Shiloh and Stones River as demonstrating what artillery could do to support tactical offensives if only the guns could be gathered together. The majority of defending infantrymen at those battles used rifle muskets.[10]

I strongly argue that it is important to get away from a monocausal approach to something as complex as a Civil War battle. No matter how important or irrelevant the rifle musket may have been, it is unconvincing to assume that just one factor determined which side of any given encounter would win the struggle. Each battle contained within itself a host of factors that influenced in small or large ways the outcome of the engagement, and the historian is well advised to be open to all of them. Whether we call this contingency or look upon it as some long-range factors combined with immediate influences, it is wise to avoid the trap of looking for simplistic answers to complicated questions.

RIFLED ARTILLERY

The third topic historians of Civil War field artillery discuss is the performance of rifled pieces. The war represented the first large-scale deployment of rifled fieldpieces in global history, even though it receives scant attention for that distinction among scholars who study European or world developments in artillery history. But American military historians who study the Civil War always pay attention to it. Their conclusions range widely across the spectrum: some believe rifled pieces were effective, while others downplay their influence.[11]

My views of rifled artillery are in the middle of that spectrum. Long-distance artillery fire tended to be ineffective because of technical problems associated with the fuzes that ignited projectiles, lack of effective indirect-fire methods, and the relatively low level of bursting power and splintering capacity of long-distance explosive ordnance. Civil War artillerists were well aware of these limitations. They deliberately crafted an arsenal for themselves that mixed smoothbores with rifles. While starting the conflict with about a dozen different types and sizes, by 1863 both sides had winnowed that arsenal down to three favored pieces—the smoothbore 12-pounder Napoleon, the 3-Inch Ordnance Rifle, and the 10-pounder Parrott rifle. The Napoleon constituted at least half the arsenal, while the two rifles together made up the other half. In this way artillerists could take advantage of whatever long-distance fire they could get out of the rifles and rely on the smoothbores for short-distance firing.

Moreover, a careful study of the type of projectiles fired during the course of the Civil War indicates that the volume of long-distance explosive ordnance steadily decreased during the conflict and the level of solid shot increased. This was because officers were tired of dealing with bad fuzes that often failed to explode their long-distance ordnance properly. They preferred simply to use solid shot, even deliberately failing to put fuzes into explosive projectiles so they could fire them as if they were solid shot. This hardly represents an endorsement of long-distance firing with rifled pieces.

The Civil War certainly did not witness a rifle revolution in terms of field artillery, nor did it witness a significant advance in long-distance artillery fire, even though there were isolated cases of good artillerists hitting targets at very long distances. If we take World War I as a model, then Civil War armies completely failed to field a modern artillery arm. But compared to the past, Civil War armies fielded a more advanced artillery force. The guns tended to be heavier (10-, 12-, and 20-pounders compared to 4- and 6-pounders half a century before) and with capabilities for longer distance firing (although not fully effective at long distance). Even though Civil War pieces represented a significantly heavier weight of projectile, the tubes and carriages were lighter by comparison with previous tubes and carriages, making for a higher level of mobility. It was easier for horse teams of the Civil War to pull ordnance than was the case in previous wars.

But these relatively small advances on the past merely represent improvement of an artillery system that had been evolving for the previous four hundred years. Within twenty years after Appomattox, new developments would sweep away most of that old system and create a new one. Civil War artillery contributed little if anything to that new system while representing one of the most advanced examples of the old system.

It may be enticing to view the Civil War as a revolution in military affairs—many historians have fallen prey to that temptation—but when weighed in the balance, there is very little support for such a view. Just as the introduction of the rifle musket represented at best a minor incremental advance in weapons technology as far as its effect on the battlefield, the introduction of new field-pieces (especially rifled ones) also represented little more than incremental advances.[12] Nearly everything concerning military operations began to change rapidly by the 1880s and continued into the 1930s and beyond. The Civil War was not, however, part of that world.

As always, I am grateful for all the help extended by the staff of libraries and archival institutions represented in the bibliography of this book. I also heartily thank Jack W. Melton Jr. for graciously allowing me to use his fine photographs of artillery projectiles and cannon. For the readers and the staff at Louisiana State University Press, especially Editor in Chief Rand Dotson, my thanks for their important support of this project. And, as always, I am grateful for the love and support of my wife, Pratibha.

CIVIL WAR
FIELD
ARTILLERY

1

. . . .

THE EUROPEAN ARTILLERY HERITAGE

C ivil War artillerists benefited enormously from a four-hundred-year heritage of European doctrine, theory, and practice. They knew little of this history, but the heritage nevertheless decisively framed their work through the inheritance bequeathed by American reliance on French practices, which in turn had been influenced by wider European practices. Nearly everything American artillerists did had been worked out somewhere and at some time in Europe long before the outbreak of the Civil War. The only really new element was the widespread use of rifled pieces and the problems and prospects inherent in their introduction.

THE BEGINNINGS

The Hundred Years' War (1337–1457) and the Italian Wars (1494–1559) saw the crude introduction of artillery into Western warfare. The English are usually credited with using field artillery at the Battle of Crecy in 1346, but their opponents, the French, led the way in developing it into an arm of field service during the latter stages of the Hundred Years War. That development continued into the Italian Wars, which also involved French forces. Observers began to differentiate between heavy siege artillery and field guns by the 1490s, but it would take more than a century of slow progress to develop a truly effective fieldpiece. Venetians created the artillery carriage, a device specifically designed to handle the needs and problems of mounting tubes for effective field service, in the 1400s. The trunnion came into being as the most effective means of adjusting elevation during that century. Historians cite the Battle of Fornovo on July 8, 1495, during the Italian Wars as one of the first engagements in which artillery was effectively used because six guns contributed to a French victory. The French also defeated their Spanish opponents at the

Battle of Ravenna on April 11, 1512, mostly by their artillery arm, marking a turning point in the rise of artillery to prominence on European battlefields.[1]

Artillery manuals appeared by the early 1500s. Armies began to streamline the many types and sizes of artillery pieces available in an effort to create a manageable arsenal. They discarded the early breechloaders as unreliable (exact machine tooling was needed to make that concept workable). Most tubes were made of bronze, but cast iron, which was cheaper but more likely to burst, also was used. The gunner's quadrant, consisting of two wooden arms and a quarter circle with a plumb bob hanging from the angle where the two arms joined, aided the gunner in setting elevation and distance.[2]

Projectiles improved dramatically. They started with a dart resembling an arrow and progressed to stone shot by the late 1300s and into the 1600s. A few lead, iron, and bronze round shots appeared as early as the fourteenth century. Scrap iron placed in a can, the original canister, dates to the 1453 siege of Constantinople. The concept of heating a shot to set fire to a structure began in Poland in the late 1500s. The weapons ranged from 10-pounders to 200-pounders (reflecting the weight of the solid shot), but the heavier pieces were impractical as field artillery.[3]

THE SEVENTEENTH CENTURY

King Gustavus Adolphus of Sweden took a major step toward developing field artillery during the Thirty Years' War (1618–48) when he fostered the improvement of a gun that was light enough to be readily transported and handled in battle. He used soldiers rather than civilian experts to fire it. The king deployed two 4-pounders as regimental guns (assigned to regiments as infantry support) and 9-pounders and 12-pounders grouped as artillery concentrations. The Swedish army also used 24-pounders as siege artillery and developed cartridge bags made of flannel to facilitate loading.[4]

According to historian Stephen Bull, artillery played "an important and integral part of both armies" during the English Civil War (1642–46). Parliamentarian forces deployed 110 guns, probably one for every thirty yards of their line, at the Battle of Marston Moor on July 2, 1644, the largest engagement of that conflict. Opposing this array were a mere 23 guns used by the Royalist force; the result was a smashing Parliamentarian victory. Bull has documented artillery-to-infantry ratios for both sides in several other English Civil War engagements. They range from one per 500 infantrymen to one per 850 foot soldiers, much higher ratios than those to be found in the American Civil War. Up to half the firings were delivered at close distance.[5]

While artillery played a larger role in the English Civil War than previous historians had thought, Bull admitted that several factors limited its effectiveness. There was a chronic shortage of ammunition, with typically fifty rounds available per gun. Many design and technical flaws limited gunners' ability to hit targets, and mobility was a severe problem. It was so difficult to manhandle these heavy pieces that commanders sometimes chose to keep them well to the rear rather than risk their capture. There was no possibility of thinking about cannon keeping up with fast-moving cavalry.[6]

Continental armies were making progress in dealing with limitations like these by the time of the English Civil War. By about 1650 an elevating screw and nut became a better way to adjust elevation than raising the butt of the tube with wooden wedges. The Dutch developed the howitzer during the 1690s. Its advantage was a curved trajectory that traced an arc somewhere between the flat trajectory of a gun and the highly arced trajectory of a mortar, allowing it to fire over the heads of friendly troops. Artillery-to-infantry ratios in the wars of Louis XIV during the late 1600s settled in at about one gun per 1,000 men, a ratio considered feasible for centuries to come. French artillerists developed the prolonge, a long rope used by the gun crew in moving the piece by hand. Louis XIV established the first artillery school in 1690 to train professionals in this technical arm. By 1680 someone had come up with the idea of the limber, a two-wheeled vehicle to which the piece could be hooked for easier transportation by horses.[7]

The French army worked at the administrative issues arising from this increasingly important service arm during the 1600s. It reduced the variety of calibers from seventeen to only six, with fourteen ounces being the smallest and 33-pounders the largest. Regimental guns comprised 3- and 4-pounders, but 8-pounders were grouped in the general artillery park. As Louis XIV's campaigns veered toward siege warfare to secure key cities along France's borders, siege artillery became increasingly important in his arsenal, which in many ways acted to limit the further development of field artillery. This is a good illustration of the fact that technological improvements were not the only influences on the development of fieldpieces—institutional and operational factors were just as significant. The French military establishment decided that siege artillery was more important in the many wars of Louis

XIV and tended to support heavy guns with long tubes to serve siege and fortress requirements.[8]

THE EIGHTEENTH CENTURY

Great advances in weapons technology and especially in administration and organization appeared in the artillery arm during the eighteenth century. The concept of boring a tube rather than casting it was developed by Swiss technician Jean Maritz, who worked in France, by 1740. In molding a tube the core tended to shift slightly and cause irregularities. Boring was more precise, safer, and produced less windage (the space between the projectile and the walls of the tube). All of this made for more accurate firing and allowed the walls of the tubes to be thinner.[9]

Methods of igniting the cannon had improved markedly. Beginning in the 1400s, a slow match, made of strands of hemp covered in various materials and burning at the rate of four inches per hour, had generally been used. It was succeeded by the quick match, burning at thirty seconds per yard and made of cotton or worsted material, during the 1600s. A quick match could be inserted into the vent, eliminating the dangers involved in pouring a small amount of loose powder into the vent and then lighting it. The quick match also was called portfire. By 1765, for greater safety, a length of quick match was inserted into a tin tube that was then inserted in the vent. Experiments to substitute another material, such as quill or copper, for the tin then took place.[10]

Cartridge bags had become common by the early 1600s and were widely used in the following century as well. Canvas primarily was used to make them, but flannel and silk also were employed.[11]

By the late 1700s the English had introduced the stock trail, a single piece of wood to replace the twin pieces more commonly used. This lightened the weight of the gun carriage. By then some armies were making the wheels of the limber the same size as those of the carriage, so as to be interchangeable, and placing ammunition chests on the limber for readier access to projectiles.[12]

Throughout the eighteenth century, solid shot was the mainstay projectile of European armies. According to some reports, it constituted 70 percent of the rounds used in battle. Canister, effective up to 400 yards, was the next-most-important projectile. The common shell (a ball filled with powder and fitted with a primitive fuze designed to burst in the air as an antipersonnel weapon) was of third importance. The powder-charge explosion inside the tube lighted the fuze placed in the common shell, the windage being wide enough to allow the flames to pass by and reach it. English lieutenant Henry Shrapnel developed a twist on the common shell by inserting iron pellets along with powder into the projectile's cavity. The pellets continued to move forward in a cone-shaped pattern after detonation. Often called spherical case or case shot, this concept was initially proposed by Shrapnel in 1784 but not adopted by the British until 1804.[13]

Administrative and organizational improvements were just as important as technical advances during the eighteenth century. By 1732 the French imposed order on the many varieties of ordnance. Jean-Florent de Vallière set the French army standard as the 4-pounder, 8-pounder, 12-pounder, 16-pounder, and 24-pounder. This array of sizes provided choices for field commanders. The Austrians settled on the 3-pounder, 6-pounder, and 12-pounder, organizing their field artillery in batteries of four to six pieces each.[14]

Jean-Baptiste Gribeauval became famous in the 1760s for improving the standard set by Jean-Florent de Vallière. His Gribeauval system standardized the size and construction of carriages, limbers, and ammunition chests as well as settled on various types and sizes of pieces. It allocated artillery on the battalion, brigade, and field-army levels for a layered organizational scheme to provide firepower where needed. The Gribeauval system also incorporated the latest in technical improvements, reducing the weight of the tube without sacrificing weight of firepower, enhancing sights to include calibration and graduation features, decreasing windage to create longer-distance firing, and employing soldiers rather than civilians to drive the carriages.[15]

Most European armies began to use the howitzer more frequently by the late eighteenth century, especially during the French Revolutionary Wars (1792–1802). Howitzers constituted one-third of the French artillery arm, mixed in batteries with guns to provide flexibility.[16]

Generally, all European armies believed in assigning artillery to small units to support the infantry. Some allocated pieces to units as small as the battalion, while others preferred to assign them to the brigade or the division. This dispersion of the big guns did not prevent officers from assembling them in large concentrations for a specific mission on the battlefield; the system of command and control was flexible. The overall ratio of guns per infantry was usually one piece for every 1,000 men, but some theorists preferred ratios three times greater. The concept of preparing artillery to keep pace with fast-moving cavalry began to appear by the 1780s in Russia and became more common the next decade. Light tubes and carriages were used, but the most important change was to let the crewmen ride on carriages and limbers or mount them on horses.[17]

Firing the piece became more of a science in the eighteenth century as experiments and tests added data to the knowledge base of the artillerist. The term "point-blank," so often bandied about by students of artillery history, had a technical definition then. When the tube was leveled horizontally, the projectile still rose a bit above the line of sight due to its parabolic trajectory. The point at which it initially rose above that level was called the first point-blank primitive and was just in front of the muzzle. The point at which it descended below that level was called the second point-blank primitive. For the 8-pounder Gribeauval gun with a charge of two and a quarter pounds of powder, the second point-blank primitive was 384 yards from the tube. Any shot at a target that lay between the first and second point-blank primitive was termed "point-blank firing." Any firing at a target that lay beyond the second point-blank primitive was termed direct firing and had to be accomplished by elevating the tube.[18]

Theorists debated the utility of different firing systems, striving to avoid volley, or salvo, firing (when all guns fire at once) because that inevitably caused lulls in the rate of fire. Independent firing would not necessarily create a steady flow of fire, but a middle course, such as ordering every second gun to discharge in turn, would even out the rate. Ricochet fire (aiming so that the projectile bounced off the ground and then into its target) gradually became more common by the late eighteenth century. It was especially effective if the ground was dry and hard. While line-of-sight firing dominated artillery practice during the era, early experiments at indirect fire can be traced to the 1750s.[19]

Doctrinal debate became more heated by the late eighteenth century. The comte de Guibert, in *Essai général de tactique,* published in 1772, provided the fullest discussion of artillery as an element of field tactics in the era. Guibert characterized it as an accessory to infantry operations, arguing it could not stand alone on the battlefield without support from foot soldiers. He advocated concentration of guns and obtaining a crossfire on the target while pushing for heavier pieces to be included in the arsenal along with better training of artillerists. Guibert learned from infantry tactics that moving artillery in column to the battlefield and then deploying from column into line was the preferable maneuver.[20]

Guibert liked oblique fire rather than frontal fire but warned that the guns should not be placed on a high hill. Doing so would create a plunging fire wherein the projectiles dug into the earth instead of ricocheted into their intended targets. The guns should not be placed either in front of or behind friendly infantry, for that allowed the enemy two targets in line instead of one. Infantry instead should be placed to the right and left of the batteries. The primary target of artillery, in Guibert's view, was the enemy infantry formation, not enemy artillery. He advocated the use of solid shot against infantry and liked the idea of mounting gun crews so they could accompany cavalry units in the field.[21] Guibert's views became widely accepted because they reflected common thought in many countries. When the chevalier Jean du Teil wrote *De l'usage de l'artillerie nouvelle dans la guerre de campagne* (*On the Use of the New Artillery*) in 1778, he generally supported Guibert's main points.[22]

Historian Christopher Duffy believed the increasing professionalization of the artillery arm led to a marked difference in the way the Seven Years' War (1756–63) was conducted a century before the American Civil War. The enlarged presence and rise in effectiveness of the big guns was noticeable. Standardization of training, streamlining of calibers and types of pieces, and improving administration and organization all were having their effect in bringing the artillery into prominence. The guns were more often used to damage enemy infantry formations than to counter the fire of enemy artillery. They continued to be assigned to smaller infantry units to provide fire support for friendly troops. During the era of the French Revolutionary Wars, at least half of a field army's guns were arrayed along the line of battle in this way, as much to bolster the sometimes shaky moral of volunteer troops as to provide protection against attacking infantry.[23]

THE NAPOLEONIC ERA

Building on the long series of developments before him, Napoleon brought the artillery arm to an unprecedented height during his many wars with a variety of European opponents. As an artillerist in the pre-Revolution French army, Napoleon employed the guns with a higher degree of concentration than anyone before him, grouping large temporary batteries for bombarding enemy positions to prepare the way for a massive assault. No one before or since could get so much out of his artillery arm as the French dictator.

Napoleon preferred to have a ratio of one piece for every 1,000 infantrymen, but in some campaigns he amassed a much higher ratio. At Austerlitz on December 2, 1805, he fielded 139 pieces to support an infantry force of 75,000 men. His allied opponents in that engagement fielded a higher ratio, 278 guns for a force of 87,000 men. French batteries usually consisted of six but sometimes as many as eight pieces and generally contained a mix of guns and howitzers. The smaller pieces, 3-pounders and 4-pounders, were becoming less popular as heavier pieces increasingly made their appearance. Six-pounders, 8-pounders, and 9-pounders were the most common, with 12-pounders representing the higher end of the spectrum and 24-pounders relatively rare. The Duke of Wellington at the Battle of Salamanca on July 22, 1812, had thirty 6-pounders, fifteen 9-pounders, nine 5.5-inch howitzers, and six 24-pounder howitzers, along with two 4-pounders that accompanied his Spanish cavalry. His French opponent, Auguste Frédérick de Marmont, had one 3-pounder, thirty-six 4-pounders, twenty-one 8-pounders, seven 12-pounders, and thirteen howitzers of unreported weight.[24]

Sighting devices had advanced by the Napoleonic era compared to the old gunner's quadrant. A tangent arrangement with a movable bar was fixed at the breech, with distances marked along the frame. The bar could be moved to the desired distance, then the fixed sight at the muzzle of the tube had to be aligned with it by using the elevating screw. Artillery of the era often had problems with enlargement of the vent that communicated between the rear of the bore and the outside. Escaping gas burned away the metal and enlarged the hole, eventually making the piece unserviceable. Lining the vent with a copper insert, called bouching, reduced the problem.[25]

All Napoleonic-era artillery was smoothbore and made of iron or brass. It was generally believed to be effective only up to 1,200 yards. The most commonly used projectile was solid shot, constituting up to 80 percent of the rounds carried into the field; about half of the rest were canister. Theory held that artillerists should fight to the last moment because short-distance fire with canister was the most effective way to deal with enemy infantry. At longer distances, solid shot plowing into troop formations was viewed as a better alternative to shell.[26]

Administratively, Napoleonic artillery was organized much as it would be in the Civil War half a century later. Batteries were assigned to divisions, where infantry commanders were in charge of using them. Artillery chiefs were responsible for the daily care and maintenance of the batteries but did not exercise command on the battlefield unless the division commander allowed it. There always existed a certain level of tension in this shared responsibility as there would be in the Civil War. Corps-level and field-army-level artillery reserves were common. Battery commanders generally deployed their pieces in an uneven line to reduce the effect of getting caught by enfilade fire on the flank, with twelve to twenty yards separating each piece.[27]

The most important effect of artillery on the battlefield was Napoleon's use of concentrations to pave the way for infantry or cavalry assaults. This became something of a trademark for the French dictator and set him apart from other commanders both before and since. It was not an original idea of Napoleon's. Du Teil had advocated such a tactic in his 1778 book. Napoleon was influenced by du Teil and tried to implement the suggestion, especially after 1808, when his opponents became better at waging war and the quality of his own troops declined. But he parted from du Teil on the issue of ammunition use. The French theorist had advocated taking no more than 200 rounds per gun to the field to reduce the strain on logistics, while the dictator preferred 300 rounds so he could pummel the enemy with heavy fire. On several occasions, Napoleon was able to mass large concentrations to good effect. At Wagram on July 6, 1809, he assembled 112 pieces to prepare a successful attack on the Austrians. But at Waterloo on June 18, 1815, his battery of 80 guns failed to pave the way to victory.[28]

It is important to point out that Napoleon *did not* use artillery concentrations in the majority of his battles. As Brent Nosworthy has noted, historians have tended to see the relative lack of artillery concentration in the Civil War as a departure from Napoleonic practice.[29] In reality, however, Napoleon was virtually alone during the many wars that erupted from his ambitions in employing artillery concentrations at all, and even he did not use them regularly. Overwhelmingly, artillery was used in dispersed fashion to support infantry units rather than grouped to focus fire on a single target, just as it would be in the Civil War to come. And, as we have seen with the Waterloo example, Napoleon's concentrations did not always achieve their purpose.

EUROPEAN DEVELOPMENTS, 1815–1861

After Napoleon, refinement of the artillery arm continued. As American artillery officer William E. Birkhimer put it, the two basic requirements were to enhance field mobility by making the pieces lighter and to reduce recoil.

These two objectives tended to counter each other, however, because reducing recoil depended a good deal on making the carriage stout and heavy. A number of other considerations, such as cost and streamlining the variety of types available, continued to be important too.[30]

Brass, an alloy of copper and zinc, tended to dominate the metals used to make tubes, but cast iron began to be popular because it was considerably cheaper. The two metals competed with each other during this period. By the 1830s wrought iron emerged as a viable alternative at about the same time that steel began to be used. The French experimented successfully with mixing different metals by shrinking a wrought-iron band over a cast-iron barrel, a technique that characterized the Parrott pieces soon to be produced in the United States. The British stock trail had a significant advantage in the struggle to lighten the carriage without reducing the absorption of recoil. It was widely adopted after the Napoleonic era, though only by the 1830s in the United States.[31]

Europeans brought back the concept of loading the piece at the breech instead of the muzzle. An Italian developed the first serviceable breechloader by 1846, while William Armstrong did the same in Britain by 1854 and Englishman Joseph Whitworth followed suit the next year. All of these models were rifled as well. Rifling became the most potentially significant innovation yet in the development of field artillery, but the 1850s represented only its introductory period. That decade and the next, the period of America's Civil War, was a transition phase into the new world of both breechloaders and rifled artillery as armies evaluated whether these innovations were superior to muzzleloaders and smoothbores. The Civil War became the first major test of rifled artillery but failed to offer a proper experiment in the use of breechloaders.[32]

Developments in the improvement of projectiles lagged behind those in other areas. The next generation of explosives, after gunpowder, was developed in Switzerland by 1846. That was called guncotton, produced by steeping cotton in concentrated nitric acid, then washing and drying it. The result was highly inflammatory and exploded with a force equal to three times the same amount of gunpowder. It also produced little or no smoke. Guncotton was at least three times more expensive and much more dangerous to make than gunpowder, both of which delayed its use for decades to come. Some Civil War officers were aware it existed. John Gibbon included a brief discussion of guncotton in his artillery manual published in 1863, but the new explosive was not available for use during the Civil War. Guncotton, however, was the wave of the future, introducing the era of high explosives that replaced gunpowder before the end of the nineteenth century.[33]

The widespread use of rifled artillery spurred the development of fuzes designed to explode long-distance shells and case shot. Because rifling reduced windage, artillerists could no longer rely on gases from the cartridge to set off the crude fuzes then in use. The most common of these was called a wooden fuze, consisting of a piece of wood tapered to fit more easily into the fuze hole of the projectile. The wooden plug was hollowed out and filled with portfire composition. A fuze like this was sometimes simply referred to as portfire. It was a time fuze because it came in varied lengths depending on how far the target happened to be.[34]

Belgian captain Charles Bormann developed the most sophisticated time fuze to replace the wooden fuze. It consisted of a circular train of powder that communicated to the main powder charge of the fuze. Bormann marked off the circular train in quarter-second intervals. Before inserting the fuze into a projectile, the artillerist used an awl to cut into the train at the interval required so it would begin burning at that point until reaching zero. The Bormann fuze allowed for firing times up to five seconds. When the burning composition reached zero, it entered the main powder charge of the fuze, which exploded and knocked out of place a small tin plate, which then communicated flame to the powder charge in the shell. As with any fairly complicated device, the Bormann fuze sometimes failed to work as intended.[35]

The English developed a more sophisticated way to ignite the powder cartridge in the tube than the old portfire and linstock methods. By the early 1850s the friction primer had come into being. It consisted of a copper tube filled with mealed powder that was inserted into the vent, with a crosspiece of copper attached to its end that contained a friction device activated by jerking on a lanyard. There was no need to light a slow-burning match. As with the Bormann fuze, however, the rate of misfires was significant.[36]

The introduction of rifles coincided with the development of what many artillerists considered the height of smoothbore development as well. Napoleon III charged French theorists to develop a fieldpiece that would combine the characteristics of a gun and a howitzer so as to streamline the wide range of varied types of pieces in French arsenals. He also wanted a substantial weight of projectile combined with lightness of tube and carriage to achieve heavier fire with higher mobility in the field. The result was the 12-pounder Napoleon, which fulfilled the emperor's specifications. It also was among the earliest pieces to dispense entirely with ornamentation of any kind, producing a sleek, streamlined, modern appearance without handles on the tube. The US Army adopted it in 1857.[37]

Whether rifles would win in their contest with smoothbores during the middle decades of the nineteenth century was an open question as far as artillerists were concerned. While modern historians tend to assume rifling was automatically superior, contemporaries made no such assumptions.[38] There were more technical problems to be worked out before rifling became dominant. For example, projectiles had to be designed to connect with the rifling to utilize its stabilizing spinning effect. Thus, round projectiles were turned into conical projectiles with an expandable base around the butt. Only the base, made of copper, brass, or papier-mâché, connected with the rifling and usually broke off from the projectile after leaving the tube.[39] In addition, rifles employed canister less effectively than did smoothbores. The spin tended to splay the balls out in irregular patterns rather than create a cone-shaped spread, and in turn the canister rounds tended to wear out the sharp edges of the rifling. The rifle's only advantage over the smoothbore was its much longer distance, and yet it could not ensure effectiveness even in that advantage. The rifled-projectile fuzes were not entirely reliable, and it would take many years to improve them.[40]

The best that can be said is that rifles and smoothbores entered a period of equilibrium in their relative value in the1850s until the 1880s. They occupied separate but connected spheres, with smoothbores excelling at short-distance fire (especially against enemy infantry) and rifles excelling in long-distance fire.

A trend developed to drop the former practice of calling the basic artillery unit a company. In Britain, that had prevailed mostly because the army preferred to organize field artillery in battalions for greater administrative ease, and the subunits were naturally termed companies. But by 1859 the British Army redesignated artillery companies as batteries, and the US Army followed suit. Most European militaries thought it was wise to keep from one-fourth to one-third of its fieldpieces in a general reserve, with the rest divided among corps, divisions, or brigades of infantry. Horse artillery, designed to accompany fast-moving cavalry, was less common than batteries designed to accompany infantry, but the Prussians and a few other European nations maintained such a force. Prussia was noted for the excellence of its horse artillery units.[41]

Rockets enjoyed a brief presence in the artillery arm during the first half of the nineteenth century. They had initially been used 500 years before but were discarded until forces of the Kingdom of Mysore used them against British troops during several wars in the 1790s. These rockets impressed the English officers, and Col. William Congreve started a Western trend to develop and use them on the battlefield. By 1799 he had created the Congreve rocket. The weapon was first used in the siege of Boulogne in 1806 and proved effective enough to be improved and retained in the arsenal. The improvements led to larger warheads until the rockets ranged in size from 6-pounders to 42-pounders, the latter reportedly capable of reaching a target 3,000 yards away. The 32-pounder charge was encased in an iron tube that was three feet, six inches long and four inches in diameter. The tube was attached to a fifteen-foot stick. The longer the stick, the longer the distance the rocket carried and the higher the trajectory. Shorter sticks produced shorter distances and flatter trajectories.[42]

Rockets possessed several advantages, including ease of mobility, with relatively few pieces of equipment to handle. They could be set up almost anywhere, and under certain conditions operatives could fire fifty rockets in five minutes. The major disadvantage was their erratic trajectories at almost any distance. Inaccuracy plagued the rocket. As artillery historian Boyd L. Dastrup has put it, "Congreve's rockets were . . . suitable only for use against unfortified targets in area bombardment."[43]

William Hale, a mechanic at the Royal Arsenal, developed an improvement on the Congreve rocket by 1845. It was controlled by rotation rather than by the dynamics of a stick, with a steel tube headed by a cast-iron compartment. Hale developed a sixteen-pound charge capable of hitting targets up to 2,200 yards away. The British Army was not initially interested, but the US Army adopted the Hale rocket in 1847. Col. Edward M. Boxer, who also improved the Congreve rocket, managed to get the British to adopt his version in 1864. Three years later authorities replaced it with an improved version of the Hale rocket.[44]

Rockets never improved enough to offer a challenge to field guns as a significant weapon, but they supplemented the long arm in minor ways. The Hale rocket was available to Civil War artillerists but made only a brief and usually overlooked appearance in the conflict.

Rockets faded away even from European use by the 1870s, when improvements in field artillery began to catapult the arm into a new era. They resurfaced, however, in the late 1930s and during World War II. Many armies used them to deliver massed firepower spread over a wide target area because of the mobility inherent in their delivery, with the Germans and Russians especially bringing them into play.[45]

2

. . . .

THE AMERICAN ARTILLERY HERITAGE

T he American experience with field artillery before the Civil War was solidly lodged within the Western artillery heritage emanating from the major European powers, mostly England and France. But there were some variations on the story influenced by American needs and limitations. Both streams of experience merged by 1861 to create the prospects and problems associated with field artillery in the Civil War.

THE AMERICAN REVOLUTION

America's first major war occurred as a result of trouble between the thirteen colonies and England. With great difficulty, the nascent central government of the rebellion, the Continental Congress, managed to assemble a respectable artillery arm for the Continental Army. That arm eventually encompassed five different calibers of guns and two different calibers of howitzers. It had a siege train consisting of two different calibers of guns and four of mortars for a grand total of thirteen different types. In contrast, the Army of the Potomac at Petersburg in 1864–65 possessed seventeen different calibers of all types of ordnance. This difference highlights the limitations faced by the Continental Congress.[1]

American artillery typically attached 3-pounders, 4-pounders, and 6-pounders to infantry brigades, while 12-pounders and 24-pounders were used as guns of position in fortifications. The Continentals tended to use 5.5-inch and 8-inch howitzers. They also used the English system of the late eighteenth century for most of the conflict. This consisted of a bracket trail (two stems of wood connected with each other, used before the development of the stock trail), while horses harnessed in single file pulled the piece. Each gun carried two side boxes, one affixed to each stem of the trail; one box contained powder fixed in bags and the other projectiles. There was no ammunition box on the limber. When in battery, the two side boxes were removed and placed on the ground three paces from the end of the trail handspike. Reserve ammunition was carried in wagons or carts, organized into a train and driven by hired civilians. Not until the siege of Yorktown (1781) did the Americans become acquainted with the more advanced Gribeauval system through their collaboration with French forces. They did not adopt the improved English block trail until many years after the Revolution.[2]

In one way the Continental Congress adopted a better system of management than either the Union or the Confederate government in the Civil War. It appointed an artillery chief, Henry Knox, for the entire long arm of the American force, a post retained until 1798. Knox acted as the chief administrator of the artillery arm and at times even assumed field command of units on campaign. While neither the Federals nor Confederates utilized a chief artillerist, in other ways the artillery organization of the Revolution was similar to that of the Civil War. Battery officers took orders from the commander of the infantry brigade to which they were attached and owed regular reports to Knox. Battery commanders, not infantry officers, were responsible for maintaining their commands in the field, but they relied on the infantry brigade's quartermaster, commissary, and ordnance officers for supplies. The same situation prevailed in the Civil War.[3]

British forces fighting in the Revolutionary War also attached small guns to infantry units but had a stronger organization of reserve pieces to accompany field armies. They grouped heavier guns into artillery brigades of six pieces each so as to keep artillery officers in charge of those reserves and concentrate fire when needed on the battlefield. The proportion of artillery to infantry was relatively high in the British forces in America. Lt. Gen. John Burgoyne had a ratio of one gun per 167 men during the Saratoga Campaign of 1777. Gen. Sir William Howe fielded one piece per 200 men at the Battle of Brandywine (September 11, 1777). The British force that captured Savannah late in 1778 had one piece for 375 men, and Lt. Col. Banastre Tarleton had two pieces for his force of 1,100 men at the Battle of Cowpens (January 17, 1781). American commanders could not afford such high ratios but Gen. George Washington did group spare guns into an artillery reserve, which he used well at the Battle of Monmouth (June 28, 1778).[4]

The Americans did not have a well-digested artillery manual. In the eyes of William Birkhimer, a post–Civil War artillery officer, they learned "the manual of the piece, with a few of the simplest manoeuvres." Birkhimer did not consider American batteries to be very mobile. Civilian drivers handled the horses on the road, but after reaching the battlefield, the gun crews took over the job of manhandling the carriages. The relatively crude level of training did not include an emphasis on rapid movement.[5]

It cannot be said that field artillery played a prominent role in the battles of the American Revolution. Shortages of carriages, inconsistent forage for horses, and miserable roads all conspired to limit its deployment and effectiveness. Heavily wooded terrain also impaired the long arm's chance of making a difference on the battlefield.[6]

1783-1846

Victory in the American Revolution resulted in a long period of administrative neglect for the artillery arm of the new nation. Severe problems of funding limited its development and threatened even the existence of field artillery. The government eventually authorized four regiments of artillery, but the companies within them were mostly armed with heavy guns for the coastal forts constructed during the era. By 1808 a company of light artillery designed for field service was authorized, but soon the secretary of war tired of the expense associated with maintaining the horses and dismounted it. By 1821 Congress authorized the mounting of one company in each of the four artillery regiments, but it was not done until 1838. Each was armed with three 6-pounder guns and one 12-pounder howitzer. Three of the four field batteries were termed "mounted" artillery, referring to the use of draft horses (the men walked or rode on carriages and limbers when needed). One of the four was termed "horse," or "flying," artillery (the men rode on horses). That sole unit of flying artillery was Capt. Samuel Ringgold's Company C, 3rd US Artillery.[7]

The Americans acquired heavier pieces during this period. The army adopted a 42-pounder in 1801, and by 1819 bigger pieces, such as the 100-pounder, came into the arsenal. But the 24-pounder continued to be the biggest gun considered suitable for field service. The 3-pounder and 4-pounder models were dropped, and the 6-pounder became the smallest used in the field. By 1835 an artillery board adopted as the standard arsenal the 6-pounder gun, 12-pounder gun, 12-pounder howitzer, and 24-pounder howitzer. The 12-pounder mountain howitzer (lighter and more easily disassembled to be transported on mules) was added in 1836. A 32-pounder howitzer was added by 1843, but it was really too heavy for effective field service and rarely used in that role.[8]

THE MEXICAN WAR, 1846-1848

William Birkhimer correctly pointed out that US field artillery first made its presence felt on the battlefield during the engagements of the Mexican War. But it was such a small part of the war effort that one can only say it was an introduction to rather than a consummation of artillery's promise. Nevertheless, an important level of professionalism was reached in this conflict, and many observers praised the role played by field batteries in nearly every engagement.[9]

In February and March 1847, Congress authorized the addition of an eleventh and a twelfth company to each of the four artillery regiments of the army. It also allowed four more light companies to be assembled by mounting one from each of the four regiments. By the summer of 1847, the army had forty-eight batteries, of which only eight were equipped as field artillery.[10]

Although small in number, American light batteries exceeded expectations in some battles. They dominated the action at Palo Alto on May 8, 1846. Capt. James Duncan's Company A, 2nd US Artillery and Maj. Samuel B. Ringgold, who had trained his Company C, 3rd US Artillery, became artillery heroes during this engagement. Capt. Braxton Bragg and his Company E, 3rd US Artillery shone even brighter at the Battle of Buena Vista on February 22–23, 1847. Mobility, accuracy of fire, and sometimes close-distance firing were the keys to success.[11]

Organization of the small artillery arm in Mexico was simple. Batteries were attached to brigades or divisions and received orders from infantry commanders. They also relied on infantry staff for quartermaster, commissary, and ordnance supply. There were too few batteries to provide a general reserve for the field army. Henry J. Hunt, who graduated from the US Military Academy in 1839, thought artillery officers were more professionally trained in the Mexican conflict than in the coming Civil War. He rose to prominence as one of the most effective artillerists of that latter conflict and after Appomattox argued it was important that infantry commanders allow artillerists the freedom to act on their own in battle. As long as the infantryman simply told the artillerist what needed to be accomplished and then let him go about it as he saw fit, the big guns could contribute greatly to the army's success. Hunt believed this occurred routinely in Mexico but did not always happen in the Civil War.[12]

ARTILLERY MANUALS

The American army fought the Revolutionary War without a comprehensive guide to training. Capt. William Stevens worked up what Birkhimer has called "the first artillery tactics published" in North America by 1797. It was planned as a three-volume set, with the first volume covering field artillery, the second heavy artillery, and the third ordnance matters. In the end, only the first volume was published. It is unclear if it ever was officially adopted by the War Department. A French officer serving in the US Army, Louis de Tousard, published the two-volume *American Artillerist's Companion* in 1809. This was more of a treatise than a manual and was never adopted by the War Department.[13]

The first book to be adopted was written by Maj. Amos Stoddard, who quickly worked it up after the War of 1812 began. Taken liberally from a book written by Col. Andrzej Tadeusz Bonawentura Kościuszko, it was adopted on August 1, 1812, and remained the official artillery manual without alterations until 1821. Birkhimer thought Stoddard's book demonstrated that the Gribeauval system had been gradually introduced since the American Revolution and that greater mobility was apparent with the increased use of horses to maneuver pieces on the battlefield.[14]

Kościuszko's original, although also a short volume, was more detailed and informative than Stoddard's extract. Translated by US Military Academy superintendent Jonathan Williams and published in 1808, it strictly adhered to the formation of the battery with a right flank and a left flank, warning against inversions (altering that rigid formation). Kościuszko advocated the double column (a front of two pieces) but allowed the single column (a front of one piece) occasionally. He had horses pull the pieces to the drilling ground or battlefield, where gun crews used ropes to manhandle them. Kościuszko's book, more a treatise than a manual, failed to clearly differentiate the three basic formations of field artillery—line, column, and in battery (the last being ready for firing).[15]

American artillerists had more instructional material to guide them in the War of 1812 than in the Revolution, but a true manual still was not available.

A three-volume work by Henri Dominique Lallemand, a former artillery officer under Napoleon and refugee to the United States, still did not fill that bill. Published as *A Treatise on Artillery* in 1820, Lallemand was the first to clearly differentiate the three basic formations of line, column, and in battery. His discussion of how to go from one formation to another was clear and concise. He also introduced the term "section" to refer to two guns and their caissons. Yet Lallemand conceived of a rigid formation for a battery, as had Kościuszko. He even numbered every piece to make it easier for the commander to deal with inversion. "Any formation which inverted the original order of the carriages was considered an inconvenience, to be escaped from as soon as possible," observed Birkhimer. Lallemand preferred the double column over the single column.[16]

Although it represented a significant step forward in battery management, the War Department adopted only parts of Lallemand's book to create an artillery manual cobbled from different sources in 1821. This compendium proved inadequate and was soon replaced. A board recommended the adoption of a book that had been translated from the French by Lt. Daniel Tyler of the 1st US Artillery. Tyler had been dispatched to France to observe artillery practice and translated the manual of the Gribeauval system. Published as *Manual for Artillery of the Garde Royal* in three volumes in 1828, it was quickly adopted by the War Department. Tyler understood that the Gribeauval system was nearing the end of its usefulness and thus inserted a recommendation that the US Army also adopt the English block trail.[17]

France, however, continued to be a source of authority for artillery even after its Gribeauval system began to fade. Capt. Robert Anderson translated the latest French tactics and published it in 1839. *Instruction for Field Artillery, Horse and Foot* was adopted by the War Department the next year. It was, as Birkhimer has argued, the best artillery manual yet to appear in the United States and underwrote the success of artillery in the Mexican War. Samuel Ringgold, however, did not like the French horse artillery system, preferring the one used by the British Army. He raised such a fuss about it that the War Department created a board, on which Ringgold served, to examine the question. By 1845 Ringgold's pressure resulted in the adoption of the English system of horse artillery. The result was "an English-Americanized revision of the French system," as Birkhimer put it.[18]

Anderson's book was a watershed in the development of a professional artillery arm in the United States. It dropped any concern for inversion and insisted battery officers learn how to maneuver in a less rigid fashion. Individual pieces and sections became the basic units of maneuver, allowing for the passage of carriages, countermarching, and moving pivots for wheeling. Anderson dispensed with general or special guides (the practice of assigning men to stand where formations were to wind up after maneuvers). He greatly reduced the use of ropes for manhandling a piece, retaining the prolonge only for dragging it to the rear, and relied on horses to move the pieces as much as possible. This required more detailed and clearly explained descriptions of how to use the horses to go from line or column into battery and back. The book greatly enhanced the level of mobility and articulation in artillery formations and maneuvers. Anderson kept the commands "as simple, short, and as few as possible," as he put it. In addition, he illustrated the work with many diagrams to explain everything.[19]

As important as it was, Anderson's *Instruction* was not fully equal to the needs of the army. As Birkhimer put it, the captain produced a basic manual of the piece and of the battery and "merely touched on" higher-level discussions about artillery management. It was not a truly comprehensive manual. A board was created in 1856 to address the situation. Consisting of Capt. William F. Barry, Capt. William H. French, and Captain Hunt, it met from November 1856 to September 1857 and then again from September 1858 to March 1860. The Barry Board's *Instruction for Field Artillery* was adopted by the War Department in March 1860.[20]

Birkhimer considered this the most complete artillery manual produced in the United States before the Civil War. It contained "a clear exposition of the principles on which field artillery rested." The board had discussed "organization, matériel, and the service of artillery in campaign, presenting a philosophical and instructive *exposé* of the general principles underlying the formation, discipline, and service . . . of an efficient field artillery." The War Department printed the first edition in 1860 and further editions in 1861, 1863, and 1864. Given its importance, the manual was reprinted in 1968 and 2005 for the use of reenactors and other interested readers.[21]

As an illustration of Birkhimer's regard, one can pause over the manual's instructions concerning the method for teaching individual members of the gun crew. The board cautioned noncommissioned officers to explain each movement and then perform it. They were not to touch the soldier except "to rectify mistakes arising from want of intelligence." The instructor was to carefully go through one step at a time but cautioned not to overdo instruction in each too long. "Great patience and the utmost precision are necessary on the part of the instructor. He should especially endeavor to excite a spirited and active deportment at every military exercise."[22]

Instruction for Field Artillery was not the only book available to those who wanted to learn about artillery matters. Roughly a dozen books were in print during the war years about various aspects of the subject. Most of them were purely technical in nature or derived from Anderson's book or the current artillery manual. Chief among them were John Gibbon's *The Artillerist's Manual* of 1860 and Joseph Roberts's *The Hand-Book of Artillery for the Service of the United States* of 1863.[23]

Gibbon served as instructor of artillery at the US Military Academy for five years and wrote his book initially for cadets. Assigned elsewhere, he converted the limited text into a more general treatise on field artillery "with a view of spreading information not popularly accessible, upon a subject of the first importance to our national defence." Published on the eve of the Civil War, it went through a second edition in 1863. Gibbon went into great detail on a number of issues not covered by the official manual, such as a description of gunpowder, the history of rifling and of projectiles, and the history of artillery in general. In contrast, Roberts prepared his book for easy reading by organizing it like a catechism, with questions and answers. He derived the information from half a dozen books, including Gibbon's work.[24]

The Confederates had difficulty gaining access to artillery books once the war began. Lt. W. Leroy Brown of Company H, 2nd Virginia Artillery tried to fill the gap. "The writer, having had access to several interesting works on the subject of artillery that are now very difficult to obtain," distilled bits of information from a dozen of them when he had "a few spare days." The result was *Notes on Artillery,* published in Richmond in 1862 (but with his name misspelled as "Broun"). Gibbon was among the dozen sources he consulted.[25]

The War Department fostered a revision of its ordnance manual right after the outbreak of the war. It was managed by an ordnance officer, Capt. T. T. S. Laidley, who finished his work by September 1861. The result was an exhaustive compilation of technical data on all aspects of ordnance for both the artillery and infantry. The Confederates also needed such a manual and adapted it from the Federal government's book. Their version was published in Richmond in 1862.[26]

Fig. 2.1. Six-Pounder Gun, Model 1841. Representative of cannon of the past, 6-pound-ers were widely used by some units on both sides of the Civil War, especially the Confederate Army of Tennessee. They were mostly phased out, however, in favor of 10-pounders and 12-pounders. LC-DIG-cwpb-02256.

HARDWARE

Civil War artillerists had at their disposal a varied arsenal when hostilities broke out. The War Department had adopted six sizes and types of cannon for service by that time. They were the 6-pounder, the 12-pounder gun, the 12-pounder howitzer, the 24-pounder howitzer, the 32-pounder howitzer, and the Napoleon (also called the 12-pounder light gun or gun-howitzer). But the details of these types varied. For example, nineteen different patterns of 6-pounders had been developed or used in the United States from 1819 to 1862, made by fourteen different manufacturers in five different kinds of metal. The

Fig. 2.2. Twelve-Pounder Howitzer and Limber. This is a wonderful photograph of a standard cannon of the prewar era that continued to see fairly wide service during the Civil War. The cannon-limber combination created a highly flexible four-wheeled contrivance ideal for negotiating rugged terrain and tight corners. The infantry camp scene in the background also is very interesting. LC-DIG-cwpb-01571.

6-pounder quickly became obsolete during the war, although phased out more slowly among the Confederates than among the Federals. In addition, several other types and sizes of ordnance were available other than the officially sanctioned arsenal of the prewar years. As a result, about a dozen different types and sizes of cannon were used in the Civil War by both sides.[27]

The most common metals in use by 1861 were bronze, iron, wrought iron, cast iron, and steel, although there was no convergence of opinion about which was superior. *Instruction for Field Artillery* concluded that bronze was better than iron. Often called gun metal or erroneously referred to as brass, bronze consisted of ninety parts copper and ten parts tin. The Napoleon was the last and best cannon made of bronze. The metal "wore and stretched through

Fig. 2.3. Ten-Pounder Parrott. One of three main types of artillery used during the Civil War, this serviceable American product became a mainstay of many batteries. Rifled, made of cast iron, and with a reinforcing wrought-iron band at the breech, its weight of projectile represented a significant upgrade from many pre–Civil War cannon. Photograph by Jack W. Melton Jr.

severe use, but seldom if ever burst," according to modern historians. It was not appropriate, however, for rifled pieces "because of its softness and rapid erosion." Iron was cheaper than bronze but not so reliable if poorly made.[28]

Cast iron tended to burst even when efforts were made to reduce that problem. Nevertheless Robert Parker Parrott, a graduate of the US Military Academy and a captain in the army, believed in it. He resigned to become superintendent of the West Point Foundry at Cold Spring, New York, in 1836. Parrott turned this privately owned manufactory into a major producer of ordnance. By the late 1850s he had adopted a water-cooling process created by Thomas J. Rodman to slowly cool the cast iron and add strength to it. Parrott also added a wrought-iron band around the breech of cast-iron tubes. Both efforts reduced but did not eliminate the tendency of breech bursts.[29]

TABLE 2.1. Specifications of Nine Popular Fieldpieces of the Civil War

	Tube	Carriage	Total Weight	Distance
10-Pounder Parrott Rifle	74 inches long, weighed 899 pounds	Weighed 900 pounds	1,799 pounds	1,900 yards (10-pound solid shot at 5-degrees elevation and 1 pound of powder)
Napoleon 12-Pounder Smoothbore	66 inches long, weighed 1,227 pounds	Weighed 1,128 pounds	2,355 pounds	1,619 yards (12-pound solid shot at 5-degrees elevation, 2.5 pounds of powder)
3-Inch Ord-nance Rifle	69 inches long, weighed 820 pounds	Weighed 900 pounds	1,720 pounds	1,850 yards (9.5-pound solid shot at 5-degrees elevation, 1 pound of powder)
6-Pounder Model 1841	60 inches long, weighed 880 pounds	Weighed 900 pounds	1,780 pounds	1,523 yards (6.1-pound solid shot at 5-degrees elevation, 1.25 pounds of powder)
12-Pounder Howitzer, Model 1841	53 inches long, weighed 785 pounds	Weighed 900 pounds	1,685 pounds	1,072 yards (12-pound shell at 5-degrees el-evation, 1 pound of powder)
20-Pounder Parrott Rifle	84 inches long, weighed 1,750 pounds	Weighed 1,175 pounds	2,925 pounds	1,900 yards (20-pound shell at 5-degrees el-evation, 2 pounds of powder)
6-Pounder Wi-ard Rifle	53 inches long, weighed 725 pounds	Weighed 1,100 pounds	1,825 pounds	7,000 yards (6-pound shell at 35-degrees el-evation, 0.75 pound of powder)
12-Pounder Whitworth Rifle	104 inches long, weighed 1,092 pounds	Weighed 900 pounds	1,992 pounds	2,600 yards (12-pound shell at 5-degrees ele-vation, 1.75 pounds of powder)
4.5-Inch Siege Rifle	133 inches long, weighed 3,450 pounds	Weighed 2,300 pounds	5,750 pounds	3,265 yards (30-pound shell at 10-degrees ele-vation, 3.25 pounds of powder)

Parrott developed a type of cannon that was cheap and quick to produce. With the outset of the Civil War, his company turned out mainly 10-pounders and 20-pounders, although it made heavier types as well. The 10-pounder

Parrott fired a solid shot 1,900 yards with a pound of powder and five-degrees elevation. The tube was seventy-four inches long and weighed 899 pounds. With a carriage of 900 pounds, the piece weighed 1,799 pounds altogether.[30]

Parrotts of all types were yet untried in battle when the firing on Fort Sumter initiated the Civil War. The same was true of the Napoleon. Named after its sponsor, Emperor Napoleon III of France, it streamlined the arsenal with a piece that combined the characteristics of a gun and a howitzer. A 12-pounder, it also could replace smaller pieces. The French developed this unusual cannon by 1853, and the United States modified it and began producing its own version, Model 1857. The US Army had five Napoleons when the war broke out in 1861 but had ordered 1,157 of them by January 1864.[31]

The smoothbore Napoleon seemed very promising. With a 2.5-pound powder charge, it propelled a solid shot 1,619 yards at five-degrees elevation. The bronze tube was sixty-six inches long and weighed 1,227 pounds. With a carriage of 1,128 pounds, the piece weighed 2,355 pounds altogether.[32] "Mobility being a prime consideration," everyone expected the Napoleon would fire a heavier projectile yet remain light enough for six horses to handle it in the field. But the proof was pending. "This gun is still upon trial," declared *Instruction for Field Artillery* in 1860. The authors predicted, however, that the Napoleon would replace all other smoothbores after it proved itself.[33]

The Napoleon represented another watershed in the development of field artillery. Prior to the mid-nineteenth century, it had been customary to add a good deal of ornamentation or at least handles onto the tube, far more so in the early centuries of artillery than in more recent eras. But by the early 1800s, it had become clear that ornamentation and handles created weak points, introducing the possibility of fractures in the tubes. The Napoleon was the first piece deliberately designed to have no such weak points. "The more sweeping the exterior curves and the more gradual the blending of one surface into another, the stronger the weapon under repeated stress," explained historians James C. Hazlett, Edwin Olmstead, and M. Hume Parks.[34]

Of all the types adopted by the US Army before 1861, the Napoleon was the most prominent, and it would play a large role in the war. But the 10-pounder Parrott, available but not officially adopted by that time, would play an equal role. Yet a third type, the 3-Inch Ordnance Rifle, was still in the developmental phase when the war began but would soon be available. Its popularity equaled that of the Napoleon and the 10-pounder Parrott. These three types carried

Fig. 2.4. Napoleon Gun-Howitzer, or Light 12-Pounder. Developed by the French under the patronage of Napoleon III, this cannon served several purposes. It represented a significant improvement over the 6-pounder in terms of weight of projectile; it supposedly combined the characteristics of a gun and a howitzer; and it was lighter than most previous types of artillery, thus increasing mobility in the field. The Napoleon also was designed without any ornamentation or handles that could lead to weak points along the tube, creating a sleek appearance. The Americans adopted it and produced hundreds for use during the Civil War. It became a favorite among many Union and Confederate artillerists and was one of the three most commonly employed types of cannon in the war. Photograph by Jack W. Melton Jr.

the bulk of artillery service on both sides of the opposing lines during the Civil War. (Because it was not ready for service until after the conflict started, the story of the 3-Inch Ordnance Rifle will be told in chapter 4.)

Civil War artillerists had other types of pieces available that were far less widely used than the big three. Charles T. James developed rifled projectiles to fit a bore of 3.8-inch caliber. He cooperated with James Tyler Ames of the Ames Manufacturing Company in Chicopee, Massachusetts, to produce field-pieces capable of using his projectiles. These pieces were generically referred to as James rifles. Rodman, whose water-cooling process aided Parrott in us-

Fig. 2.5. Whitworth Gun. A sophisticated British weapon, it was the best breechloader of the Civil War era. The gun had a fairly long range and accuracy but was used quite sparingly by both sides in the conflict. The Whitworth had a spiraled, hexagonal-shaped barrel on the inside that its projectile fitted exactly, imparting a vigorous spin on firing. In this photograph, taken in Richmond right after the war, the breech block is open and the trail is stenciled with "Richmond Arsenal 1864." The Whitworth's complicated mechanism, special projectiles, and imported British-made equipment lessened its usefulness on the battlefield. LC-DIG-cwpb-03639.

ing cast iron for his tubes, also developed a 3-inch rifle made of wrought iron that found its way into use.[35]

Several types developed in Britain were imported to the United States. Sir Joseph Whitworth produced a highly advanced rifled gun in 3-pounder, 6-pounder, and 12-pounder versions, all of them breech loading. The Federals used at least four Whitworth 12-pounders during the war, and the Confederates employed a few more. Given the nature of its design, with precise tooling so the movable breech would not allow gases from the powder explosion to escape and a projectile molded as an eight-sided object to exactly fit the rifling, the crew had to learn how to operate this touchy piece of artillery.[36]

Capt. Theophilus A. Blakely of England developed a 12-pounder with a

Fig. 2.6. Six-Pounder Wiard Gun. An impressive weapon developed by Norman Wiard, a Canadian working in the United States, the specially designed carriage allowed for a much greater elevation, up to around thirty-five degrees, than any other cannon of the era. Only a handful of batteries North and South, however, employed this unique type of artillery. LC-DIG-cwpb-02744.

wrought iron reinforcing band wrapped around the breech. The Confederates supplied at least two batteries with this type. Norman Wiard of Canada developed a steel piece in 6-pounder and 12-pounder versions. It was distinguished by a reinforcing band that covered the back half of the tube and was mounted on a specially designed carriage that increased the elevation of the tube from zero to thirty-five degrees. At least three batteries in the Union army were armed with Wiard pieces. The 14th Ohio Battery used six of them on April 6, 1862, at the Battle of Shiloh, lost them to the Confederates, but recovered the pieces the next day. They were so badly damaged by the retreating Rebels that the unit replaced them with three 6-pounder brass rifles and one 6-pounder smoothbore.[37]

The primary difference between a gun and a howitzer was that the latter was chambered, with a recess at the back end of the tube for the powder charge to enter. This compressed the explosion of the powder to add more velocity to the projectile and created a higher trajectory. With an elevation system that was slightly higher than that of the gun, more recoil pressure was exerted down through the carriage rather than backward. This put more strain on the wheeled wooden carriages and contributed to a persistent problem with breakdowns, especially at the axles.[38]

While guns and howitzers had a long history in North American and European warfare, rifling was new and not yet tested in a major war on either continent. The addition of spiraled grooves to the interior of the bore was the major factor in the increased distance firing of a rifle, though not the only one. Designers also tried to increase the distance by elevating the tube higher than smoothbores. Wiard's carriage allowed for tube elevations up to thirty-five degrees, in contrast to most other smoothbore and rifled pieces, which could be elevated only up to five degrees. Because Wiard's design was not widely used, elevation potential remained very limited during the Civil War.[39]

Rifled artillery required a projectile of a different design, elongated in shape rather than the common spherical shot or shell. This allowed for a greater weight of projectile for any given caliber and offered the opportunity for a different type of fuze. The rifling combined with the elongated shape imparted greater stability of flight so that the forward end of the projectile landed head on, allowing the placement of a contact fuze to explode it.[40]

Designers had to tackle the problem of making the projectile fit into the rifling grooves and yet be small enough for easy insertion. Dr. John B. Read of Alabama patented the process of applying a sabot, made of material that expanded on firing to catch the grooves, at the back end of the projectile. This concept was applied to many rifled projectiles, varying in the type of material used in construction. If the designer wanted to ignite a fuze at the forward end of the projectile with flames from the powder charge, he could make grooves in the sabot material for that purpose.[41]

A variation on this concept was the forcing cone, whereby the rear part of the projectile was tapered with a larger ring of sabot material around it. The powder discharge forced the ring forward, expanding as it moved along the increasing diameter of the projectile. In contrast, other projectiles were fitted with flanges or studs projecting from the back end that fitted into the grooves; this was mostly a British design and worked best with breechloaders. These projections eliminated the option of lighting the fuze at the forward end of the projectile with powder blast because there was no possibility of flame or gases passing by them.[42]

A handful of designers who produced projectiles also made guns for them.

Sylvanus Sawyer of New England developed his own rifle cannon to go along with his rifled projectile. The combination was not a success. Sawyer made the rifling grooves in his cast-steel tube much deeper than usual; most artillerists came to believe that shallow grooves were best. Even though the Ordnance Department approved his product, the Union army rarely used it. Parrott was another example of a designer-manufacturer who made both cannon and projectiles, although his projectiles were not new creations of his own design. James was yet another projectile maker who arranged for a partner to make cannon for him.[43]

Three well-known men made projectiles and fuzes but not cannon. John Absterdam of New York City was joined by Benjamin Hotchkiss and John Schenkl, the latter two making the two most commonly used projectiles for rifled artillery during the Civil War. Hotchkiss applied a sabot made of lead that often broke into fragments close to the muzzle and threatened friendly personnel. Schenkl applied a sabot made of papier-mâché, which also broke up early in flight but was less dangerous to those nearby. Schenkl also made fuzes.[44]

Different kinds of gunpowder were used to fire small arms, cannon, projectiles, and fuzes. For small arms, small grains were needed to make the powder burn faster. For artillery, large grains were called for because of the need to produce a slower buildup of pressure in the tube. Mealed powder, made very fine but not into dust, was needed for fuzes to create an exact rate of combustion.[45]

Before the Mexican War, American artillery relied on the wooden fuze to explode shells. Consisting of a hollow wooden tube filled with powder, it was capped by a paper cover and had markings on the outside denoting burning time. The markings went down as low as tenths of an inch. The crew cut it at the desired timing just before inserting it into the projectile. An improved paper fuze was developed by 1846, but by the onset of the Civil War, both types were out of favor.[46]

Newer devices were widely used by the time of the Civil War. The Bormann fuze was the most popular. Developed by the Saxon army officer Charles Bormann, who also served in the Belgian army, it was available in Europe by 1835 but was not tested in the United States until 1852. The US Army approved it in further tests two years later. The key innovation was that Bormann created a horizontal powder train rather than a vertical one. He fully sealed the train to prevent moisture from seeping in. Bormann marked times along the pewter casing so that gunners could cut it at the desired distance. His fuze was still ignited by flames from the cartridge explosion, and both sides of the train from the cut ignited. One merely flamed to a dead end, but the other flamed into a chamber, where it ruptured a thin sheet of tin and communicated to the powder charge in the projectile.[47]

Bormann's horizontal powder train proved to be more reliable than the vertical train used in the wooden and paper fuzes. It allowed the fine powder to be better compacted because it was laid out in a thin stream as opposed to the heavier concentrations in the vertical train. But the horizontal train imposed a limitation on distance, allowing no more than five seconds because of the constricted space to lay out a circular, horizontal track. Since heavy artillery needed distances up to thirty-five seconds, the Bormann fuze was relegated to field artillery. When George Wright and Hotchkiss modified the Bormann fuze to increase it to twelve and fourteen seconds, the track demanded so much space that a flat-nosed projectile had to be developed for it. This changed the aerodynamic aspects of the projectile's flight and was not successful. Also, the original Bormann fuze became less useful when rifled artillery grew in prominence. It was a flame-ignited fuze, and rifling decreased the windage needed for the flame to go from the powder charge to the front of the projectile.[48]

To explode rifled shells, one had to cut grooves in the saboting material, as noted earlier, or rely on percussion fuzes. Both methods were employed during the Civil War. Hotchkiss cut grooves, while Parrott used the percussion method. Schenkl also developed a percussion fuze that had two safety devices to avoid accidents.[49]

ARTILLERY ORGANIZATION

While the hardware of artillery was continuing to evolve toward rifling and improved fuzes for projectiles, the method of organizing the arm atrophied. Congress insisted on budget constraints, and therefore all but three light artillery companies were dismounted after the Mexican War. The expense of maintaining horses was the most burdensome part of the artillery budget. From 1848 to 1861, Congress and various secretaries of war remounted some companies, only to take away their horses a couple of years later in what Birkhimer called "a paroxysm of economy." Company M, 2nd US Artillery, for example, was three times dismounted and later remounted.[50]

Hunt later wrote of "the active and persistent hostility of the War Department" during this period, but the artillery officers fought back and managed, by 1861, to achieve a stalemate. Only one of the eight field companies remained unhorsed on the eve of the Civil War, although all seven of the mounted companies made do with just enough horses for training purposes as a compromise.[51]

EVE OF CONFLICT

Artillery historians Hazlett, Olmstead, and Parks have written that the Civil War occurred in a significant transition phase. The most important element in that transition was the introduction of rifled pieces and the question of whether they would outperform smoothbores. It also was a period of shifting from bronze and iron to steel as the best metal for making tubes and from ornamentation to a streamlined, functional shape. The introduction of modern breechloaders completed the list of transitional elements of the 1860s period.[52]

The same transition was taking place in Europe simultaneously, but no major wars broke out on the continent to test these new devices and concepts. While considerably lagging behind European developments before the Mexican War, the Americans rapidly caught up with them from 1846 to 1861. The Civil War therefore became the first major conflict to employ rifled artillery on a large scale, to see if steel was more durable than the older metals, to employ the streamlined tube by the thousands, and to at least hint at the effectiveness of breechloaders. The new rifled projectiles and fuzes developed by the 1860s were equally important in testing the effectiveness of new hardware. As historian Boyd L. Dastrup has put it, "the new field artillery met its first real test during the American Civil War."[53]

3

· · · · · · · · · · · · · · · · · · ·

WAR FOOTING

Before 1861 the regular army maintained its artillery as a peacetime organization designed to train recruits. That meant each battery kept only four guns and a reduced number of horses. Because the unit trained with empty ammunition chests, it was possible to keep the number of horses to a bare minimum. Of course, this pleased congressmen who wanted to spare the taxpayer every penny. But in time of conflict, the batteries had to upgrade rapidly to a war footing. That meant six guns each, filled ammunition chests, and more horses. According to the official artillery manual, a six-gun battery on war footing consisted of five officers, 150 men, and 110 horses.[1]

It was a relatively simple matter to expand the peace establishment of a battery to its war footing because the essentials were already in place. But it was more difficult and time consuming to create a battery from nothing. Because the nation relied on a volunteer army raised from the populace by state governments, the majority of all artillery units North and South were volunteer batteries and regiments. It is not surprising there would be variation in the method and organization of this volunteer artillery force as different state governments experimented with different ways of going about the process.

In some cases, governors had the advantage of prewar volunteer artillery companies to draw on. The 1st Rhode Island Artillery grew from a long tradition of volunteer artillery units in that state, stretching back to the Artillery Company of Newport, organized in 1741, and including the United Train of Artillery of 1774 and the Providence Marine Corps of Artillery of 1801.[2]

The Washington Artillery of New Orleans, organized in 1838, was the best known prewar artillery unit in the South. Its first and only company had served in the Mexican War, and four new companies were organized in May 1861. The battalion entered Confederate service in Virginia. Eighty-one men were left behind in New Orleans to act as a reserve, but by February 1862 they became the nucleus of a fifth company that took the field in the western theater soon after the fall of Fort Donelson.[3]

No more than a few dozen volunteer and state militia batteries existed before the Civil War. Only five of the twenty-eight batteries fielded by Louisiana, for example, had been organized before the outbreak of hostilities. The level of preparedness for the field among all of these prewar units was very uneven.[4]

Using Louisiana as a guide, more than 80 percent of all the artillery units used by both sides in the Civil War had to be created from scratch. State governments did this with vigor if not efficiency, simultaneously organizing even larger forces of infantry and cavalry. For example, Illinois ultimately created 152 infantry regiments, seventeen cavalry regiments, and thirty-three batteries for the war. The artillery accounted for 16.3 percent of the state's military units, while the cavalry accounted for 8.4 percent. The infantry regiments constituted the bulk of the state's contribution, slightly more than 75 percent of its military units. When counting the men in each of the three arms, the artillery was by far the smallest in number.[5]

The cost of creating batteries was enormous. The state government spent $8,835 to recruit, uniform, and partially equip Battery G, 1st Rhode Island Light Artillery. But it took much more to fully equip a six-gun battery—as much as $50,000—and the central government had to bear most of that burden. The process was aided by generous individuals who contributed personal funds. Capt. John D. Imboden spent $298 to buy tents for the men of his Virginia battery. Capt. Thomas H. Brem "advanced the money to fully equip" Battery C, 1st North Carolina Artillery. It was later refunded by the government, "but in a depreciated currency." The Chicago Board of Trade financed not only an artillery battery but also three infantry regiments for war service. One member of the board pledged $5,121 for the battery.[6]

ARTILLERY ORGANIZATION

The manual clearly laid out the organization of artillery. In a battery of six pieces, two were designated as the right section, two the center, and the last two the left section. In a battery containing eight pieces, there were right, right-center, left, and left-center sections. The manual defined the term "battery of manoeuvre" as all the fighting elements of the unit. In other words, it referred to the guns and their assigned caissons, all properly manned, horsed, and equipped, ready for maneuvers in the field. The supporting elements accompanied the gun and maneuvered with it.[7]

The gun crew was referred to as a detachment, and each man was given a number. When the 24th New York Battery organized in 1863, each detachment consisted of one sergeant, one corporal, one gunner, and twelve men. Two detachments served each section, the latter commanded by a lieutenant. The artillery manual stipulated that the junior lieutenant should be in charge of the center section, with the senior lieutenants in charge of the flanking sections. It also noted that a lieutenant should be in charge of the line of caissons. A driver was needed for each pair of horses in the six-horse team that pulled a gun and for each pair that pulled a caisson.[8]

Support personnel included two artificers, the chief of whom was in charge of the battery forge. A mechanic, often called an artificer, was in charge of the battery wagon, which contained the unit's tools and repair material. The battery was allowed three or more wagons to convey forage, camp equipment, and other supplies. Two buglers, a man to carry the unit's guidon, and a two-horse ambulance also were allowed.[9]

The seven members of the gun detachment who loaded and fired the piece were the essential personnel who worked the crew-served weapons. "A gun detachment of artillery was like a machine," wrote John H. Rhodes of Battery B, 1st Rhode Island Light Artillery. "No one worked individually but all in unison and with the precision of clockwork, every man on time and in time."[10]

John D. Billings described how the gun detachment worked in the 10th Massachusetts Battery. A sergeant was in charge of the detachment, but a corporal acted as gunner. Seven other men worked under these two noncommissioned officers to fire the piece. Number 1 was in charge of sponging out the powder residue from the previous round and ramming home the new charge. Number 2 was responsible for placing the new charge in the tube. Number 3 thumbed the vent by using a rawhide cover over his thumb to close it while Number 1 pushed in the sponge. This prevented air from igniting any leftover powder that could prematurely set off the new charge. Number 3 also was responsible for pricking open the new cartridge through the vent once it was seated at the end of the tube in order to expose the powder. Number 3 also worked the handspike on the trail of the piece at the order of the corporal.

TABLE **3.1.** War Footing of a Six-Piece Battery

Full Battery	Members of Gun Detachment	Duties of Members of Gun Detachment
One Captain	Sergeant	Commander
Four Lieutenants	Corporal	Gunner
Two Staff Sergeants	Number 1	Sponge tube and ram home new charge
Six Sergeants	Number 2	Place new charge in tube
Twelve Corporals	Number 3	Thumb vent, help with trail handspike
Six Artificers	Number 4	Insert friction primer in vent, attach lanyard, tug on it at order of gunner
Two Buglers	Number 5	Help limber and unlimber piece, carry ammunition to Number 2
Fifty-Two Drivers	Number 6	In charge of limber, cut fuzes and place them in projectiles
Seventy Crew Men	Number 7	Carry ammunition to Number 5
110 Horses		

Number 4 inserted the friction primer into the vent, attached the lanyard, and tugged on it to fire the piece at the corporal's command. Number 5 helped the other men limber and unlimber the piece and carried powder cartridges to Number 2. Number 6 was in charge of the limber. He cut fuzes and placed them into the shell, giving the rounds to Number 7, who carried them to Number 5.[11]

Number 3 had one of the most important jobs in the team. A mistake by him could kill or injure other members of the detachment. He was enjoined to make sure the vent was fully covered and halt the sponging by calling out "stop the vent" before the sponge was pushed into the tube if that became necessary.[12]

The support personnel of the battery played a role in maintaining unit efficiency. Artificers repaired breakdowns in the field. "There were emergencies often arising in our career which very much depended upon this artificer's genius," wrote A. J. Bennett of the 1st Massachusetts Battery. Three drivers were required for every piece and three for every caisson. One driver, as mentioned earlier, took care of two horses. One pair of horses constituted the lead team, the next behind it was the swing team, and the last was termed the wheel team. It could require up to twenty-five men to man and support

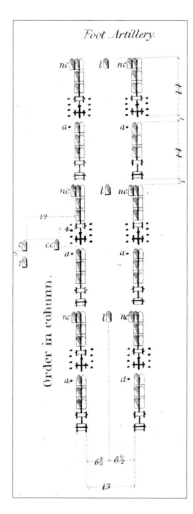

Fig. 3.1. Order in Column. This sketch illustrates a six-piece battery formed in double column, or a column of sections. It was the most commonly used of several types of column formations available to battery commanders. The caisson of each piece, with its attached limber, is placed immediately behind the piece, and the sketch shows the exact place for every member of the gun detachment. Anderson, *Instruction*, 123, plate 4.

one piece in the field, although that number varied since a piece could operate with a skeleton crew. Some of the support personnel received higher pay than the gun detachment because of their skilled trades.[13]

FORMATIONS BY THE MANUAL

The most important preparation for war was learning the formations and maneuvers contained in the army's tactical manual. *Instruction for Field Artillery* contained a wide array of information about how to form and move guns

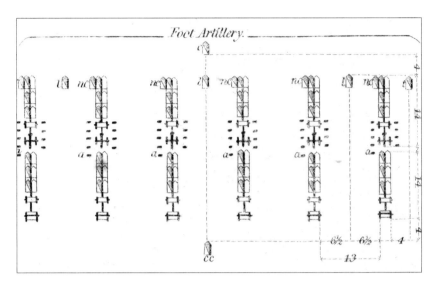

Fig. 3.2. Order in Line. Formation of a six-piece battery in line but not ready for action. The first echelon consists of the piece and limber with their six-horse teams. In the second echelon are the caissons with limbers and six-horse teams. The solid rectangles represent where each member of the gun detachment should stand. Anderson, *Instruction,* 123, plate 5.

on the battlefield, along roads, and on review. Like the infantry and cavalry manuals, it tightly focused on the primary tactical level, that of formations and maneuvers. The secondary tactical level, dealing with what today would be called operations, was barely touched on, but that did not lessen the importance of *Instruction for Field Artillery.* Formations and maneuvers constituted the foundation of small-unit tactics.[14]

There were three basic formations for field artillery. Batteries could be formed in column, in line, or in battery. All three were designed to press the guns, caissons, personnel, and horses into as small a space as possible without causing chaos. In general, the manual mandated an interval of only two yards between carriages.[15]

The most common formation in column was by section, which placed two pieces side by side, followed by another section to the rear, with a third behind the second. Each gun detachment formed on foot in two ranks and marched two yards behind its piece. When in line the battery formed two lines, the first consisting of the gun and its limber, while the second consisted of the caisson and its limber. The unit was not ready for action in this formation; that is why the third formation, in battery, was devised. In battery consisted of three lines, with the first composed of the pieces detached from their limbers and pointing toward the target. The second line consisted of the limbers with their ammunition chests, while the third line consisted of the caissons with their reserve supply of ammunition.[16]

The column formation could be altered to a column of pieces rather than a column of sections. This would stretch the battery out in a long, thin column. Yet a third option was a column of half battery, but that was recommended only for a unit consisting of eight pieces rather than six. The manual recommended the column of sections as the default column formation and reiterated that no matter what the formation, each caisson had to stick to its piece wherever it went.[17]

The column of sections also was sometimes called the double column because, compared to the column of pieces, it was twice as wide. It was best to make the center section the head of the column and the right and left sections take post to the rear. That made it easier to deploy from column into line because each of the flanking sections would have a clear way to move to the front without interfering with each other. As Henry L. Scott, author of the 1861 *Military Dictionary,* put it, "the deploy is then toward both wings at the same time, and more promptly performed." The artillery manual stipulated that the two sections following the center section should each form a column of one piece, while the center section formed a column of two pieces. The authors did not offer a rationale for this; perhaps it was easier for an individual piece to move forward without another piece to its flank. If the battery consisted of only four pieces, the center two guns could form the head of the double column.[18]

The manual specified the distances between material and personnel within formations. The term "interval" referred to the space between carriages, right to left, whereas "distance" referred to the space between one line of carriages or personnel and the one ahead or behind it. Generally, as mentioned earlier, a distance of two yards should be maintained when in column. When in line, the manual called for intervals of fourteen yards between carriages but still a distance of two yards. For horse artillery (operating with cavalry), the intervals were increased to seventeen yards.[19]

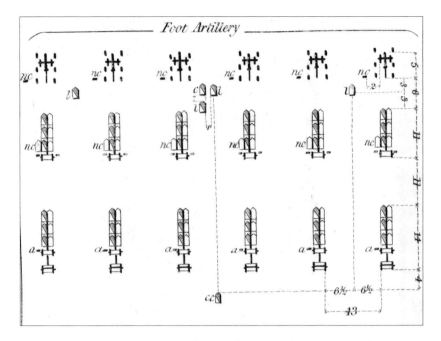

Fig. 3.3. Order in Battery. This image depicts a battery ready for action. In the first echelon are six pieces, with the members of the gun detachments in their assigned places. The second echelon consists of the six-horse teams and the limbers, which have been disconnected from the pieces. In the third echelon are the caissons, led by their six-horse teams and limbers. Anderson, *Instruction,* 125, plate 6.

Separating limbers from pieces in order to go into battery could be done in two ways. One was termed the "about," in which the drivers made a turn of 180 degrees so as to point the piece toward the enemy before unhooking the limber from the gun and sending the former to the rear. The other was to unhook the two carriages first and then manhandle the piece around to point toward the target. If already in line, the second option was the best. The members of Battery F, 1st Ohio Light Artillery preferred the second option at all times. "Instead of making the 'about' with the guns attached to the limbers, it was our way to come to a halt, unlimber, and turn the pieces by hand. By the time the limbers could be brought about we were ready to commence firing." In battery was the only formation in which the piece and its attendant caisson were separated. Otherwise, they were so important to each other that the two

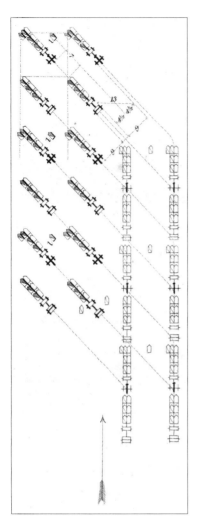

Fig. 3.4. Oblique March. This maneuver allowed a six-piece battery to change its direction of approach at a forty-five-degree angle from its original line of march. In this sketch, the battery is marching in double column and alters its direction to left oblique. Anderson, *Instruction*, 135, plate 10.

pieces of equipment linked together were often called "the piece" rather than reserving that term only for the gun.[20]

Keeping proper alignment while in any formation was considered important. It was a mark of discipline and an aspect of aesthetics as well. Normally the focus of alignment was on the drivers of the wheel horses, the team closest to the limber. In other words, if a battery was in line, one could stand opposite the wheel driver on one flank, look across the entire formation, and see that all other drivers were in line with him. When in battery, the drivers and their horses were detached from the guns, so the line of sight was taken along the wheels of the pieces.[21]

If the interval between pieces was too wide while the battery was in line, the only way to correct it was a slight forward movement. The center section, which was the guiding subunit of the six-piece battery, moved straight forward while the two flanking sections advanced at a slight oblique to close on it. If the interval could not be corrected by a slight movement such as this, then one piece from any section was advanced at least four yards, and all the others were ordered to move up and form on it. The short intervals mandated for the in-battery formation were dropped when the unit was actually on the battlefield and under fire. Then it was desirable to open the intervals and adjust the pieces to the lay of the land "so as to obtain the greatest advantage from their fires."[22]

The manual stipulated the exact spot each member of the gun detachment was to assume when in battery. Number 1 stood two feet from the right wheel and Number 2 two feet from the left wheel. Number 3 placed himself just behind Number 1, and Number 4 just behind Number 2. Number 5 stood five yards to rear of the left wheel and Number 6 to the rear of the limber, while Number 7 stood to the left of Number 6. The chief of caisson stood four yards to the rear of the limber and to its left, while the chief of the piece took his position at the trail handspike.[23]

THE MANUAL: MANEUVERS

The board that prepared *Instruction for Field Artillery* offered some theoretical discussion of their subject. They noted that the maneuvers of all three arms of the service—infantry, cavalry, and artillery—were "regulated by the same general principles." As the major arm, the infantry influenced the maneuvers of the other three more than the cavalry and artillery influenced foot maneuvers. "Infantry forms of command" were adapted as far as possible to the needs of the artillery. The board also admitted that the artillery manual contained more maneuvers than were likely to be needed in practice, but it saw this as useful. Learning all the maneuvers well meant that battery commanders would be so thoroughly prepared for war that "the most difficult circumstances may not present anything that is unknown." Cooperation with infantry and cavalry was the key. The battery commander needed to under-

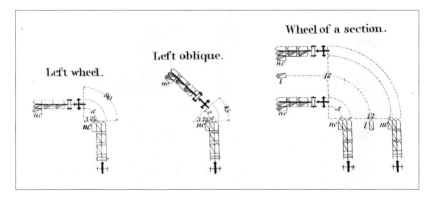

Fig. 3.5. Left Wheel, Left Oblique, and Wheel of a Section. Three maneuvers are illustrated in this image. On the left is a left wheel of ninety degrees by one piece, led by its six-horse team and limber. In the middle, a piece conducts a left oblique of forty-five degrees. On the right, a section conducts a left wheel of ninety degrees. Anderson, *Instruction,* 119, plate 2.

stand the maneuvers of those two arms if he wished to work in close union with them. The best way to maneuver a battery was by the section rather than the half battery or the piece.[24]

Instruction for Field Artillery contained full details about how to maneuver in column formation. This included changing the direction of the march, countermarching so as to redirect in the opposite direction of movement, going from column of sections to column of pieces and back again, moving by the right flank, breaking sections, and going from column into park for the night.[25]

When moving from line into column or from column into line, one section usually served as the guide, shifting first while the other two sections moved according to its movement. There was an exception to that rule, which involved each section wheeling on its own while in column so that, when they finished the wheel and faced either left or right, they would be in line. While moving straight ahead in line, one section served as a guide as the others closed on it.[26]

It often was necessary for either sections or individual pieces to move past one another. This took place in as small a space of ground as feasible and thus required dexterity on the part of the drivers. Passage of fixed obstacles such as buildings was just as important and delicate. When confronting an obstacle

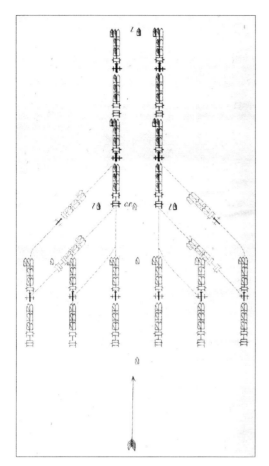

Fig. 3.6. Forming Double Column. This diagram explains how a six-piece battery could ploy from the order in line into a double column, guiding on the center section, with the two flanking sections moving into column behind the center section. Anderson, *Instruction,* 148, plate 20.

to the front, the battery captain indicated which section needed to deal with it, then it was up to the chief of that section to decide how to do so. He could accomplish the task by "closing on one of the adjoining sections, removing from it, breaking his section, or halting it and forming in column in rear of one of the adjoining sections." These were a large number of options; the section chief had to make a quick decision as to which one to employ. After negotiating the obstacle, he also had to resume his place in the line. When confronted by a narrow passage through a fence or a mountain defile, similar maneuvers were required to narrow the formation so the battery could pass through the gap.[27]

When in battery and ready for action, it often was necessary to change

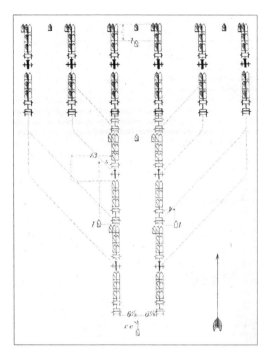

Fig. 3.7. Deploying from Double Column Forward into the Order in Line. This diagram illustrates how a six-piece battery could deploy from a double column into the order in line by guiding on the center section; in other words, the second and third sections of the column are deploying right and left into line to flank the center section. This process was the reverse of going from line to double column. Anderson, *Instruction,* 150, plate 21.

the direction of fire to meet a new threat on the flank. This involved moving most of the pieces into a new line facing right or left, leaving one in place, but changing its direction of fire, to serve as a guide for the rest. The detachment of the guiding piece simply moved the trail to point the gun in the new direction while the other crews manhandled their pieces some distance to create the new line extending from that flanking piece. If several batteries were in line and had to redirect their fire to right or left, a similar maneuver was used except that, rather than one piece, an entire battery, usually the one in the center, became the guide.[28]

Wheeling a battery involved shifting its front to right or left while in motion. This was called wheeling on a moving pivot. There was no wheeling on a stationary pivot for artillery as there was for a line of infantry. "In the wheelings," stated *Instruction for Field Artillery,* "the lead driver enters the new direction without making his horses pull; the middle driver does the same; and it is not until the wheel driver is in the new direction that the traces are stretched." A half wheel changed the direction of movement by a forty-five-degree angle rather than ninety degrees. The half wheel also was referred to as an oblique movement. The terms "about" and "countermarch" referred to reversing the direction of movement 180 degrees so that it was opposite the original direction.[29]

Moving by the flank while in line was relatively easy. Each piece turned right or left and then moved forward in a column of pieces until the desired distance had been achieved, then each once again faced to the front.[30]

The manual included instructions for firing a battery while on the move. This involved half of the guns firing to cover the advance of the other half. The right half, for example, moved forward until a certain distance ahead that did not endanger it from friendly fire, then opened on the target to cover the advance of the left half. The process was repeated until the object of the maneuver had been accomplished. The same move could be done by sections as well. Firing became more complicated when a battery was formed en echelon, which meant that each piece was a few yards forward or backward compared to its neighboring piece. The distance between their locations could not be so great as to expose one piece to the fire of its neighbor. The manual pointed out that one gun should never open fire until the horses of its neighboring gun were safely out of the way when deploying into battery successively, piece by piece.[31]

TRAINING

Although the formations and maneuvers associated with artillery training were roughly similar to those found in infantry and cavalry, it did not seem so to the men. "To be an expert artilleryman was much of an education," commented P. C. Hoy of Bradford's Mississippi Battery. John W. Chase of the 1st Massachusetts Battery agreed. "I tell you Artillery practice is a big thing to learn," he declared to his brother.[32]

Artillery training started at the most basic level. The men grouped into squads and practiced the elementary formations and maneuvers also learned by the infantry. Artillerists pointed out that they actually used very little of these formations and maneuvers, but learning them instilled discipline and military bearing. Often they learned them while temporarily armed with castoff muskets. After that, the men practiced standing-gun drill. That was the process of stepping from line into their respective positions around the gun and its limber, ready for action, and stepping back into line again. This was done without horses. The next level of training was in firing the piece.

Fig. 3.8. Battery A, 1st Pennsylvania Light Artillery (Keystone Battery). The battery has assumed the Order in Battery and is ready for firing. The pieces are in the first echelon, their limbers constitute the second echelon, and the third echelon consists of caissons and their limbers. LC-DIG-ppmsca-33218.

"In this operation each man must know his precise place," wrote Billings of the 10th Massachusetts Battery, "and fit into it as accurately as if he were a part of a machine."[33]

There were, in short, many levels of training, from the individual soldier to the squad to the gun detachment. The men also engaged in section drills and battery drills. The last named was the largest because, with all of the horses involved, battery drills required a lot of space. A heavy course of training could involve up to six hours each day, divided into three segments, from early morning to late afternoon.[34]

The men entered a new level of training when they mixed drill with firing, starting with blank cartridges. Jacob Roemer's Battery L, 2nd New York Light Artillery received 321 rounds of blanks along with 290 rounds of real ammunition when it was ready to practice firing. Even a year later Roemer used blank cartridges to continue training his men. Firing blanks also was a way to accustom new horses to the sound of battle.[35]

Artillerists practiced getting on and off the caissons and limbers for times when the battery had to move quickly. They were assigned places to sit so as to minimize the danger of falling off. The artillery manual warned that officers should not resort to this too often as it increased the weight the horses had to pull. After experience, detachment members were expected to be able to mount and dismount even while the carriages were moving at a walk to save time.[36]

The manual also contained instructions on how to dismantle a piece and put it back together. At least some units practiced this process. The 9th Massachusetts Battery "became quite proficient in it."[37]

Cross-training the members of each gun detachment so they could perform every duty involved in firing and reloading the piece was essential. The manual stressed the importance of explaining to each member why it was necessary for him to pack all this information in his long-term memory. The primary reason for cross-training was the attrition rate of gun detachments under fire. Once in action, a piece often had to be worked with a small crew, with men required to double up on their duties. The manual required officers to train detachments with reduced numbers so they could adjust to this situation while under fire. *Instruction for Field Artillery* worked out an elaborate chart indicating which man was to substitute for another, accounting for anywhere from eight men down to two men left in the gun detachment.[38]

Because the gun detachment centered on a crew-served weapon, each member was expected to know the various parts of his piece. They were quizzed by being asked to point out the various components of a gun. Bradford Nichol of Rutledge's Tennessee Battery "marked off minutely" each part of the piece and carriage for his men "and made them answer the different names" and tell him how each part was to be used.[39]

Even though they did not work the guns, the drivers intensely drilled in their own duties. With three drivers for every gun and caisson, these men played the key role in formations and maneuvers. Drivers were drilled as to the fastest way to prepare their horses using the specially designed harness made for them. They also had to understand the various formations and maneuvers and learn how to move the teams and carriages. Once in battery, the drivers' work was largely done, but some batteries also trained them in working the piece so as to replace fallen members of a gun detachment.[40]

Bugle calls were typically used in training because, once learned, they were easier to hear and recognize than verbal orders. Many of the smarter horses learned to associate a particular call with a particular movement and could respond to it even without coaxing from the driver. The buglers of Lamkin's Virginia Battery possessed "a music book with a call for every movement of the entire drill," and it is likely other batteries had such books as well.[41]

All of this training worked best if it was preceded by thorough study of the manual. Officers required an hour or two of "book learning" every day as the basis of drill. It was important to explain the reason for formations and maneuvers to them so they in turn could convey this to their men. Officers also underwent regular recitations in the manual. Artillerists often referred to this as "going to school" because they included oral exams. Noncommissioned officers also were required to participate.[42]

When Joseph William Eggleston transferred from an infantry unit to Lamkin's Virginia Battery, he found that he was well ahead of the men in his understanding of artillery drill. The battery had been recruited from the mountains, and its members possessed low levels of education. On conducting his first drill, Eggleston impressed them with how much he knew. When he told them he had read Joseph Roberts's *Hand-Book of Artillery,* one man blurted out, "'Book, I did not know you could learn this from a book.'"[43]

The ultimate level of training was a sham battle, but such exercises were comparatively rare. Battery A, 1st Rhode Island Light Artillery conducted a practice battle along with infantry and cavalry units during its training period. The men fired blank cartridges during the sham engagement. When Battery B, 1st Illinois Light Artillery staged its own mock battle, it did so by firing only friction primers and pitting one section against another.[44]

Artillerymen found sham battles stimulating and often reported the same level of excitement associated with drilling. The key factor was that both consisted of a good deal of movement at a quick pace. The swirling action impressed many observers and participants alike. "It was the grandest yet most awful spectacle that war affords," concluded Henry H. Eby of the 7th Illinois Cavalry. Adding to the excitement and elevating the level of danger, accidental explosions sometimes took place during drill. When moving with loaded caissons, there were occasions, as with the Good-Douglas Texas Battery, when poorly packed rounds loosened and went off.[45]

Taking pride in their level of accomplishment, many members of volunteer artillery units tried to compare themselves to the US Army. About half of the regular artillery was assigned to the Army of the Potomac early in the war. Historian L. Van Loan Naisawald believed the regulars provided a benchmark for the volunteer units to aspire to match. He also believed the volunteers eventually came to equal their quality.[46]

Jacob Roemer viewed the regulars as setting the standard and appreciated any "courtesies received from them." So did Capt. Thomas W. Osborn of Battery D, 1st New York Light Artillery and Capt. John J. Good of the Good-Douglas Texas Battery. "We are so well drilled that the folks around here think that we are all regulars," crowed John Reiley of the 19th Ohio Battery. When the experienced 1st Wisconsin Battery was called on to drill opposite Battery G, 5th US Artillery at New Orleans late in the war, Dan Webster and Don C. Cameron thought the regulars were "perhaps a little more like a machine in their movements." But "we could come into battery, load, fire, limber-up and move to a new position quicker than they could at their best."[47]

Volunteer artillerists understood how important training had been once they entered the field. Difficult formations and maneuvers they failed to learn on the drill ground became deadly weaknesses under fire. Battery E, 1st Illinois Light Artillery had obtained its horses only ten days before the Battle of Shiloh and had managed to train them for only three days. The drivers were unable to limber to the rear in a timely manner to save their pieces from capture on April 6.[48]

Bad training was as disastrous as no training. Capt. Charles S. Cotter seemed to use a drill "after his own style than the regular artillery tactics" when he put Battery A, 1st Ohio Light Artillery through its paces. Col. Charles Wainwright, chief of artillery for First Corps at Gettysburg, was appalled at the performance of Capt. Michael Wiedrich's Battery I, 1st New York Light Artillery on July 2. "Wiedrich . . . made wretched work of it." His men were "utterly ignorant as to ranges, and the old man [he was fifty years old] knew little more himself. I had to go to each piece myself, set their pendulum haussée, and show them just what length of fuze to use."[49]

TARGET PRACTICE

Army regulations allowed for a limited amount of target firing with blank cartridges but reminded officers that "practice in gunnery is a heavy expense to the government." The regulations did not discuss target shooting with live ammunition, but some batteries engaged in it as part of their training. Orders to conserve ammunition limited the extent to which this was possible.[50]

Battery commanders improvised when it came to selecting a target to shoot at. Some stacked fence rails to make a pile ten feet wide about a mile from the firing point, banked up earth into a berm, or selected an abandoned house half a mile away. The 18th Indiana Battery fired at "an old wheat sack hung in a fence corner" at three-quarters of a mile distance one day and at "a white Sycamore tree" two miles away on another day. Batteries camped near a large body of water fired across the liquid expanse. The 1st Maryland Artillery (CS) fired canister at flocks of ducks on the Potomac River, with nearby infantrymen securing those hit for their dinner.[51]

Artillery practice sometimes endangered civilians. Officers sent out to ensure that the way was clear near Centreville overlooked a house that soon after was potted with rounds. A sick woman and three children were inside it at the time, "all scared nearly to death," recalled Edward Porter Alexander. A fourth child became so wild with fright that he ran into the woods and only later was found. Fortunately no one was injured. The 5th Massachusetts Battery also came close to killing a woman while practice firing in the vicinity of Washington, DC, because no one told its officers that a cluster of houses was located on the other side of a hill their target occupied.[52]

The distance of artillery practice varied widely. The 1st Connecticut Battery fired at 1,600 yards, while Battery L, 2nd New York Light Artillery fired at 735 yards and then 1,795 yards. The 5th Massachusetts Battery fired at a tree one and half miles away, hitting it two or three times out of twenty rounds. For these neophyte artillerists, the distance made all the difference. The 18th Indiana Battery initially hit a target placed three-quarters of a mile away but, on another day, could not touch one placed two miles away. The men of Rutledge's Tennessee Battery needed several rounds to even come close to a target placed 845 yards away, finally landing one only a foot from it.[53]

Target firing with live ammunition taught the gunners how to adjust elevation and range. Gunners of the 5th Massachusetts Battery were not told that a stump was 1,000 yards away when they opened on it in foggy conditions. They misjudged the distance, setting the elevation at four degrees, but later when the fog began to dissipate changed it to one and three-quarter degrees to land several rounds very near the stump.[54]

Batteries raised in 1862 seem to have practiced live firing more intensely than those organized earlier in the war. When the 18th Ohio Battery joined with the 19th Ohio Battery for target training in December 1862, both units fired at a locust tree almost daily. Their practice was "pretty wild" at a distance of 1,300 yards but calmed down when brought 400 yards closer to the tree.[55]

Target practice with live ammunition accustomed the men to the noise and excitement of firing and taught them to respect the punching power of their guns. They did much better at shorter distances than long, foreshadowing the problems associated with firing rifled pieces. Target practice also taught the men to consider unintended consequences. Jacob Foster used a large plantation as a firing range because it was so big that his firing would not endanger any nearby properties.[56]

CONTINUED TRAINING

The artillery continued drilling and target firing even after the men had undergone the test of battle. New recruits and fresh horses were continually being added to batteries, and it was necessary to train them. Even veterans became rusty if not put through their paces between campaigns. The men, who thought they already knew enough, sometimes resented these refresher courses in drill and target practice, but they were useful in honing a unit's combat efficiency.[57]

Artillery units constantly trained throughout their war service. They also drilled in large groups, several batteries together. Units that had little opportunity to train early in their service made up for it later. "We drill at every gait from the walk to the gallop and every thing in the Tactics," reported Lt. Harry C. Cushing of Battery H, 4th US Artillery in February 1863. Recitations for officers and noncommissioned officers continued. Battery B, 1st Rhode Island Light Artillery drilled with a brigade of infantry in May 1863, which was "very instructive both to the infantry and artillery." Wainwright mandated recitations in tactics and regulations three days a week and drill at least two or three hours each day, with priority given to battery-level drill. Sham battles continued, and some units competed in drill competitions, with a prize awarded the winner.[58]

Target practice became an important part of refresher training. When Swett's Mississippi Battery and the Good-Douglas Texas Battery fired at a target 1,200 yards away in August 1863, although both units had endured several battles, neither could hit it. Target practice took on a more intense and professional tone as the war lengthened. Officers still set up improvised targets, such as shelter-tent halves, but they fired more rounds during each session and assigned men to observe and record the effect of every shot. A thorough report, required by the artillery chief of the Army of the Potomac early in 1864, included the name of the gunner, the number of rounds fired, the distance, the elevation, the length of fuze, the type of ammunition, and the results of the firing.[59]

Training was vitally important, no matter when it took place. Ordered to cross a railroad and go "forward into battery, left oblique, march!," during the Peninsula Campaign, members of the 1st Company, Richmond Howitzers executed the maneuver perfectly. Robert Stiles "was amazed to see every piece, limber, caisson and man in the exact mathematical position in which each belonged, and every man seemed to have struck the very attitude required by the drill-book."[60]

FORMATIONS IN THE FIELD

As Stiles reminds us, the link between training and performance on the battlefield was vitally important. One was intricately tied to the other. A survey of reports and personal accounts demonstrates that most artillerists learned the formations and maneuvers well enough to perform them effectively under fire. Many could execute them with assurance, others could just get by, while a small minority utterly failed.

The column formation was universally employed by artillerists during the war. It was the only way to move a battery along a road. Columns were used in moving toward the battlefield. Deploying into line took place only when the battery was ready to go into action. Going into battery took place at the last moment in this approach to combat.[61] Reports often did not specify the type of column, but that could be because the double column (one section, or two pieces, wide) was the default style. Columns of pieces were used quite often, especially if there was a narrow space through which the battery was to pass. For example, Battery B, 1st Rhode Island Light Artillery moved along Caroline Street in the town of Fredericksburg during the engagement on December 13, 1862. Other batteries adopted the column of pieces to pass through woods, deploying into line on open ground beyond.[62]

The echelon formation was widely used on many battlefields, especially when one battery aligned next to another to protect each other's flank.[63] Another use of the echelon formation was to better fire in several directions as needed. Lt. Michael Leahy positioned Battery B and Battery K, 1st US Artillery in echelon at the Battle of the Staunton River Bridge on June 25, 1864. The two units formed "nearly a half circle, enabling the fire to be changed to any direction with but little maneuvering."[64]

Adjusting the intervals between pieces often accompanied an echelon formation. Lt. George B. Winslow set the pieces of his Battery D, 1st New York Light Artillery "into *échelon,* at about two-thirds the usual intervals and distances, the better to command the slope of the hill and both flanks" at Chancellorsville in May 1863. John Cheves Haskell contended that increasing the intervals while in echelon formation enabled him to protect one piece with the crossfire of another when he had no infantry support.[65]

It often became necessary to ignore the regulation interval between pieces even when batteries were not formed in echelon. Because of limited space, Maj. Thomas W. Osborn put five batteries at half regulation intervals on top of Cemetery Hill at Gettysburg. Some interval was essential for the gun detachment to work properly, so there was a limit to closing it. While some officers thought six yards was too little, others believed eight yards was barely enough. Increasing the interval was seen as a way to lessen damage from return fire by spreading the battery out a bit.[66]

It was not uncommon to place sections anywhere from 200 to 800 yards apart to take advantage of terrain features or to spread out their fire. This forced battery commanders to move from one to another section to supervise their performance. Lt. Lyman A. White of Bridges's Illinois Battery indicated that operating in sections rather than as a battery was the common mode during the Atlanta Campaign.[67] But only rarely did officers form their units in half battery.[68]

Many commanders adopted several formations during the course of a single engagement. Capt. Jacob T. Foster advanced his 1st Wisconsin Battery across the heavily wooded bottomland of the Yazoo River during the Chickasaw Bayou Campaign on December 27, 1862. He began by passing through woods in column while following an infantry brigade, then formed line at double interval in a field that had scattered trees and logs in the way. Then he formed in battery near Mrs. Lake's house and waited two hours. After that, "we formed into column" and went forward and left to the bank of Chickasaw Bayou, where the men formed in battery once again.[69]

MANEUVERS IN THE FIELD

Conducting complicated maneuvers in the field represented the height of tactical proficiency, especially under battlefield conditions. Movement was the key to tactical success. One aspect of this is speed, or the gait of the horses.

The manual identified four speeds. The slowest was the walk, but it often was inadequate if a battery had to keep up with infantry. Next was the trot, followed by the trot out (which was a more rapid trot), and then the gallop. When decreasing speed, the order was gallop, trot out, trot, and walk.[70]

While Lt. Tully McCrea of the 1st US Artillery claimed that he rarely saw a battery go into battle at anything above a walk, the evidence in reports and other personal accounts indicate that a faster gait was common. Officers used the trot and the trot out.[71] They used the gallop just as often but were careful not to exhaust the horses.[72] Interestingly, some commanders moved their animals at a double quick, even though that was an infantry term that appeared in the artillery manual only when instructing officers how to move their gun detachments on foot; it did not apply the term to horses.[73]

Changing front while in battery could be accomplished in different ways. When Confederate infantry appeared to the right of the 2nd Maine Battery on July 1 at Gettysburg, Capt. James A. Hall conducted "a partial change of front by hand" in their direction and fired double canister to stop them. Capt. James Stewart ordered his Battery B, 4th US Artillery "to change front forward on the left piece" to meet a similar emergency that day. Lt. Andrew T. Blodgett executed the same maneuver but to the rear in the battle of July 22, 1864, during the Atlanta Campaign. In addition to changing the front of the entire battery, some commanders did this for only half the battery or for just one section.[74]

Officers often called for a wheeling movement while batteries were still in motion.[75] They also employed the left or right oblique quite often.[76] Gun detachments became adept at moving by the flank. Capt. Putnam Darden employed this maneuver because his Jefferson Artillery's fire was blocked by friendly infantry to his front at Stones River on December 31, 1862. By sliding to the side, he uncovered his front and opened fire.[77] Conducting an about was one of the more difficult maneuvers to perform, especially under pressure, but several battery commanders managed it. The maneuver is rarely reported and must have been rarely utilized.[78]

Fences impeded artillery movement across the battlefield. Unlike infantry, which could crawl across a fence if needed, the big guns needed a passage through it. If the gunners could not easily pull it apart, they took axes from the battery wagon and chopped a hole through it.[79]

Officers felt comfortable advancing and retiring by pieces, sections, and half battery. Each subunit advanced from 200 to 1,000 yards at a bound to wait for the others to move in succession, often firing at the same time.[80] In addition, many batteries conducted several maneuvers during the course of a single day of battle. Battery E, 2nd Illinois light Artillery occupied six positions on April 6 at Shiloh, conducting different maneuvers to assume them. Capt. Josiah H. Burton of Battery F, 1st Illinois Light Artillery "fired in almost every direction and moved his battery many times" during the engagement of July 22 outside Atlanta.[81]

For the most part, artillery officers used the correct wording for every maneuver as stipulated by the artillery manual, but sometimes they varied the language. Jacob Roemer was careful to give the exact wording to reach a position during the Second Battle of Bull Run in August 1862 because his men were comparatively new to service; he never gave those exact words again on future battlefields. With repeated experience his men came to understand his meaning no matter his exact wording.[82] When Capt. James Stewart moved his Battery B, 4th US Artillery into a dangerous spot at Cold Harbor in June 1864, he gave the standard orders for the movement but then added something "not included in the 'Light Artillery Manual,'" recalled Augustus Buell. "'Come on, boys! Follow me!!—Charge!!!'" Buell affirmed, "We all knew what it meant." When staff officer Thomas H. Malone instructed Smith's Mississippi Battery to open fire at Stones River, Lt. William B. Turner "gave the order to his men in his own peculiar slang and drawling, whining voice." Then "his bright, intelligent Lieutenant Smith translated it into military phraseology."[83]

The manual spelled out the process of moving artillery pieces by hand when they were in battery. It was obvious that, if the piece was to be moved only a short distance, it was better for the gun detachment to do it themselves rather than to limber up the horses.[84] But there are many examples of gun detachments moving artillery pieces a considerable distance in battle. These usually occurred when the battery commander did not want to expose his horses to enemy fire. Lt. Lester I. Richardson ordered his men to move their pieces up "a little more than" the length of the recoil so they could creep forward after every round on June 18, 1864, at Petersburg. Capt. Louis Hoffmann's 4th Ohio Battery did the same at Chickasaw Bayou, gaining "ground yard by yard." The total distance moved in some cases was fifty to one hundred yards. Remarkably, some gun detachments did this even while advancing up a slope.[85]

MOVING

Artillery handbooks stressed the need for speed when an alarm was called. To be caught with horses unharnessed and the battery in park on the approach of an enemy was humiliating, so speed drills often were worked into training. The 5th Company, Washington Artillery managed to hitch up and be ready to move, during drills, in anywhere from four to fifteen minutes. The latter timing seems to have been more common for most units, with a number of other batteries reporting that it took ten, fifteen, or twenty minutes to go from a restful state to a condition of readiness.[86]

The handbooks specified the rate of marching once the battery began to move. John Gibbon thought a pace of two and a half miles per hour was ideal; a battery could double that speed if the horses moved at a trot for half the time. Gibbon recommended a halt of ten minutes every hour for rest and to allow the column to close up. He thought a battery should not try to move more than forty miles in one day. Drivers should reduce their horses to a walk at least fifteen minutes before halting for a short rest and at least one hour before going into camp for the night.[87]

The manual stipulated that each gun detachment should be divided so that half marched with the gun and the rest with the caisson. In this way the men could lend ready assistance to both carriages when overcoming difficulties in the road. The carriages should maintain a distance of at least two yards from each other and cross ditches at a slant to put less strain on the teams. Every battery had some extra horses, and they could be added to the teams to negotiate steep slopes, but the manual cautioned not to place more than ten horses on a carriage because it was too difficult to manage such a large team.[88] Naturally, the men wanted to ride on the carriages, but the manual strictly forbid this except for two circumstances. The first was when the battery was ordered to move at a trot, a pace too fast for footmen to keep up, and the second was "to make a rapid crossing in the vicinity of the enemy."[89]

A battery could make good time in the right conditions. There are reports of artillery moving fifty miles in twenty-six hours, although the average rate of travel for Maj. Gen. William T. Sherman's guns during the Carolinas Campaign was up to eighteen miles per day.[90] Difficult road conditions, of course, slowed the rate of travel. Four miles from Gettysburg on July 1, Lt. William Wheeler responded to an order to move his 13th New York Battery as fast as possible. The "roads were very stony, and my wheels were in very bad condition, but ahead I went; the gun-carriages rattling and bouncing in the air; feed, rations, kettles and everything else breaking loose from the caissons, the cannoneers running with all their might to keep up." He refused to allow the detachment to mount the carriages for fear they would be thrown off.[91]

Night marches were very difficult, and Charles Wainwright believed the cost was too high to attempt them, especially if through unknown and wooded country. When forced to move his artillery through side roads on the night of November 6, 1863, his equipment suffered from running into trees, breaking wheels and harnesses and losing implements. "I think that $3,000 would not cover the loss to [the] government in my command alone," he wrote.[92]

The manual indicated that artillery could ford a stream as long as the water was no more than three feet deep. When crossing a pontoon bridge, everyone was to dismount except the wheel driver, and he was to keep twenty yards between carriages. It was dangerous to place nearly all the weight of one gun and its limber on one pontoon, a consideration that influenced the placement of the floating bridge. If there was no more than eighteen feet between the middle of one pontoon and that of its neighbor, then artillery could safely move in a continuous stream across the bridge.[93]

Many times artillerists had to improvise a stream crossing. Members of the 25th Ohio Battery wrapped tarpaulins around the boxes of two army wagons and took them off the wheels to use as ferry boats when crossing the White River in Arkansas. The stream was 350 feet wide, and the water was too cold for anyone to swim across it with one end of the rope that was needed to pull the improvised boats across. Not even a mule would swim the river by itself with the rope attached to its tail. So the battery men took the powder out of a 6-pounder case shot and stuck a piece of wood in the fuze hole, tying a cord to the wood and the end of the rope to the other end of the cord. They fired the projectile with only two ounces of powder to get the rope across the river.[94]

Stream crossings could be very dangerous. Several accidents occurred as carriages rolled off narrow bridges, especially in the dark, leading to the drowning of horses and the injury of drivers. When pieces fell into creeks, they were retrieved by pulling them out with other teams.[95]

Movement produced friction, which in turn created wear and tear on equipment. On the march the men greased all wheels every five days, using hog's lard as the best lubricant. Collars and saddles rubbed the horses' skin and produced sores if they were not unsaddled and rubbed down. The men also covered the elevating screws when on the march to prevent them from "being clogged with dirt."[96]

PARKING

Given the large equipment drawn by teams of horses, instructions on how to arrange everything when stopping were needed. Bivouac referred to a quick settling for sleep during a march and thus was not as complicated as a semi-permanent park. Gibbon recommended selecting a bivouac site one hundred yards from any houses and placing the carriages at internals of four yards, the pieces in one line and the caissons in another; forges and battery wagons constituted a separate line. From two to four sentinels should be posted to secure the bivouac site.[97]

For a longer-lasting camp, two plans of park were recommended. Augustus Buell described them as the half-battery plan and the section plan. The substantial difference between the two was that the former placed all the men's tents, the poles upon which they hung the harness, and all their horses to both sides of the park, with guns, caissons, and battery wagons taking up the interior. The latter plan allowed the men, harness poles, and horses to remain with their section inside the park. According to Buell, the men preferred the section plan so they could camp together, placing their tents in front of their own gun. Buell indicated that batteries often adopted a third plan not laid down in the manual. This was adapted from the cavalry camp and involved placing all the tents of a battery in one line facing the line of horses, with the guns and caissons in yet a third line.[98]

Descriptions of park arrangements by artillerymen reveal that sometimes they adhered to regulations and other times adapted according to their own notions. When Battery M, 1st Illinois Light Artillery created a park after the fall of Atlanta, a couple of officers and three enlisted men staked it out. They arranged a variation of the manual by placing the horses on either side of the park and within it as well, mixing them with the guns and the men's tents.[99]

Posting guards was vital whether the unit was in bivouac or in a longer-term park. The 7th Massachusetts Battery placed one sentinel to watch the guns and caissons and two to watch the horses. The former was to make sure no one meddled with the guns and caissons and prevented any citizen from entering the park. The two men with the horses prevented their being stolen, caught any that broke loose, and helped those that got entangled with the picket rope.[100]

CONCLUSION

To move from a peace establishment to a war footing was a challenge in 1861. The small force of regular artillery and the handful of prewar volunteer and militia batteries found it relatively easy to make the transition. But the newly created volunteer batteries, constituting 80 percent of the artillery force used in the Civil War, had to learn everything from scratch. The officers and men had the well-developed artillery manual and a number of good handbooks to guide them, but this could only be a starting point. Months of training, which continued far beyond their initial service period, and the hard experience of campaigning and battle constituted the heart of their preparation for war.

Artillery did not necessarily have more to learn than infantry or cavalry, but its training was vastly different from the other two arms of the service. It was the only arm that used crew-served weapons, demanding a higher degree of teamwork and a higher level of technical knowledge. Weaponry and other hardware mattered more to the artillery than to the other arms, and each member of the gun detachment was compelled to understand his weapon. Artillerymen also managed large teams of horses in contrast to the infantrymen, who did not have to bother with a horse, or a cavalryman, who only had to manage his own mount. Batteries were small units, the equivalent of an infantry or cavalry company, but they were more complex and more independent than either counterpart in the other two arms.

An artilleryman's worth was measured entirely by the fire of his piece. Another step in gaining a war footing, therefore, was the acquisition of proper artillery weapons, especially in an era of transition from smoothbore to rifled pieces. Finding the right hardware and using it effectively in the field was all important to the success of the artillery arm.

4

. . . .

HARDWARE

Civil War armies used about a dozen different types and sizes of artillery pieces. These weapons varied in their technical capabilities, the size and weight of their projectiles, and the type of metal they employed. Weight of projectiles ranged from six pounds to thirty pounds, and constituent metals included brass, bronze, steel, wrought iron, and cast iron. About half the pieces used in the war were rifles, and the rest were smoothbore.[1]

The conflict offered artillerymen ample opportunity to evaluate the effectiveness of their weapons. A number of Federals liked the Napoleon and worked to acquire it for their units. Henry J. Hunt, longtime artillery chief of the Army of the Potomac, was among those who preferred the French-designed weapon. Another regular officer, Harry C. Cushing, joined Hunt in that opinion, but many volunteer artillerists preferred the sleek new weapon too. John Merrilles rejoiced when these "splendid guns" were added to Battery E, 1st Illinois Light Artillery.[2]

According to ordnance chief Josiah Gorgas, the Napoleon was the favorite Confederate fieldpiece of the war. "The simplicity and certainty of the ammunition of this smooth-bore, its capacity for grape and canister, its good range, and its moderate draught, as it was not too heavy for four horses, were certainly strong reasons in its favor. At the distance at which the serious work of the artillery was done, it was an over-match for rifled artillery."[3] Philip D. Stephenson of the 5th Company, Washington Artillery, agreed that the Napoleon was "the best gun for all round field service." He admired the appearance of the piece as well. "They were beautiful, perfectly plain, tapering gracefully from muzzle to 'reinforce' or 'butt,' without rings, ridges, or ornaments of any kind. We were proud of them and felt towards them almost as if they were human."[4]

Fig. 4.1. 3-Inch Ordnance Rifle. Developed from a prototype made by John Griffen, this cannon was sponsored by the US Ordnance Department and became available at the opening of the Civil War. Made of wrought iron, it was one of the three most commonly used cannon of the war and remained a mainstay of the American artillery force long after Appomattox. Photograph by Jack W. Melton Jr.

Quite a few officers sought to add the Napoleon to their units. Confederates widely believed it was more effective against personnel, especially at short distances, and could deal with an enemy battery at 800 to 1,000 yards distance. For many, Napoleons were "undoubtedly the most efficient field-guns in service." Surprisingly, a handful of Napoleons were rifled. Of about five hundred surviving pieces today, six have rifling. Some also were made of wrought iron rather than bronze.[5]

Of the dozen or so major types of pieces employed in the war, the 3-Inch Ordnance Rifle was the only one developed just as the conflict began. It was adapted from a weapon previously manufactured by John Griffen, superintendent of Safe Harbor Iron Works in Lancaster County, Pennsylvania, in 1854. Griffen's innovation was to use wrought iron welded together rather than hammered to make the tube. Officers of the US Ordnance Department altered elements of his design to make a piece fit for army use by 1861. The 3-Inch Ordnance Rifle also was sleek in design to reduce the number of stress points to almost zero. The Phoenix Iron Company of Phoenixville, Pennsylvania, parent company of Safe Harbor Iron Works, made 543 of these rifles from November 21, 1861, to November 25, 1862, and another 327 from the latter date to April 1865. The army had to condemn only 15 of these weapons and paid between $330 and $350 each for those it retained. All of the Phoenix pieces were made of wrought iron. Only one other civilian firm made the 3-Inch Ordnance Rifle, Singer-Nimick Company of Pittsburgh, producing six pieces made of cast steel instead of wrought iron.[6]

The tube, which was 69 inches long and weighed 820 pounds, had seven grooves, which were 0.84 inches wide and 0.075 inches deep, with one turn in eleven feet. It fired 1,850 yards at five-degrees elevation, about the same as a 10-pounder Parrott. The 3-Inch Ordnance Rifle was mounted on a standard carriage made for the 6-pounder bronze field gun, which was not entirely suited to it. Like the carriage used for the 10-pounder Parrott and the James rifle, the increased recoil created by the rifling led to damaged trail and cheek pieces for the Ordnance Rifle. The carriage weighed 900 pounds, making for a total weight of 1,720 pounds for the piece.[7]

The 3-Inch Ordnance Rifle, according to one artillerist, "eventually became the favorite" piece in the Union army. "They delivered their fire with an accuracy and certainty not excelled by any pieces upon the field," concluded Capt. Job B. Stockton about his battery's ordnance. The wrought-iron process, which involved wrapping several layers of iron to form the tube, produced exceptionally strong cannon. There is no evidence that any Ordnance Rifle burst during the war.[8]

Confederate gunners who were on the receiving end of the 3-Inch Ordnance Rifle called it "the most accurate field piece" of the Civil War. It "was a dead shot at any distance under a mile. They could hit the head of a flour barrel more often than miss, unless the gunner got rattled." Some Confederates thought it was superior to the Napoleon. Because of its origin, the Ordnance Rifle was not available to Confederate units unless they captured it on the battlefield. When Capt. Joseph Graham's Company C, 1st North Carolina Artillery received an Ordnance Rifle that had been taken at Gettysburg, the men considered it "our new treasure."[9]

The Federals who used the 3-Inch Ordnance Rifle offered varied comments about its effectiveness. Most believed it was superior to the 10-pounder Parrott only because of the latter's tendency to burst. But Capt. Richard Waterman of Battery C, 1st Rhode Island Light Artillery thought the Parrott was superior to the Ordnance Rifle at distances of 900–1,500 yards. The Ordnance Rifle bested a Confederate Whitworth at 2,700 yards during the Battle of Fredericksburg but only because Charles Wainwright, who liked the weapon, personally directed its fire. At Chancellorsville Wainwright observed the effect of both the Ordnance Rifle and the 10-pounder Parrott at distances of 2,700–3,000 yards and concluded there was no difference in accuracy. Still, he preferred the Ordnance Rifle because of its lighter weight. Many battery commanders replaced other types with Ordnance Rifles whenever they had a chance to do so.[10]

But the Ordnance Rifle was not uniformly praised by the Federals. Henry Hunt referred to it as "the feeblest [piece] in the world," and others considered its "weight of metal" too light. When dealing with infantry at close distance, the Napoleon surpassed the Ordnance Rifle because it could handle canister better.[11] The only piece that could rival the 3-Inch Ordnance Rifle at long distance was the 10-pounder Parrott, which was praised by many Federals. In fact, within the Army of the Tennessee, the 10-pounder Parrott was preferred to the Ordnance Rifle. Still, a Confederate artillerist was stunned by the Ordnance Rifle's superiority over the 6-pounders he used.[12]

While the 10-pounder Parrott was widely praised, the heavier 20-pounder version was liked by some and disliked by others. One 20-pounder Parrott "was better than a whole 6 pdr pop gun battery," as A. C. Waterhouse put it after the war. Nearly 300 of them were made for the Union army from September 1861 through July 1864, and they found their way into many field units. Tredegar Iron Works at Richmond manufactured some for the Confederates, but the quality was poor. Even so, when Bradford's Mississippi Battery acquired three 20-pounder Parrotts captured in May 1864, P. C. Hoy thought they "were beauties, if such a thing as a gun could be called so."[13] Hunt rated the 20-pounder Parrott as inferior to other pieces. "The gun is too heavy for field purposes," and the 4.5-inch siege gun was better suited for situations demanding a heavier piece. It was difficult to find reliable projectiles for the 20-pounder Parrott, and "the guns themselves are unsafe," he observed. Of twenty-two 20-pounder Parrotts used at Antietam in September 1862, two of them burst.[14]

The James rifle received divergent evaluations. While Gov. Richard Yates believed its performance at Fort Donelson in February 1862 warranted the purchase of many more for army use, Lt. Stephen Carr Lyford reported it was "almost universally condemned" by the men. Lyford, chief of artillery in the Army of the Tennessee, cited "its liability to clog and its accuracy being thereby impaired" as the chief reason. He also noted that it was two or three times more expensive than better types and could not "endure half the number of rounds" as the 10-pounder Parrott.[15]

The 4.5-inch siege rifle, Model 1861, was designed for heavy work in fixed positions but found its way into the field. The Army of the Potomac had two batteries of these cast-iron rifles from late 1862 until early 1864. No one reported any problems with the performance of the piece but all found it too heavy for field service. Sherman shipped them to his army group for the bombardment of Atlanta in July and August 1864. "In accuracy, range, and certainty of flight and explosion," the 4.5-inch siege rifle left "nothing to be desired," commented Brig. Gen. William F. Barry, Sherman's artillery chief. Other types positioned in the gray area between light and heavy guns included 30-pounder Parrotts and 32-pounder guns.[16]

English-made pieces were well liked by both Union and Confederate artillerists. The 3-inch Blakely guns "would shoot a mile as well as a half, and they were very accurate, too," commented a North Carolina man. Artillerists also liked the Whitworth gun for its convenience of loading at the breech. "Their accuracy was amazing, while the unnecessary, unsightly, dangerous, and detestable ramrod business was entirely discarded, and the rapidity of fire increased."[17] US citizens living abroad purchased six Whitworth pieces for the Union army. They constituted a battery in the Army of the Potomac during the Peninsula Campaign and then shifted to the defenses of Washington, DC. By August 1863 Brig. Gen. Richard Arnold believed there were eight Whitworth guns in the Union army. The Saint Louis Arsenal manufactured the special eight-sided projectile used in them.[18]

The Federals were impressed by the technical aspects of the Whitworth but not by its impracticality. The rifling consisted not of grooves cut into the barrel but "by making the bore itself hexagonal with a rapid twist." It only fired solid shot, but the round was "planed down to fit the bevels of the bore exactly," and the powder charge, which was contained in a tin case, also fitted the bore exactly. It had tremendous distance and accuracy, but the caliber was too small to do a lot of damage to the target. Moreover, the distance was so great that gunners could hardly tell the effect of their shots unless the round kicked up a lot of dust. The rifle itself was too heavy for easy maneuvering in the field. All of these limitations caused the Whitworth to be little used by either side.[19]

Civil War artillerists preferred some types of metal over others. Iron was deemed better than brass by some. The latter metal tended to become hot with rapid firing, which led to premature discharges. Bronze pieces tended to wear out sooner than those made of other metals. Bronze was good enough for smoothbores and had the advantage of being easily melted down for reuse. Wrought iron was cheaper than steel, and some thought it lasted longer. While some gunners liked steel, ordnance chief George D. Ramsay cautioned that it had not received enough of a trial even as late as July 1864. "We should . . . not accept the virtue of steel as an established fact until it is thoroughly tried in the forms in which it is to be used," he concluded about the metal that ultimately exceeded all others in use after the war.[20]

One of the more important questions to be answered in the Civil War was whether rifled artillery proved its worth in field conditions. As Maj. Gen. George B. McClellan put it, "rifled ordnance was just coming into use for the first time in this country" when the war broke out. It was "a mere matter of theory" as to whether they were worth employing in large numbers.[21]

Artillerists rarely declared fully in favor of rifles or smoothbores. They were aware that rifles were better at longer distances and often noted that smoothbores were better at shorter distances. Within their own spheres, both rifles and smoothbores worked well, which is why Civil War artillerists wanted to mix the two types in their units. Barry reflected this way of thinking as he praised the 3-Inch Ordnance Rifle, the 10-pounder Parrott, and the 20-pounder Parrott equally with the Napoleon as long as each piece was used in consonance with its special strengths.[22]

SIGHTING DEVICES

Civil War artillerists used several devices to set the elevation of their pieces for distance firing. The old gunner's quadrant was not popular, so the breech sight and gunner's level were more often employed. The most complicated sighting device was the pendulum-hausse. Unlike the breech sight and gunner's level, which were set on top of the tube near the breech, the pendulum-hausse rested on a special seat that extended from the butt of the tube. It had a lead-filled ball that swung freely to mark the vertical plane. All three of these devices had slides to set the elevation for distance firing, with the gunner visually aligning them with the front sight of the tube.[23]

We have only limited information about whether and how sighting devices were used in the field. Confederate battery officers included references to sighting devices in their reports of Stones River. The men of Scott's Tennessee Battery "used the pendulum hausses with tolerable satisfaction." But far more officers indicated that they had never been issued sighting devices of any kind or found them unnecessary. "We could make little or no use of them," wrote Lt. L. G. Marshall of Carnes's Tennessee Battery. "Our chiefs of pieces much preferred to watch the effect of their shots, and regulate the elevation accordingly."[24]

Capt. William L. Ritter of the 3rd Maryland Battery (CS) did not participate in the fighting at Stones River, but he noted in other battles that the impact of firing tended to press the butt of the tube upon the elevating screw and depress it a bit. If a piece was engaged in very intense and rapid firing, the gunner often forgot to adjust elevation to compensate for it. There would be no time to use a sighting device in conditions such as these; the gunner had to rely on his experience and presence of mind.[25]

Federal officers gave very few references to the use of aiming devices. Capt. Edward W. Rogers noted that three of his gunners took along their breech sights when abandoning their pieces in the Confederate attack on Fort Stedman in March 1865 to prevent the enemy from using them. This would imply that the use of sighting devices was perhaps more common among Union batteries than among Confederate units.[26]

VENTS

The vent was an important element of the piece. A narrow hole allowing communication between the end of the barrel and the outside of the tube, it had to be as small as possible to limit the escape of gases when the piece was fired. At 0.2 inches in diameter, it was big enough to allow the primer to operate. "Large vents are more rapidly injured than small ones," noted Joseph Roberts in his handbook, and the wear and tear on a vent was a sure sign that the piece had been used for a long time. Repeated firings of bronze pieces tended to melt the tin in the metal of the vent and thus widen it. John Gibbon noted that a vent piece made "of pure copper screwed into the gun" was best. If it became too wide, it could easily be removed and replaced.[27]

But there are many reports of widened vents even after relatively limited firing. Three of the 10-pounder Parrotts in Battery D, 5th US Artillery suffered "materially" enlarged vents during the Peninsula and Seven Days Campaigns in 1862.[28] Some officers referred to vents burning out, sometimes until one could stick a finger into them.[29] Others noted that vents literally blew out of the tube when the piece was fired. They found, as Gibbon asserted, that vents made of copper proved to be much more resistant to widening.[30]

Artillerists learned to deal with this problem. When the vent of his piece enlarged during rapid firing at Cedar Mountain on August 9, 1862, Edward A. Moore of the Rockbridge Artillery noticed that much more smoke was gushing from it. He told his captain, who advised him it would cause wild shooting, so Moore took his piece to the rear. But Capt. Jacob T. Foster continued firing when the vent of a 20-pounder Parrott partly blew out; he just fired more slowly. During the Siege of Vicksburg, which witnessed an enormous amount of firing, Federal gun vents often enlarged or blew out; they were replaced at the ordnance depot established at the Yazoo River near the siege line. The problem seemed more acute among the various Parrott pieces than other types.[31]

Making it impossible to use the vent was the quickest way to disable a gun. Driving a spike into the hole was the typical method. Some Confederates who captured guns at Fort Stedman had no spikes, however, so they hammered away at the vents to dent their circumference enough so the pieces could not be used when the Federals reclaimed the fort. Capt. George R. Swallow of the 7th Indiana Battery managed to spike his own gun at Stones River without meaning to do so. The "vent of my left piece became filled with friction primers" because someone had neglected to see that the one primer was taken out before inserting another. Other ways in which a vent could be made a hindrance was to place the cartridge with a seam under the opening, which made it more difficult to prick open the fabric to expose the powder. In Lumsden's Alabama Battery, a piece of wet cartridge bag jammed in the vent of one piece during ramming and had to be driven out with a punch and hammer.[32]

IGNITION

By 1861 igniting an artillery piece by using fire had become old fashioned. Even so, portfire made an appearance now and then. Not only was it defined as a

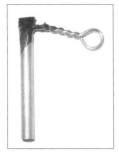

Fig. 4.2. Friction Primer. This small device, shown here as a reproduction example, was the best detonation method for cannon by the time of the Civil War, replacing linstock and portfire. The Number 4 of the gun detachment inserted it into the vent. Then he attached to it the hook on the end of the lanyard, stretched the lanyard taut, and tugged sharply when ordered. This pulled the horizontal piece of the primer through the end of the vertical piece, creating sparks that communicated down the vertical tube into the powder charge. The friction primer was issued to batteries in larger numbers than the rounds they possessed because they sometimes failed to go off properly, and crews often dropped them in action. Photograph by Pratibha A. Dabholkar.

fuze containing portfire combustibles, but the term also referred to a slow-burning cord that smoldered for a lengthy period of time when lit. Contained in a metal tube at the end of a stick, it could be inserted into the ground until needed. Capt. William N. Pendleton was familiar with portfire from his West Point cadet days and used it during the first engagement of his Rockbridge Artillery in July 1861. It was lighted just in case the friction primer did not work but proved to be unnecessary; it was never lighted again in the battery.[33] Nevertheless, portfire is included on the receipt for a number of ordnance stores received by the Norfolk Virginia Artillery in November 1863, which indicates that ordnance officers must have taken it more seriously than did gunners. The Norfolk unit, armed with 10-pounder Parrotts, also received 764 friction primers.[34]

Civil War artillerists, understandably, preferred the friction primer. Consisting of a small brass tube full of powder with a cross tube at top and a wire that, when jerked by a long cord called a lanyard, created friction to ignite the powder, it was the most effective method of igniting a cannon yet developed. One hundred primers were packed in a tin box for shipment to units, and ordnance officers were advised to issue 50 percent more primers than the number of rounds on hand to allow for waste and carelessness.[35]

Although advanced in design and concept, the friction primer did not always work. Confederate captain David D. Waters found that a "great number of friction-primers . . . were worthless" during the Battle of Stones River. "I

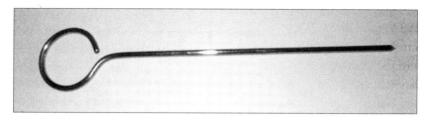

Fig. 4.3. Vent Pick, or Priming Wire. The Number 3 of the gun detachment was responsible for exposing powder to the action of the friction primer by punching a hole in the
fabric of the powder charge after it had been rammed home to the end of the tube. He
inserted a pick like this reproduced example through the vent before Number 4 inserted the friction primer. Photograph by Pratibha A. Dabholkar.

was compelled to make on the field quill-primers, which answered the purpose." Capt. Theodore S. Thomasson of the 1st Kentucky Battery (US) used
850 friction primers to fire 561 rounds during the second day of fighting at
Nashville in December 1864. A week later, while firing for two hours near
Columbia, Tennessee, he used 60 primers to fire 40 rounds.[36]

Thomasson did not explain why he expended so many primers, but we can
assume it was a combination of faulty devices and careless dropping by his
men. Archaeologists who dig battery-emplacement sites often find unfired
friction primers. They also find dropped, unfired small-arms ammunition
when they dig infantry positions. In the excitement of battle, it was natural
for artillerymen and infantrymen alike to fumble with small items and lose
control of them.[37]

But faulty manufacturing also accounted for many of the bad primers.
Capt. Charles Semple, chief ordnance officer of Breckinridge's Division at
Chickamauga, blamed Confederate arsenals for the problem. Lt. Francis W.
Dawson, assistant to the ordnance chief on Lt. Gen. James Longstreet's staff
in 1863, identified the problem as the wire breaking "at the point where it enters the tube." He thought the only solution was to use brass wire, but it was
very difficult to find such material in the Confederacy. Nevertheless, Dawson
moaned that "too frequently in action a fine shot is lost by the delay consumed
by replacing a primer which has failed to explode."[38]

An adjunct to the friction primer was a priming wire, or vent pick, to be
inserted into the hole to poke open the cloth covering of the cartridge and

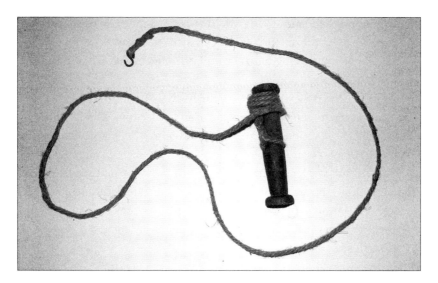

Fig. 4.4. Lanyard. The Number 4 also was responsible for handling the lanyard. As shown in this reproduction example, it consisted of a coarse cord with a wooden handle on one end and a metal hook on the other end. Photograph by Pratibha A. Dabholkar.

expose powder to the action of the primer. Although this method worked smoothly in countless instances, sometimes things went wrong. More than one gun became temporarily unserviceable because the priming wire stuck in the vent. Often this was due to powder residue building up and catching the wire. After eighteen rounds, a rifle gun of Burton's Louisiana Battery was rendered unserviceable when the priming wire broke off in the vent, leaving a portion stuck in it. At the Battle of Big Bethel on June 10, 1861, a piece of the Richmond Howitzer Battalion fell silent because the man who worked the priming wire lost his cue and stuck it in the vent just before, rather than after, the cartridge was rammed home. The rammer bent the end of the wire so sharply that it was impossible to pull it out of the vent.[39]

The other adjunct to the friction primer was the lanyard, a long cord with a hook on the end. The gunner attached the hook to the primer, stood a short distance to the side, and gave a steady jerk on the handle at the other end when ordered to fire. For countless times this method worked very well, but if one forgot his lanyard in the confusion of battle, it was difficult to know what to do about it. An enterprising infantryman of the 7th Connecticut, who took charge of a gun abandoned by the 4th New Jersey Battery near Chester Station in May 1864, confronted this problem with ingenuity. Pvt. Seth A. Clapp of Company K found a length of telegraph wire and used it as a substitute.[40]

BREAKDOWN AND DISABLING OF TUBES

The tube was the most basic component of an artillery piece, and *Instruction for Field Artillery* cautioned men to take good care of it. They were to wash it inside and out after every firing, depressing the tube to drain all water. Every particle of burnt powder and fragment of cloth cartridge had to be extricated from the rifling grooves. Evidence indicates the men took these injunctions seriously. As soon as a campaign was over, gun crews "took the powder stains off the guns and burnished them up outside and in, bright as a new cent," as John Merrilles put it.[41]

Gun crews could do nothing about a tube with a fault in it. Cracks appeared after firing, making it unsafe to try another round, and bursting could happen without warning. A 30-pounder Parrott near Gen. Robert E. Lee's headquarters exploded at the thirty-ninth round fired at the Battle of Fredericksburg. Lee and Longstreet were standing nearby, and Brig. Gen. William N. Pendleton, Lee's chief artillerist, was but ten feet from the piece, yet no one was injured. But all too often bursting tubes took out members of the gun crew. Parrott rifles were especially prone to bursting. A 20-pounder "flew literally all to pieces," during the North Anna phase of the 1864 Overland Campaign in Battery C, 11th Georgia Artillery. "Only one small piece left on carriage," wrote Capt. John T. Wingfield, and six men were injured. "From the number of pieces it flew into, it is judged the metal was very sorry."[42]

Besides bursting, another common way a tube became disabled was by getting a round wedged in the bore. This happened "from some unknown cause," as Lt. H. Shannon of the Warren Light Artillery put it, at Stones River. Of forty-three pieces belonging to the Left Wing of the Union army at that battle, one piece was disabled by Confederate fire while four others were disabled through some fault of their own or of the gun detachments. Artillerymen had a device called a worm to extract rounds from the tube, but many batteries seem not to have had one available when they needed it.[43]

When battery commanders indicated the cause of a projectile blocking the tube, it was "carelessness in loading" as Lee put it. Edward A. Moore of the Rockbridge Artillery explained one such action in more detail. During the Valley Campaign of 1862, he was about to place a cartridge in the tube when the rammer, Jim Ford, suggested they place and ram the cartridge and the shell at the same time rather than separately. "The charge stopped half-way down and there it stuck," Moore recalled.[44] Another cause for wedging was that ammunition did not exactly fit the bore. In Humphreys's Arkansas Battery two pieces "were rendered useless by ammunition too large." Jacob Roemer asserted that the tube of one of his pieces became so hot while firing at Cedar Mountain "that the bore became too small to permit a shot." He let the tube cool a couple of days and then was able to extract the round.[45]

Dismounting (separating the tube from the carriage) was the most visible form of disabling a piece, eliciting cheers from gun crews when they managed to accomplish that feat in an enemy battery. But sometimes a piece "dismounted itself," as Maj. Roger P. Chew put it. Such tubes had to be tied up under the limbers or caissons and transported because it was too difficult to remount them under fire. Capt. Hubert Dilger reported that his men "secured the dismounted piece below the caisson in the manner prescribed" in the manual at Second Bull Run. Men of the 1st Minnesota Battery slung a tube below the limber rather than the caisson on the first day at the Battle of Corinth in October 1862.[46]

It may seem incredible that artillerymen should bury a fieldpiece to prevent its capture by the enemy, but John Watson Morton claimed his men did so after Maj. Gen. Nathan Bedford Forrest's raid on Memphis in August 1864. Fearful of being cut off, they buried two steel Rodman rifles in the middle of the road. "The deep mud helped to hide traces of the grave." Morton hid the limbers and caissons in a nearby swamp. Later when it was safe, he returned and dug them all up.[47]

Lt. Edward P. Newkirk of Battery M, 1st New York Light Artillery tried to disable a 12-pounder howitzer captured at the Battle of Averasboro because he had no need to keep it. The task proved more difficult than anticipated. Newkirk placed it in a small hole and set maximum elevation, put a cartridge in and packed the rest of the tube with sand and broken pieces of brick. When fired, "the only effect seemed to be the driving of the gun into the ground for more than half its length." So, he rammed a shell in the tube, spiked the vent, and burned the carriage.[48]

CARTRIDGES AND SABOTS

The bags that contained the powder charge were made of various materials, but there was no uniform opinion on the best to use. *Instruction for Field Ar-*

tillery argued for wool with no admixture of cotton, but the *Ordnance Manual* allowed cotton or paper. Gibbon listed woolen material, such as "wildbore, meino, or bombazetti," and flannel as acceptable. He noted that cotton had a tendency to burn and should not be used. Capt. Frank P. Amsden did not identify the kind of fabric of twenty-five cartridges that he lost "through the flimsiness of the material the bags were made of," but he blamed the Washington Arsenal for making them.[49]

Early in the war, the men of Guibor's Missouri Battery (CS) used local material to improvise artillery supplies. They obtained flannel, needles, and thread from a dry-goods shop and tried to make cartridge bags. "My first cartridge resembled a turnip," recalled W. P. Barlow. "But we soon learned the trick, and at the close ranges at which the next battle was fought our home-made ammunition proved as effective as the best."[50]

The gunpowder inside the bag had to be coarse grained to burn slower and provide propulsive power to move the projectile. It often was called cannon powder. Rifle powder was much more fine grained but inadequate for artillery use because it burned so rapidly that it essentially exploded at once. In general, the size of the powder charge was one-twentieth the weight of the projectile.[51] The amount of powder had an effect on efficiency. Maj. Robert H. Fitzhugh conducted an investigation of one hundred cartridges belonging to the 11th New York Battery and found that twenty-three had one ounce less powder in them than was required. Five others had various other defects, while only seventy-two appeared serviceable.[52]

Sabots were inserted between the cartridge and the projectile. For smooth-bores, they were made of wood and attached to the projectile with straps. Sabots were necessary for smoothbores because the projectiles were round in shape. The flat wood provided an even surface for the exploding powder to act uniformly on the projectile. Affixing the projectile, sabot, and cartridge in one unit was termed "fixed" ammunition. Apparently the sabot was small enough that it did not trap bits of cartridge cloth between itself and the inside of the tube. Its straps came loose after leaving the tube as did the sabot, and all flew along the line of fire.[53]

Rifled projectiles were conical in shape and did not need a separate wooden sabot. Instead, designers fashioned sabots to be built onto the end of the projectile. The rear end of some of these conical projectiles were cone-shaped, and thus a layer of material could be applied around them that would expand upon the explosion of the powder charge to catch the rifling grooves and impart spin to the projectile as it left the tube. The Schenkl shell used papier-mâché as the saboting material. Consisting of paper and glue or paper, flour, and water, this material dried hard enough to serve the purpose. It also had the advantage of being less harmful to friendly troops when it disintegrated and fell off the projectile in flight. This method worked as long as the papier-mâché remained in good shape, but a sabot of this type was liable to be damaged in transit or weakened by foul weather. In addition, Robert Fitzhugh found on testing papier-mâché sabots on the target field that the material sometimes did not take the grooves well enough to spin the projectile properly.[54]

The other common material used in sabots was lead. It was more reliable but could be dangerous to friendly troops when a battery fired over its own infantry. Most of the sabot material seems to have flown quite far. For example, archaeologists found "105 thin fragments of lead sabot" lying 270 yards in front of the position of a battery of James rifles on the battlefield of First Bull Run.[55]

CARRIAGES

Carriages have been an underappreciated component of an artillery piece. Historians have focused heavily on the tube and its technical capabilities while paying scant attention to the wooden-and-metal apparatus that supported it. The carriage not only gave the tube its mobility but also offered a platform whereby it could be pointed. It also absorbed the inevitable recoil when the powder charge was fired. According to Joseph Roberts, "lightness and strength combined, great mobility and flexibility, and a low center of gravity, in order to surmount all difficulties in the field" made for good carriages. The apparatus had "to resist the concussion in firing, and the severe jolting produced when moving rapidly over uneven ground."[56]

The Ordnance Department was using three basic carriages by the outbreak of the war. One was designed for the 6-pounder gun and the 12-pounder howitzer, another for the 24-pounder howitzer, and the third for the 12-pounder gun and the 32-pounder howitzer. Ordnance officers tried to use a preexisting carriage for any new piece, modifying it as necessary. For example, the Napoleon used a modification of the carriage designed for the 24-pounder howitzer.[57]

Carriage wheels were a standard height of fifty-seven inches in diameter. There was no advantage to making them bigger. The hub was called a nave, from which fourteen spokes emanated to the rim. The term "felloes" denoted the sections of wood, seven in number, that together constituted the wooden part of the rim, with a circular iron rim on the outside. The spokes did not extend directly out of the nave but were pushed outward a bit to create "a convexity or 'dish' which gave elasticity and protected them from shock," according to modern historians. "The 'dish' also served to make the carriage wider with decreased length of axletrees." This same type of wheel was used for limbers, caissons, battery wagons, and battery forges.[58]

White oak was the preferred wood for carriages because it was, as Gibbon noted, "tough and pliable." White ash was used for the sponge and rammer staves, while black oak was used to make ammunition chests. The wood had to be thoroughly dried, and all was painted olive green. Metal parts were painted black.[59]

It was important for the carriages to be properly manufactured, especially to absorb recoil. Modern photography indicates that when fired, the wheels of a Civil War artillery piece rose off the ground a bit and, when settling back, rolled toward the rear. This could be reduced by decreasing the diameter of the wheel or by increasing the diameter of the axle. The overall weight of the carriage could also reduce recoil; if too heavy, it would limit mobility as well.[60]

BREAKDOWN OF CARRIAGES

Most commentators believed that a problem with faulty carriages arising by 1862 was caused by private contractors. "Most of the trails are almost worthless, the wheels are fast falling to pieces, and the different parts are fast giving way," complained Lt. Edmund Kirby of Battery I, 1st US Artillery after the Seven Days Campaign. "These carriages were made by Wood and Brothers, contractors, New York," he reported.[61]

But the problem was not limited to Wood and Brothers. Many reports surfaced about carriage breakdowns on the battlefield. They began with Shiloh and the Peninsula Campaign in April 1862 and included both Union and Confederate batteries. The two problem areas centered on the axle and the trail; both components were responsible for managing the recoil of the piece. The axle also received a lot of stress when moving the piece over rough terrain.

Many battery commanders reported that an axle broke or fractured while firing. At times they blamed it on high tube elevations, which added more stress to the axle. Lt. Malbone F. Watson fired a gun in his section of Battery I, 5th US Artillery 150 times "at an angle of between five and six degrees" at Second Bull

Fig. 4.5. Making Gun Carriages. The large artillery force created by both sides during the Civil War demanded expansive manufacturing, both by civilian firms and governmental establishments. This image illustrates the handcrafting of artillery carriages by skilled workers. The demand was so high that several firms supplied the Union army with faulty carriages, made in a hurry with bad wood and iron, which broke down at an alarming rate in 1862. While the problem lessened the next year, it never went away before the war ended. *Frank Leslie's Illustrated Newspaper,* August 17, 1861, 217.

Run. The axle broke "completely through the center, letting the muzzle down on the ground."[62] Other officers noted that recoil was the cause of axle breaks. No fewer than four pieces in one battery of Maj. Gen. John Pope's Army of Virginia lost their axles due to recoil at Second Bull Run. Some officers noted that such recoil-related stress was increased if firing on muddy, clay-like ground.[63]

Bad iron fastenings also caused breakdowns. Firing double charges of canister led to broken iron straps on the axle of a piece in the 4th Indiana Battery at Stones River. In another instance, "faulty construction of the iron part" played the main role in breaking two pieces of Battery E, 1st Illinois Light Artillery at Shiloh. Capt. Stephen H. Weed of Battery I, 5th US Artillery had lost the axles of five pieces by July 5, 1862, because "of the most villainously poor character" of iron used on them.[64]

Axle problems continued in 1863. Wainwright had eighteen 3-Inch Ordnance Rifles in the First Corps, Army of the Potomac at Gettysburg. Six of them broke axles because of recoil. Two James rifles in the 4th Indiana Battery broke their axles at Chickamauga in September, while the straps of an axle on a 12-pounder howitzer in the 3rd Iowa Battery broke at the Battle of Helena the preceding July. It was possible to replace an entire axle on the battlefield if one had been transported in the battery wagon. Lt. John K. Bucklyn of Battery E, 1st Rhode Island Light Artillery, however, had to ride "to every battery on the field to borrow one" at Gettysburg.[65]

The 1864 campaigns witnessed no abatement of axle breakdowns nor any changes in the cause. Three pieces of Battery A, 1st Pennsylvania Light Artillery became "disabled by the breaking of the understraps, occasioned either by the severity of the recoil or the inferior quality of the iron used," wrote Lt. Wallace F. Randolph. When the sergeant of a piece in Battery B, 1st Rhode Island Light Artillery noticed his rounds veering off to the right, he found that the axle had cracked enough in the middle to tilt the top of the wheels closer together, causing the carriage to lean and influence the trajectory. He probably would not have noticed the crack otherwise. But axles also broke while the piece was transported along roads or cracked while the battery drilled over rough ground or as it tried to cross a ditch.[66]

Axles were the most important component of the carriage. One factor in this problem was that many carriages were not designed to work with new tubes like the 3-Inch Ordnance Rifle. The increased power and recoil of the new ordnance tended to be too much for those originally designed for lighter pieces. The poor quality of iron that went into the straps merely exacerbated the issue. Although thoroughly reported, the axle problem was never resolved during the war. To a significant degree, it inhibited the effectiveness of artillery on the battlefield.

The trail was the second-most-important component of the carriage. It absorbed recoil and settled the piece on a level plane and was manipulated to traverse the tube for range of firing. With the handspike, the trail was relatively easy to use for maneuvering by a trained crew.

Trail breakdowns were not as common as axle problems, but they caused a decline of combat effectiveness. Officers reported that sometimes recoil "badly cracked" the trail. Some specified the area around the elevating screw as the weak point, while others noted the places where iron plates or handles were located. Hard or frozen ground increased the possibility of fracture, and the problem varied from battle to battle. At Chickamauga, only four Confederate trails out of 175 pieces broke. But of four pieces of Lt. David H. Kinzie's Battery K, 5th US Artillery, the trails of three broke during the Battle of Fredericksburg. Kinzie was not shy about assigning blame for these problems. He examined the broken trails and found they were "made out of very bad material, part of the wood being completely rotten," noting that Wood and Brothers of New York were the culprits. "I also noticed that the stocks were made out of one piece of wood, and not in two parts, as required by the Ordnance Manual."[67]

It was a bit easier to replace broken trails than broken axles. Artificers could fashion new ones out of raw materials in the field. When the 5th Massachusetts Battery opened fire during the Peninsula Campaign, the trail of one piece broke completely at the elevating screw; the gun had been placed in a cornfield, and the rows prevented it from recoiling naturally. Rather than send it back to the depot at Washington, DC, artificers selected a live oak tree, cut it down, and hewed out a replacement trail with axes. They worked all night to ready it for use the next day. The unit historian admitted it did not look pretty but was more serviceable than the original. Captured by the Confederates at Gaines's Mill in late June 1862, the piece returned to Federal hands at Chancellorsville, its improvised trail intact.[68]

The story of the 5th Massachusetts Battery piece was unusual. For most axle and trail mishaps, the result was a disabled gun. The trail problem, although nearly as widely reported, like the axle problem remained unresolved by war's end.

BREAKDOWNS IN OTHER CARRIAGE ELEMENTS

Other components of the carriage also suffered breakdowns, but not as often as axles and trails. Marches along rough roads and crossing ditches pounded the wheels of carriages, but those could be replaced by the spares carried on the caissons. Thomas W. Osborn asserted that his men could replace a wheel in three minutes even under fire. The artillery manual also included details about how to conduct emergency repairs on wheels to keep the pieces rolling.[69]

There are some reports of elevating screws breaking during combat. Maj. Gen. Ulysses S. Grant's ordnance chief during the Vicksburg Campaign noted that the elevating screws of the 30-pounder Parrotts were too weak, "especially at the point where they enter the socket attached to the trail." If they

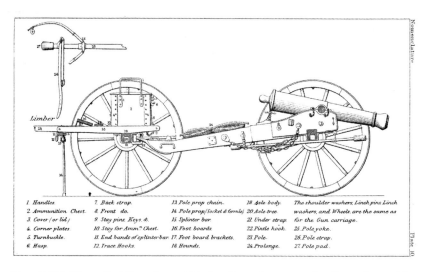

1. Handles.	7. Back strap.	13. Pole prop chain.	19. Axle body.	The shoulder washers, Linch pins Linch
2. Ammunition Chest.	8. Front do.	14. Pole prop(Socket &ferrule)	20. Axle tree.	washers, and Wheels, are the same as
3. Cover (or lid.)	9. Stay pins. Keys &.	15. Splinter bar.	21. Under strap	for the Gun carriage.
4. Corner plates.	10. Stay for Amm". Chest.	16. Foot boards.	22. Pintle hook.	25. Pole yoke.
5. Turnbuckle.	11. End bands of splinter bar.	17. Foot board brackets.	23. Pole.	26. Pole strap.
6. Hasp.	12. Trace Hooks.	18. Hounds.	24. Prolonge.	27. Pole pad.

Fig. 4.6. Side View of a 6-Pounder and Limber. It was important for all members of the gun crew to know all parts of the piece, its carriage, and its limber. Illustrations such as this were important learning tools. The different parts are identified by the legend and its accompanying numbers for easy study. *Instruction for Field Artillery,* plate 10.

could be strengthened and their sockets made heavier, "these screws would be the best that have been introduced into the service."[70]

When Brig Gen. William F. Barry served as artillery chief of the Army of the Potomac, he noted that the huge expansion of the artillery arm in 1861–62 was the chief cause of all carriage breakdowns during the early part of the conflict. Contractors cut too many corners in frenzied efforts to fulfill government orders, even using rotten wood for key elements of the carriage. Barry tried to replace bad workmanship with better; judging from unit commander reports, he never solved the issue.[71]

The problem of breakdowns among all elements of an artillery unit is a subject that has hardly been mentioned by military historians. While damage to equipment from enemy fire highlights their studies, disabling due to faulty construction or bad material has been neglected. We do not have comprehensive information about the subject from the men who suffered the most from breakdowns, the Civil War artillerist; they often reported it for individual batteries in specific battles but compiled no overall data on the problem. In only a handful of available reports did a battery officer indicate the number of breakdowns compared to the number of pieces available to him in a given engagement. But even from this small resource, we can gain some clue to the proportion of the problem. In five instances, the percentage of breakdowns in a given unit in a given battle ranged very widely, from 2.2 percent to a whopping 75 percent. That averages to about 25 percent overall.[72]

That may or may not have been an accurate reflection of breakdowns for all units engaged in Civil War combat, but it lands pretty close to the only information available concerning artillery breakdowns in another war. From August 1914 to April 1915, a total of 805 French field guns broke down due to mechanical failure, representing 19.3 percent of all 75-mm fieldpieces the French possessed at the start of World War I. In the First Battle of Champagne, from December 20, 1914, to March 17, 1915, the French Fourth Army lost 10 percent of its fieldpieces in the first six days of fighting, "far out-stripping losses due to enemy action," according to one historian. Given the complexity of the 75-mm piece compared to Civil War artillery, that may reflect well on the French and poorly on the nineteenth-century Americans. At any rate, breakdowns are an underappreciated factor in artillery effectiveness, and more work needs to be done on the subject for a full understanding of the long arm.[73]

LIMBERS

Carriages tended to be the most vulnerable piece of equipment of a Civil War battery because of the heavy weight they carried and the stress exerted by firing. The other components suffered far fewer breakdowns in the field. The limber was a two-wheeled contrivance that served as the hauling and maneuvering device for the piece while in transit. It set up a compound four-wheeled conveyance (limber plus carriage) that was more flexible than a single four-wheeled wagon because, unlike the rigid wagon, it consisted of two separate vehicles joined together. The limber plus carriage could make tight turns and negotiate uneven terrain without upsetting. Because the caisson had to keep pace with the piece, a limber was added to it as well. A limber was also added to the battery wagon, which also was a two-wheeled vehicle.[74]

The gun carriage connected to the limber via a lunette, or metal ring, attached to the end of the trail. This ring slipped over a pintle hook on the axle of the limber. On the other side of the limber, a long pole extended to which the six-horse team was hooked to pull both limber and carriage. An ammuni-

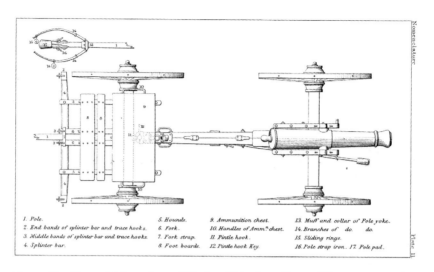

1. Pole.	5. Hounds.	9. Ammunition chest.	13. Muff and collar of Pole yoke.
2. End bands of splinter bar and trace hooks.	6. Fork.	10. Handles of Amm.ⁿ chest.	14. Branches of do. do.
3. Middle bands of splinter bar and trace hooks.	7. Fork strap.	11. Pintle hook.	15. Sliding rings.
4. Splinter bar.	8. Foot boards.	12. Pintle hook Key.	16. Pole strap iron. 17. Pole pad.

Fig. 4.7. Top View of 6-Pounder and Limber. This view offers a different perspective on the equipment, one not obtainable by someone standing on the ground. *Instruction for Field Artillery,* plate 11.

tion chest was added to the limber to serve as the most immediate source of cartridges and projectiles for the gun. It was removable and divided into three sections for different kinds of projectiles.[75]

The only real problem with a limber was the tendency of the pole to break. It was a long and relatively thin piece of wood with six horses hooked to and often struggling against it. Especially when horses were hit in battle, they often fell onto the pole and broke it, rendering the limber inoperable.[76]

CAISSONS

The two-wheeled caisson held the readily available reserve of cartridges and projectiles for the piece, while the larger reserve resided in the ordnance train well to the rear. The caisson held three ammunition chests and carried a spare wheel for either its own use, that of the limber, or that of the piece. In an emergency a caisson could substitute for a limber by hitching it to a piece and moving it out of danger. Hunt suggested early in 1864 that caissons should carry all the ammunition needed by both artillery and infantry units so the Army of the Potomac could dispense with ordnance trains altogether. He

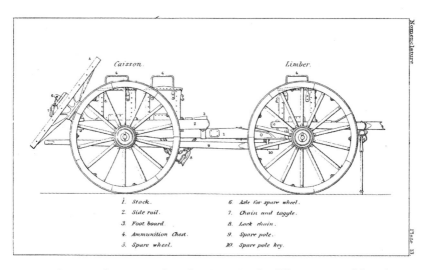

Fig. 4.8. Side View of Caisson and Limber. Knowing the different parts of the caisson and its limber also was important. Members of the gun detachment and members of the driving teams often had to fill in for their comrades, and cross-training improved their efficiency. *Instruction for Field Artillery,* plate 13.

thought the caissons could bring more ammunition to the battery positions and avoid sending units out of line when they ran out of rounds. The suggestion probably was impractical and never implemented.[77]

"No positive rule can be laid down with respect to the caissons in presence of an enemy," concluded the authors of *Instruction for Field Artillery.* They thought it best to charge a noncommissioned officer with keeping the caissons close enough for resupplying the pieces but not so close as to be exposed to heavy fire.[78] Battery commanders praised the noncommissioned officers who performed this task well. Capt. Josiah W. Church of Battery D, 1st Michigan Light Artillery commended Sgt. S. E. Lawrence for "obeying orders promptly and watching our movements" to save the caissons when Church retired at Chickamauga. Capt. Cullen Bradley of the 6th Ohio Battery praised Cpl. E. H. Neal for "keeping the caissons well screened, and for keeping the battery well supplied with ammunition" at Stones River.[79]

As Church and Bradley well knew, the primary job of anyone placed in charge of the caissons was to keep them close to the pieces. "We moved the guns in line each followed by its caisson," wrote Joseph William Eggleston of the Nelson Virginia Artillery, "or as it was technically called we moved forward 'in battery.'" When stationary, the caissons could be placed fifty or even two hundred yards behind the pieces, as was done in two batteries at Chickamauga. When Capt. Daniel T. Cockerill told the caisson drivers to take their rigs to a spot behind Battery F, 1st Ohio Light Artillery at Stones River, five of them misunderstood and left the field. Only one placed his caisson where Cockerill wanted it; the rest were found hours later.[80]

Similar to carriage problems, the axles of caissons had a tendency to falter in the field. Those of two caissons in Battery G, 1st Rhode Island Light Artillery broke at Antietam, making a total of ten that had done so since the unit took the field. An axle break caused a wheel to fall off a caisson of Battery A, 1st Rhode Island Light Artillery during the Seven Days Campaign. The usual recourse when these breakdowns occurred was to abandon the vehicle, but in one battery a blacksmith was able to repair a broken caisson axle on the field at Gettysburg.[81] If members of the gun detachment happened to be riding on a caisson when the axle broke, they were subject to severe injuries. This happened on Lt. Gen. T. J. "Stonewall" Jackson's flanking march at Chancellorsville. The road his column used was rutted, and when a caisson's axle broke, it threw two men sitting on the ammunition box "violently to the ground," breaking the ribs of one and disjointing the hip of the other.[82]

Conveying ammunition was the sole purpose of the caisson. It was the final element in a long system of logistics that started with government arsenals and private munitions suppliers. Cartridges and projectiles were packed at the point of origin in wooden boxes painted olive green on the outside, with the type of ammunition lettered in white on each end. Inside the box information concerning the place of manufacture and the date the cartridges and projectiles were made was listed.[83]

Caissons sported three ammunition boxes capable of holding forty rounds each, while limbers carried one box. The boxes often were referred to as ammunition chests. Each was divided into compartments designed to accommodate different types of projectiles. *Instruction for Field Artillery* urged artillerists to place some tow between the rounds to prevent them from hitting each other. It also suggested a proportion of different types of projectiles that could be altered by preferences. If a battery commander favored solid shot, case shot, or shell, he could raise the proportion accordingly, but that would create problems in terms of finding the right kind of space in the ammunition boxes.[84]

When Cpl. Bradford Nichol inspected the ammunition boxes of Rutledge's Tennessee Battery in November 1861, he recorded what he found inside. There were eight canister rounds, twenty-eight spherical case shot, and ten solid shot in the ammunition box of each limber. There also were thirty-one canister rounds, thirty-eight spherical case shot, and sixty-one solid shot in the three boxes on each caisson.[85]

Despite the manual, some artillerists did not pack these rounds carefully enough in either limber or caisson. On several occasions ammunition boxes suddenly exploded at the most unexpected moment. This happened when the battery was moving and a projectile shifted, usually causing injuries. For example, a man was mortally wounded, two horses killed, and another injured when a limber chest exploded while Battery M, 2nd US Artillery was on the move in June 1863.[86]

WEAR AND TEAR

Beyond poorly made material, another factor in artillery service was wear and tear over time. Even well-made tubes, carriages, limbers, and caissons endured hard service in the field. When temporarily assigned to consolidated Battery L and M, 3rd US Artillery, John Watkins of the 19th Ohio Battery found that the regulars' 10-pounder Parrotts were still in pretty good shape but their carriages were "badly worn and the harness all out of repair." Following the stress of Second Bull Run and the Maryland Campaign, many batteries in the Army of Northern Virginia were rendered almost unserviceable and needed refitting.[87]

The long campaign against Vicksburg greatly stressed Grant's artillery arm. Many pieces had been fired more than three thousand times during the course of the six-week siege. Capt. Jacob T. Foster gave up his "beloved twenty pounder parrots [sic]" because a board of inquiry condemned them. "The rifling was completely worn out." Members of the battery saw the effect of this wear and tear on the quality of their firing just before the pieces were condemned; one-third of their shots widely missed the target.[88]

Many carriages for fieldpieces were falling apart by the end of the Vicksburg Campaign. They had "traveled hundreds of miles, mostly in a hot climate," reported Grant's chief of ordnance. "Many trails and axles were broken by the firing and in some cases the wheels were injured."[89]

MISCELLANEOUS HARDWARE

Artillery required a wide variety of big and small pieces of equipment. The battery wagon, a two-wheeled vehicle, was "a long bodied cart with a round top with the lid hinged." The wagon contained a variety of material, spare parts, and tools, amounting to more than 125 items. "It was the Battery's storehouse," recalled Jacob Roemer, and "a huge trunk on wheels" according to another artillerist. A traveling forge, with a fireplace and bellows, also was issued to every battery. The artificers were in charge of the battery wagon and traveling forge.[90]

The list of miscellaneous materials issued to a battery was almost staggering. The 5th Company, Washington Artillery received a resupply of everything on June 8, 1863, which included 160 types of materials, 33 types relating to the work of the carpenters. Battery possessions included everything from oils and liniments to keys for locking the ammunition chests.[91]

While some items in the battery's possession were seldom used, many of them were important components. Several buckets made of rubber, sheet iron, or oak were needed for sponging the tube and greasing the wheels. The thumbstall consisted of buckskin "stuffed with hair" and was two and a half inches long and one inch thick. A strap three inches long was attached to it so the man using it could secure the other end to his wrist for easy access performing the important task of closing the vent during cleaning and reloading. Tarpaulins made of heavy canvas and impervious to rain measured twelve feet by fifteen feet. These typically were used to cover the carriages and harness but could be used to shelter six to nine men from the weather. The prolonge, a rope twenty-six feet, seven inches long, was used to manually pull the piece to the rear. Covers made of leather protected the vent against rain.[92]

Artillerists received several unique issues of personal gear and clothing because of their employment with the guns. Heavy epaulets made of brass were initially issued to protect their shoulders against saber cuts by enemy horsemen, but they were soon discarded as unnecessary. The men, however, liked their government-issued trousers for their reinforced seats, due to their practice of riding on vehicles.[93]

Whether artillerists should be issued personal weapons to defend themselves was a matter of debate. The army decided before the outbreak of war that noncommissioned officers, drivers, and cannoneers should have sabers,

TABLE 4.1. Typical Equipment and Material Issued to a Battery

---

4 12-pounder Napoleons
4 carriages, limbers, caissons
1 forge and limber
1 battery wagon
8 sponges and rammers
4 sponge buckets
4 vent covers
8 tar buckets
8 water buckets
4 pendulum-hausses
8 thumbstalls
8 lanyards
8 tarpaulins
4 linstocks
many carpenter tools
1 quart of sperm oil
2 pounds of beeswax
1 gallon of linseed oil
1 gallon of spirits of turpentine
50 pounds of olive paint
1 pound of black paint
12 nose bags
1 elevating screw
4 rammer heads
4 sponge heads
5 keys for ammunition chests
44 ammunition boxes
96 12-pounder shot fixed
96 12-pounder canister fixed
336 12-pounder shell fixed
40 spokes

Source: Receipt, June 8, 1863, Cuthbert H. Slocomb Service Record, Washington Artillery, M320, NARA.

but most men found them to be a nuisance. "What can a man do with a sword dangling around his legs," complained Ira Butterfield of the 1st Wisconsin Battery. In units assigned to accompany cavalry, revolvers also were found to be of little use, but noncommissioned officers kept their sabers and revolvers as symbols of authority. Battery B, 4th US Artillery, however, retained all its sabers for use only at monthly inspections.[94]

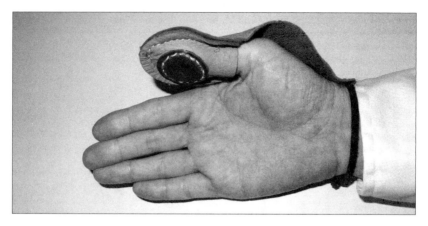

Fig. 4.9. Thumbstall. This small but important piece of equipment, shown as a reproduction, allowed a gun detachment's Number 3 to close the vent while Number 1 sponged out any leftover powder and smoldering pieces of fabric from the previous charge before inserting a new cartridge. Air entering the tube through the vent could prevent the sponging from eliminating all such hazards; if they remained, they could set off the new powder charge with disastrous results for Number 1. Many such accidents led to facial burns and the loss of hands or arms. Conscientious vent men were known to keep their thumb over the vent even when wounded in a valiant effort to save their comrade. Photograph by Pratibha A. Dabholkar.

Most commentators believed that the artillerists' main reliance had to be on effective serving of the big guns rather than on personal weapons. "They should be taught to look upon their pieces as their proper arm of defense," John Gibbon wrote of them. Sherman agreed. "That's right, boys, that's right. Remember, your guns are your only safety. Don't depend upon pistols or sabers, but upon your twenty-pounder rifles," he told members of the 1st Wisconsin Battery. Now and then officers issued infantry muskets to their artillerists. Every man beyond seven per piece in Battery C, 11th Georgia Battalion received a musket and ammunition partway through the Petersburg Campaign, but ordnance officers failed to give them cartridge boxes to hold the ammunition.[95]

CONCLUSION

Every battery was a traveling community of men, horses, and an array of material that was an entity in itself. While the four or six guns were the centerpieces, they were by no means all that had to be requisitioned, stored, and maintained by artillerists. Everything concerned with supplying a battery had been worked out through long practice before the war. There was little need for innovation during the conflict. Civil War artillerists had at their disposal good guns and a working method to fall back upon that was solid and enduring.

5

. . . .

FIRING THE BIG GUNS

As a crew-served weapon, field artillery was a complicated tool of war. Seven men operated it, with direction from two others, all of them working as a team engaged in a deadly business. Each man had to do his part in the process before the next step could proceed. If someone did something before he was supposed to, it literally could be deadly for his comrades. Beyond questions of safety, the members had to work together to aim as well as load the piece. There were many factors that affected accurate shooting.

The gunner, a corporal, was primarily responsible for aiming the piece. The sergeant told the rest of the crew what type of projectile to use, how long to set the fuze if using explosive ordnance, and when to stop firing. All of these details came from the officer in charge of the section or the battery.[1]

The commands were carefully explained in the artillery manual. "Load" meant, of course, to load the piece and then wait for further orders. "Commence firing" gave authority to fire as well as to immediately reload and continue firing until told to stop. If more than one piece was to fire, that indication could be, "Section—commence firing."[2]

Every type of piece recoiled, but it was not for a great distance. According to John Gibbon, the 6-pounder gun recoiled up to two yards, while the 24-pounder howitzer recoiled ten yards. If resting on a wooden platform wetted by rain, the recoil was longer due to less friction. "By hand to the front" was the command for moving the piece back to its firing position. The gunner also had to readjust the aim after every firing.[3]

Some battlefield conditions interfered with the recoil and return of the piece. William Meade Dame of the 1st Company, Richmond Howitzers recalled that his unit took position in a plowed field at Spotsylvania in May 1864,

Fig. 5.1. Sighting a Fieldpiece. The corporal of the gun detachment straddled the train and bent down to get a good line of sight along the top of the tube, elevating the piece by turning the screw under the barrel. In these motions he set both the range (lateral aiming), adjusting it as needed by moving the end of the trail, and the distance (commonly called the range), using the elevating screw. Because of the recoil of the piece, most of this had to be redone after every round. *Frank Leslie's Scenes and Portraits of the Civil War* (New York: Mrs. Frank Leslie, 1894), 279.

and the men had great difficulty moving the piece back into firing position. They used fence rails to impede the recoil, even though an ordnance officer warned that the tube would burst if recoil was not allowed to run its course. They found this to be untrue. Their barrier allowed them to fire faster without having to run the piece forward again. Interestingly, the wheel ruts caused by the recoil and return of pieces in Battery B, 4th US Artillery served the gunners well at Cold Harbor a few weeks later. Smoke so obscured the field that they could not see how far or in what direction to return the piece, so they used the ruts as their guide.[4]

Other battlefield conditions affected the quality of firing. If the carriage rested on uneven ground, the shot tended to veer toward the direction of the lower wheel. A strong wind blowing across the flight path of the projectile could influence the trajectory. Even under ideal conditions all projectiles traced a parabolic trajectory that was well known by artillerists.[5]

The crew manhandled the piece, usually without any artificial aids, during firing. Anderson's artillery manual of 1840 had provided instructions for using the bricole, a harness with a rope attached so that each member of the crew could add his weight to manhandling the piece. The 1860 manual dropped the bricole and replaced it with the prolonge, a long rope without a harness attachment. While the *Ordnance Manual* indicated the prolonge was eighteen feet long and three and a half inches in circumference, made of four strands of hemp, Gibbon stated it was twenty-six feet long.[6] One end of the prolonge was to be attached to the trail of the piece and the other to the limber. The purpose was to fire the piece while retreating slowly. It avoided the time and effort to limber and unlimber the piece repeatedly every few yards. "It is but seldom that this mode of moving and firing is necessary," proclaimed *Instruction for Field Artillery,* "and it will only be resorted to when circumstances require it."[7]

But firing by prolonge occurred quite often during the Civil War. The 1st Iowa Battery did it at Pea Ridge in March 1862, and when advancing Confederates approached Battery H, 5th US Artillery a month later at Shiloh, the regular cannoneers retired "with fixed prolonge, firing canister into them as it went." Examples of this technique also occurred on the second day at Stones River, on July 2 at Gettysburg, on the first day at Chickamauga, during the Atlanta Campaign, and at Third Winchester (September 19, 1864). Firing by prolonge "required soldierly qualities more often lacking than existing," concluded Thomas W. Osborn. "It required an officer of steel nerves, the most perfect discipline of the men and obstinate bravery in both."[8]

In most cases reports simply mentioned the use of a prolonge in firing without providing details. Capt. Thomas H. Carter, Lt. Gen. Jubal Early's artillery chief, stated that it was used in the regulation way, attaching the piece to the limber and firing in retreat. But other officers simply reported that the men, rather than horses and limbers, pulled the piece without providing details of the method. Capt. Charles A. Phillips retired his 5th Massachusetts Battery this way when pressed by Confederates in the Peach Orchard at Gettysburg. Phillips himself took the end of the rope, "throwing it over my shoulder," as six of his men took hold along its length. "We kept the gun moving as fast as we could" over ploughed ground until reaching firmer soil, but they did not fire along the way.[9]

As Phillips demonstrated, the prolonge could be used to manually extricate a piece out of danger. It also was used to pull a piece stuck in a muddy road. When the 9th Massachusetts Battery found itself in this predicament during the Seventh Offensive at Petersburg, three prolonges were attached to one piece, and sixty men pulled it out.[10]

FIRING SYSTEMS

Artillerists had a number of ways to deliver fire on their targets. Direct fire was the term applied to making the projectile hit its target without hitting anything along the way. Grazing fire involved the projectile striking the ground at a shallow angle not exceeding ten degrees and then rising slightly to bounce several times at the end of its flight. Plunging fire meant the projectile buried itself in the ground at first strike. Horizontal, parallel, or rolling fire was a slight variation on grazing fire. It started with the axis of the piece horizontal (or parallel) to the ground and the line of sight falling about seventy-five yards ahead. The projectile bounced many times close to the end of its flight but never rose above the level of the muzzle. This type of firing was considered effective for reaching targets beyond the normal distance of the piece. Finally, ricochet fire involved the projectile bouncing off an object and changing course on the way toward the target.[11]

Several of these firing methods involved bouncing the projectile off the ground or some other object, but this was relevant only to smoothbores and spherical projectiles. The elongated projectiles of rifles tended to bury themselves on first impact. While they could and did bounce off objects such as trees, they were not well suited for this action. Moreover, Civil War officers rarely reported using these bouncing or ricocheting methods in action even with smoothbores. Confederate artillerists tried ricochet fire at Batteries L and M, 3rd US Artillery during the Jackson Campaign in Mississippi in July 1863 but failed to hit their target.[12]

Bouncing and ricocheting required firm, hard ground and demanded a more sophisticated approach to sighting the piece. Since half of the field artillery used in the Civil War was rifled, this alone cut down the possibilities of employing these methods by 50 percent. Smoothbore artillerists did not seem to bother with the complications involved in bouncing their shots, preferring to employ direct fire. It is not even certain that the ricocheting fire received by the regular batteries at Jackson was deliberately planned by the Confederate gunners.

Another firing system indicated how many pieces should open at the same time. *Instruction for Field Artillery* listed firing by piece (starting from the right or left piece), section, half battery, and full battery. At Chancellorsville, the commander of Manley's Battery ordered his men to "fire one gun at a time, so we could get the range. It served us well, as the gunners were able to be more effective in their aim." Battery M, 1st Illinois Light Artillery developed a reputation as the "Revolving Battery" because its commander liked to begin with volley fire and then shift to individual fire. Many officers employed firing by section.[13]

Firing by the full battery, often called volley fire, became a point of debate. Gibbon advised against it, arguing that the enemy could take advantage of the intervals between volleys to return fire. Civil War officers generally ignored his advice. They employed firing by the full battery many times and claimed it was effective. Capt. Wilbur F. Goodspeed used it several times during the Atlanta Campaign, once firing volleys for two hours at Confederate earthworks.[14]

Brig. Gen. John M. Corse lavishly praised Battery H, 1st Missouri Light Artillery for firing by full battery during the Atlanta Campaign. "The true effect of artillery was here best found in volley firing. While one or two guns fired consecutively at an object for a week may produce no effect, six guns fired together and repeatedly will overcome any possible obstacle in a very short time. The great success of this battery throughout this entire campaign is owing to the fact that its fire has ever been concentrated, and by battery or in volleys."[15]

RATE OF FIRE

An associated issue was how fast the crew could reload, aim, and resume firing. Gibbon reported the standard rate of fire as one round every thirty to forty seconds with the 6-pounder. "The mean rate is about one shot per minute," he wrote of the 12-pounder, "but when close pressed, and firing at objects not difficult to hit, two or three shots per minute can be fired." Howitzers fired more slowly than guns, amounting to one and a half minutes per round. Joseph Roberts broke down the rate of fire based on type of projectile, with two solid shots or two spherical case fired per minute. He thought canister could be fired faster, three rounds per minute, because it demanded less care to aim. This is faster than the artillery rate of fire in the Napoleonic era, which has been estimated at twenty to thirty rounds per hour.[16]

Civil War artillerists estimated the potential rate of fire with varying conclusions, depending on the skill and experience of the gun crew. "It does not take longer for a well-drilled battery to load and fire a cannon than for a sportsman to load and fire a fowling piece," wrote Thomas W. Osborn. Augustus Buell believed it took a bit longer to load a rifle than a smoothbore, but no matter the type, most Civil War artillerists were confident in their ability to fire fast. While exercising the School of the Piece in the manual, one gun crew of the 10th Massachusetts Battery loaded and fired in forty-nine seconds. Estimates of possible ratios in actual battle ranged from one round per minute, Gibbon's mean rate, to much higher ratios. Edward Porter Alexander thought it could be from thirty "carefully aimed shots in an hour, to 100 hurriedly aimed." James Dodwell of Battery I, 1st Illinois Light Artillery asserted that, if pressed heavily, a crew could fire six rounds per minute, which seems almost impossible.[17]

We can judge actual fire rates in combat from a number of reports filed by officers, although they vary widely. Commanders set the rate and often mandated a relatively slow pace. For example, Lt. Jerome B. Stephens of Battery C, 1st Ohio Light Artillery ordered one round from each piece every five minutes for two hours during the Atlanta Campaign. Battery L, 1st New York Light Artillery fired one round from each piece every three minutes during the Overland Campaign.[18]

But when not restrained by orders, gunners often fired much faster, very often hitting and exceeding the one-round-per-minute mean established by Gibbon.[19] Many achieved two rounds per minute.[20] On July 3 at Gettysburg, Eleventh Corps artillery fired from two to four rounds per minute. "That is about as rapidly as the chief of the gun could take good aim," wrote Osborn. But he also noted that at Chancellorsville his battery had "under pressure . . . fired nine shots a minute from every gun, or 54 shots a minute from six guns, and every one with good aim."[21]

We can trust Osborn, for he was a thoroughly professional artillerist. But one wonders at the report spread by Tobias Charles Miller that gun crews in the Chicago Board of Trade Battery fired six rounds per minute per piece at Stones River. Even more difficult to swallow is that one gun in the 3rd Company, Richmond Howitzers fired eleven rounds in one minute at Cold Harbor.[22] It might have been remotely possible that an especially good gun crew could do this for a short while, but it lies well beyond the norm.

PROBLEMS OF RAPID FIRING

Rapid firing had drawbacks. During their first heavy exchange at Stones River, gun crews of the 8th Wisconsin Battery ran out of water and had to empty their canteens into the sponge buckets. The men of the Rowan Artillery (Company D, 1st North Carolina Artillery) skipped that step by emptying their canteens directly into the barrels after firing 655 rounds in succession. If the tube was made of bronze, rapid firing could cause the metal to expand just enough to create problems with ramming. This happened with the Pee Dee South Carolina Artillery after 160 rounds.[23]

Rapid firing also led to a fast expenditure of ammunition. Most commentators assumed these rounds also were largely wasted due to poor aiming. "The rule is, *fire slowly and cautiously,* and observe well the effect of the shot," instructed W. Leroy Brown in his Confederate artillery handbook. He allowed only one or two well-aimed rounds per minute. Roberts told his readers that "ammunition should at all times be carefully husbanded," especially at the start of a battle.[24]

At Fredericksburg, Charles Wainwright reported that First Corps guns fired 5,782 rounds. "I estimate that one-quarter of the amount fired was thrown away by the excitement of officers and men." That amounted to 1,445 rounds wasted. Many officers were concerned about running out of ammunition in rapid firing and having none left for emergencies. With his supply line nearly cut by Confederate cavalry, Maj. Gen. William S. Rosecrans cautioned his artillerymen to save ammunition during the Battle of Stones River. "Well, be a little more deliberate and take good aim," he told Capt. Cullen Bradley of the 6th Ohio Battery. "Don't fire so d—d fast!" Concern for wasting ammunition on the battlefield continued to the very end of the war. Lt. Valentine H. Stone of Batteries C and I, 5th US Artillery reported, "my guns were fired deliberately, and I am satisfied that not a round of ammunition was thrown away" during the Battle of Fort Stedman.[25]

No one was more concerned about this problem than Henry J. Hunt, artillery chief of the Army of the Potomac. Alarmed at reports that some batteries fired three hundred rounds in small skirmishes, he attacked the problem vigorously in December 1862. Hunt repeated instructions already set out in an order dated September 12 that officers should never exceed one round per gun every two minutes except when firing canister at short distance. Even this rule was meant for emergencies; one round per gun every four to six minutes was "as rapid firing as should be permitted" in normal situations. He worried that the higher the demand for ammunition, the greater likelihood of shoddy manufacturing by private contractors who tried to meet it.[26]

Hunt lectured his officers, warning them that rapid firing would not be allowed as an excuse for pulling their guns out of action when they ran out of rounds. "In future, batteries will not be permitted to leave their positions under this plea." Instead, officers should send caissons back to the ordnance train as soon as they were empty. "An officer who expends ammunition improperly proves his ignorance of the proper use of his arm, and a want of capacity for the command of a battery."[27] For Hunt, careful firing was a major component of field effectiveness, especially for rifled pieces. "The value of the rifled cannon consists principally in its accuracy; accuracy requires careful pointing, with close observation of the effect, and these require time." Hunt argued that twelve rounds, carefully pointed and observed, were more effective than fifty rounds fired poorly at a target more than 1,000 yards away.[28]

Hunt addressed a related issue too: the habit of stockpiling ammunition next to a piece to sustain rapid firing. Sometimes the crew left such piles behind when retiring in a hurry. Hunt thus forbade the practice of stockpiling. He believed that slowing the pace of firing would avert this ill-advised tactic.[29]

In the Army of the Potomac, most artillery officers took Hunt's reservations with rapid firing to heart. "The firing was deliberate and apparently no shots were thrown away except from defective fuses," wrote the artillery chief of the Third Corps about Fredericksburg. Battery commanders in their reports referred to their "careful supervision," economical expenditure, and accuracy of fire. "I have expended no ammunition without a specific object and have endeavored to make every shot valuable," stated Capt. Edwin B. Dow.[30]

But not everyone agreed with Hunt on this point. During the Atlanta Campaign, most artillery and infantry officers thought there was nothing wrong with rapid firing or a heavy expenditure of ammunition. When Thomas W. Osborn came from the Army of the Potomac to join the Army of the Tennessee as chief of artillery, he decided not to stop this practice even though he considered it wasteful. The corporate culture of this western army encouraged both rapid firing and heavy expenditure during a successful campaign, and Osborn felt uncomfortable trying to fight against the current of opinion.[31]

STRIVING FOR ACCURACY

The accuracy that Hunt encouraged was affected by many factors in addition to the rate of firing. Gibbon noted that even if firing several pieces of the same caliber, with the same charge, and at the same elevation, each would deliver the round at slightly different distances. The causes included wear and tear on the bore and vent, slight irregularities of the projectiles, air pressure and temperature, the type of metal used to make the tube, and the nature of the recoil. Gibbon urged cannoneers to let recoil have its way rather than try to restrain it, as the piece would work more accurately that way. Roberts even cited the rotation of the earth as a factor in accuracy. He believed a shot fired in the northern hemisphere would veer slightly to the right.[32] All these factors only slightly affected accuracy; gunners could hardly be expected to account for them, especially on the battlefield. Cannoneers simply gauged the distance as accurately as possible and adjusted the piece accordingly. Much depended on the skill of a few men.

The artillery manual urged cannoneers to practice judging distance. One way to do so was to use the naked eye to estimate the distance and then measure it to see if they were right. Artillerists then relied on a table of distances for instructions on how to set elevation and cut fuzes for different types of pieces and at different distances. Only at point-blank distance was it unnecessary to set elevation, but only a handful of references mention point-blank firing in the field. Battery K, 1st New York Light Artillery fired percussion shells at this distance at Chancellorsville as did the 10th Massachusetts Battery at Burgess's Mill in October 1864.[33]

Mostly, Civil War cannoneers relied heavily on tables of distances. Augustus Buell noted that a shell was lighter than case shot, so their prescribed distance was a "trifle greater for each elevation." He also reported that his comrades had to be more careful in timing the fuzes of shells than case shots since the former had to explode closer to the target.[34] These tables of distances were so important to gunners that they often posted them where they could be easily accessed. One Napoleon, made at the Confederate arsenal in Columbus, Georgia, had the table of distances carefully pricked on the soft bronze near the breech of the tube; a gunner could readily glance at it while working the piece.[35]

Demand for printed copies of the table of distances can be seen in correspondence. Edward P. Alexander requested "printed tables of ranges and elevation" for the 10-pounder Parrott from the Ordnance Bureau. A few days later he made his own table of distances for the Whitworth and the 20-pounder Parrott and distributed them to four batteries.[36] But Gibbon warned his readers that any published table of distances "should be considered simply as a means of limiting the number of trials to be made before finding out the range of a gun, and not as giving accurate results which will be the same under all circumstances." This sound advice was reinforced by evidence from the field. Lt. W. M. Polk of Scott's Tennessee Battery reported that the table of distances used by the Federals, which he employed at Stones River, did not "answer as well as it should" because it was made for much better powder than that available to the Confederates.[37]

If a gunner had a good eye, he could estimate distance quickly, perhaps discussing it with his section commander. But some men had great difficulty estimating distance. Maj. Davis Tillson, artillery chief of the Third Corps, Army of Virginia, withdrew a section from the field after it became clear the commander could not fix the distance.[38] Nevertheless, most gunners could estimate distance visually with consistent accuracy. The support for this conclusion lay in how well the projectiles found the intended target. Jacob Roemer praised his gunners at the Battle of Campbell's Station on November 16, 1863, for stopping a Confederate infantry advance. The rounds "exploded at just the right point. Therefore the eyes of the gunners must have been very good to judge the distance so accurately. It was this very exactness in cutting the fuses that made our shots so effective." But Capt. Max Van Den Corput relied on Confederate signal officers to give him the exact distance between his battery, planted on top of Lookout Mountain, and the Craven House, located part way down its slope. After several weeks of occupying the mountain, the signal men knew the exact location of the house and conveyed that information to Corput's gunners.[39]

Typically, artillerists found the exact distance by first estimating it and then observing the effect of a round or two. Men who observed this fire often fell down on the ground to see it under the cloud of cannon smoke. They also stationed themselves a few yards away from the piece and often used a pair of field glasses. It sometimes took several rounds to find the exact elevation and fuze length.[40] Lt. William B. Turner's Mississippi Battery employed both visual estimates and observation at Stones River. Turner "walked out in front of the guns, . . . looked toward the enemy, and began, as if to himself," counting from 100 to 455 yards as he mentally measured the distance. Then he ordered fuzes cut and authorized the first round. His best gunner immediately threw himself onto the ground, "resting upon his left hand, and looked under the smoke, to see the result." On his report Turner ordered the guns to fire at 500 yards.[41]

On a few occasions artillerists could measure distance before it was necessary to fire. Federal troops in a fort at Winchester set up markers for artillery practice, and the 1st Company, Richmond Howitzers happened to take post at that spot during the Second Battle of Winchester in June 1863. The battery received unusually accurate fire until someone noticed the marker, and the guns advanced a few yards to get away from the place. Capt. Henry M. Stuart of the Beaufort Volunteer Artillery also measured distance before the Battle of Honey Hill in November 1864. He noticed a small creek in front of the Confederate earthwork. "I had stepped off the distance from this stream to our guns," he reported, "and cut the fuses for the shrapnel carefully."[42]

It was possible to gauge the distance by observing enemy return fire. Joseph Roberts noted that counting the number of seconds between the flash of enemy guns and the report of the discharge was the starting point. Then one had to multiply "the number by the velocity of sound in the air," which was 1,092.5 feet per second if the temperature was 33 degrees Fahrenheit. How one could do all this while dodging artillery rounds is difficult to fathom, but Lt. Samuel N. Benjamin of Battery E, 2nd US artillery used some of this method at Fredericksburg. "The distance was determined by counting the time between the flash and the report of the enemy's guns," he wrote.[43]

Whether by "actual survey," as Capt. Lyman Bridges put it, or by other means, gunners managed to obtain enough information about distance. When his captain told Lt. William L. Ritter of the 3rd Maryland Battery (CS) to go out and see how far a Federal work party was located near New Hope Church in late May and early June 1864, Ritter and another officer crept forward as close as they dared. He "marked the trees with his eye" before leaving and managed to tell the gunners how to find the tree visually and use it as a marker for their fire.[44]

The fact that fuzes often did not work well—a topic to be discussed in the next chapter—was helpful in gauging distance. Capt. J. H. Pratt noticed that Federal gunners were having trouble finding the exact distance to hit his Texas battery during a skirmish in the Little Rock Campaign of September 1863. That is, they did until one of his own shells failed to explode. Pratt believed the Federals examined the dud, noticed how his men had cut the fuze, and adjusted their own firing accordingly, after which their rounds began to tell.[45]

There is relatively little information in battle reports about the exact elevation batteries used in any given engagement. When reported, it often was a modest two, four, six, or eight degrees. Capt. Josiah W. Church tried to hit targets on top of Missionary Ridge during the battle for that eminence in November 1863, beginning at ten-degrees elevation (the round sailed entirely across the ridge) before reducing to seven degrees to squarely hit a Confederate battery. Capt. Thomas F. Vaughn of Battery A, 3rd Illinois Light Artillery found that seven and a half degrees failed to reach his target during the Little Rock Campaign. He "then turned the elevating screw way down, which is 9 1/2 degrees, the full elevation without sinking the trail," but the round still fell short. In contrast, there are reports of other officers setting elevation at twenty-five degrees and even forty-five degrees with different pieces, but these accounts provide no details and are not fully reliable, given the extreme elevations cited.[46]

The coordination between estimating distance and setting the fuze was crucial. Men in the 5th Massachusetts Battery believed they did their best shooting with six-and-a-half-second fuzes at an elevation of four and three-quarter degrees during the Seven Days Campaign. Capt. Charles D. Owen of Battery G, 1st Rhode Island Light Artillery fired at a Confederate battery one mile away at Antietam. He set the fuzes at eight seconds and his elevation at four and one-quarter degrees, silencing the battery in twenty minutes. Capt. William Hexamer's Battery A, 1st New Jersey Light Artillery silenced a Rebel battery with 150 rounds by setting the fuzes at four seconds and the elevation at four degrees. Hexamer bested another battery with 30 rounds, using two second fuzes and two degrees of elevation. He then fired at a third target, two infantry regiments, using two and a half second fuzes at two-degrees elevation.[47]

Some artillery officers added the distance to the target when reporting fuze length and elevation. Captain Hexamer fired at a distance of 3,800 yards with twelve and a half seconds at eleven degrees at Fredericksburg. At Chancellorsville Capt. R. Bruce Ricketts used fifteen-second fuzes at fourteen degrees to reach a Confederate battery 3,600 yards away, but the distance was too great for him to determine if it was effective. Lt. Redmond Tully's Battery D, 1st US Artillery fired at Confederate earthworks 1,000 yards away with two-second fuzes and two-degrees elevation.[48]

These statistics indicate that officers estimated the combination of fuze length and elevation differently and with varying results. It was very difficult to estimate distances given all the impediments to clear vision on the battlefield. We can conclude that, despite the table of distances, gunners to some degree engaged in a guessing game when they estimated distance, fuze length, and elevation in preparation for firing. But they got better at this game with repeated experience in the field.

Many artillerists tested the extreme distance of various types of ordnance. The Napoleon could throw solid shot 1,800 yards "with ease and accuracy," reported Capt. Theodore Miller of Battery E, 1st Pennsylvania Light Artillery. Roemer was convinced his 3-Inch Ordnance Rifles could fire solid shot up to three and a half miles. When Battery C, 1st Pennsylvania Light Artillery was ordered to hit Confederate guns two and a half miles away at Fredericksburg, Capt. Jeremiah McCarthy tried his 10-pounder Parrotts, but "only a few" rounds "reached the desired point." Twenty-pounder Parrotts easily hit targets one and a half miles away at the Battle of Chattanooga, and 3-Inch Ordnance Rifles fired at targets 3,000 yards away.[49]

Lt. Samuel N. Benjamin's Battery E, 2nd US Artillery contained four 20-pounder Parrotts and planted a famous shot in a building used by Confederate sharpshooters during the Siege of Knoxville. The first round, fired from 2,500 yards away, took effect. "During the whole war I saw no prettier single shot," remembered engineer officer Orlando M. Poe, "though its accuracy may have been accidental."[50]

Even the limited use of Whitworth rifles registered on the consciousness of those who received its fire. At Fredericksburg a Whitworth opened up with telling effect from 2,700 yards away, and Union artillerists fought back. After some effort Capt. James A. Hall's 2nd Maine Battery of six 3-Inch Ordnance Rifles silenced it. At Chancellorsville another Confederate Whitworth hammered Union wagons at a distance of three miles.[51]

DIRECT AND INDIRECT FIRE

The term "direct fire," as noted earlier, was used by Civil War contemporaries to denote firing so that the projectile did not hit anything else before it reached the target. This type of firing was emblematic of a key aspect of artillery fire in that era—the gunner had to see the target in order to aim the piece. But after the Civil War, when technical capabilities enabled field artillery to fire at great distances, it became possible to hit targets well beyond the vision of the gunner. This came to be termed "indirect fire," and a new definition of the term "direct fire" also was developed. Today direct fire is defined as taking place within the line of sight of the gunner and not over twenty-degrees elevation. Anything beyond line of sight and twenty degrees is currently termed indirect fire.[52]

Line of sight was all important to Civil War gunners, while neither the manual nor the handbooks discussed indirect fire. Modern archaeologists have developed the concept of view sheds, what someone can see of the landscape from a given point, and a handful of them have applied it to artillery execution on Civil War battlefields. Topographic wavelengths are defined as the distance between the crests of neighboring ridges or hills or, alternatively, the distance between valleys. Longer wavelengths gave advantages to rifled artillery, and shorter wavelengths offered advantages to smoothbores. Conducting studies of battlefields to draw conclusions about view sheds and the performance of field artillery is a fruitful new direction in Civil War studies.[53]

Civil War artillerists often commented on the limitations of their line of sight. When a general urged Lt. Henry W. Kingsbury of Battery D, 5th US Artillery to open on a Confederate battery shielded by a patch of woods at Malvern Hill in June 1862, Kingsbury told him "that it was useless to fire at objects we could not see." The Union defeat at Brice's Cross Roads in June 1864 took place in unusually thick woods, which greatly hampered artillery support. "It was no position at all," Capt. John A. Fitch of Battery E, 1st Illinois Light Artillery told a board of inquiry. "I could not see for any distance. I could not judge the distance the enemy were from me, or whether the ground rose or fell in our front. I could not judge of the effect of our firing, nor tell when we got range."[54]

Even though thick brush began 40 yards in front of his guns, Fitch cut the fuzes for 450 yards because that was where he guessed the Confederates were located. On other fields artillerists fired at the smoke rising from opposing batteries on the other side of trees. At other times they aimed at the muzzle flashes that appeared through the haze and vegetation. Columns of dust raised by thousands of moving feet also became a targeting point.[55]

Many infantry officers urged their artillerists to shell woods. Brig. Gen. Charles Griffin, a former artillerist, ordered Lt. Lester I. Richardson of Battery D, 1st New York Light Artillery to indiscriminately rake the trees at Spotsylvania to discourage the Confederates from massing infantry. Richardson fired solid shot "at no visible object, and what I could see, with no effect." At times gunners fired case shot into woods, but solid shot was the preferred projectile for this job. During the Fourth Offensive at Petersburg, Griffin ordered his artillery to use solid shot and aim "at so low an elevation as to strike the ground at the edge of the woods and enter on the ricochet" when firing into timbered areas.[56]

For good reason, Joseph Roberts urged gunners not to fire at night as it was a waste of ammunition. There are many instances of nightfall putting an end to combat during the Civil War, indicating that artillerists fully understood this point. But it was possible to effectively fire in the dark if conditions were right. The night of May 2, 1863, was cloudless with a bright moon shining to enable some degree of accurate shooting at Chancellorsville. Also, gunners could arrange artificial aids. Edward Porter Alexander "marked points of direction to Banks' Ford for night firing" on the afternoon of May 4 at Chancellorsville. He began to shell the ford at 10 P.M. and believed it was effective in harassing the Federal withdrawal from the battlefield.[57]

In fact, many artillerists began to see the utility of firing at a target not visible to the gunner, representing the first wave of thinking about what a later generation termed indirect fire. Alexander argued it was not necessary for batteries to be positioned on high ground, where they were visible to enemy artillery, in order to find and hit targets. They could be placed in ravines where, sight unseen, the crew "only need the direction & the approximate distance. Signals from other points can tell them when they are about right, & then, safe themselves, they can do the most effective artillery work in the world." But in this Alexander referred to enfilading fire, which did not need much accuracy.[58] Still, as he indicated, artillerists sometimes used an observer to gauge the effect of indirect fire. To hit a Confederate battery shielded by woods at Spotsylvania, Capt. Charles A. Phillips estimated its location and ordered his 5th Massachusetts Battery to open fire. "I rode to the right about half a mile and got within about 300 yds of the rebel battery." From there he could see where his shells landed and sent an orderly back to inform the gunners how to alter their fire. His battery drove the Confederate guns off the field.[59]

Signal officers proved to be excellent artillery spotters, although they were never intended to do such work. The newly created Signal Corps consisted of officers trained in reconnaissance and, using a system of flag waving, to convey messages by line of sight between signal stations. On many occasions, if they happened to be near a battery, they offered their services in directing fire on targets unseen from the ground. Capt. Thomas W. Osborn planted 250 rounds from Battery D, 1st New York Light Artillery onto Confederate troops hidden by a patch of woods, relying entirely on "telegraphic signals of one of the signal corps posted in the top of a high pine tree," during the Seven Days Campaign. By all accounts this fire was effective at breaking up the troop concentration. Earlier, during the Peninsula Campaign, an observer in a balloon telegraphed reports "assisting to regulate the range of our guns," claimed telegrapher J. Emmet O'Brien.[60]

A handful of signal officers were very active in assisting the artillery during Sherman's Atlanta Campaign. Lt. Samuel Edge regularly worked with Union batteries in the static trench lines near Atlanta. At times he worked from a signal station high up a tree and at other times placed a colleague in the tree while he relayed information to a nearby battery. At least according to Edge, this system worked well.[61] Armed with powerful telescopes, signal officers could have provided a boon to artillerists if they had been trained to work with the big guns and if enough officers had been assigned to this duty. But cooperation between signal officers and artillery commanders was haphazard at best. An unidentified signal officer "had the kindness to come to our battery with a telescope," reported Capt. Arnold Sutermeister during the Atlanta Campaign. With that scope Sutermeister was able to get a clear view of a Confederate fort on the Chattahoochee River too far away for the naked eye. "Could we procure the services of a signal officer for a short time every day or two it would be of great advantage to us," he asserted.[62]

There is no doubt that signal officers could have significantly increased the effectiveness of field artillery during the Civil War, but it has to be pointed out that the problems limiting line of sight were far more complex than could be solved by using a powerful telescope. At times targets were in sight and then disappeared. Lt. Lester I. Richardson fired at a moving column of Confederate infantry at Cold Harbor until it marched into a ravine, but Richardson continued to fire into the ravine at random hoping he might continue to inflict damage. There were many instances where troops were dimly visible but it was difficult to tell if they were friend or foe.[63]

Perhaps the greatest inhibition against indirect fire was not a physical but an intellectual roadblock. The culture of field artillery in the 1860s did not even recognize this concept much less encourage officers to explore ways to achieve it. Capt. John A. Tompkins expressed this culture of conservatism, which ran high in the Army of the Potomac, while writing his report of Antietam. He admitted that his men fired at a Confederate battery "which was hid by a ridge" but hastened to assert that otherwise "every shot was fired at a visible enemy, the guns pointed with care, and the accuracy of aim and length of fuse noticed."[64]

AVERAGE DISTANCE OF FIRING

Many factors affected the distance of firing, but rifling was the only one that was new to the Civil War era. The average distance of actual firing on the battlefield becomes a significant point as a way to gauge the effect of rifled artillery on field operations.

Based on statistics from 336 examples of firing in which the distance was reported, the average distance between muzzle and target was 917 yards, roughly half a mile. There was almost no pattern among these 336 examples. Field artillery in the East fired at about the same distance as that in the West, and no difference between Union and Confederate fieldpieces could be detected.

The only pattern evident related to type of target. In 50 examples the reports indicated that the guns were firing at opposing infantry, with an average distance of 489 yards. This is roughly a quarter of a mile, about half the average distance for all 336 examples and just beyond the recommended distance of canister. In 77 other examples, reports indicated the target was artillery, and in these cases the average distance came to 1,122 yards, close to three-quarters of a mile. Unfortunately, the reports did not consistently indicate whether the pieces were smoothbore or rifled.

If we consider the bracket between 489 yards and 1,122 yards, it is obvious that the capabilities of both smoothbores and rifles fell easily within that pocket. These findings fail to support an argument that rifles were hugely successful or were used in dramatically different ways than smoothbores under battlefield conditions. Nor do they support an argument that smoothbores were more successful than the new rifles. The relative importance of smoothbores and rifles can be said to have achieved a state of equilibrium.

TOTAL ROUNDS FIRED

Another consideration when assessing field effectiveness concerns the total number of rounds fired in an engagement and those used over a longer period of time. Depending on circumstances, some batteries fired comparatively little. For example, the 20th Ohio Battery did not see action at all on the first day at

Chickamauga and fired only 85 rounds on the second day. But more commonly batteries fired at least 500 projectiles in a given engagement, even large ones, which amounted to 80–100 rounds for each piece, depending on whether the battery contained four or six guns. When the Amherst Virginia Artillery fired 1,600 rounds at Third Winchester, Henry Robinson Berkeley thought it was "about four times as much as we have ever used in a fight before."[65] A single gun detachment firing 200–300 rounds on one day of battle was quite common throughout the Civil War.[66]

At Rosecrans's order his artillery chief, Col. James Barnett, provided detailed information about the Union guns at Stones River. Among other things, he listed the number of rounds fired by each battery. The totals ranged from a low of 7 rounds to a high of 2,299 rounds, the latter by the combined Batteries H and M, 4th US Artillery. The highest number fired by a battery that was not consolidated was 1,650 rounds. A total of 20,307 rounds were fired by all Federal artillery during the three-day battle. That amounted to 781 rounds per battery on average, or 130 rounds per gun, assuming that each battery contained six pieces.[67]

John Fitch, who served as Rosecrans's provost judge, provided detailed information concerning the artillery in a book he authored about the Army of the Cumberland at Stones River. The average weight of the 20,307 rounds fired during the battle amounted to 10 pounds and the powder charge to send them on their way averaged 1.5 pounds. That came to a total weight of 203,070 pounds of projectiles and an expenditure of 30,360.5 pounds of powder. At an estimated average cost of $0.07 per pound, the metal used in making the 203,070 pounds of projectiles came to $14,214.90. At an average cost of $0.20 per pound, the total expenditure of powder came to $6,072.10. Fitch reported that the use of artillery at Stones River cost the Federal government $20,287. "This is taking the most economical view of the subject," he cautioned.[68]

Statistics for Gettysburg indicate a conservative expenditure of ammunition despite the great role played by artillery on both sides. The Army of the Potomac fired 32,781 rounds, about one-third of its supply, averaging 270 rounds for each of the 362 pieces on the field. The Army of Northern Virginia was even more conservative, firing about 22,000 rounds, or half its available ammunition, averaging 150 rounds for each of 272 pieces. Terrain did not limit artillery firing at Gettysburg, but it played a large role at Chickamauga, where the Army of Tennessee fired only 4,568 rounds, or only 38 projectiles for every piece. Federal artillery fired 7,325 rounds in that two-day battle.[69] Typically, more rounds were fired to support an infantry attack than to repel one. At Chickasaw Bayou Battery G, 1st Michigan Light Artillery fired 335 rounds per piece in supporting a major Union attack on December 29, 1862, while Confederate pieces fired a total of 120 rounds to stop it.[70]

"It has been stated," wrote historian L. Van Loan Naisawald, "that the Union artillery arm fired a total of five million rounds of ammunition during the Civil War." This amounted, in his view, to an average of four rounds per piece every day of the conflict. While Naisawald did not provide a source for his information, we can arrive close to that figure by other means. The ever-reliable Jacob Roemer calculated the total expenditure of the two batteries he consecutively commanded during the Civil War as 9,780 rounds. Extrapolating this number as an average for the 460 Union batteries, together they fired 4,498,800 rounds during the war. Using Roemer's statistic for the 292 Confederate batteries, Rebel artillery expended 2,855,760 rounds during the conflict. Combining the two belligerents, 752 batteries fired a grand total of 7,354,560 rounds from 1861 to 1865.[71]

By far, the Civil War was the biggest artillery conflict ever to occur in the Western Hemisphere. It was comparable to any prior war that had occurred in Europe as well and exceeded the number of guns and rounds fired in most previous European conflicts. Yet it has never been given the attention it deserves among global military historians for being a significant test case of field artillery effectiveness.

6

. . . .

PROJECTILES AND FUZES

The tube was the delivery device for the projectile, but the fuze ignited explosive ordnance used in that device. Projectiles and fuzes were important elements in artillery effectiveness, and their story is multilayered and complex.[1]

Artillerists relied on four basic types of projectiles during the Civil War. Solid shot was the oldest type available, in use literally since the dawn of the artillery age four hundred years before the firing on Fort Sumter. It was still useful for hitting enemy troop formations. At 600 yards a solid shot could penetrate five to six feet of "newly thrown-up earth," according to John Gibbon. It remained a standard part of the issue to batteries in the field.[2]

But shells were more commonly used in the Civil War than solid shot. The term applied to projectiles that had only a bursting charge inside that broke up the casing into fragments that damaged targets. Shells could be effective even if they burst on the ground. When fired from smoothbores, they were round, like solid shot, and used a flame-ignited fuze to burst the charge. In rifled pieces shells assumed an elongated shape and were typically set off by a percussion fuze placed in the nose.[3]

With eight ounces of powder, the 12-pounder shell broke into twelve to fifteen fragments. When exploding in motion, the fragments in front continued to fly forward at a fast rate, while those in back flew backward at a much slower speed. Gibbon thought the fragment pattern could extend as much as 300 yards in diameter. He believed shells produced "a greater moral effect" than solid shot because of the noise and suddenness of the explosion. It therefore was useful against cavalry because it frightened horses.[4]

The Confederates improved on the performance of shells by shaping the

Fig. 6.1. Solid Shot with Wooden Sabot for 12-Pounder Howitzer. The oldest type of projectile in history, solid shot was still used in the Civil War for a variety of reasons. Smoothbores fired round projectiles, which necessitated a wooden sabot to more evenly catch the gases expanding through the tube from the powder explosion. The metal straps broke away and dropped the sabot after the round left the muzzle. This is an original solid shot from the Civil War. Photograph by Jack W. Melton Jr.

cavity as a polygon to break up the casing into a predetermined number of roughly equal fragments. Semple's Alabama Battery received many polygonal shells, all for the Napoleon and all fixed, in the late summer of 1863. By February 1865 the Confederates manufactured polygonal shells for Coehorn mortars along the lines at Petersburg. These small projectiles broke into twelve "diagonal pieces," according to Federal artillery officers who examined the fragments.[5]

Case shot was a shell that, in addition to a bursting charge, contained musket balls in the cavity. Also called shrapnel or, when designed for smoothbores, spherical case, resin or melted sulphur was poured into the cavity to seat the balls securely. A 6-pounder case shot contained 37 bullets, 12-pounders held 76, and 24-pounders 175. The exterior of case shot was thinner than in a shell to reduce the size of the bursting charge and make more room for the musket balls.[6]

The purpose of case shot, as Joseph Roberts put it, was "to extend all the advantages of canister shot, to distances far beyond the reach of that projectile." It had to explode in the air to achieve its potential, and that required a time fuze. The optimum bursting took place fifty to seventy-five yards short of the target so that the impetus of the trajectory would spray the fragments and bullets forward in an expanding pattern. It also had to explode fifteen to twenty feet (or twenty to fifty feet according to some experts) above the ground. This

TABLE 6.1. Four Popular Projectiles of the Civil War

	Diameter	Length	Weight	Sabot
12-Pounder Case Shot (Smoothbore)	4.50 Inches	Fitting 4.62-Inch Caliber	9 Pounds, 10 Ounces	Wood Cup
Schenkl Shell	2.92 Inches	9.19 Inches	8 Pounds	Papier-Mâché
Hotchkiss Shell	2.94 Inches	6.63 Inches	8 Pounds, 7 Ounces	Lead Band
10-Pounder Parrott Case Shot	2.86 Inches	8.50 Inches	11 Pounds, 7 Ounces	Wrought-Iron Cup

would "allow the cone of expansion of the bullets to cover the largest possible area." All this demanded gunners who could estimate distance and fuzes that worked consistently well.[7]

A 12-pounder case shot could spread fragments of the casing and the musket bullets in a pattern up to 800 yards wide. But at that great distance, the chances of hitting anyone was greatly diminished. The closer one stood to the point of explosion, the more danger he faced. As with shells, case shot could damage cavalry formations more heavily than infantry, as the man-horse combination offered a bigger target for the increased number of missiles it spread.[8]

W. Leroy Brown thought that case shot was "the most formidable projectile in the hands of an artillerist." Another Confederate called it "the most terrible shot used by Arty at any range over 500 yards." That was in some ways true but in other ways misleading. The technical limitations and the difficulty of exploding case shot exactly on target created a mixed record. John Watkins of the 19th Ohio Battery told his friend that case shot was "a nasty thing ... if they burst," a comment that pointed to the problem of effective fuzes.[9] In some circumstances case shot worked well. Confederate gunners used it to repel a Union attack on the base of the Mule Shoe Salient at Spotsylvania on May 18, 1864. William S. White described victims as "literally torn into atoms; shot through and through by cannon balls, some with arms and legs knocked off, and some with their heads crushed in by the fatal fragments of exploded shell. Horrible, horrible!"[10]

Case shot became so popular with some artillerists that others criticized them for it. Henry J. Hunt told his subordinates in the Army of the Potomac that "there is too much shrapnel used." He preferred solid shot "in almost all cases." Edward Porter Alexander would not have agreed; he considered solid shot "the least effective ammunition."[11]

Canister was the second-oldest artillery projectile in history, a simple piece of ordnance containing cast-iron balls that sprayed out in a cone-shaped pattern on leaving the muzzle. It should not be confused with grapeshot, which was primarily a naval ordnance consisting of larger balls grouped around a wooden stick. Grapeshot was useful for tearing up the sails and rigging of naval vessels, but it had been a feature of land warfare for some time as well. By the Civil War, however, it no longer was used on land, but contemporaries often employed the term when referring to canister.[12]

Gibbon noted that the canister balls were not evenly distributed throughout the dispersal cone; most of them flew near its center, thus concentrating the destructive potential. The full cone pattern did not develop until the cluster of balls had traveled about one-tenth of the way toward the aiming point. The cone was at its maximum extent from 300 to 450 yards from the muzzle. Beyond 450 yards the pattern dissipated a great deal. This meant that there were two sectors wherein infantrymen were less exposed when receiving canister fire. The first was very close to the gun delivering the charge, and the other was at the farthest extent of the distance from the gun to the target. If the ground was hard, the artillerist could maximize the effect of canister by counting on some of the balls to ricochet.[13]

Canister seems to have had greater space between the projectile and the bore of the tube, what was termed "windage" in artillery parlance. William S. White noted that "the flame from the gun seems to go much farther than" with other types of ordnance. But the increased windage did not diminish canister's effect. *Instruction for Field Artillery* encouraged the use of double charges of canister up to 150 yards but reminded artillerists that they should use only one powder charge to fire the double load.[14]

Experience on the battlefield led to a campaign to increase the number of balls in each canister round. Artillerists complained that twenty-seven shot per round, packed in a tin casing with sawdust, did too little damage when fired from smoothbores at short distance. After Gettysburg, where this issue moved to center stage, Hunt recommended the weight of the balls be reduced from seven ounces to two or three ounces and their number increased so that sixty to eighty balls filled each round. He believed the new arrangement would render canister more effective at distances less than 200 yards. By March 1864 the new smoothbore canister round was ready, containing seventy-two balls of three ounces each. There is no indication, however, that artillerists were satisfied with it.[15]

The introduction of rifles complicated the use of canister. The spin imparted to the round by the rifling led to a less predictable pattern than the cone shape produced by smoothbores. The 3-Inch Ordnance Rifle had a slightly smaller bore than the Napoleon, which meant the balls had to be arranged in a different way. Instead of occupying four tiers, they were packed in seven tiers, making them spread out faster, while the balls of the smoothbore canister remained in a more compact group for a longer time. Because of this, everyone agreed that short-distance canister fire by rifles was not as effective as when delivered from smoothbores.[16]

EVALUATIONS OF PROJECTILE DESIGNS

Civil War artillerists frequently evaluated the different makes and designs of their projectiles after testing them in combat. While opinions varied, there were certain streams of agreement. Schenkl projectiles tended to receive higher ratings than any other, with Hotchkiss projectiles next in order of preference. A number of also-rans, including Dyer and James projectiles, were largely rejected, while Parrotts rested comfortably in the middle of this spectrum.

Many officers praised John P. Schenkl's products. These rounds had a tapered lower half around which was wrapped the sabot material. On firing, that material slid forward to catch the grooves. The 5th Massachusetts Battery tested his percussion shells during the Peninsula Campaign. The men fired at "a pile of dirt" that Confederate soldiers had been working on at a distance of 2,400 yards, and all of the shells burst properly. Based on evidence such as this, Brig. Gen. William F. Barry, McClellan's artillery chief, requested more Schenkl projectiles for his rifled pieces. Many officers continued to prefer this type throughout the war. As late as July 1864, reports indicated they "worked admirably."[17]

The praise was not unmixed with criticism. Lt. Albert Vincent of consolidated Batteries B and L, 2nd US Artillery, fired 150 Schenkl percussion shells from June 6 to 13, 1863. He noted approvingly that three-fourths of the rounds exploded properly, unconcerned that a quarter of them failed to do so.[18] Col.

Fig. 6.2. Three-Inch Schenkl Shell without Sabot. All rifled projectiles were elongated rather than spherical and demanded a different type of sabot. John P. Schenkl, whose projectiles were among the most widely used in the Civil War, designed them with a tapered rear around which was wrapped papier-mâché. On discharge, the papier-mâché was forced forward to fill in the spiraled rifling, which imparted spin to the projectile. This is a photo of an original 3-inch Schenkl shell without the sabot. The plug to hold the percussion fuze is in the forward end. Photograph by Jack W. Melton Jr.

Henry L. Abbot, in charge of the siege train of the Army of the Potomac during the Petersburg Campaign, noted that Schenkl's projectiles did not consistently take the rifling grooves in Parrotts. He also reported that sabot pieces had too much tendency to break away from these rounds and endanger friendly troops. In short, even Schenkl's projectiles had significant problems.[19]

On the other hand, there were artillery officers who swore by the projectiles designed by Benjamin B. Hotchkiss, but they were in fewer number than the Schenkl advocates. These rounds employed a unique design, best explained by the historian of the 5th Massachusetts Battery as "a compound shot consisting of two parts of cast iron, with the rear cap fitting over the forward portion. Around the joint was placed a band of lead so locked into both parts of the shot as to prevent its flying off after it leaves the piece. The explosion of the charge forces the rear part forward, expanding the lead, forcing it into

Fig. 6.3. Three-Inch Hotchkiss Shell with Sabot. Benjamin B. Hotchkiss designed his widely used rifled projectile differently than Schenkl. He made it in two pieces that fitted together in a way to allow for lead to be applied in a band around the middle to act as a sabot. The rear end moved forward on discharge and forced the lead to expand and catch the rifling. This material often broke off soon after leaving the barrel and showered any friendly troops in its line of flight, injuring some on occasion. Since papier-mâché was lighter than lead, it tended to be less dangerous. This is an original 3-inch Hotchkiss shell fitted with a time fuze in the plug at the forward end. Photograph by Jack W. Melton Jr.

the grooves, and cutting off windage." But even those who admired the Hotchkiss products admitted they did not burst properly all the time. After firing Hotchkiss shells and case shot at Chancellorsville, Capt. James H. Cooper of Battery B, 1st Pennsylvania Light Artillery stated they "worked well, most of them exploding at or near the point fired upon." Other men noted the tendency of sabot pieces to fall on friendly troops, a problem with all rifled projectiles. As late as March 1865 officers reported "insufficient bursting charges in many of the Hotchkiss 3-inch shell and case-shot."[20]

One can find fewer comments on Parrott ammunition than on Schenkl and Hotchkiss types. Barry noted that sand cracks lessened the reliability of Parrott ammunition during the Carolinas Campaign. Lt. Col. William H. Ross, artillery chief of the Fifteenth Corps, disliked Parrott products for another reason: "The powder in the shells is insufficient and poor."[21]

Fig. 6.4. Ten-Pounder Parrott Shell with Sabot. Schenkl and Hotchkiss were primarily projectile designers and manufacturers who made their products to be used in a variety of different types of artillery pieces. But Robert P. Parrott was primarily a cannon designer and maker who also designed and made projectiles to be used mostly by his own cannon. This is a photo of an original 10-pounder Parrott shell with a percussion fuze in the plug. The sabot is a wrought-iron cup at the rear end that expanded to catch the rifling. By 1864 the US Ordnance Department mandated that only Parrott projectiles be used in Parrott pieces. Photograph by Jack W. Melton Jr.

Almost everyone considered Dyer and James projectiles inadequate. Capt. Alexander B. Dyer had developed a rifled projectile before the war that Ordnance Bureau chief Brig. Gen. James W. Ripley endorsed for use. A large number were issued to the Army of the Potomac during the Peninsula Campaign, but their performance was strikingly bad. Lt. Charles A. Phillips of the 5th Massachusetts Battery fired many and found that only two worked properly; the rest "turned over, burst in the air, and flew round in all sorts of ways." Capt. Charles D. Owen of Battery G, 1st Rhode Island Light Artillery reported at Antietam and Fredericksburg that the Dyer projectile failed to take the grooves in rifled pieces. Even as late as the Atlanta Campaign, these products were being used in a limited way but still produced negative commentary.[22]

Sometimes the problem lay not in projectile design but in manufacturing. Because several arsenals and private firms made them and stamped their mark on ammunition boxes, it was possible for artillerists to identify their products. They generally gave the Allegheny Arsenal near Pittsburgh high marks but roundly condemned the Saint Louis Arsenal.[23]

By 1864 the Ordnance Bureau began to regulate what types of projectiles should be used with certain types of pieces. Brig. Gen. George D. Ramsay, who had replaced Ripley as bureau head, mandated that only projectiles produced by Parrott be used in Parrott rifles. Hotchkiss projectiles could be used in the smaller-caliber Parrotts if no Parrott ammunition was available, but Schenkl projectiles were never to be used in Parrott pieces. Ramsay also prohibited the use of Parrott projectiles in 3-Inch Ordnance Rifles.[24]

Confederate-made ammunition was notorious for poor quality. "I have mighty little confidence in" the 20-pounder Parrott ammunition produced at Richmond, wrote Col. Frank Huger. "They either burst in . . . the gun, or else they don't go straight." When he examined one projectile, Huger found that the cavity in the middle was "off center by a lot," meaning that one side was twice as thick as the opposite side. "No wonder they don't go straight."[25] Problems such as this led the Confederate chief of ordnance, Brig. Gen. Josiah Gorgas, to establish a facility controlled by his department to produce ordnance for both the artillery and the infantry. Gorgas believed one could not expect uniform standards by farming out production to private concerns. The government created a plant at Macon, Georgia, under the control of Lt. Col. John W. Mallet, which seems to have improved the quality of Confederate ordnance.[26]

CHEMICAL PROJECTILES

The Civil War witnessed a few efforts to deploy crude types of chemical weapons. Defined as "agents, intended to kill or disable by virtue of their chemical properties," inventors of the time discussed the idea of placing agents such as cayenne pepper, black pepper, snuff, and mustard seed in artillery shells. They extended the list to more serious agents such as chloroform, chlorine, arsenic, strychnine, sulfur, and various acids.[27] Virtually all of this lay in the realm of discussion. At the end of the Overland Campaign, William N. Pendleton read of a "stink-shell" in a newspaper and contacted Lee's ordnance chief. "The question is whether the explosion can be combined with suffocating effect of certain offensive gases, or whether apart from explosion such gases may not be emitted from a continuously burning composition as to render the vicinity of each falling shell intolerable. It seems at least worth a trial." W. Leroy Brown was by that time working in the Ordnance Department and wrote an endorsement on Pendleton's dispatch. "Stink-balls, none on hand; don't keep them; will make if ordered." But there is no indication that this was done.[28]

FIXED AMMUNITION

Artillery ammunition could be delivered to units in the field either fixed (with the powder cartridge attached to the projectile) or as two separate pieces. The former facilitated loading by cutting down a step or two in the process. But there are very few references to fixed ammunition in the sources. When Capt. Charles Swett received projectiles for his Mississippi Battery on September 6, 1863, the receipt included 154 rounds of fixed ammunition divided between thirty-four solid shot, thirty-two canister, and eighty-eight shells.[29]

Swett's fixed ammunition was solely for the Napoleons in his battery. He received 131 rounds for his rifled pieces, but none of them were fixed. Even the 135 blank rounds received were not fixed. George A. Farr of Battery M, 4th US Artillery asserted that his unit also received fixed ammunition only for its smoothbores. Joseph Roberts noted in his handbook that fixed rounds were never issued for heavier ordnance such as 24-pounders and 32-pounders. The *Ordnance Manual* warned that dismantling a fixed round was dangerous, in itself a potent reason for not issuing a large number of them.[30]

EXPEDIENT PROJECTILES

The Confederates often placed unusual components in their projectiles because they fell short of standard material, especially early in the war. At the Battle of Carthage on July 5, 1861, the men of Guibor's Missouri Battery filled canister rounds with short iron rods cut up by blacksmiths. At the Wilson's Creek battlefield of August 1861, archaeologists have uncovered canister pieces "made from round stock or rods" as well as "square or bar stock."[31] Some Confederate guns at Stones River fired short pieces of railroad iron in lieu of standard projectiles. John Henry Otto of the 21st Wisconsin saw something "twisting round high in the air." It buried itself in the mud and when dug up was found to be a section of railroad iron fifteen inches long. At Second Winchester Union gunners insisted that opponents fired short sections of railroad iron at their batteries.[32]

The Federals also made expedient rounds, although not due to shortages. Many infantrymen offered artillerists their musket balls to use as canister. Battery B, 1st Illinois Light Artillery used "bags of bullets, which we had prepared for close work," on the first day at Shiloh. Men of the 33rd New Jersey saved balls from cartridges that became damp. "When we had enough to fill a stocking," wrote Stephen Pierson, they gave them to the 13th New York Battery for use in its Napoleons. "Your *stocking legs* saved us," a battery sergeant told Pierson after the Battle of Peach Tree Creek on July 20, 1864. Members of the 11th Illinois saved "pieces of iron, taps or bolts" during the Siege of Vicksburg. They filled empty peach cans and offered them to Battery D, 1st Illinois to use in its 24-pounders. "The cans would be torn to pieces and scatter the contents far and wide," recorded George Carrington.[33]

ROCKETS

The US Army had retained the equipment and theory of rocket use before the Civil War even though it had no active rocket batteries. The *Ordnance Manual* differentiated between signal rockets and war rockets, the latter designed on the Hale rocket system and measuring three inches in diameter.[34]

Both sides made an attempt to create rocket units when the war began. In the North Maj. Thomas W. Lion, a former English officer, led the creation of the Rocket Battalion, putting together two companies by December 1861. He practiced firing modified Hale rockets across the Potomac River after receiving his armament—four rocket tubes mounted on a carriage—reaching distances of up to three miles. With four carriages he could fire sixteen rounds in a salvo. Lion wanted to place a hollow head on each rocket, fill it with shrapnel balls, and affix a time fuze to maximize the effect. The tubes were eight feet long and had a bore of two and a quarter inches. The only problem was that the rockets traced wild trajectories, flying off in any direction. After several trials the idea of a rocket battalion was dropped. Lion's two companies converted into normal artillery units, with Battery B becoming the 14th New York

Battery.[35] The idea of creating a rocket battery resurfaced early in 1863 when a man named G. H. Snelling urged it on Hunt, who was not convinced. "We have never had a properly organized or instructed artillerist" to fire rockets, he admitted, and he had no time to organize a unit now.[36]

Much the same applied to the Confederate army. Soon after First Bull Run, Edward Porter Alexander searched Richmond for rockets and tubes with the intention of making Battery E of the Sumter Battalion, a Georgia artillery unit, into a rocket battery. After acquiring them he tested the equipment but found the firing to be too unpredictable.[37]

Someone organized a rocket unit that was attached to Brig. Gen. J. E. B. Stuart's cavalry brigade after the Seven Days Campaign. Stuart used a battery armed with Congreve rockets to strike the Union fortified camp embracing Harrison's Landing. The unit "had been gotten up by some foreign chap who managed it on this occasion," recalled W. W. Blackford. "They were huge rockets, fired from a sort of gun carriage, with a shell at the end." The effect was less than encouraging. The rockets went straight enough during the initial part of their trajectory, but if they hit anything in flight, they continued in a very erratic way, even coming back toward the Confederates. Surprisingly, Capt. John C. Tidball of Battery A, 2nd US Artillery praised the Confederates for firing "with great precision a score or so of war rockets" at the camp.[38]

Capt. Samuel T. Wright's Halifax Artillery acquired thirteen rocket launchers by the latter part of 1862, when it served in southeast Virginia, and used them in two engagements with Federal forces conducting movements toward Franklin on the Blackwater River. The first use occurred on October 3, 1862. "No one was wounded," recorded the historian of the 11th Pennsylvania Cavalry, "but the fearful noise and hissing of the rocket shells was rather disquieting." Another Federal move toward Franklin resulted in a more serious engagement on December 2, but it proved to be a disaster for the Confederates. Union troops captured seventy rockets of 12- and 15-pounder sizes. Wright's battery gave up its rocket launchers by the spring of 1863.[39]

On the frontier, Capt. John S. Greer's Texas battery organized late in 1863 and early in 1864, acquiring rockets as its primary armament by June of that latter year. It never employed them in action and gave up the temperamental weapons within a month. On the other side of the Confederacy, Federal forces improvised a rocket unit by detailing men from the 74th Pennsylvania and 127th New York, launching rockets several times during raids and reconnaissance movements in the area around Charleston, South Carolina, in the summer of 1864.[40]

Hale rockets were more often mentioned in plans for these batteries than Congreve rockets. When Alexander tested the Hale late in 1862, he observed how it traveled through the air. "The rocket moves off slowly at first, the rear end gyrating around the path of the head in a decreasing circle until it falls into it when the flight immediately becomes straight." Relic collectors have found Hale rockets on the battlefield of Seven Pines and have assumed the Confederates had used them.[41]

FUZES

By the Civil War, great advances had been made in developing modern fuzes to ignite explosive projectiles, but many technical problems hampered their effective use in the field. Several manufacturers produced them. Parrott at the West Point Foundry made both projectiles and fuzes. While he could turn out projectiles for an average price of six cents per pound, he manufactured a percussion fuze for ninety cents per pound, fifteen times more than the cost of the round. The reason for this disparity was the complexity of the fuze; although small, it was very delicate.[42]

Wooden and Paper Fuzes

The wooden fuze was the oldest in existence and still saw some use. Made of a length of wood, tapered toward one end and filled with mealed powder, it had marks on the outside that indicated time of burning. The artillerist cut if off at the desired time and inserted it into the projectile. The wooden fuze was a flame-ignited time fuze, the gases and flame of the powder explosion passing by the projectile (windage) and igniting the fuze in a split second before the projectile left the tube. Everyone recognized that wooden fuzes burned irregularly and so relegated them mostly to mortars rather than to fieldpieces.[43]

Paper fuzes were more reliable than wooden ones. They consisted of a paper case to hold the mealed powder placed inside a wooden or brass fuze plug. These burned at a standard rate differentiated by color. The yellow fuze burned at the rate of one inch in five seconds, green at seven seconds, and blue at ten seconds. All of them were made two inches long in the factory and the gunner had to cut them according to the time desired. For example, a blue fuze was capable of burning twenty seconds but could be cut to any time less than that. Relic collectors have found examples of paper fuzes in tan color as well and with times ranging up to forty seconds. The paper fuze, like the wooden variety, was a flame-ignited device.[44]

Paper fuzes were quite simple and easy to use. According to Gibbon, they came to be favored for heavy ordnance, while the Bormann fuze was favored in the field artillery. But there is evidence of their use in fieldpieces as well. Capt. Overton W. Barret of Barret's Missouri Battery (CS) reported favorably of them at Stones River. "My shells, ignited by red, green, and black fuses, were the most effective and accurate projectile which I used in this battle."[45]

But many artillerists complained of paper fuzes that failed to perform as expected. They "worked very indifferently" during the Peninsula and Seven Days Campaigns. Barry noted that they burned reliably when cut up to about eight seconds, but beyond that point they were "very uncertain; at 12 seconds often burning no longer than five or six seconds." At sixteen seconds, the actual burn rate was even shorter, decreasing in time the longer the setting. Barry believed that "careless mistakes have been made in marking the time on the outside of the cases" at the factory.[46] Other officers found different problems with paper fuzes as well. Charles Wainwright noticed that it was difficult to cut and place the fuze in wet weather without dampening the mealed powder. At Fredericksburg Capt. William Hexamer of Battery A, 1st New Jersey Light Artillery found that some of the fuzes were "entirely too small in diameter and could not be used without rolling [additional] paper around" them. Capt. James H. Stokes of the Chicago Board of Trade Battery, after examining a number of paper fuzes, concluded that the mealed powder was "stuck in [the paper] with mucilage, which, forming a glazeing to the powder, forbids ignition." He suggested that crews "dip the fuse in alcohol or turpentine, which, as a necessary accessory, is not always on hand."[47]

Confederate artillerists consistently complained of "failure to ignite" as a problem with their paper fuzes. "They proved inefficient, not preserving the range," wrote Lt. William B. Turner of Smith's Mississippi Battery after Stones River. The only problem encountered by Capt. Felix H. Robertson of Robertson's Florida Battery was with paper fuzes; all the other types worked well. Robertson thought the issue lay with the "faulty manner of driving the paper well into the wood."[48]

Despite these limitations, paper fuzes continued to be employed throughout the war. Capt. Theodore S. Thomasson used them to fire 69 percent of his rounds on the second day at Nashville. He reported no problems but noted that he used 400 paper fuzes to fire 389 rounds. His men probably dropped 11 fuzes in the heat of action. That loss rate, only 2.7 percent, is a small measure of waste in combat.[49]

Bormann Fuze

The Bormann fuze dispensed with paper and consisted entirely of metal. Gibbon called it "by far the best and most regular of any now in use." It held the mealed powder in a circular train, did not have to be driven into the fuze plug, and could be kept indefinitely in the projectile unlike the paper fuze, which had to be fired soon after insertion. Lead, or an alloy of lead, covered the powder train and could be easily cut with an awl, exposing powder at the desired setting. One of the few limitations of this flame-ignited fuze was that it allowed a maximum of only five seconds burn time. According to one artilleryman, that is why it was used only in smoothbore ammunition in his battery.[50]

But actual practice in the field yielded substantial criticism of the Bormann fuze. Some Confederate artillerists at Stones River praised it. The fuzes "operated in accordance with the tables, as we had taught the gunners," wrote Lt. L. G. Marshall of Carnes's Tennessee Battery. But Captain Barret found fault with the Bormann, calling it "very inferior" without explaining his view. Federal artillerists lodged several complaints. Barry wrote that the Bormann "does not give the satisfaction we ought to expect." James Stokes found fault with the mucilage used to seed the mealed powder in the train. He also thought the "thin partition" of metal that separated the train from the bursting charge sometimes broke through too early and caused a premature explosion.[51]

But other Union and Confederate officers had ideas about why Bormann fuzes produced premature detonations. W. Leroy Brown argued that crewmembers failed to screw the fuze into the plug properly, allowing flame to pass between the thread of the screw and the shell casing. Acting on that assumption, Brown taught personnel how to screw the Bormann in tightly with a fuze wrench and then apply a glaze made of white lead and litharge (lead oxide) on the "exterior rim of the fuze." After that, "very few premature explosions" took place. Both Hunt and Barry also identified carelessness in screwing the device into the plug as the problem.[52]

There is no indication that defects in the Bormann fuze were rectified. George Wright of Washington, DC, worked up an improvement on it by lengthening the burn time from five seconds to twelve seconds. But because this took place late in the war, this version of the fuze saw little service.[53]

Concussion Time Fuze

In contrast to the flame-ignited time fuzes, important developments in creating a pressure-activated time fuze took place during the Civil War era. One concept was to take advantage of the force exerted by the powder cartridge that sent the projectile on its flight. Called a concussion time fuze, it could be placed in a spherical projectile with the fuze facing the breech of the tube so the powder explosion could press directly on it. That pressure pushed the fuze deeper into the plug, breaking a membrane and activating the timing mechanism. In March 1864 Hunt reported to his subordinates that "every effort is now being made to provide a concussion shell for the" Napoleon, but there is no evidence that it was used during the war.[54]

Percussion, or Impact, Fuze

Another method of using pressure to set off a projectile was not at the point of firing (concussion) but at the point of impact (percussion). Placing a detonating device at the forward end of an elongated projectile worked because the forward end could be counted on to squarely hit the target. The general principle was best illustrated by the Parrott percussion fuze, which employed two pieces. Inside the device a slider rammed backward when the projectile hit something and pushed an anvil cap that exploded, creating the fire necessary to set off the bursting charge. The slider also was called a jumper, both names reflecting the fact that it moved within the fuze. Of course, this action was inhibited by the projectile landing on soft ground, but in general it worked pretty well. A safety device was necessary to prevent premature explosions. Adding a couple of prongs strong enough to prevent the slider from hitting the cap but weak enough to break when the projectile hit the target worked well.[55]

Several manufacturers made percussion fuzes, including James and an Englishman named Bashley Britten, who patented his version in Britain in March 1861. More than one Confederate officer also developed a percussion fuze. While serving in the Ordnance Bureau, W. Leroy Brown patented one in May 1863 that he claimed could be used in spherical projectiles. Capt. Isidore P. Girardey, also working with the Ordnance Bureau, patented his own device the following month. It could "convert a time-fused projectile into a percussion-fused device," according to historian Charles H. Jones.[56]

The percussion fuze represented a major step in the evolution of projectile fuzes, and it came about solely because of the deployment of rifled artillery. Many artillerists assured their correspondents that percussion fuzes were more reliable than time fuzes, and Hunt recommended them when firing all explosive ordnance.[57]

Combination Fuze

A logical idea was to devise a fuze that combined timing and pressure. Called the combination fuze, it doubled the chances of exploding the ordnance. One system backed up the other to lessen the chances of duds. Both Schenkl and Sylvanus Sawyer developed combination fuzes that protruded from the elongated shell. Exposed as they were, both were subject to heat caused by friction while flying through the air. Success rates varied. Using them in heavy artillery late in the Petersburg Campaign, Schenkl combination fuzes worked only 55 percent of the time, while Sawyer designs worked 85 percent. Hotchkiss developed a combination fuze that mixed a Bormann fuze with his own percussion fuze, thus combining a flame-ignited device with a percussion device. It saw less use than the Schenkl and Sawyer versions.[58]

Field satisfaction with combination fuzes varied. The device had the reputation of being the most reliable fuze, but practice did not support that view. Capt. John A. Reynolds of Battery L, 1st New York Light Artillery found that in many cases the rammer caught the fuzes. The Number 1 man had to turn the rammer, or work it off the device somehow, but that altered the fuze and led to faulty shots. Reynolds had the end of his rammers reamed out to create a deep cup, which seemed to take care of the problem.[59]

Lt. Albert O. Vincent of consolidated Batteries B and L, 2nd US Artillery, used sixty Schenkl case shot with combination fuzes while supporting cavalry at Beverly Ford in June 1863. He found that only six to eight exploded "within the time indicated," while barely one-fourth of the sixty "exploded at all." Vincent's detailed explanation is worth quoting in full: "The 'latch spring' of many of the fuses will not lie flat on the top of the *rotator,* but works, *up* and *down,* the 'latch pin' out of its bed, and prevents the fuse to turn after the *time* has been regulated. With others, the holes through which fire is communicated to the bursting charge cannot be made to force the proper opening of the case, or outside fuse play, but always pass the proper hole, and confine the flame in the small plug until, by chance, it escapes and communicates with the bursting charge, not one exploded by concussion." This assessment indicates the delicacy of the mechanism and why it tended not to work. "I like the principle of the combination fuse," Vincent concluded, "but its imperfect construction renders it useless."[60]

The Federal Ordnance Bureau, considering the varied limitations of all fuzes, wisely relied on a variety of fuze types. In June 1862 it ordered from the Cyrus Alger Iron Company of South Boston, Massachusetts, a total of 70,000 rounds of explosive ordnance. The bureau requested 16,666 combination fuzes, enough to set off 23.8 percent of those rounds, while ordering 23,334 time fuzes, enough to set off 33.4 percent of them. It also ordered 30,000 percussion fuzes, enough for 42.8 percent of the rounds. The procurement strategy was to lessen dependence on one system of bursting long-distance ordnance. For 50,000 of the 70,000 rounds ordered, or 71.5 percent, the bureau specifically mentioned Schenkl versions of projectiles and fuzes, including 20,000 Schenkl case shot and 30,000 Schenkl percussion fuzes.[61]

FUZE IMPROVEMENTS

Some degree of improvement took place on both sides during the war. While some men aimed at making it possible to use one type of fuze on many different types of projectiles, others tried to enhance the reliability of fuzes to work under the stressful conditions of combat.

Dyer, chief of the Federal Ordnance Bureau, before the war had invented an adapter to enable a fuze designed for one projectile to be used in others. Some 100,000 were purchased by the government by 1863, but complaints concerning them led to the adapter being mostly dropped the next year.[62]

On the Confederate side, C. A. McAvoy of Richmond developed an igniter for flame-activated time fuzes affixed to rifled projectiles. It consisted of a wooden cylinder with a lead weight inside, "suspended from an iron pin by a serrated wire," according to Charles H. Jones. "The interior of the lead weight contained fulminate compound which ignited when it pulled free upon firing." In essence the McAvoy fuze igniter was similar to a combination fuze that mixed pressure activation with flame ignition.[63]

The McAvoy igniter was highly praised by some artillery officers. Maj. S. P. Hamilton declared it "a perfect success" after using many at Chancellorsville. But Maj. Robert A. Hardaway had the opposite opinion, estimating that only one out of fifteen exploded properly. He speculated that gunners pounded the fuze and igniter into the shell too vigorously and knocked off mealed powder. When he tried inserting them himself, taking great care, they seemed to work better. Nevertheless, McAvoy's flame igniter was widely used. The Norfolk Light Artillery received 192 of them in November 1863 along with 370 other fuzes.[64]

HOW EFFECTIVE WERE FUZES?

The issue of fuze effectiveness is a story of potential not realized. None of the fuzes available to Civil War artillerists worked fully well. For every type, design, or product, one finds praise and condemnation from the officers who utilized them in the field. Of all the elements that made up artillery effectiveness, fuzes were the weakest link.

It would be wrong to overemphasize this point. For every time a fuze failed, there was another time when the same type or design worked, otherwise artillery would have been totally ineffective. But fuzes both enabled field artillery to operate at an acceptable level and limited that effectiveness too. At the very least, we must conclude that fuzes represented a mixed technical achievement.

It is interesting that this limited achievement took place at a time of tremendous ferment in fuze development. Historian Edward B. McCaul Jr. has pointed out that while only 8 patents had been issued for artillery fuzes from 1855 to 1860, 83 were issued from January 1861 to December 1864. A total of 115 patents were issued for artillery fuzes from 1855 to 1872. Of that number, 14.8 percent applied to flame-ignited time fuzes, 7 percent to concussion time fuzes, 37.4 percent to percussion or impact fuzes, and 25.2 percent to combination fuzes; the rest applied to fuze accessories. Most of these devices were never tested or adopted by the Union army.[65]

But McCaul's conclusion that this level of inventiveness produced a fully reliable fuze by the end of the conflict was incorrect. He noted a good deal of improvement from initial problems that surfaced early in the conflict, so that "by the end of the Civil War the modern artillery fuze had been created and fully tested." McCaul argued that inventors listened to complaints and corrected defects. By 1865, in his view, the army was equipped with far-better artillery fuzes than it possessed in 1861.[66]

The fault with this conclusion is that McCaul failed to read reports by artillery officers written throughout the four years of the war. Those reports clearly indicate that fuze problems did not go away. Despite all efforts they persisted and were never solved. These included rounds that burst prematurely or did not burst at all, and they began from the start of the war. For example, to test the quality of his ordnance, Confederate major Francis A. Shoup fired thirty rounds of 6-pounder case shot near Bowling Green, Kentucky, in February 1862. Only nine of the thirty "exploded accurately," while five burst "within limits" and twelve "not at all." The remaining four fell "entirely short."[67]

The period from April to December 1862 produced the most reports of unreliable fuzes during the entire war; the problems affected both belligerents and were not confined to only one type of fuze. It did not matter that the devices, on examination, appeared to be perfect. Even percussion fuzes did not always work properly. More than one of them actually exploded in midair rather than on impact. Consolidated Batteries B and L, 2nd US Artillery fired thirty-four shells on May 7 and another fifty-one shells on May 23, 1862; fully one out of three failed to explode. At Fredericksburg eleven out of twelve shells fired by the 4th New York Battery did not detonate, while only 15 percent of those fired by Battery C, 1st Pennsylvania failed.[68]

Secondary factors besides faulty fuzes accounted for some of the failure to burst. Maj. Thomas S. Trumbull believed that when a shell failed to take the groove of a rifled piece, it affected the working of the percussion fuze. "The centrifugal force, operating on the plungers of those shells which fail to take the grooves, caused the explosion of the caps in air." Other officers found cartridges filled with "different kinds of powder or of various quantities, which made accuracy almost impossible." Capt. Andrew Cowan of the 1st New York Battery opened some case shot and found one with no bursting charge and another filled with iron filings instead of gunpowder. Others found shells with holes in the casings due to air pockets. Lt. Samuel N. Benjamin of Battery E, 2nd US Artillery threw away fifty-three shells and case shot at Fredericksburg, "they being unfit for use, having large flaws in their butts."[69]

Reports of failure to burst reduced in 1863 but did not disappear. "I don't think we succeeded in bursting ten shells out of every hundred fired," reported Col. Frank Huger, battalion commander in Longstreet's Corps during the Knoxville Campaign. Capt. Joseph W. Church of Battery D, 1st Michigan Light Artillery found that only two-thirds of the twenty-five rounds he fired on one day of the battle at Chattanooga burst properly, blaming this on damp fuzes. Another artillery officer cited corroded plugs; coating the fuzes with spirit of turpentine seemed to help. The problem may have been that the partitions separating the component parts of the devices were too thin, breaking when rattled by the process of firing, as Brig. Gen. John M. Brannan reported of such problems during the Chattanooga Campaign. "Our artillery men complain that they cannot do half the execution they could if their ammunition was good, or even *ordinary*," wrote Lt. Benjamin W. Underwood of the 72nd Illinois at the Siege of Vicksburg.[70]

Lt. William A. Ewing of Battery H, 1st US Artillery tried to find out why twelve of thirteen Schenkl percussion shells failed to burst. "The concussion produced by the explosion of the charge, causes the 'Plunger,' to strike the *lead* in the bottom of the fuze-plug so forcibly as to *imbed itself therein*," he reported. "The soft lead fills the space between the outside of the plunger and the inside of the fuze-plug, holds the plunger as in a vice, and prevents its flying forward when the shell strikes the ground or other object." Another officer believed that placing a washer under the plunger might solve the defect.[71]

Problems persisted into 1864. Just before the Overland Campaign, Hunt instituted a rigorous program of target practice. At least eleven batteries took part from April 19 to 21, 1864. When the 11th New York Battery fired eighteen percussion shells, only ten worked. It then fired six case shot with combination fuzes, and only one of them exploded. On the other hand, some officers reported success with their fuzes. Capt. Romeo H. Start of the 3rd Vermont Battery counted only two premature explosions when he fired 395 rounds during the Battle of the Crater on July 30, 1864. But Lt. Elbert W. Fowler of the 10th Wisconsin Battery lamented that "not over half of the shells" he fired during the Carolinas Campaign exploded properly.[72]

Improvement for some batteries and continued problems for others was the scenario for the latter half of the war. From the low point of 1862, a moderate and uneven level of improvement three years later is the best conclusion to make of fuze reliability. Of the sixty-four reports used in the foregoing discussion concerning the failure of explosive ordnance to burst as intended, thirty-seven of them (57 percent) were written in 1862, sixteen (25 percent) appeared in 1863, and eight (12.5 percent) were submitted in 1864.

COPING WITH BAD PROJECTILES AND FUZES

Battery commanders developed ways to deal with bad projectiles and fuzes. A higher-ranking officer told the commander of Battery I, 2nd Illinois Light Artillery to use up all his unreliable ammunition in target practice before the start of the Atlanta Campaign so he could requisition more. But the battery fired so much ordnance that it raised questions, so the commander secretly buried the rest of his bad rounds.[73]

A better strategy was to refuse inferior ammunition when it arrived. Capt. Peter Simonson, artillery chief of the First Division, Fourth Corps, became so disgusted with damp powder in the bursting charge that he ordered his two battery commanders to inspect all ordnance supplies before signing for them. From early May until June 9, 1864, they rejected more than 400 rounds of ammunition.[74]

Another strategy was to convert explosive ordnance into solid shot. By not inserting a fuze into a shell or case shot, gunners created another round of nonexplosive ammunition. This practice appeared at the Battle of Fredericksburg soon after the fuze problems had become endemic. At least two Federal batteries fired shells as solid shot on December 13, 1862. Battery A, 1st Maryland received Confederate rounds that failed to burst. When Capt. John W. Wolcott examined them, he found they also were explosive rounds that had no fuzes. The gunners in Parker's Virginia Battery took the trouble to empty the bursting charge from a shell before firing it as solid shot, but no one else appears to have bothered with that step. Twelve percent of the rounds fired by the 1st Massachusetts Battery on one day at Chancellorsville were shells "used as solid shot." Forty percent of the projectiles fired by Independent Battery D, Pennsylvania Artillery at the Battle of the Crater were shells fired without fuzes.[75]

Still another strategy for coping with bad fuzes was to increase the use of genuine solid shot and decrease the use of explosive ordnance. Collecting 134 examples of firing, wherein battery commanders specified how many and what type of ordnance they expended in a given engagement, the statistics reveal interesting results. The data set contains statistics for the years 1862–65, but because the reports tend to be meager in 1865, they can be dropped for our purposes. In 1863 the rate of increase in the use of solid shot was 193 percent compared to 1862. In 1864 the rate of increase was 582 percent compared to 1863 and 1,873 percent compared to 1862. Use of solid shot increased at a faster

TABLE 6.2. Expenditure of Projectiles, 1862–1865

	1862	1863	1864	1865	Total
Case Shot	4,884	7,779: increased 59% since 1862	49,124: increased 531% since 1863, increased 906% since 1862	1,459	63,246, or 37.2% of total rounds fired in war
Shell	3,954	5,435: increased 37% since 1862	60,408: increased 1,011% since 1863; increased 1,428% since 1862	1,179	70,976, or 41.6% of total rounds fired in war
Canister	1,291	1,928: increased 49% since 1862	3,276: increased 70% since 1863; increased 154% since 1862	119	6,614, or 3.8% of total rounds fired in war
Solid Shot	1,212	3,509: increased 190% since 1862	23,918: increased 582% since 1863; increased 1,873% since 1862	996	29,635, or 17.4% of total rounds fired in war

Note: Results based on 134 reports submitted during these years.

rate than that of canister, shells, or case shot with but one exception: the rate of increase in shell expenditure in 1864 was higher, but only if one compares it to 1863. In every other way, solid shot expenditure rose at a higher rate than that of any other projectile.

Artillerists started the war using low rates of solid shot because there was so much excitement about the introduction of rifles and long-distance explosive ordnance. Then reality set in; rifles did not have a revolutionary effect on operations for many reasons, chief among them being persistent problems with fuzes. Many battery commanders therefore bypassed explosive ordnance and relied instead on solid shot, producing a steadily increasing expenditure of that type of projectile during the war.

"At close quarters, we could hold our own very creditably," recalled Alexander of Confederate artillerists, "but when it came to extreme ranges, a considerable percentage of our rifle shell would tumble, or explode prematurely, or not explode at all. This made accurate shooting almost impossible." They attempted solutions such as putting leather washers under fuzes or coating them with white lead but to little avail. Alexander noted the emotional effect of faulty ordnance on gun crews. "An unreliable fuse or a rifle-shell which 'tumbles' sickens not only the gunner but the whole battery. . . . There is no encouragement to careful aiming when the ammunition fails, and the men feel handicapped."[76]

Battle reports, target practice, and statistical analysis reveal many problems associated with fuzes and projectiles; fixing them was another matter. Schenkl traveled to the Peninsula to witness the erratic performance of his percussion fuzes at Yorktown in the spring of 1862. Several times officers visited arsenals to inform the manufacturers of problems or to investigate why faulty ordnance supplies were sent to units. But these measures failed to solve the problems that limited the effectiveness of long-distance artillery fire in the Civil War.[77]

MIX OF PROJECTILES

Despite the problems, artillerists had to soldier on and make do with what they were issued. *Instruction for Field Artillery* suggested that 400 rounds of ammunition should be available to each piece in every battery, half of it carried in the ammunition chests on the limber and the caisson, the other half in the wagon train. Army commanders, however, developed their own ratios. Grant's Army of the Tennessee carried 300 rounds per gun during the Vicksburg Campaign, and Maj. Gen. Oliver O. Howard reduced that figure to 250 rounds per gun at the end of the Carolinas Campaign.[78]

For a battery of six Napoleons, *Instruction* suggested 504 case shot, 168 shells, 168 canister, and 504 solid shot per piece. But for a mixed battery consisting of four 12-pounder guns (pre-Napoleon weapons) and two 24-pounder howitzers, the manual suggested 224 case shot, no shells, 112 canister, and 560 solid shot per 12-pounder piece and 112 case shot, 168 shells, 42 canister, and no solid shot per howitzer. It can be seen that the manual authors tried to determine the optimum spread of projectiles to match the type of piece, favoring smoothbores with canister and solid shot while allotting rifles a good deal of explosive ammunition.[79]

The actual mix of projectiles kept on hand during field service varied widely from those suggestions. Battery A, 1st Illinois Light Artillery received 120 rounds at Fort Donelson on February 14, 1862. It consisted of 62.5 percent shells, 25 percent solid shot, and 12.5 percent canister. Battery G, 1st Ohio Light Artillery took 600 rounds into the second day of fighting at Shiloh. Sixty percent of them were shells, 33.3 percent were canister, and 6.7 percent were solid shot. The 4th Ohio Battery consisted of two 12-pounder howitzers and four 6-pounder rifle guns when it fought at Chickasaw Bayou. The available ammunition reflected that division of pieces within the unit. For the two howitzers, 61.9 percent of the supply consisted of shells, while 20.7 percent was case shot and 17.4 percent was canister. For the four 6-pounders, 52 percent were shells, 44.5 percent was canister, and 3.5 percent was solid shot.[80]

It was difficult to know how many rounds of each type of projectile might be needed in combat. Hunt wisely made only estimates on that score while preparing for the Overland Campaign. He suggested each battery acquire "12 to 16 solid shot, 8 to 12 shrapnel, 4 shell, 4 canister to each chest for 12-pounders; 25 to 30 shell, 15 to 20 shrapnel, 5 canister to each chest for rifle guns."[81]

But could anyone really estimate what was actually needed? Capt. William W. Buckley provided a clue when he listed all the ammunition available to his Battery D, 1st Rhode Island Light Artillery at the start of the Knoxville Campaign. He also listed what he expended from November 16 to December 4, 1863, and further reported on what was left. This campaign, which mixed pitched battle with siege-like conditions, was a good mix of operational modes. Buckley used significantly fewer rounds of solid shot and canister than the proportion of those two types in his initial supply while using significantly more case shot than his original proportion. Only with shells did Buckley essentially use the same proportion of rounds as represented in his initial supply. In other words, he guessed wrong in three of the four projectile categories.[82]

A mix of projectiles offered battery commanders choices when they decided what to fire during battle. For example, Battery K, 4th US Artillery "opened with canister, shot and spherical case, according to the range and the work to be accomplished," at the start of the Seven Days. Commanders often fired spherical case from smoothbores and shells from rifles. Battery G, 1st Missouri Light Artillery fired a wide variety of projectiles (case shot, canister, shells, and solid shot) from its Napoleons, while firing only case shot and shells from its Parrotts.[83]

Lt. George H. Briggs's 5th Indiana Battery, consisting of two 3-Inch Ordnance Rifles and two Napoleons, fired 6,494 rounds during the Atlanta Campaign. The Napoleons expended more solid shot (1,291) than the rifles (20). Both types of cannon fired roughly the same number of case shot (1,594 from Napoleons and 1,403 from the rifles), but the Napoleons fired significantly

TABLE **6.3.** Projectiles Available, Expended, and Remaining for Battery D, 1st
Rhode Island Light Artillery during the Knoxville Campaign

	On Hand, November 15, 1863	Expended November 16–December 4, 1863	On Hand, December 5, 1863
Solid Shot	96 (10.7% of supply)	25 (4.9% of rounds used)	71 (18.5% of remaining rounds)
Canister	120 (13.5% of supply)	28 (5.5% of rounds used)	92 (23.9% of remaining rounds)
Shell	388 (43.5% of supply)	216 (42.5% of rounds used)	172 (44.8% of remaining rounds)
Case Shot	288 (32.3% of supply)	239 (47.1% of rounds used)	49 (12.8% of remaining rounds)
Total	892 (100% of supply)	508 (57.0% of original supply)	384 (43.0% of original supply)

more canister (eighty-one compared to fifty five) than the 3-inch pieces. The biggest difference lay in shell expenditure. While the Napoleons only fired 477 rounds, the rifles used 1,573 rounds. Moreover, the rifles divided their shell expenditure into time fuze (957 rounds) and percussion fuze (616 rounds), while the Napoleons only used time fuzes.[84]

The same battery could fire a different pattern of projectiles from one day to another. The Napoleons of Battery H, 1st New York Light Artillery devoted 90 percent of their rounds to solid shot and the rest to shells at Cold Harbor on May 30, 1864. Yet four days later they fired 42.5 percent solid shot, 40.7 percent case shot, and 16.8 percent shells.[85]

Extended experience taught battery commanders to suit projectiles to the type of cannon, even though all types were generally capable of firing most of the ordnance available. Capt. Lyman Bridges was in charge of thirty-four pieces in the Fourth Corps during the Tennessee Campaign of November–December 1864. At Franklin his 12-pounders fired all the solid shot and some of the case shot, while the 3-inch rifles fired all the shells, using percussion fuzes, and some of the case shot. Both types of cannon also fired canister and shells with time fuzes. At Nashville Bridges's 12-pounders fired most of the canister, while the 3-inch rifles fired most of the shells with percussion fuzes. The artillery of the Twentieth Corps developed this streamlining to a greater degree during the Carolinas Campaign. Its 12-pounders fired only solid shot and case shot, while the 3-inch pieces fired only case shot and shell with time fuzes or percussion fuzes.[86]

PROJECTILE AND FUZE EXPENDITURE

Understanding the total expenditure of different types of projectiles and fuzes for the entire war can illuminate the choices made by battery and section commanders as to the best types to use. To that end, we can use data from 134 examples (discussed earlier) of artillery firing across the board in the Civil War, Union and Confederate, in both eastern and western theaters. The total number of rounds fired amounted to 170,471. The most numerous type was shell, at 70,976 rounds, representing 41.6 percent of the total. Next in importance was case shot, at 63,246 rounds, or 37.2 percent of the total. Solid shot, at 29,635 rounds, or 17.4 percent, and canister at 6,614 rounds, or 3.8 percent, each fell far below the first two types of projectiles.

Statistics for the 19th Ohio Battery confirm the reliability of this data set. Serving from 1862 to 1865, this unit fired a total of 5,298 rounds. Of that number 2,306, or 43.7 percent, were shells. Case Shot, numbering 2,027 rounds, represented 38.3 percent of the total. The Ohio gunners fired 731 rounds of solid shot, or 13.8 percent of the total, and used 234 rounds of canister, or 4.2 percent of all the rounds they expended.[87]

While popular images of Civil War combat tend to feature the use of canister, this projectile type was the least important to most artillerists. Short-distance firing at infantrymen represented the most dramatic use of cannon imaginable, but the number of times it happened paled in comparison to the number of times batteries fired long-distance explosive ordnance at artillery, infantry, and cavalry. Solid shot was significantly more important to batteries than canister, although it did not compare to shell and case shot.

The fact that explosive ordnance represented 78.8 percent of all projectiles fired during the Civil War highlights the importance of fuzes. But the data set of 134 examples yielded limited information on the use of fuzes; twenty-nine of them offer a useable sample. A total of 41,123 fuzes were mentioned in these twenty-nine reports: 25,955, or 63.2 percent, were time fuzes, and 15,168, or 36.8 percent, were percussion fuzes. Looking at expenditure over time, there was a marked decline in the use of time fuzes and a corresponding increase in the use of percussion fuzes from 1862 to 1864. Time-fuze employment

TABLE **6.4.** Expenditure of Time and Percussion Fuzes, 1862–1865

	Number Used in 1862	Number Used in 1864	Total Number Used from 1862 to 1865
Time Fuze	528 (73.9% of fuzes used)	25,173 (63.4% of fuzes used; 4,667% increase compared to 1862)	25,955 (63.2% of fuzes used)
Percussion Fuze	186 (26.1% of fuzes used)	14,508 (36.6% of fuzes used; 7,700% increase compared to 1862)	15,168 (36.8% of fuzes used)
Total	714 (100%)	39,681 (100%)	41,123 (100%)

Note: Results based on 29 reports submitted during these years.

dropped from 73.9 percent of the total in the former year to 63.4 percent by the latter year. Percussion-fuze employment increased from 26.1 percent in 1862 to 36.6 percent two years later. In fact, the rate of increase (7,700 percent) in the use of percussion fuzes nearly doubled the rate of increase in the use of time fuzes (4,667 percent). This seems to indicate a greater frustration with the problems associated with time fuzes compared to percussion fuzes, or perhaps it hints at a growing reliance on rifled projectiles, since percussion fuzes could not be used on smoothbore ammunition.

Statistics from two batteries support the data sample. At Shiloh Battery H, 5th US Artillery fired 37 rounds of explosive ordnance from two 10-pounder Parrotts. Gunners used time fuzes for 26 of those rounds (70.3 percent) and percussion fuzes for 11 (29.7 percent). In contrast, Battery I, 1st New York Light Artillery fired 144 rounds from December 12 to 20, 1864, during the March to the Sea, using time fuzes for 47.3 percent and percussion fuzes for 52.7 percent.[88]

Four reports offer enough information to tentatively compare the frequency with which officers chose combination fuzes over percussion fuzes. A total of 1,295 fuzes were mentioned in these reports. Of that number, 735 (56.7 percent) were combination and 560 (43.3 percent) were percussion. But all that this small data set tells us is that, for at least some officers, the combination fuze played a significant role in their operations.

CONCLUSION

While projectiles and fuzes play a large role in the books that have been written by specialists in Civil War artillery hardware over the years, what has been lacking in that literature is an investigation into how those projectiles and fuzes were actually used in the field. *The War of the Rebellion: A Compilation of the Official Records of the Union and Confederate Armies* offers a wealth of information and considerable data on that subject. This chapter represents an initial exploration of that important information to indicate that fuze problems were endemic and persistent throughout the Civil War, significantly limiting artillery effectiveness North and South. Despite efforts to deal with those limitations, the problems never were solved. They especially limited the success of rifled pieces, dampening the initial enthusiasm for them that had burgeoned among officers at the start of the war. Statistics on projectile use also indicate that battery commanders tended to downplay long-distance explosive ordnance by not inserting fuzes into those projectiles, using them instead like solid shot, and by increasing their use of actual solid shot and decreasing the use of long-distance explosive rounds.

The Civil War represented the fullest introduction of rifled artillery in world history to date, and yet that type of cannon failed to realize its potential on the battlefields of 1861–65. Technical capabilities, especially in the area of fuzes, were the key to understanding why this took place. The Civil War occurred on the cusp of a new age in artillery technology but was too early in that transition period to present with confidence the trajectory of developments that would lead artillery to the future.

7

. . . .

BATTERIES, BATTALIONS,
AND REGIMENTS

Mobilizing an artillery arm was a joint venture by the state governments and the central government of both sides in the Civil War. The central government issued a call for troops, setting a quota for each state, and the governors raised the necessary units. The states organized artillery, cavalry, and infantry formations, establishing their official designations. They sometimes furnished arms, clothing, and equipment but more often transferred those units to the central government as soon as possible. The central authority was then in charge of them, feeding the men and providing them weapons, clothing, and other equipment as needed.

The basic artillery units of the Civil War were the battery, battalion, and regiment. They were mostly created by the various state governments, with some input from the central government, and endured for the entire service of the unit. All three forms of organization—battery, battalion, and regiment—were employed by state governments, although the central government, at least in the North, had a definite preference for one of them.

The Federal government had a prewar artillery organization of its own that it reinforced after the outbreak of hostilities. The US Artillery, or the regulars as they often were called, came to include five regiments with a total of sixty batteries. The Federal authority also raised a large force of Black troops by the end of the war, which included at least half a dozen batteries. These Black troops fell into the category of Federal volunteers because they were not meant to be a permanent organization beyond the end of the war. The Confederate government also organized a small number of infantry units sponsored by the central authority but apparently no artillery.

The Federal government tried to influence the mobilization process employed by state authorities. "We prefer independent batteries to regiments of artillery," wrote Secretary of War Simon Cameron in September 1861. This was ironic given that the regular artillery was organized entirely as regiments. Cameron also pointed out that those state volunteer batteries should consist of four 6-pounders and two 12-pounders each. State governors, however, largely ignored these recommendations. They continued to organize batteries, battalions, and regiments, even though the central authority continued to prefer independent batteries. By September 1862 the War Department laid out the organization of all kinds of units in the "Volunteer Army of the United States." In this order a clause indicated that "as a general rule, artillery will be called for and received by batteries, thus rendering the field and staff unnecessary." This was the primary reason for the government's insistence on battery organization. With a regiment, it would have had to pay the salaries of colonels, lieutenant colonels, majors, and the regimental staff members. With the state volunteer artillery organized mostly as batteries, however, the central government could save a lot of money.[1]

Another reason for the War Department's policy was that the artillery regiment was essentially of no use in wartime. None of the volunteer or regular artillery regiments served together as a unit. The batteries always were detached from their regiments to separate stations.[2] In the prewar period the regimental organization made sense for administrative reasons because batteries were not attached to infantry units. Regimental field and staff handled the paperwork necessary for the independent artillery arm. But during wartime, the batteries were assigned to infantry units and relied on infantry staff to supply them.

The Federal government maintained four regiments of artillery before the war and authorized the creation of a fifth regiment after Fort Sumter. The law establishing that fifth regiment used the term "battery," for the first time, to designate the twelve subunits of the regiment. Before that, the terms "company" and "battery" had been used interchangeably in the regular artillery arm.[3]

The states did pay some attention to the central government when organizing their artillery arm. In the North ten states out of twenty-four (41 percent) created artillery regiments, but they mixed the forms of organization by creating independent batteries too. Of the 460 Union batteries that served during the war, 163 (35.4 percent) were in a regimental organization; the rest, 297 (64.5 percent), were independent batteries. In short, a slim majority of the Union volunteer artillery arm was organized as the Federal government preferred.

In the Confederate service four of fourteen states (28 percent) created regiments or battalions. The latter organization fell somewhere between the regiment and the independent battery, consisting of between two and eleven companies of artillery. The North never created an artillery battalion, either among the state volunteers or among the regulars, but it was not uncommon in the South. Of 292 Confederate batteries, 37 (12.6 percent) served in regiments, 19 (6.6 percent) served in battalions, and 236 (80.8 percent) served independently. The Confederate government never expressed a preference for battery, battalion, or regiment.

The artillery regiments of the North and South were white elephants, serving no real purpose. Col. Charles Wainwright was the commander of the 1st New York Light Artillery in addition to filling other roles in field service. He struggled to find the time and energy to keep up with the massive paperwork involved in regimental administration. In January 1864 his regiment consisted of 1,139 men, "a fair-sized army in itself," as another wrote of the 1st Ohio Light Artillery. "The [New York] regiment is widely separated," complained Wainwright, "and will never act together as a regiment, but so long as it maintains its organization, I want to do all I can to keep up a regimental pride."[4] Everyone recognized that the artillery regiment was of little utility, but some argued it gave ambitious officers an opportunity to rise in rank. If not for the regiment or battalion, the highest level an aspiring officer could attain was captain, even though his level of responsibility was higher than that of an infantry company commander.[5]

RATIO OF ARTILLERY TO INFANTRY

Administrators were guided by theories concerning how many artillery pieces were needed to properly support infantry. During the Napoleonic Wars, the ratio ranged from one to five guns per 1,000 men. *Instruction for Field Artillery* adopted a wide range too, noting that anywhere from one to four pieces per 1,000 men was acceptable. John Gibbon settled on two to three pieces per 1,000 men.[6] But there existed a general idea that new troops, especially those raised from the untrained masses, needed a higher ratio of artillery than veterans. Acting on that assumption, William F. Barry recommended to McClellan that he should field three guns per 1,000 men when building the Army of the Potomac. Barry noted that the ratio could be decreased as the infantrymen became experienced.[7]

Veteran artillerist Gen. Braxton Bragg thought Confederate armies in the West had too high a ratio of guns to men. He railed against Maj. Gen. Earl Van Dorn's Army of the West, which sported ninety-four guns for a force of only 16,000 effectives, amounting to one gun per 170 infantrymen. "No treasury could stand such expenditures," Bragg complained, "and the resources of no country could supply material for guns, ammunition, harness, horses, and forage; besides, it would effectually destroy the efficiency of any force to be thus encumbered by the most unwieldy of arms." The lesson was not learned. Lt. Gen. John C. Pemberton's Army of Mississippi and Eastern Louisiana had a ratio of one gun per 215 effectives in January 1863.[8]

Ordnance chief Josiah Gorgas agreed that Confederate field armies had too much artillery. Due to the constant drain of troop strength, he also thought it better to model the ratio as the number of guns per brigade rather than 1,000 men. Gorgas recommended a maximum of five pieces per brigade. Robert E. Lee argued that the Army of Northern Virginia needed a large artillery arm to contend with the Army of the Potomac, which not only had a lot of guns but also ones "of larger caliber, longer range, and with more effective ammunition."[9]

The Army of the Potomac outgunned Lee's force because it tended to have a larger infantry component, which led to a larger artillery component as well. John C. Tidball thought it maintained a pretty constant ratio of two and a half pieces per 1,000 men throughout the war. Before the Atlanta Campaign, Sherman's army group had about three pieces per 1,000 men, but he reduced it to a bit less than two per 1,000. By the time he prepared for the Carolinas Campaign, Sherman reduced it further to one piece per 1,000 men.[10]

The percentage of artillerymen as a component of any infantry unit varied from 6 percent to 12 percent. They comprised 7.1 percent of the personnel in Brig Gen. Peter J. Osterhaus's Ninth Division, Thirteenth Corps, Army of the Tennessee early in May 1863. Osterhaus's ratio increased to 8 percent later that month. In the Confederate Army of Tennessee, the division led by Maj.

Gen. John P. McCown had an effective strength of 3,940 men after Stones River, with 8.6 percent of them serving in the artillery. That was higher than the 6.1 percent average in Bragg's army during the summer of 1863.[11]

Field artillery's primary role was to support the infantry, and the battery was its basic unit. Army commanders distributed them by assigning typically one battery for each brigade, keeping some of the batteries as a general reserve for the field army.[12]

ARTILLERY RESERVE

Every sizeable field army had a general artillery reserve controlled by the chief of artillery. As early as the Peninsula Campaign, the Army of Northern Virginia fielded a relatively large general reserve. By late May 1863 its reserve consisted of thirty-six pieces, representing 13.3 percent of all guns in Lee's army. When a third corps was created soon after, it largely led to the draining of this general reserve because, according to Edward Porter Alexander, "we could not maintain it."[13]

Shortage of resources also led to a small general reserve in the Confederacy's western field army. Bragg had created a reserve for the Army of the Mississippi in the fall of 1862, but it consisted only of three batteries that Bragg himself controlled. Two of those batteries were detached from the larger force, which was redesignated the Army of Tennessee, in December 1862. Bragg increased his general reserve to four batteries and named an officer to control it in February 1863.[14]

Under Maj. Gen. Don Carlos Buell and Maj. Gen. William S. Rosecrans, the Union Army of the Ohio / Army of the Cumberland had a large general reserve. Maj. Gen. George H. Thomas later maintained it at twelve batteries (half of them regular troops) while assigning eighteen batteries to his divisions.[15]

Barry, Sherman's chief artillerist, saw to it that each of the three field armies in the Atlanta Campaign maintained a reserve. Thomas's Army of the Cumberland (three corps) had twelve batteries, Maj. Gen. James B. McPherson's Army of the Tennessee (two and a half corps) had four batteries, and Maj. Gen. John M. Schofield's Army of the Ohio (one corps) had two batteries. But Sherman did not allow those army commanders to keep their reserves with their commands. He stationed them in rear areas: Thomas's and McPherson's at Nashville and Schofield's at Chattanooga. All three commanders could draw on their reserve artillery for replacement batteries. In other words, Sherman made it a strategic rather than a tactical reserve because he did not want to encumber his army group with them.[16]

HUNT'S ARTILLERY RESERVE

Henry J. Hunt was an early advocate of the reserve-artillery concept and did all he could to promote and justify such an organization in the Army of the Potomac. He pointed out that it played a crucial role during the Peninsula and Seven Days Campaigns and praised McClellan for authorizing the creation of such a large reserve force.[17]

Hunt believed it was important for him to control not only the reserve guns but also the ammunition train that accompanied them. At Malvern Hill the engaged batteries needed replenishment, but their ammunition trains got tangled up and could not reach them in time. Hunt saved the day by resupplying many batteries from the 100 wagon loads of artillery ammunition in the reserve. He continued this formula during the Maryland Campaign, where seven of sixty-two batteries (11.2 percent) with the army were placed in the reserve. At Fredericksburg the proportion of batteries was nine of sixty-nine (13.0 percent), twelve of seventy-one (16.9 percent) at Chancellorsville, and twenty-two of sixty-seven (32.8 percent) at Gettysburg.[18]

But Hunt added a twist, creating what he called his "special reserve" of artillery ammunition separate from the ammunition train belonging to the army-level reserve. It carried twenty rounds per piece over and above the official allowance. Hunt assigned a trusted officer to control the special reserve and a battalion of heavy artillerymen acting as infantry to escort it. If the ammunition train for his general reserve became depleted, he could call on the special reserve. Maj. Gen. Joseph Hooker had ordered it be disbanded after Chancellorsville, but Maj. Rufus Ingalls, his chief quartermaster, continued to furnish Hunt with the wagons without telling Hooker.[19]

The artillery reserve of the Army of the Potomac was in a class by itself in the Civil War. Hunt's innovative management turned it into "that solid rock of dependence," as John C. Tidball put it. Thomas W. Osborn felt complimented when ordered to place his company in the general reserve because "only the choice batteries of the Army are selected for that command." In September 1863 the reserve consisted of 115 officers and 3,154 enlisted men, the equivalent of an infantry division at that stage of the war. Its sixty-seven pieces needed 254 wagons to keep them supplied.[20] William E. Birkhimer believed it was the most impressive artillery reserve in American history. It was "placed upon a proper footing, to be used both for purposes of fighting and of supply, commanded by officers conversant with its functions, and capable of developing, organizing, and directing its powers." John C. Tidball thought "it was in reality an artillery division."[21]

Imagine Hunt's troubles when his reserve was threatened with dissolution. Two weeks into the Overland Campaign, Grant decided it was unnecessary. He came from the West, where artillery reserves were small if they existed at all, and told Maj. Gen. George G. Meade, commander of the Army of the Potomac, to send the reserve pieces back to Washington. Grant's primary purpose was to lessen the strain on logistical support for the army. Hunt was determined "to hold on to all the organizations" possible. He could not stop the disbandment of the reserve and the assignment of those batteries to corps and division, but he could try to lessen the effect of Grant's streamlining on his artillery force. Hunt proposed that all six-gun batteries in the Army of the Potomac be reduced by sending away two pieces from each. The two sections left in each battery would retain all caissons and gun detachments that belonged to the section sent away. In this fashion Hunt complied with Grant's desire to lessen the number of pieces traveling with the army, but he would only need to reacquire two pieces for each battery to bring the artillery force back up to its original strength. Meade convinced Grant to concur; the lieutenant general also allowed Hunt to retain his special ammunition train, but the reserve artillery was disbanded.[22] "So goes an organization which it has required nearly three years to bring to its present condition of efficiency," Hunt moaned.[23] But it was better than sending away entire batteries. Grant deserves some credit for approving this plan; his goal had been to reduce logistical problems, and Hunt's plan did so only slightly.

When the order promulgating the plan was issued on May 16, Wainwright kept all caissons, ammunition, and horses of the sections sent back to Washington and used them to replace worn-out material and draft animals. Although Hunt's plan was designed to prevent entire batteries from being sent to the rear, some of the units left the army anyway and for unexplained reasons. Batteries D and H, 1st Rhode Island Light Artillery was an example. The gun detachments of Battery H were detailed to act as heavy artillerymen in the forts protecting Washington until reassigned to light artillery duty in October.[24]

Hunt lost his artillery reserve but saved most of its elements. Batteries worn down had previously been transferred to the reserve to recuperate. Now they went to Hunt's ammunition train, which "became the nucleus around which a new reserve grew up, without special orders, and merely from the force of circumstances." But that improvised reserve lacked the "administrative machinery of its predecessor."[25]

By September the army was tied down in extensive earthworks at Petersburg, negating the need for streamlined logistics. With a heavier demand for artillery support, Hunt ordered all batteries to requisition two more pieces if they had the manpower to work them. Most of the army's artillery units could meet Hunt's manpower requirements (130 men for each battery armed with rifles and 140 men for each battery armed with Napoleons), and they began to rebuild to six pieces each. Hunt recreated the army's artillery reserve and then informed Meade's headquarters of his actions. He further informed Grant's chief of staff that it was wise to keep one-third of the guns in the reserve. No one protested Hunt's actions, and his favorite command was reborn without prior official approval.[26]

HOW MANY PIECES?

Artillerists argued about how large the basic artillery unit should be throughout the war. *Instruction for Field Artillery* noted that batteries "on the peace establishment" should contain four pieces but those "on the war establishment" should have six or eight pieces. Personal opinion played a large role in this issue. Soon after taking charge of the Army of the Ohio, Rosecrans wanted to increase the size of his thirteen batteries that contained only four guns by adding two more to each one. In contrast, Lt. Joseph W. Martin sent away two of the six pieces in his 6th New York Battery because he considered "that four guns, with full detachments and good horses, would be capable of doing better service than six guns badly horsed and imperfectly manned."[27]

A survey of battery organization across the board reveals a mix of four-gun and six-gun batteries throughout the war, at least among Federal forces. The size of batteries in Sherman's army group during the Atlanta Campaign varied a great deal. The Army of the Cumberland used twenty batteries near the end of the campaign; thirteen of them contained six pieces, five had four pieces, one had five pieces, and another had nine pieces. At the same time, of the eighteen batteries in the Army of the Tennessee, eight fielded six cannon, another eight had four cannon, and two had three cannon. In Schofield's Army of the Ohio, five batteries contained four pieces, one had three pieces, and one had two pieces. Thomas pushed for the reduction of six-gun batteries in his army, and all of them in the Twentieth Corps were reduced to four pieces by September 1864.[28]

In the Confederacy, artillery chief Francis A. Shoup recommended a reduction to four-gun units in the Army of the Mississippi right after Shiloh. The most immediate reason was a shortage of men and horses, but Shoup also argued that "the nature of our country renders four-gun batteries preferable." Gen. Pierre G. T. Beauregard accepted the recommendation and also required streamlining calibers within each battery and retaining six horses to pull every carriage. Most units complied, but more than a year later three batteries in the army contained six guns each.[29] Artillerists in the Army of Northern Virginia also preferred four-gun batteries. At the start of the Overland Campaign, forty-two of the army's fifty-one batteries, or 82.4 percent, contained four pieces. One battery used six pieces, and the rest either three or five cannons each.[30]

Surprisingly, a handful of artillery units wound up with seven or more guns. Even though *Instruction for Field Artillery* allowed for this, it is difficult to understand why it was done. If six guns were an unwieldy unit, imagine how unmanageable were eight or nine pieces. In fact, every battery that had eight guns soon reduced to six. Nevertheless, McClellan recommended the regular batteries in the Army of the Potomac be increased to eight pieces each in September 1862. His reason was distrust of the volunteer batteries; McClellan considered his regulars more reliable, and he was worried that ten out of twenty-six of the regular batteries had been reduced to four guns due to manpower shortages. His suggestion was not approved.[31]

Very often battery commanders had little choice about how many pieces they controlled. Combat losses, breakdowns, and finding out that some types of cannon did not work well were all circumstances that played a role in how many cannon they could use.[32] The example of Battery I, 1st Illinois Light Artillery indicates how often not only the number but also the type of cannon changed a lot over time. It had received four 6-pounder bronze James rifles when organizing in the fall of 1861. Soon after, two 10-pounder Parrott guns were added. Before the Battle of Perryville in October 1862, two Napoleons replaced two of the James rifles, making three sections with one type each.

At some point after October 19, 1863, six Rodman guns replaced all of those types. The Rodmans were 6-pounder cast-iron smoothbores. On July 16, 1864, these were replaced by six 3-Inch Ordnance Rifles. The following September the battery was reduced to four pieces for the rest of the war.[33]

On the Confederate side, Graham's Virginia Battery started in June 1861 with three 6-pounder brass guns and one 12-pounder brass howitzer. The next month it increased to a six-gun unit by receiving two 10-pounder Parrotts and in January 1862 became an eight-gun battery with the addition of two 8-pounder iron rifles. By April 1862 it had reduced back to a six-gun battery by getting rid of a 6-pounder and an 8-pounder. The following month the battery exchanged the remaining 8-pounder for a third 10-pounder Parrott and was told to send its original two 10-pounder Parrotts "to Richmond to be busted." By late June 1862 Graham's company received another 10-pounder Parrott and a Napoleon, giving up its 12-pounder howitzer. In September 1862 the battery gave up its last 6-pounder gun and received another Napoleon plus two 20-pounder Parrotts; it lost the 20-pounders in battle on July 27, 1864. During its complicated history, Graham's Battery started with four pieces, went to six, up to eight, then back to six, reduced to four, increased to five, again reduced to four, and ended with six pieces. It used a total of six different types of cannon. This was, perhaps, an unusual story, but it demonstrates how contingencies played a large role in determining how every battery commander operated.[34]

MIX OF PIECES

As the history of Battery I, 1st Illinois Light Artillery and Graham's Virginia Battery illustrate, the question of how many pieces should constitute a battery was tied to the question of whether those pieces should be a mix of types or only one kind of cannon. Overwhelmingly, batteries were mixed in terms of the type of piece, the weight of projectile, and whether they were rifles or smoothbores, guns or howitzers. This was so because Civil War artillerists had so many different types available. It made sense to mix batteries so as to have a choice of capabilities within each unit.

In addition to choice, batteries became mixed in part because of the need to organize a large artillery arm quickly, and often officers accepted whatever happened to be available. With time and experience, many artillerists preferred to abandon the mixed battery and fill an entire company with one type

TABLE **7.1.** Mix of Pieces in the Army of the Potomac, 1862–1864

Type of Piece	Number and Percentage of Total, Peninsula Campaign[a]	Number and Percentage of Total, Antietam[b]	Number and Percentage of Total, August 31, 1863[c]	Number and Percentage of Total, March 29, 1864[d]	Number and Percentage of Total, May 20, 1864[e]	Number and Percentage of Total, October 31, 1864[f]
Napoleon	88 (28.0)	112 (34.7)	136 (38.4)	124 (45.0)	88 (42.7)	120 (43.7)
3-Inch Ordnance Rifle	82 (26.1)	102 (31.6)	152 (42.8)	121 (44.0)	102 (49.6)	124 (45.3)
10-Pounder Parrott	104 (33.2)	58 (17.9)	53 (14.9)	16 (5.9)	16 (7.7)	24 (8.8)
20-Pounder Parrott	20 (6.3)	30 (9.3)	6 (1.6)	6 (2.2)		6 (2.2)
12-Pounder Howitzer	10 (3.2)	16 (4.9)				
12-Pounder Parrott	4 (1.3)					
32-Pounder	6 (1.9)					
12-Pounder Dahlgren Boat Howitzer		5 (1.6)				
4.5-Inch Siege Rifle			8 (2.3)			
Unspecified Siege Gun				8 (2.9)		
Total	314 (100)	423 (100)	355 (100)	275 (100)	206 (100)	274 (100)

[a] *OR*, 5:19–21.
[b] Johnson and Anderson, *Artillery Hell*, 38–39.
[c] *OR*, 29(2):130–31.
[d] *OR*, 33:760–61.
[e] "Journal of Siege Operations," 26, Box 1, Henry Jackson Hunt Papers, LC.
[f] *OR*, 36(1):284–86.

of cannon, although this was by no means a universal trend. It tended to take place only in the major field armies of both belligerents.

The mixed battery was part of the artillery doctrine of the United States. *Instruction for Field Artillery* pointed out that a 6-pounder battery consisted of 6-pounder guns and 12-pounder howitzers. A 12-pounder battery consisted of 12-pounder guns mixed with either 24-pounder or 32-pounder howitzers.

TABLE 7.2. Mix of Pieces in First Corps, Army of Virginia at Second Bull Run; in Fourteenth Corps at Stones River; and in Thirteenth Corps in September 1863.

First Corps, Army of Virginia, July 21, 1862[a]	Number and Percentage of Total	Fourteenth Corps (later renamed Army of the Cumberland) at Stones River[b]	Number and Percentage of Total	Thirteenth Corps, September 26, 1863[c]	Number and Percentage of Total
10-Pounder Parrott	13 (22.8)	Napoleon	10 (7.3)	Napoleon	7 (10.3)
6-Pounder (Brass Smoothbore)	10 (17.5)	3-Inch Ordnance Rifle	4 (2.9)	3-Inch Rodman	10 (14.7)
6-Pounder Wiard (Steel)	8 (14.1)	10-Pounder Parrott	34 (24.8)	10-Pounder Parrott	8 (11.7)
3-Inch Ordnance Rifle	6 (10.5)	12-Pounder Howitzer	24 (17.5)	12-Pounder	3 (4.5)
12-Pounder Mountain Howitzer	6 (10.5)	6-Pounder Smoothbore	36 (26.3)	12-Pounder Howitzer	11 (16.2)
12-Pounder Wiard (Steel)	4 (7.0)	Unspecified James Rifle	23 (16.7)	30-Pounder Parrott	8 (11.7)
12-Pounder Howitzer (Brass)	4 (7.0)	6-Pounder Wiard	2 (1.5)	6-Pounder	6 (8.8)
6-Pounder Rifle (Brass)	4 (7.0)	12-Pounder Wiard (Steel) gun	2 (1.5)	Unspecified James Gun	9 (13.3)
6-Pounder (Iron Smoothbore)	2 (3.6)	16-Pounder Parrott	2 (1.5)	3.5-Inch English Piece	6 (8.8)
Total	57 (100)		137 (100)		68 (100)

[a] OR, 12(3):494.
[b] OR, 20(1):235–41.
[c] OR, 26(1):739.

Napoleons were to constitute the entire armament of other batteries only because they theoretically combined the effect of a gun and a howitzer. But for the mixed battery, the artillery manual recommended that two-thirds of the armament should be guns and one-third howitzers. Barry followed that recommendation when he assembled pieces for the Army of the Potomac. He also wanted half the pieces to be rifled.[35]

Shifting from mixed batteries to uniform batteries proceeded steadily in the Army of the Potomac. Table 7.1 shows the army reducing from seven different types in 1862 to four by 1864, but two of those four types made up only 8 percent of the total. Napoleons and 3-Inch Ordnance Rifles constituted nearly 90 percent of the armament in 1864 compared to a bit more than half in 1862.[36]

The Army of the Ohio / Army of the Cumberland started the war with mixing of types and gradually shifted to uniform batteries. The army used only three batteries on the second day at Shiloh, yet those units fielded six different types of cannon. At Stones River Rosecrans employed nine different types of ordnance, with few batteries uniform in type. But by late 1863 seven of eight batteries placed in one division of the Army of the Cumberland's artillery reserve were uniformly armed. By the time of the Tennessee Campaign in the fall of 1864, Fourth Corps batteries fielded a total of thirty-four pieces, but only two types were represented. These statistics demonstrate that the trend toward uniform batteries was quite steady under Rosecrans and Thomas.[37]

The five major field armies of the war, those which experienced the longest and hardest service, all shifted from mixed to uniform batteries. Field armies of secondary importance or of short-term service did not streamline and often had to accept the cast-off pieces from mainstream units. When Barry took charge of Sherman's artillery, he weeded out odd calibers and sent them to ordnance depots or assigned them to garrisons. Those discarded pieces served the geographic departments, where they protected supply lines and garrisoned cities behind the front lines.[38]

Mixing of types was more common among Confederate units than Federal, primarily because of the South's low capacity for manufacturing cannon. Rebel armies relied heavily on capturing Union pieces. An army that depended on such a method for replacing pieces could not be choosy.[39] Yet the trend toward uniform armament did appear sporadically in mainline Confederate field armies. At Antietam only five of Lee's fifty-nine batteries had uniform ordnance. Alexander's battalion did not get uniform types in each battery until September 1863, while other units retained mixed types to the end of the war. Federal artilleryman Augustus Buell thought Lee's ordnance after the surrender at Appomattox constituted "a miscellaneous lot."[40]

While howitzers were accorded a high level of importance early in the mixed-

TABLE 7.3. Mix of Pieces in the Army of Northern Virginia at Antietam and during the Overland Campaign

Antietam[a]	Number and Percentage of Known Type	Overland Campaign[b]	Number and Percentage of Total
Napoleon	27 (13.9)	Napoleon	94 (47.9)
3-Inch Rifle	40 (20.7)	3-Inch Rifle	32 (16.3)
10-Pounder Parrott	36 (18.6)	10-Pounder Parrott	48 (24.4)
12-Pounder Smoothbore Howitzer	34 (17.6)	12-Pounder Howitzer	6 (3.1)
20-Pounder Parrott	4 (2.0)	20-Pounder Parrott	12 (6.2)
6-Pounder Smoothbore	45 (23.2)	24-Pounder Howitzer	4 (2.1)
3.5-Inch Blakely Rifle	2 (1.0)		
24-Pounder Smoothbore Howitzer	4 (2.0)		
Whitworth Rifle	2 (1.0)		
Unknown Type	52 (21.2 of Known and Unknown Type)		
Total of Known Type	194 (100)		196 (100)

[a] Johnson and Anderson, *Artillery Hell,* 47.
[b] *OR,* 36(1):1053–54.

batteries phase, they were weeded out toward the end of the conflict. Capt. Louis Hoffmann possessed four rifles and two howitzers in his 4th Ohio Battery but fired his guns about twice as much as his howitzers at Pea Ridge in March 1862. If Hoffmann's experience is an indication, artillery officers seem to have found guns more useful than howitzers.[41] By 1864 major field armies had largely cut out the howitzer from their armament. The three types chosen included two guns, the 3-Inch Ordnance Rifle and the 10-pounder Parrott, and the Napoleon, which supposedly combined the benefits of a gun and a howitzer. Mixed batteries went from having howitzers as one-third of their armament to having them as only half of one piece, so to speak, in the streamlined phase of the war.

In terms of type of piece, officers went from about a dozen different kinds and makes to only three. Two of those three, the 3-Inch Ordnance Rifle and the 10-pounder Parrott, were designed by Americans and manufactured in the United States. The other, the Napoleon, was designed by the French but manufactured in the United States.

FROM LIGHTER TO HEAVIER ORDNANCE

In terms of the weight of projectile, the mixed-battery phase of the war saw everything from 6-pounders to 24-pounders. In the streamlined phase that followed, artillerists settled on 10-pounders and 12-pounders, while the 3-Inch Ordnance Rifle fired a round that weighed nine and a half pounds. Projectiles of nine and a half to twelve pounds represented an increase in projectile weight over the past, but they fell far short of the heaviest projectile weight available to officers.

By late 1862 Lee wanted to get rid of anything less than the Napoleon, the 10-pounder Parrott, and the 3-Inch Ordnance Rifle from the Army of Northern Virginia. "Batteries composed of such guns would simplify our ammunition, give us less metal to transport, and longer and more accurate range of fire," he wrote. A few 20-pounder and 30-pounder Parrotts were acceptable as well. The Federals outgunned his army, which was "discouraging to our artillerists." As the Army of Northern Virginia built up, William N. Pendleton boasted that its artillery was becoming "more formidable than it has ever been before. The Yankees will not again have their way with us at long range any more than at close quarters."[42]

The process of upgrading took longer than expected, but the spirit of it was caught by Capt. E. S. McCarthy of the Richmond Howitzers. "The day of 6-pounders being passed" is how he justified a requisition for 3-Inch Ordnance Rifles. The Napoleons began rolling in soon after Chancellorsville. By November 1863 all 6-pounders had been turned in, but not all of them had yet been replaced by better ordnance.[43]

A similar process of conversion took place, although more slowly, in the Army of the Mississippi / Army of Tennessee. At the end of 1862, 6-pounders and 12-pounder howitzers still constituted 85 percent of the armament, and their limitations were felt at Stones River. "Six-pounder batteries cannot maintain a fight with long-range guns," declared Capt. Overton W. Barret. After that battle Bragg began to weed out anything less than a 12-pounder,

TABLE 7.4. Mix of Pieces in the Army of the Mississippi / Army of Tennessee, 1862–1864

Type of Pieces	Ordnance Department, Army of the Mississippi, July 8, 1862[a]	Army of Tennessee, November 1863[b]	Army of Tennessee, April 30, 1864[b]	Army of Tennessee, September 20, 1864[b]
Napoleons		48 (33.1%)	64 (53.4%)	90 (72.6%)
3-Inch Rifle		19 (13.1%)	6 (5.0%)	
10-Pounder Parrott		12 (8.2%)	10 (8.4%)	
12-Pounder Gun	6 (6.2%)			
12-Pounder Howitzer	36 (37.2%)	28 (19.3%)	38 (31.6%)	12 (9.7%)
Unspecified Rifle Gun	14 (14.4%)			22 (17.7%)
6-Pounder	41 (42.2%)	22 (15.1%)		
24-Pounder Howitzer		4 (2.7%)		
20-Pounder Parrott		4 (2.7%)		
Unspecified James Rifle		7 (4.8%)		
Unspecified Blakely Rifle		1 (1.0%)	2 (1.6%)	
Total	97 (100%)	145 (100%)	120 (100%)	124 (100%)

[a] OR, 17(2):643.
[b] Daniel, Cannoneers in Gray, 109, 128, 167.

preferring the Napoleon on the assumption that it was an all-purpose cannon and easier to manufacture. By April 1864 the army had completed the process of upgrading to heavier pieces. When the men of Lumsden's Alabama Battery were transferred to the defenses of Mobile in 1865, they once again used 6-pounders. "They seemed like pop guns in comparison with the 12 pounder Napoleons that we had handled so long," the men recalled after the war.[44]

Mainstream Union armies also underwent a process of shifting from light to heavier guns, but it proceeded more quickly and smoothly than among the Confederates. Col. Charles P. Kingsbury, chief of ordnance in the Army

TABLE 7.5. Mix of Pieces in the Army of Mississippi and Eastern
Louisiana, 1863, and the Defenses of Mobile, 1865

Army of Mississippi and Eastern Louisiana, January 18, 1863[a]	Number and Percentage of Total	Light Artillery in Mobile Defenses, February 21, 1865[b]	Number and Percentage of Total
6-Pounder Gun (Bronze)	25 (44.7)	Napoleons	12 (50.0)
12-Pounder Howitzer (Bronze)	16 (28.5)	3-Inch Rifle	2 (8.4)
3-Inch Parrott Rifle	9 (16.2)	10-Pounder Parrott	2 (8.4)
12-Pounder Gun (Bronze)	2 (3.6)	12-Pounder Howitzer	4 (16.6)
24-Pounder Howitzer (Bronze)	2 (3.6)	20-Pounder Parrott	4 (16.6)
Unspecified Parrott Rifle Gun	1 (1.7)		
Unspecified James Rifle Gun	1 (1.7)		
Total	56 (100)		24 (100)

[a] *OR*, 17(2):843.
[b] *OR*, 49(1):1002.

of the Potomac, recommended as early as the Peninsula Campaign that all 6-pounders be weeded out and replaced mostly by Napoleons. That piece probably was "the most efficient part of our artillery," he believed, and McClellan readily agreed.[45]

When Rosecrans's command lost many guns at Stones River, the general requested eighteen Napoleons and twelve 3-Inch Ordnance Rifles or 10-pounder Parrotts as their primary replacements. He also wanted half a dozen 24-pounder howitzers. When the Washington authorities agreed, his army significantly upgraded the quality of its armament.[46]

SMOOTHBORES VERSUS RIFLES

Of all the choices presented to artillery officers in terms of selecting types of cannon, none were more significant than the choice between smoothbores and rifles. The Civil War was the first major conflict in global history to employ

TABLE 7.6. Rounds Fired by the Army of the Cumberland and the Army of the Tennessee during the Atlanta Campaign

Army of the Cumberland	Rounds Fired and Percentage of Total[a]	Army of the Tennessee (Fifteenth and Seventeenth Corps)	Rounds Fired and Percentage of Total[b]
Napoleon	29,643 (33.4)	Napoleon	12,204 (28.5)
3-Inch Ordnance Rifle	35,321 (39.7)	3-Inch Ordnance Rifle	13,842 (32.5)
10-Pounder Parrott	14,786 (16.6)	10-Pounder Parrott (Fifteenth Corps only)	4,171 (9.8)
20-Pounder Parrott	5,059 (5.6)	12-Pounder Howitzer (Fifteenth Corps only)	1,493 (3.6)
24-Pounder Howitzer	3,368 (3.7)	20-Pounder Parrott	9,239 (21.6)
4.5-Inch Siege Rifle	201 (1.0)	24-Pounder Howitzer (Seventeenth Corps only)	1,230 (2.9)
		6-Pounder James (Fifteenth Corps only)	91 (1.1)
Total	88,378 (100)		42,270 (100)

[a] *OR*, 38(1):185.
[b] *OR*, 38(3):63.

significant numbers of rifled pieces. Therefore its battlefields became testing grounds for the effectiveness of rifled ordnance. Federal and Confederate officers commented a good deal on rifles, but their conclusions were mixed; some preferred smoothbores, while others became firm advocates of rifles.

Hunt recalled that early in the conflict younger artillery officers were eager to use rifles "as the latest improvement." The Ordnance Department also promoted them, probably because it was sponsoring its own version of the type in the 3-Inch Ordnance Rifle. But older artillery men cautioned everyone that the day of the smoothbore was not yet over, and McClellan wisely listened to them. He insisted that half the armament accompanying the Army of the Potomac be smoothbore. In the West artillerists seemed to prefer rifles early in the war, a situation deplored by Brig. Gen. Albin F. Schoepf. "We are

TABLE 7.7. Mix of Pieces in and Rounds Fired by Sherman's Army Group during the Carolinas Campaign

Type of Pieces[a]	Number and Percentage of Total	Rounds Fired and Percentage of Total[a]
Napoleon	30 (44.1)	1,621 (41.2)
3-Inch Ordnance Rifle	34 (50.0)	2,201 (55.9)
20-Pounder Parrott	4 (5.9)	111 (2.9)
Total	68 (100)	3,933 (100)

[a] OR, 47(1):177, 184.

depending on them [rifle pieces] to the exclusion of other and (under certain circumstances) more appropriate guns." He wanted each battery under his command in Kentucky to give up two rifles for smoothbores.[47]

Some officers parted from the mainstream and strongly preferred rifles over smoothbores. Jacob D. Cox complained of the conservatism of regular artillerymen who believed the Napoleon was superior to any rifle. He was certain that rifles surpassed smoothbores even at short-distance fighting and were more mobile. "They were so much lighter that we could jump them across a rough country where the teams could hardly move a Napoleon," he wrote. "We could subdue our adversaries' fire with them, when their smoothbores could not reach us."[48]

But McClellan and Schoepf were wise to argue for a mix of rifles and smoothbores, and most Union artillerists came to recognize the need for short-distance as well as long-distance ordnance. The only real question was whether to include rifles in the same unit as smoothbores or separate them into their own batteries. During the first half of the war, the tendency was to mix them. When streamlining became popular, however, the trend shifted to separating them into their own units.

PERSISTENCE OF SMOOTHBORES

Taking all the evidence into account, one can find more defenders of the smoothbore than of the rifle. "I am out with the rifled guns," admitted Confederate Frank Huger. He knew they could be useful but argued that smoothbores should constitute two-thirds of the armament. Brig. Gen. John D. Imboden, an artillerist and cavalryman, also believed in smoothbores. "In open ground at 1000 yards, a 6-pounder battery of smooth guns, or, at 1500 to 1800 yards, a similar battery of 12-pounder Napoleons, well handled, will in one hour discomfit double the number of the best rifles ever put in the field."[49]

Surprisingly, some artillerists felt insulted when ordered to convert their smoothbores to rifles. Capt. W. Irving Hodgson wondered if his 5th Company, Washington Artillery was being punished when compelled to give up its smoothbores. One possible explanation for this attitude could be that firing at short distance, the acknowledged province of the smoothbore, was viewed as demanding more courage and grit than long-distance fighting. Similarly, Capt. Thomas W. Osborn took it as a compliment when he was ordered to exchange his 3-Inch Ordnance Rifles for Napoleons. "This exchange was given or made as a special and marked compliment to the battery for the services it had performed."[50]

The Army of the Mississippi / Army of Tennessee retained a higher-than-average proportion of smoothbores throughout the war. At Shiloh 85 percent of its pieces were smoothbores. At Chickamauga Napoleons accounted for 49.4 percent of the rounds fired by Hill's Corps artillery and 57.2 percent of the rounds fired by Breckinridge's Division artillery. But during the first half of the Atlanta Campaign, Lt. Gen. Leonidas Polk's Army of Mississippi (which soon was incorporated into the Army of Tennessee as a corps) had so many Napoleons that they accounted for 83.5 percent of the artillery firing.[51]

But even many enthusiastic supporters of smoothbores had to admit that if opposed by a rifle battery, Napoleons were inadequate. All the enemy had to do was establish a position beyond the smoothbore's potential for firing at long distance. "I found that the lack of long-range guns was a great drawback to our batteries," admitted Capt. David D. Waters at Stones River. Battery commanders tried to place their pieces where they could be most advantageously used, the rifles farther back and the smoothbores closer to the enemy.[52]

Hunt found it ironic that one of the purposes of the Napoleon was to simplify logistics by combining the capabilities of the gun and the howitzer in one piece. But, at the same time, rifles came to insert a new logistical problem. They used a wide and puzzling array of ordnance. The Schenkl, Hotchkiss, and other projectile types and the varied types of fuzes to explode them "would get mixed in the same battery, and affect its efficiency," he recalled.[53] In other words, rifles created a lot of trouble even as they provided hope of effective long-distance firing. Even with streamlining, Osborn found a confusing mix of types when he became artillery chief of the Army of the Tennessee in August 1864. "The armament was by far too varied for an army in the field, consisting of four calibers of rifled guns and three of smooth-bore." He reduced it further to only two calibers of rifled and one of smoothbore. While complexity of supply affected both types, rifles posed more logistical difficulties than smoothbores.[54]

Moreover, uniform batteries created some organizational difficulties. At Nashville Fourth Corps commander Brig. Gen. Thomas J. Wood told his artillery chief to shift the all-rifle and all-Napoleon batteries around so that every division would have access to both types. Col. Charles H. Tompkins, artillery chief of the Sixth Corps, placed all his rifle batteries in one temporary division in his artillery brigade and the smoothbore batteries in another to compensate for the lack of mixing these two types in the same battery.[55]

CONCLUSION

In the end, most artillerists admitted that smoothbores and rifles occupied separate but interlocked positions. At short distance smoothbores prevailed, while at long distance rifles ruled. Union and Confederate armies maintained roughly an equivalent number of both types. By the end of the war, the smoothbore contingent was filled by one kind of cannon, the Napoleon, while the rifle contingent was shared between the 3-Inch Ordnance Rifle and the 10-pounder Parrott.

Reflecting its position as a war of transition from smoothbore cannon with lighter weight of projectile to rifled pieces with heavier weight of projectiles, the Civil War witnessed a streamlining process that took artillerists from a choice of a dozen types of cannon to only three types. They continued to prefer mixed batteries until the concept of uniform batteries became popular in the five major field armies. While smoothbores and rifles had their advocates, the consensus was to keep an even number of both types on hand. Hard and continuous campaigning had inspired these shifts over time in the five major field armies, while other formations continued to use varied types of cannon, weights of projectiles, and mixes of smoothbores and rifles while organizing their artillery arm.

8

. . . .

UNION ARTILLERY BRIGADES AND
CONFEDERATE ARTILLERY BATTALIONS

S peaking to the Massachusetts Historical Society in 1888, Henry J.
Hunt complained of a fundamental problem during his extensive
Civil War service. Because "the operations of field artillery are in
the main auxiliary to those of other troops, its annals are comparatively pro-
saic, especially when its action is controlled, not by its own officers, but by
those of other arms."[1]

Hunt referred to the fact that field artillerists were commanded by infantry officers who had the authority to tell them how to use their guns. In the
administrative structure artillerists relied on infantry quartermasters, ordnance officers, and other staff personnel to fill their supply needs. Because
there were no units larger than the regiment, artillery officers could not rise
above the rank of colonel; most could not rise above that of captain because
their state had not organized artillery units larger than a battery. The artillery
arm was the most technical branch of the three, yet its highly intelligent officers had few outlets for their ambition. In short, a range of important issues
cropped up early in the war concerning its management for effective use in
the field. These issues dealt with the upper level of military management, the
level existing above the basic or primary organizational level of the battery,
battalion, and regiment.

For the first half of the war, artillery management consisted of dispersing
batteries by assigning them to infantry brigades or divisions. The commander
of those infantry units not only had full command of them during battles but
also was administratively responsible for them between engagements. Dissatisfied with this arrangement, artillery officers in the Army of the Potomac

and the Army of Northern Virginia (but not anywhere else) pushed for the creation of larger field units of guns, grouping batteries into what the Federals would call artillery brigades and the Confederates would term artillery battalions. Artillery officers led these brigades and battalions, but their authority over them was limited. Jealous of losing control, infantry officers stipulated that the artillery commander had full administrative control over the brigades and battalions between battles but did not command them while engaged in combat.

Thus, the story of artillery management falls into two phases. During the first half of the war, dispersal ruled. During the last half, concentration was the order of the day. Artillery officers widely applauded the change from dispersal to concentration, and historians have uniformly supported their viewpoint. But the story is not so neat or simplistic. We need to consider whether dispersal was as bad as artillery officers and historians have portrayed and whether concentration was a real improvement in artillery management. The answer to both questions complicates our previously uncomplicated perception of the issues.

DISPERSAL OR CONCENTRATION?

Given its primary purpose of supporting infantry and cavalry, officers other than artillerists were primarily responsible for developing the dispersal system. In his 1846 *Elements of Military Art and Science,* Henry W. Halleck urged the distribution of guns along the entire line of battle, while West Point professor Dennis Hart Mahan warned against concentrating the pieces because it would be more difficult to extricate them from the battlefield in case of a reverse.[2]

But *Instruction for Field Artillery,* authored by artillery men, offered the opposite view. "The *effect* of field artillery is generally in proportion to the *concentration of its fire.* It has therefore for its object, not to strike down a few isolated men, and here and there to dismount a gun, but by a combined and concentrated fire to destroy an enemy's cover; to break up his squares and columns; to open his ranks; to arrest his attacks, and to support those which may be directed against him."[3]

Authors of artillery handbooks supported the official manual. Joseph Roberts strongly urged the concentration of guns. "The effects of the fire will be in proportion to the number of guns brought together," he wrote. The authors of *Revised United States Army Regulations* also supported this view, writing that the "fire of artillery being formidable in proportion to its concentration," dispersal was the wrong policy. In contrast, Francis J. Lippitt's *A Treatise on the Tactical Use of the Three Arms* argued that concentration was important for offensive action but dispersal was best for defensive operations.[4]

Artillery officers uniformly praised concentration. Dispersal tended to waste ammunition, according to John C. Tidball, because infantry officers "always wanted their batteries to fire whether their positions enabled them to do so with effect or not." Even on the march, artillery and infantry moved at differing speeds, and it was not easy for one to accommodate the other. It also was easy for foot soldiers to resume their march, while artillery horses had "to overcome the inertia of a heavy load at every start, thus causing an unnecessary expenditure of animal vitality at every halt." The worst aspect of dispersal, according to Tidball, was that batteries were "employed in such a desultory manner as greatly to weaken their effect as a whole.... The fact of their being tied down to the narrow limits of small infantry commands rendered their employment other than in a scattered and feeble manner, impracticable." Confederate artillerists echoed their Union opponents in this argument. Robert Stiles called the dispersal system "that very defective organization."[5]

Historians have strongly sided with Civil War artillerists. Jennings Cropper Wise, a historian and army officer born in 1881, wrote of "pernicious brigade distribution," blaming it on "the prevailing custom of the time." L Van Loan Naisawald called the practice "a tactic that belonged to the vanishing era of the smoothbore musket." Larry Daniel, in his admirable study of artillery in the Army of the Mississippi / Army of Tennessee, represents the persistence of this historical interpretation. He argued that Confederate artillery in the West was "largely ineffective" during 1861–62. "The brigade-battery organization simply did not lend itself to the massing of guns in battle."[6]

But there is a basic problem with the argument that the dispersal system inhibited concentration. Historians point to three examples to prove their argument that massing guns proved effective on the battlefield. Those three include the Confederate concentration of fifty-three pieces at Shiloh on April 6, 1862; the Federal massing of thirty-seven pieces at Malvern Hill on July 1, 1862; and the Federal concentration of fifty-eight pieces at Stones River on January 2, 1863. Ironically, all three instances of effective massing took place in field armies that were practicing the dispersal system at the time. That system obviously did not prevent officers from concentrating their guns at Shiloh, Malvern Hill, and Stones River when they wanted to do so. It should also be pointed out that in all three cases infantry officers fully supported and even facilitated the massing of those guns.[7]

It is a matter of further irony that, after the shift to the concentration system in 1863, historians find few examples of effective massing of pieces on the battlefield. The Army of the Potomac had not yet implemented the concentration system when it fought at Chancellorsville, yet the Federals created not one but four masses of guns during the battle. They concentrated thirty-eight pieces near Fairview on May 2, 1863, but lost that position to Confederate counterbattery fire. The Federals also assembled three concentrations along a heavily fortified line protecting their retreat across the Rapidan River on May 4. Those consisted of thirty pieces on the left, forty-eight in the center, and thirty-two on the right.[8]

Joseph Hooker finally authorized the creation of artillery brigades after Chancellorsville, and several concentrations appeared at Gettysburg. The Confederates, who also had organized their guns into artillery battalions by now, used 135 pieces to pound the Union line in preparation for Pickett's Attack on July 3, 1863, a concentration that utterly failed to prepare the way for victory. The Federals grouped a number of batteries in several places to deal with their enemy, especially on the high ground of Culp's Hill, Cemetery Hill, Cemetery Ridge, and Little Round Top. A total of 126 Union guns replied to the Confederate bombardment on the last day of the battle.[9]

Advocates of concentration tend to point to Gettysburg to prove their point. Tidball argued that the engagement "fully demonstrated the great power and influence in battle of this arm when properly managed." Naisawald also thought Gettysburg demonstrated the success of the artillery brigade system. But no one among contemporaries or modern historians point to any similar massing of guns during 1864–65, when the concentration system spread throughout the Union and Confederate armies. While Lee did mass twenty-nine pieces to repel a Federal attack at Spotsylvania on May 18, 1864, far more often batteries were sent to brigades and divisions when called on. If this represented a reversion to the dispersal system, then perhaps that system had been a useful one after all.[10]

Tidball bemoaned the reversion to dispersal in the last year of the war and blamed it on infantry officers. "They still insisted on having batteries assigned to them for the march and for the battle, and upon one pretext or another generally managed to have them temporarily under their control." In his view this negated "a great deal" of the good in the new system of management, and "a great deal of the viciousness of the old system" was "left still to plague the service." What Tidball refused to admit was that the infantry officers wanted batteries not out of nostalgia, but out of necessity.[11]

Flexibility was the key to any good system of artillery management. Dispersal did not prevent concentration during the first half of the war, and concentration did not lead to more massing during the last half of the conflict. Contemporaries and modern historians place too much emphasis on concentrating the guns. Artillery did make a difference on the battlefield by closely supporting infantry units, especially when repelling an enemy attack, and the best way to do this was to spread out batteries along the infantry line. Even William E. Birkhimer, a postwar artillery officer who strongly favored concentration, was forced to admit in his history of the arm that there were times when dispersal of batteries to small infantry units was necessary. Even after creating artillery battalions, Lee's guns were dispersed to support various infantry units when the Federals began the Fredericksburg Campaign of November–December 1862. After the battle they were brought back to the battalion again.[12]

The shift from dispersal to concentration midway through the war had not changed the way artillery was handled in battle, but it made a big difference in administration. Artillery officers serving at levels higher than that of the battery or regiment were now in charge of training, inspection, and supply of the guns for entire corps. They could maintain levels of readiness for the field more effectively than infantry commanders and infantry staff members. That actually was the most important benefit of concentration, not the ability to mass guns on the battlefield.

EVALUATING DISPERSAL

In order to better understand the history of field artillery during the first half of the Civil War, it is important to take dispersal seriously as a useful operational system. There were limitations in that system, of course, but there also were strengths. It had worked for centuries, and there was nothing new in the Civil War that required its abandonment. The creation of artillery brigades and battalions, a genuine innovation within the history of American field artillery, was only an adjustment of the old dispersal system rather than a radical departure from it.

Friction between Infantry and Artillery Officers

The main source of friction between artillery and infantry officers in the dispersal system was how best to use the guns in battle. Accentuating this problem was the fact that battery commanders had to take orders not just from their immediate brigade or division leader but also from any infantry officer who outranked them. Capt. W. Irving Hodgson's 5th Company, Washington Artillery was attached to Brig. Gen. James Patton Anderson's Second Brigade at Shiloh. Anderson instructed him what to do at the start of the engagement. Then Brig. Gen. Daniel Ruggles told Hodgson to fire at a Federal camp for a while, during which time Anderson's troops moved away and Hodgson lost contact with them. Ruggles told him "to go wherever I heard the most firing," and Hodgson also took orders from Brig. Gen. James Trudeau of the Louisiana state forces, who was acting as a volunteer aide for Beauregard. He also was told what to do by Maj. Gen. William J. Hardee, by one of Hardee's aides, by Lt. A. R. Chisolm (also an aide to Beauregard), and by other staff members. Hodgson lost count of the many men who gave him orders that day.[13]

There was nothing necessarily wrong with taking orders from a variety of people, even though it could be wearing on the nerves. But real friction occurred when those officers were ignorant about the proper use of artillery and refused to admit it. They placed batteries on exposed ground where the men and horses were needlessly sacrificed or put them too far from infantry support. Infantry officers sometimes ordered their attached guns to open fire even though the artillerists knew the distance was too great for their pieces. They sometimes ordered fire on what artillerists believed were friendly troops or to fire even when there was no visible target of any kind to aim at. Another fairly common problem was that sections of a battery were ordered away to another position by an infantry officer who failed to inform the battery commander what he was doing.[14]

When Thomas W. Osborn discovered during the Atlanta Campaign that an infantry officer had placed a battery 300 yards in front of the picket line without fieldworks and no infantry nearby, he protested. The brigade commander "asked with all seriousness 'What is artillery for if not to protect the infantry?'" Osborn could not understand this attitude. "The ignorance of some of our general officers in regard to the proper uses of artillery is simply stupendous," he wrote. "How necessary it may be, and often is, to have men in command of artillery who have made it their special study."[15]

Artillery officers employed several strategies to mitigate bad orders from infantrymen. Often, they suggested better ways to employ their guns, and the infantry officer usually deferred to them. For example, Capt. Charles H. Morgan "objected strongly" to the positioning of a section from his Second Corps artillery at Fredericksburg, "and the project was given up."[16] Interceding with higher authority often worked. Officers of the 1st Connecticut Battery and the 5th New Jersey Battery avoided taking an exposed position by appealing to Brig. Gen. Alfred H. Terry. "Capt. Rockwell and Capt. Warren you are at liberty to place your batteries where you think they can do the most good," Terry said. "I leave it with you, because I know that I can rely on your judgment."[17]

At times artillery officers simply ignored orders. When Brig. Gen. George G. Meade and Brig. Gen. Truman Seymour told Capt. James Thompson to reposition his Battery G, 2nd US Artillery to fire to the right at the Battle of Glendale in June 1862, he refused. When Brig. Gen. Philip Kearney told him the same thing, Thompson did so but aimed his guns once again to the left as soon as Kearney rode away. He was proven right because, soon after Kearney's interference, Confederate infantry appeared in the direction selected by the captain.[18] More than one artillery officer merely gave the appearance of obeying bad orders, as had Thompson. Forced to take up exposed positions, they refused to open fire and thus drew no attention to themselves from the enemy. At other times, they remained in the dangerous spot for a while but soon left it when the infantry officer went away.[19]

The real problem stemmed from personnel issues rather than from the system itself. Some infantry officers insisted on having their way and engaged in vendettas against the artillery. Maj. Gen. Henry Heth proved to be a constant thorn in the side of Lt. Col. William Thomas Poague. At Cold Harbor Heth insisted that Poague place two batteries in an exposed position to cover his division's left flank. "That was the place and the only place for artillery," as Poague remembered Heth's words. The result was a bloody fiasco. At a distance of only 250 yards, the two batteries were decimated, their commanders killed, several of their pieces disabled, and Poague himself narrowly escaped death.[20]

On the Federal side, a similar situation developed for Charles Wainwright, artillery chief of the Fifth Corps. Division commander Charles Griffin, a former artillerist, constantly fought with him during the Overland Campaign. Hunt was called in for an opinion and sometimes admitted that placing pieces in exposed positions was an acceptable risk. At other times he found the division commander's choice of ground "utterly untenable." Griffin demanded that the colonel fire his pieces almost continuously. "I was helpless to prevent it," Wainwright admitted. One battery fired 250 rounds from each piece every day for three days, expending "a whole campaign allowance of ammunition." Wainwright estimated that at least two-thirds of those rounds were utterly wasted. He believed that Griffin "was scared, and made a noise to keep his men's courage up."[21]

By the end of May, Griffin managed to separate as many batteries from Wainwright as possible. He talked corps leader Maj. Gen. Gouverneur K. Warren into permanently assigning three batteries to his division, which Meade supported when Hunt appealed to him. "I know that Griffin is set on breaking up the brigade organization of the artillery because it did not originate with him and because he commands a division," thought Wainwright. "I find myself rapidly being deprived of all command," he wrote by June 22. Griffin even ignored the colonel when the artillery chief tried to detail battery men to other duties, displaying a blatant contempt for his position.[22]

A similar situation developed in the Second Corps. On May 10, to cover the fall back of troops over the Po River, division leaders Brig. Gen. Francis C. Barlow and Maj. Gen. David B. Birney interfered with the placement of artillery. They put pieces into exposed positions that masked the fire of guns farther to the rear despite protests by artillerists. The poor placement reduced the amount of artillery support available and led to the loss of at least one piece.[23]

Maj. Gen. Winfield S. Hancock, Second Corps commander, had little sense about how to use artillery and refused to admit it. He and Hunt began a long feud at Gettysburg. When Meade reached the Pennsylvania town at 2 A.M. on July 2, he gave Hunt full authority to command the guns and authorized him to use his name in orders. Unfortunately, Meade failed to issue these instructions in written orders, and Hunt in turn failed to inform Hancock of his intention to direct the operations of Second Corps guns.[24]

Hunt developed an artillery plan when the Confederates massed 150 pieces on the morning of July 3. He was determined to husband his firepower to break up the expected infantry attack before it reached the Union line, or at least to disrupt and damage the gray formations on the way. There was no time to go through Meade's headquarters, so Hunt rode along the Union line from right to left, instructing battery commanders to wait fifteen to twenty minutes after the start of the Confederate bombardment before they replied to it. They also were to carefully select only the best targets for counterbattery fire, preserving a supply of ammunition to pound the impending infantry assault. He made it to the left end of the line just when the Confederates opened their bombardment.[25]

Partway through the shelling, Hunt inspected the ammunition chests to gauge how much the pieces were expending and visited Cemetery Hill. He engaged in a conversation with Thomas W. Osborn, who was then artillery chief of Maj. Gen. Oliver O. Howard's Eleventh Corps. In discussing the situation, Osborn suggested the guns suddenly cease firing to lure the Confederates into the open before the Federals ran out of ammunition. Howard liked the idea, as did Hunt. While Osborn spread the word among his batteries, Hunt rode along the line to do the same. It took ten minutes to quiet the guns between Cemetery Hill and Meade's headquarters in the center of the Union line, and a few more minutes to silence the rest.[26]

Hancock became angry that the army's artillery chief had stopped the shelling along his sector, the Union center, but one of his artillerists agreed with Hunt. Capt. Charles A. Phillips of the 5th Massachusetts Battery considered the bombardment a "foolish cannonade" and was glad to stop firing. A short time later Hancock rode up and ordered him to resume firing, and Phillips obeyed. Shortly after that, Maj. Freeman McGilvery, who commanded a brigade in the army's artillery reserve, stopped Phillips again. Then McGilvery and Hancock yelled at each other. "My troops cannot stand this cannonade and will not stand it if it is not replied to," the general told the artillerist. McGilvery replied that his gunners were standing it and the infantry could do so as well. Besides, he did not consider himself under Hancock's authority.[27]

Events soon overwhelmed this argument. The Confederate guns fell silent, and the infantrymen began their famous charge. Most of the Federal batteries had enough rounds to contribute to its repulse, verifying Hunt's tactics. It is true that the infantry's nerves were strained by the Confederate bombardment, but most of Hancock's men stayed the course. It was far more important to save artillery rounds for punishing Confederate infantry at close distance than to waste it in long-distance counterbattery fire.[28] But because Hancock forced some of his batteries to continue firing to the last minute of the bombardment, Union artillery support was seriously reduced in opposing Pickett's Charge. "We lost not only the fire of one-third of our guns," Hunt argued, "but the resulting cross-fire, which would have doubled its value." Those batteries had no long-distance ammunition left to punish the Confederates, opening only when they came within canister distance. In contrast, the guns controlled by McGilvery punished them the whole way. If McGilvery had obeyed Hancock, Hunt believed, the Confederates would have broken the Second Corps line. "As it was, the escape was a very narrow one."[29]

After the war, Hunt blamed army regulations concerning the relationship between artillery and infantry for what he considered a near disaster on July 3. But again it was not the system; the real problem lay in Meade's failure to inform the army that he had vested Hunt with full authority to command the guns. Hancock would not have acted as he did in face of that authority from his superior.[30]

Hancock and Hunt continued to rub each other the wrong way for the rest of the war. Before the start of the Overland Campaign, Hancock pushed to have batteries assigned to divisions even before the first shot was fired. In September 1864 he took personal charge of batteries along his sector of the line at Petersburg and handpicked a battery commander to direct the firing. When Hunt sent a different artillery officer to manage the firing, Hancock appealed to Meade, who gave him permission to do things his own way. "It is impracticable to issue orders forbidding Genl Offs to order firing," Hunt informed a subordinate in December 1864. All that could be done was to record who ordered what type of firing and the result of that order, then complain when necessary.[31]

On Christmas Day Hunt admitted that infantry officers ruled on the battlefield. "In a defensive line, all the troops of all arms *on* the line must be under the commander responsible for the safety of the line. The artillery on such a line is merely auxiliary, and its operations must be under the control of the officer who commands the line." Hunt, aptly described as "the soul of our artillery," the man who "has made it what it is by far the best arm in the service," had to admit defeat in his quest for artillery independence.[32]

Cooperation between Infantry and Artillery Officers

It should be noted, however, that most of the vicious struggles over artillery control on the battlefield occurred during the last half of the war, when concentration was the policy, and in the Army of the Potomac, the army that first considered creating artillery brigades. That army witnessed more cooperation between artillery and infantry during the dispersal phase of the first half of the war, once again pointing to the viability of that system compared to concentrating batteries as far as combat control was concerned. Jennings Cropper Wise has written that the first year of the war "taught that division and brigade commanders as a rule neither understood nor were capable of handling artillery in camp, on the march, or in action." But, based on the evidence, that was not at all true.[33]

Many infantry commanders handled their guns well. Some of them fully understood artillery, while others gave their artillerists complete freedom to do as they pleased on the battlefield. There was a high degree of cooperation between many infantry and artillery officers during the dispersal phase of the early war, and it continued into the concentration phase of the later war.

A number of infantry commanders who understood artillery gave very precise instructions to their batteries. They told artillerists to employ solid shot and shrapnel for counterbattery fire and canister against infantry. Other infantrymen merely told battery officers to follow the brigade and make themselves useful. Wainwright found division commander Joseph Hooker easy to work with at the Battle of Williamsburg in May 1862. The two reconnoitered together, and Wainwright suggested a spot for his guns, but Hooker admitted he could not guarantee infantry support there. So the colonel suggested a second place that both agreed upon.[34]

At Antietam Lee gave detailed instructions to Lt. John A. Ramsay of Company D, 1st North Carolina Artillery. He asked Ramsay to use his telescope and identify troop concentrations in the distance. On receiving this information, Lee told him to "elevate your guns and continue the fire until these troops . . . come near your line of fire, then change your position to the ridge on the right of the line and fire on the troops beyond the creek."[35]

A few infantry commanders had previously served in the artillery and, unlike Griffin, cooperated with their battery officers. Maj. Gen. John B. Magruder "dearly loved artillery service," wrote John Ramsay. Peter J. Osterhaus understood the big guns, using them more adroitly than the average division leader. At the Big Black River in May 1863, Osterhaus minutely examined the terrain to select the best spot for his favorite unit, the 1st Wisconsin Battery, and was slightly wounded by return fire as he watched the guns support a successful infantry attack.[36]

The best scenario was tight cooperation between infantry and artillery officers. If that was not possible, the second best was for the infantry officer not to interfere with his artillerists. Division leader Brig. Gen. Horatio P. Van Cleve told his artillery chief "to fight on my own hook, and do the best in my power" at Stones River. When Howard gave Wainwright full authority to command the guns on Cemetery Hill at Gettysburg, the colonel told his colleagues not to "take orders from any man with a star on his shoulders who might choose to give them." Howard fully respected Osborn's abilities as well. "He never after [Gettysburg] gave me an explicit order on a battlefield," wrote Osborn. "I learned his plan and cooperated with him to the best of my ability and judgment." When Jacob Roemer appealed to division leader Orlando B. Willcox about an order to assume a bad position, Willcox gave him carte blanche. "Go back and take any position that will suit you, provided you can protect the infantry and your own Battery, and hereafter, if you think you can do better in some other position than in that to which you may be assigned, exercise your own judgment."[37]

Infantry-artillery cooperation mostly depended on the individuals involved rather than on the system used. The dispersal system worked as well as one could expect, given the variety of personalities involved. But the concentration system did not support a higher level of artillery effectiveness on the battlefield since infantry officers continued to command the guns in combat. The true benefit of the concentration system lay in the administrative power it vested in artillery officers between battles, when the guns were directly under their personal supervision rather than under the care of brigade or division commanders and infantry staffs. This enabled the batteries to be maintained at a higher state of readiness for the field.

EVALUATING THE CONCENTRATION SYSTEM

The idea for the concentration system began in the Army of the Potomac late in 1861, but resistance to it delayed its implementation in the form of artillery brigades until May 1863. Officers in the Army of Northern Virginia started thinking about concentrating their guns in the fall of 1862 but implemented the plan almost immediately, becoming the first field army of the war to organize batteries in the form of artillery battalions. In both northern and southern armies, the idea and its implementation began in the eastern forces and spread to the West; the Confederate Army of Tennessee enacted the concept in 1863, while the Federals in the Army of the Cumberland and the Army of the Tennessee did so in 1864. The concept held little relevance for small, secondary, or temporary forces and thus was primarily a feature of artillery management in mainline field armies. It never became a universal phenomenon throughout either national force.

The Federal Artillery Brigade

The first suggestion to concentrate artillery in the Army of the Potomac appeared in December 1861, when Hunt urged McClellan to place all batteries into a corps so the chief of artillery could administer their wants more effectively. "At present the batteries scramble for what they can get, and the supplies depend more upon the whims and caprices of officers of other arms than upon the knowledge and experience of their own. This leads to great waste without securing efficiency." But McClellan failed to act on that recommendation.[38]

Wainwright testified to the problem Hunt tried to alleviate. As artillery chief of Hooker's division, he ran afoul of Brig. Gen. Henry M. Naglee, who refused "to allow his commissary to issue to the batteries." Only when Wainwright appealed to Hooker did he obtain rations for his men. While temporarily serving Third Corps headquarters, Wainwright thought Maj. Gen. Samuel P. Heintzelman viewed the artillery chief on his staff as "a sort of inspector of artillery."[39]

Wainwright became artillery chief of the First Corps in September 1862. When told he was responsible for "the efficiency of the batteries of the corps in every respect," the colonel confessed to his dilemma. "I do not see exactly how I am to carry it out with the batteries attached to the several divisions, and subject to the orders of the division commanders." He could not rely on the artillery chiefs of the divisions. "It is impossible to get them to do anything more than forward a few reports." The quartermasters and commissaries on division staff generally were indifferent to the batteries and resented the extra trouble of supplying them.[40]

On September 25, 1862, Wainwright suggested to Hunt the creation of an artillery brigade for each corps to be headed by an artillery officer with a staff of his own. All batteries in the corps would be grouped under this chief's control "to refit and instruct them. During an engagement or when necessary on the march they could be sent to the divisions, either all of them or a part."

Initially Hunt did not like the idea, but Wainwright continued to hone his proposal and convinced First Corps commander Maj. Gen. John Reynolds of its utility.[41] By November 26 Hunt had warmed up to the plan and urged Wainwright to write a proposal he could submit to Maj. Gen. Ambrose Burnside, current commander of the Army of the Potomac. Burnside flatly rejected the plan, but Wainwright believed the Battle of Fredericksburg demonstrated the limitations of the dispersal system. The colonel had no control over reserve artillery ammunition in First Corps, and infantry division leaders mismanaged their guns or were indifferent to them. The artillery chiefs did "little more than look after their own battery, and do not dare to state their objections to anything their division commander may order."[42]

When Hooker replaced Burnside early in 1863, Hunt and Wainwright urged their proposal on the new commander. Hunt always stressed the administrative benefits to artillery from the concentration system. He listed these benefits as "seeing it supplied with horses, men, and ammunition; and [seeing] that it is properly instructed and properly equipped; that the ammunition is of proper quality; [and] that the officers are fitted for their duties." He also defined the operational, or executive, duties as "the command of the troops, with the right to issue orders outside of those relating to its internal economy and administration." While Hunt and Wainwright sought operational control, they had far less chance of achieving it than administrative control. Despite his eloquence and Wainwright's good relations with Hooker, neither could convince the general even to grant them administrative control over the batteries. "The [dispersal] system had already worn a groove from which it was difficult to extricate it," John C. Tidball later wrote.[43]

Hunt discovered that Hooker's chief of Staff, Maj. Gen. Daniel Butterfield, was the chief cause of this failure. Butterfield advised Hooker to reject the artillery brigade concept based on his understanding that European armies maintained the same system prevailing in America. But the visit of a Swiss general to the Army of the Potomac changed his mind. Hunt pumped the visitor for information and found that Europeans generally divided management along lines similar to Wainwright's proposal. That convinced Butterfield, who afterward urged Hunt to propose it again to Hooker.[44]

Nothing was done before the Battle of Chancellorsville, but that engagement offered Wainwright an opportunity to promote his concept. During the critical day of fighting, May 3, 1863, he visited Hooker, who still was a bit stunned by the collapse of a pillar onto his head at the Chancellor House. When the army commander asked how things looked, Wainwright told him the artillery was in chaos. Because Hunt was away on another part of the field, Hooker asked Wainwright to take charge of it, but the colonel insisted on written orders to lend him authority. With that piece of paper, he rejoiced "at such an admission of the principles of artillery organization which I had been contending for."[45] Wainwright visited all corps commanders and not only showed them Hooker's order but also assured them he had no intention of interfering with their authority. Yet Wainwright told artillery officers to obey no operational orders from infantry officers. The next day he met Hunt and relinquished control of the artillery to him. After the battle the batteries were sent back to their assigned infantry units.[46]

Hooker took the lesson seriously. By May 12 he became a convert to the artillery brigade concept and implemented it the next day. Each of the seven corps received a brigade, with four to eight batteries each. In addition, the Cavalry Corps received two brigades, and the army's large artillery reserve was divided into five brigades. Because there were so few high-ranking artillery officers, the fourteen brigades were commanded by four field officers, nine captains, and one lieutenant. Quartermasters and commissaries were assigned to the new organizations.[47]

The artillerists liked the new arrangement. John W. Chase of the 1st Massachusetts Battery looked forward to more food, hoping "that we can get what belongs to us in the way of rations which is more than we ever have got."[48]

Resistance to the new arrangement grew in some quarters. In the Fifth Corps, division leader Griffin, as we have already seen, emerged as a "very bitter" critic of the brigade system in October 1863. Meade considered abolishing the system altogether just before the onset of the Overland Campaign. Soon after that drive began, Warren, as we have already seen, emerged as another bitter enemy of the concentration concept. We can only guess that the impetus for all this opposition lay in the natural impulse for men to guard their turf within an organizational structure. Infantry officers had always commanded artillery within their formations, and many wanted to continue doing so.[49]

But the brigade system survived these challenges. Grant approved it, even though it was something new to his experience. According to Wainwright, the general in chief told Hunt "that he knew nothing about [artillery management], had forgotten most of what he had learned at West Point, and was totally ignorant as to the organization in other [foreign] armies. He says that he commenced out West by assigning one battery to each brigade, but found out his mistake. He approves the brigade organization."[50]

The concentration system spread to other major Union field armies slowly and uncertainly. The transfer of the Eleventh and Twelfth Corps from the Potomac army to Tennessee in October 1863 brought the concept to the Army of the Cumberland. When those two corps merged to form the Twentieth Corps in March 1864, the new organization retained the brigade system while the rest of the Army of the Cumberland haltingly converted to it. The Fourth Corps did not form artillery brigades until July 18, and the Fourteenth Corps followed on July 24, although they were called battalions rather than brigades in the latter unit.[51]

In contrast to the East, there was no interservice fighting in the West. "The organization of the Artillery Brigade has been an era for good," reported Capt. Lyman Bridges. "The batteries can be more promptly equipped and supplied, all unnecessary marches avoided, the labor equally distributed, and all the artillery of the corps used to advantage. The animals of the batteries are in much better condition than when the brigade was organized."[52] It is important to note that in Bridges's comments no mention was made of massing the guns for tactical purposes, a practice that neither the Federals nor the Confederates employed during the Atlanta Campaign. The advantages of concentration were purely administrative, not operational.

When Howard brought in Osborn as chief of artillery for the Army of the Tennessee in early August 1864, Osborn discovered his new command still relied on the dispersal system. The army's artillery was "by far its worst or most slipshod organization." Osborn managed to introduce the brigade system soon after the Atlanta Campaign ended.[53] But the administrative benefits of the brigade system remained severely muted in the Army of the Tennessee. Howard soon embarked on a series of long campaigns under Sherman during which administrative as well as operational control of the batteries were given to division commanders for extended periods. In the Right Wing, Sixteenth Corps, long detached from the Army of the Tennessee, artillery brigades were not formed until January 1865.[54]

The artillery brigade concept worked well in the Army of the Cumberland, never had a fair trial in the Army of the Tennessee, and suffered severe blows from some infantry officers in the Army of the Potomac. Concentration never facilitated the massing of guns for a specific tactical mission on the battlefield even though, when allowed to operate as intended, it greatly improved the administration of the artillery arm.

THE CONFEDERATE ARTILLERY BATTALION

Confederate artillery officers developed a similar plan for concentration later than the Federals but implemented it sooner. At some time in late 1862, Lee's artillery chief, Brig. Gen. William N. Pendleton, argued that the dispersing of batteries "hinders unity and concentration in battle." While he deviated from his Federal counterparts in mentioning the massing of guns on the battlefield, Pendleton also stressed the administrative advantages of concentration. He complained that brigade and division commanders could not devote enough attention to their batteries. The dispersal system "was not promotive of greatest efficiency in this arm." Pendleton suggested a system very similar to that of Wainwright except that he used the term artillery "battalion" rather than "brigade."[55]

Lee began creating the new units in the Army of Northern Virginia late in 1862, endorsing them as "advantageous." On January 7, 1863, the Adjutant and Inspector General's Office in Richmond spelled out guidelines for creating artillery battalions across the Confederate army.[56]

But there were problems. Orders failed to provide the new battalions with adequate staff officers. Battalion commanders tried to compensate, forcing their staff to perform double duty (the quartermaster also acted as commissary of subsistence). Thomas H. Carter pointed out that his new artillery battalion contained 691 men and 356 horses, yet he had fewer staff members than an infantry regiment of 300 men. "Multiplying officers may be a great evil," Carter told Pendleton, "but not so great as inefficient artillery. A few horses saved would pay the salary of these officers."[57]

Despite these problems, officers in the Army of Northern Virginia tended to cite massing of the guns as an advantage of the new battalion system. Even Lee noted that point. While none of them placed this advantage at the center of their evaluation of the system, it is worth taking it seriously. The army had not massed guns to an appreciable extent during the dispersal system of the first half of the conflict, in stark contrast to the Federals. Lee's artillery did mass at Chancellorsville and at Gettysburg as well as on a handful of occasions during the campaigns of 1864; his subordinates tended to credit that trend to the new battalion system.[58]

Whether the battalion system resulted in a higher level of maintenance is not easy to see in the Army of Northern Virginia. Shortages of staff officers combined with general logistical and supply problems throughout the Confederacy probably negated much of the administrative benefit to be derived from the concentration system. The battalions could hardly be expected to counteract the fact that the Confederate supply system was breaking down. Pendleton tried to improve the battalion by proposing congressional legislation to appoint a full staff for every unit, including a chaplain and two surgeons, in October 1864. Lee made some revisions in the proposal and sent it to the War Department, which sent it to Jefferson Davis for an opinion. Davis did not like it at all due to pecuniary concerns and a fear of enlarging the military establishment.[59]

In the West the Army of Tennessee began to organize artillery battalions in April 1863. In some units it was not done until October of that year. Not until Gen. Joseph E. Johnston replaced Bragg in early 1864 was the process completed. Johnston allocated one battalion for each division and detailed officers from batteries to serve as battalion staff. In contrast to Lee's army, the battalions were sometimes called regiments.[60] But the battalion system in the Army of Tennessee was eliminated in November 1864. While preparing for his invasion of Union-held Tennessee, Gen. John Bell Hood broke it up and assigned battalions to divisions on a permanent basis rather than just on days of battle. "All orders and directions to the battalion from the division commanders will be promptly and strictly obeyed," he wrote. As one artillery officer noted with understatement, this order "changed the status of the artillery" for the rest of the war.[61]

The extent to which the artillery battalion concept penetrated beyond the two main Confederate field armies is unclear. In Lt. Gen. Richard Taylor's Department of Alabama and Mississippi, Maj. Charles W. Squires led a battalion consisting of six batteries in the summer of 1864. It apparently encompassed all the artillery units in the department and was a rare example of the concept extending outside the two mainline forces.[62]

Although unevenly applied across the Confederate army and imperfectly instituted in the two mainline forces, the artillery battalion represented the first attempt to create an administrative unit for higher-level artillery management in American history. "The Confederates were the pioneers in the plan of artillery organization and administration," declared historian William E. Birkhimer. He asserted that both Austria and Prussia instituted similar units after their war in 1866, and France did so after its disastrous conflict with Prussia in 1870–71. In neither the Union nor Confederate armies were the artillery brigade or the artillery battalion authorized by acts of Congress. Instead, they were improvised by the armies due to "the necessities of war."[63]

THE FEDERAL ARTILLERY CHIEF

The creation of Union artillery brigades and Confederate artillery battalions represented an interesting new step in higher-level management. In contrast, the position of artillery chief, allowed by law on the staff of field forces down to the division level, was an old tradition. But the exact responsibilities and powers of that position remained unclear in the Civil War. During the era of dispersal, he was little more than another staff officer, exercising no administrative or operational authority while shuffling reports and inspecting batteries. The era of concentration vested him with administrative authority but no operational control. No matter which system prevailed, many artillery chiefs were dissatisfied with their position.

No one was more dissatisfied than Henry J. Hunt. Starting the war as commander of Battery M, 5th US Artillery, he soon was placed in charge of McClellan's artillery reserve and then replaced Barry as chief of artillery, Army of the Potomac, on September 5, 1862. The army commander mostly restricted him to administrative matters and allowed Hunt only limited operational influence. "It was through you that I kept myself informed as to the condition of all the artillery," McClellan wrote in July 1863, and "through you that I took the steps necessary to ensure its efficiency for action, movement, & its proper employment in battle." McClellan gave Hunt detailed instructions on how to handle the guns in engagements while relying on him to administer the guns with an inadequate staff as best he could between battles.[64]

When Burnside replaced McClellan in November 1862, he continued this arrangement without change. Hooker, who replaced Burnside in late January 1863, created a good deal of trouble for Hunt. The new army commander made it clear that the artillery chief would be restricted to administration unless he decided to grant him command for a specific and limited purpose. Hooker treated Hunt as just another staff member. He did not share operational orders with him, only feeding the artillery chief enough information so he could perform specific tasks, and even directed that the artillery reserve report to his own adjutant general rather than to Hunt. These were foolish measures that could only lessen the army's efficiency.[65]

Hunt was deeply disappointed. "My position is a painful one in some respects," he wrote Burnside in April 1863. "I have been deposed from my duty of the Art'y of the army, and notified that I am 'a mere staff officer' that my duties are such as a Major (in the words of Gen. Hooker) or a lieutenant (in the words of his chief of staff) can do just as well as I can." Hunt swallowed his pride and tried to survive the Hooker regime.[66]

Hooker's artillery management at Chancellorsville was a disaster. Chief of Staff Butterfield ordered the batteries around without expertise. We have already seen that even Hooker came to realize his system was not working during the course of the campaign and asked Wainwright to take full control of the guns. Wainwright did what he could but admitted the task was daunting.[67]

As a result, Hunt's position was far more secure after Chancellorsville. Hooker finally consented to the creation of artillery brigades but soon after was relieved from command. The relationship between Meade, Hooker's successor, and Hunt was bumpy at the start because the latter pushed for enlarged authority, clearly spelled out in writing, that the new army commander hesitated to provide. This tug developed right after Gettysburg, a battle in which Hunt exercised more operational control over the guns than at any previous time, although without written authority to do so. It continued into August, when Hunt, out of frustration, offered his resignation as artillery chief. While Meade was open to his departure, Chief of Staff Brig. Gen. Andrew A. Humphreys intervened and talked the two into a compromise. Hunt and Meade worked well together after that, even though the latter always supported the infantry side of any argument over artillery management.[68]

On August 21, 1863, Meade issued General Orders No. 82, which spelled out the duties and limitations of Hunt's role. The chief's responsibilities were both "administrative and executive" in nature. He was "responsible for the condition of all the artillery" and could command all batteries when they were not attached to infantry units. Hunt's executive powers, however, were limited. He could not interfere with corps- or division-level control over batteries during engagements and had to issue all his orders in Meade's name. Even the deployment of batteries in the army reserve had to be approved by Meade. In short, when it came to maintaining the batteries, Hunt had full sway; when it came to fighting them, he was one of Meade's staff officers.[69]

Wainwright was disappointed that Hunt did not achieve more independence, but twenty years later artillery officer and historian Birkhimer highly praised this order. Meade had, in his view, spelled out a good working relationship between the artillery chief and the army commander far better than any previous arrangement. "The order very nicely balances the various parts of a delicate machinery, the disjointing of which had caused serious inconvenience."[70]

Hunt reacted against Meade's order by proposing to reorganize the artillery in February 1864. He suggested the vesting of the artillery chief with full executive as well as administrative power by creating an artillery corps on the same level as the seven infantry corps and the Cavalry Corps of the Army of the Potomac. That would require his promotion in rank and a full staff. Meade rejected this proposal, as did Grant later.[71]

But Hunt remained a tireless and vocal proponent of enlarged responsibilities for artillery chiefs. His last try took place when planning the Grand Review in Washington, DC, at war's end. Hunt proposed that all batteries in the Army of the Potomac be grouped as an artillery corps, with himself at its head. "Forty batteries in one mass moving up Pennsylvania Avenue battery-front will be a sight worth seeing," commented Wainwright. But Meade doubted such a mass of carriages could negotiate the narrow streets of Georgetown at the end of the review, and the proposal was rejected. Instead, each artillery brigade marched at the rear of its corps.[72]

Hunt and Wainwright were unusual; no other Federal artillery officers thought so much about their branch of the service, especially in relation to the other branches. None pushed so persistently for enlarged organization and authority. In the process they contributed to a more turbulent, even poisonous atmosphere in the Army of the Potomac concerning artillery-infantry relations than existed in any other field army, North or South. And in the end, other than creating artillery brigades, they failed in their objectives.

In the Army of the Cumberland, Rosecrans defined the duties of artillery chiefs as inspectors of artillery, and a similar move took place in the Army of the Tennessee. The introduction of artillery brigades elevated the artillery chief in that it vested him with administrative power, but not executive. No one in either western army complained about it.[73]

THE CONFEDERATE ARTILLERY CHIEF

In 1875, when James Longstreet thought Lee's former artillery chief blamed him for the defeat at Gettysburg, the ex–corps commander asked a former staff member's opinion. "The idea of such an old *granny* as Pendleton presuming to give a lecture or *knowing anything about* the battle of Gettysburg," responded Thomas J. Goree. "Although nominally *Chief of Artillery,* yet he was in the actual capacity of Ordnance Officer and, as I believe, miles in the rear. I know that I did not see him on the *field* during the battle. It was a notorious fact and general[ly] remarked that he was almost entirely ignored by Genl. Lee, as Chief of Artillery, and the management of it given to the Corps Chiefs of Artillery."[74]

Goree was not alone in his opinion. Edward Porter Alexander remarked that Pendleton had "practically hidden himself out all day where nobody saw him" at Malvern Hill, and "no orders could find him." Many artillerists hoped he would be replaced by someone younger, more vigorous, and more up to date with developments in his branch.[75]

But these judgments were unfair. Pendleton was nothing like Hunt, but he had administrative ability even if lacking command presence on the battlefield. Pendleton understood that administrative care underwrote battlefield performance. He described his role in helping place the guns at Fredericksburg. "To do this systematically requires exact care on my part to have all the batteries, guns, etc., classified, so that every man may know his place, and every gun be rendered fully available at the right point and at the requisite moment." Moreover, he developed the concept of the artillery battalion and pushed it through to reality.[76]

An 1830 graduate of the US Military Academy at West Point who started the war as a battery commander at age fifty-two, Pendleton organized Lee's artillery arm, rearranged the assignment of batteries, and improved cooperation between the branches of service. Lee relied heavily on his services and never considered replacing him with a younger man. Pendleton obtained more and better ordnance, laid out fieldworks for the guns, and drafted legislation concerning artillery management for consideration by Congress. The War Department appreciated his skills and sent him to the Army of Tennessee before the onset of the Atlanta Campaign to evaluate its artillery. His role as a troubleshooter outside his field army was something Hunt never experienced.[77]

Lee appreciated another aspect of Pendleton—his religious stature. The artillery chief was an Episcopal minister and "a most lovable man," according to Jennings Cropper Wise. From the beginning, Pendleton held prayer meetings every morning and night and continued to preach after becoming artillery chief in the summer of 1861. On a typical day in June 1862, he performed "needful public duty in the early morning" and then preached at three different locations during the day. "It is good for me,—I trust it is for others,—for me thus to exercise my sacred calling while occupying this strange position." He responded to all requests from fellow artillery officers for his "Christian counsel."[78] "I had last week a long and pleasing talk with General Lee on the great question of religion," Pendleton wrote in June 1863. "I visited him on duty. He was alone and introduced the subject. He is in earnest. Wept a good deal as we talked of Jackson. He is deeply concerned for the spiritual welfare of the soldiers." Lee greatly valued Pendleton's spiritual support and personal friendship.[79]

Although not appreciated by the younger officers, Pendleton played an important role as Lee's artillery chief. In all other field armies, many men rotated in and out of the position, leaving behind little evidence of their presence. To illustrate this phenomenon, Capt. Smith P. Bankhead served for a short time as chief of artillery, First Corps, Army of the Mississippi, but did not like the position. "Believing that I could render more efficient service with my own battery than on the staff of the general," he petitioned for release from his duties.[80] In fact, it is difficult to determine how many men held the position of artillery chief in the Army of the Mississippi / Army of Tennessee when Beauregard and Bragg commanded it. At Shiloh Beauregard failed to mention having one when he led the army on the second day. Nor did Bragg mention an artillery chief at the Battle of Perryville. He had an acting chief at Stones River but apparently none at Chickamauga or during the Chattanooga Campaign.[81]

Johnston tried to find a good chief after assuming command of the Army of Tennessee early in 1864. Pendleton recommended a promising young officer from Lee's army; Johnston preferred Maj. Gen. Mansfield Lovell but accepted Brig. Gen. Francis A. Shoup. After Hood took over the army, he appointed Shoup as his chief of staff and named Col. Robert F. Beckham as artillery chief on July 26, 1864. Hood abolished the battalion as an administrative unit on November 14 and with it the position of chief of artillery. Beckham became artillery chief of Lee's Corps and was mortally wounded on November 29 during the advance toward Franklin. Capt. Charles Swett filed a report on the army's artillery following its disastrous Tennessee Campaign, but his title was inspector general of artillery.[82]

Only in the Army of the Potomac and the Army of Northern Virginia did the artillery chief cut a significant figure in artillery management. But even in those two forces, he was limited to administrative work and rarely given authority to command the army's guns in battle.

AN ARTILLERY BUREAU

On March 25, 1864, the officer who commanded British field artillery in Canada visited Hunt in Virginia. This Colonel Turner "spent the day and night with me," Hunt recalled, and filled him in on British artillery organization. The most striking bit of news was that all field units were grouped in one organizational structure, "that is a single corps for administration and promotion," Hunt told Wainwright.[83]

Turner's visit recharged earlier efforts to push for a similar organization in the United States. Regular artillery officers had advocated the dissolution of their artillery regiments and replacing them with a corps that encompassed all regular batteries in one administrative unit headquartered in Washington. After the Battle of Antietam, Hunt and McClellan had written a proposal to this effect, joining the Ordnance Corps with the proposed Artillery Corps and adding pontooniers. Although General in Chief Henry W. Halleck and Secretary of War Edwin M. Stanton had supported the proposal, Congress failed to act on it.[84]

Another push in this direction took place in the winter of 1863–64 before Turner's visit. Barry, Tidball, and other regular officers wanted to do away with the artillery regiments in the regulars but without replacing them with an artillery corps. Sen. Henry Wilson, Republican of Massachusetts and chairman of the Senate Military Affairs Committee, accepted the proposal for consideration.[85] Wainwright liked this latest development and supported it with a proposal to eliminate volunteer artillery regiments, replacing them with a corps organization for each state, complete with field officers and staff members, under control of the state governor. His scheme would have opened many opportunities for higher rank. Wainwright enlisted the support of Hunt, Republican senator Edwin D. Morgan of New York, Gov. Horatio Seymour of New York, and Vice Pres. Hannibal Hamlin. But like the Barry-Tidball effort, this failed to go any farther.[86]

All schemes to replace the artillery regiment with an artillery corps failed. A similar fate befell the effort to create an artillery bureau in Washington, DC. The artillery was the only major element of the military system without such a bureau. It is ironic that many infantry officers considered the artillery chief to be just another staff member, but they failed to recognize that all other staff members had a Washington bureau to support their work. Staff positions in ordnance, commissary of subsistence, adjutant general, medical care, and quartermaster all worked not only for the general they were assigned to in the field but also for a chief of bureau in their own specialization located in Washington or in Richmond. Only the artillerist worked only for his general.

Hunt and Barry were key players in the push for an artillery bureau. After serving as McClellan's artillery chief from August 1861 until September 1862, Barry became inspector of artillery for the entire Union army, but it was an anomalous position at best. In a practical sense he took charge of the guns placed in the defenses of Washington and at Camp Barry, a large outfitting facility near the capital. But there was no true head of the national artillery vested with authority to maintain all batteries across the nation at a high and consistent level of readiness—or even to maintain an archive to document its history—as there was for all the other bureaus.[87]

In April 1863 another major effort to create an artillery bureau surfaced. Barry informed Hunt that he had been asked to draft an order to organize one, although who originated that push is unknown. Barry needed his input, stating, "I want to strike this iron while it is hot."[88] The result was "A Bill for the Better Organization of the Artillery of the U.S. Army," jointly drafted by Barry and Hunt. It identified the regimental organization as useless and called for the creation of a chief of artillery for the US Army at the rank of major general. He would be in charge of a combined force of regular and volunteer batteries consisting of 75,000 artillerists, 1,300 fieldpieces, and 10,000 horses. The bill called for abolishing the Ordnance Department and merging most of its functions into the new bureau. It recommended that two-thirds to three-fourths of the guns in the field be assigned to divisions for battle and the rest retained in corps-level reserves. Most of the bill spelled out the many levels of rank needed to staff the bureau, which included one major general, seven brigadier generals, three colonels, and so on down to battery level.[89]

The Barry-Hunt proposal was the most ambitious effort to improve artillery management in the Civil War. It would have revolutionized the way field guns were administered. Brig. Gen. Truman Seymour suggested to Hunt that, if it was approved, Brig. Gen. Thomas W. Sherman would be the best candidate to head the bureau.[90] But this last reform effort of the war also failed to win enough support in Congress. Hunt was frustrated but not defeated. In January 1865 he tried to persuade Grant's chief of staff, Brig. Gen. John A. Rawlins, of his views. He argued that the artillery was more in need of a bureau than other support services because it actually engaged in combat rather than merely supplied fighting men with material. Artillery "forms one of the most powerful and costly elements of an army," he wrote. "Concentration is favorable to discipline, instruction, efficiency, and especially to economy." Hunt met with Grant in March 1865 but could not persuade the general in chief to support his proposal.[91]

Three problems blocked any effort for radical change in artillery management during the Civil War. First, Congress was reluctant to increase expenditures by enlarging the administrative network. Second, infantry officers were jealous of their control over the artillery. Last, thanks to the professionalism and dedication of most artillery officers, the arm already was largely fulfilling its role in the war effort. There is little doubt that an artillery bureau in Washington would have increased its effectiveness, but whether it would have made a huge difference is open to question. The fact that so much of this discussion centered on creating more slots of higher rank for ambitious artillery officers must have made everyone wary of the proposal. It tended to give the impression that artillery men wanted the enlarged apparatus largely to fulfill career goals.

THWARTED AMBITIONS

This last point must be taken seriously. Whenever Pendleton proposed a reorganization of artillery in Lee's army, one of its main purposes was to open new high-rank slots for officers. These efforts always came to naught for the same reasons that they did in the northern army. In fact, a great deal of Pendleton's time was taken up with efforts to obtain promotions for his officers.[92] But there always were too few slots to satisfy the hunger for advancement. "It is notorious," wrote Maj. Melancthon Smith of the Army of Tennessee, "that in our branch of the service (light Arty) promotion has been very slow, scarcely any at all, & I have in my command, Captains, who still occupy the positions in which they entered the service at the beginning of the war whilst in the other branches promotion has been rapid." Smith himself had tried more than a year before to transfer to a cavalry command, where he hoped to become a colonel, but without success.[93]

Similar problems existed in the Federal army. Congress authorized only one brigadier general for every forty companies of artillery. At Gettysburg the Army of the Potomac fielded 320 guns, over 8,000 artillery men, and 7,000 horses, roughly the equivalent of two or three infantry divisions. Yet there was only one brigadier general and four officers above the rank of captain to manage this large resource.[94]

"The false organization of the artillery arm in our service" not only limited its effectiveness but also provided "no way of rewarding . . . officers by deserved promotion," wrote Charles Wainwright. William T. Sherman agreed, noting that artillery officers "seem almost debarred promotion." Hunt exaggerated when he argued that the lack of a higher level of artillery management and promotions for deserving officers, all due to a false sense of economy among lawmakers, reduced artillery effectiveness by one-third to one-half.[95]

Of 583 generals in the Union army, 29 of them (4.9 percent) had been in the artillery service before the war. But of those 29, only 3 (Barry, Hunt, and John M. Brannan) held artillery commands when they were generals during the conflict. The rest (including Brannan for a time) held infantry commands after they transferred from the artillery service. A slightly higher percentage of Confederate generals fell into this category. Of 425 generals in gray, 26 (6.1 percent) had seen artillery service before the war. Only 4 of them (Pendleton, Alexander, Shoup, and Armistead L. Long) held artillery commands or staff positions when they were generals in the conflict.[96]

A further problem developed when artillerists left their arm for duty in other branches. John Gibbon retained his commission as captain of Battery B, 4th US Artillery while he commanded a brigade, division, and corps in the Army of the Potomac and a corps in the Army of the James. That barred Lt. James Stewart from promotion to captain even though he led Battery B with sterling success throughout most of the war.[97]

CONCLUSION

The effort to get away from dispersal to concentration was not, as historians have claimed, primarily for the purpose of massing guns on the battlefield. The primary purpose was to ensure better maintenance and administration of the batteries. Even in the concentration period, command of batteries in battle was in the hands of infantry officers. Those infantrymen produced a mixed record; some of them were ignorant about how to use the big guns, but some directed artillery very well. Another category, infantrymen who allowed their artillerists a free hand on the battlefield, also contributed to the success of both the dispersal and concentration systems.

The concentration system originated in the East and spread slowly and uncertainly to the West. But only in the East did artillerists continue to argue for more high-level artillery management. All efforts to push for an artillery bureau to match those of the quartermaster, ordnance, commissary of subsistence, adjutant general, and ordnance failed due to congressional resistance and the infantry's desire to retain control over the guns.

Hunt argued that the failure to create higher levels of management impaired the effectiveness of artillery. That is not strongly convincing. Dedicated battery and brigade commanders largely fulfilled their mission despite this failure. Much of this pushing for higher levels of management was motivated by a desire to open high-level slots for promotion of ambitious officers. It is difficult to believe that artillery effectiveness would have increased by one-third to one-half, as Hunt argued, if these slots had been available, and that was another reason for his failure to push through the creation of an artillery bureau. Institutional resistance greatly limited the expansion of the artillery management systems for many reasons during the Civil War.

9

. . . .

SOLDIERING WITH THE BIG GUNS

About 147,000 Federals and 62,000 Confederates served as artillerists during the Civil War. They were considered to be soldiers of a different order than those who served in the infantry and cavalry. According to *Instruction for Field Artillery,* members of the arm ought to be "intelligent, active, muscular, well-developed, and not less than five feet seven inches high." Henry J. Hunt thought they should be at least five feet, eight inches tall.[1]

Officers firmly believed that the value of their arm lay primarily in the quality of the personnel. "Batteries derive all their value from the courage and skill of the gunners," wrote John Gibbon, "from their constancy and devotion on difficult marches; from the quickness and capacity of the officers; and especially from the good condition and vigor of the teams, without which nothing can be undertaken." Joseph Roberts urged all artillerymen to stick to their guns at any cost on the battlefield. "Never until the VERY LAST EXTREMITY" should a piece be abandoned. The last rounds fired at a closing enemy would be the most destructive and the most important.[2]

Lt. Albert N. Ames of Battery G, 1st New York Light Artillery screened replacements sent to his unit during the heavy campaigns of 1864. He rejected three of nineteen because they were "not intelligent enough to learn readily & I doubt if they ever will make a decent soldier as they have not got the necessary brains." John H. Rhodes of Battery B, 1st Rhode Island Light Artillery agreed with Ames. He wanted men "quick to understand, also being able to perform the duties of two or more posts at the gun. . . . A slow, awkward person should hold no place in a gun detachment of light artillery." Above all, a good artillerist had to have grit. He "has to stand up and take his medicine like a little man," wrote Augustus Buell.[3]

Confederate adjutant Robert A. Stiles thought an artillerist needed "imperturbable *self-possession,*" the ability to stand up to punishment with a hardened attitude toward death and dismemberment. Those who could "step over the dead and dying bodies of their comrades . . . in the discharge of the doubled and trebled duties now devolving upon him" made superb artillerymen.[4]

William F. Barry, who served in both theaters, believed that the western states provided more good artillerists than the older states of the East. "The western life of officers and men, favorable to self-reliance, coolness, endurance, and marksmanship, seems to adapt them peculiarly for this special arm." He found Sherman's artillery "unusually reliable and effective" compared to that in the Army of the Potomac.[5]

Most enlisted men caught the sense that the artillery was a special branch of the army and often expressed pride in their arm. This esprit de corps was fostered by the many reports of heroism by enlisted men that were filed by their officers. Pvt. David W. Camp was only fourteen years old when he replaced the Number 5 man at a piece in Battery G, 1st Ohio Light Artillery at Shiloh. Camp worked "with the skill and bravery of an old soldier," reported his captain. Sgt. S. W. Allen of Battery D, 1st Michigan Light Artillery stayed with his gun at Chickamauga, firing his revolver to the last round "and came near being run through with a rebel bayonet, when he made his escape." More than one enlisted man was noted in reports for throwing an enemy shell out of the battery before it exploded, saving the lives of his comrades. A supreme act of courage was to keep the thumb on the vent to prevent premature discharge even though hit by bullets. Stiles witnessed an example of this at the Battle of Williamsburg when a member of the Fayette Artillery was hit in the leg and head but kept his thumb on the vent until the downward pressure of his falling body pulled it off.[6]

Enlisted men developed an appreciation of their guns. Many admired the aesthetics of the tube, speaking of it as "a thing of beauty." They became familiar with each piece and felt as if they were losing a comrade if they had to give one up. "Day and night every man has to stay right by his pieces," wrote John Merrilles. They "sit by it, eat by it, and sleep by it." Many gave names such as the Green Mountain Ranger, Black Bet, Sallie, and Do Do Baby to their pieces.[7] "My boy[s] love their Guns all most to Idolitry and well they may for they have helped them out of many tight places," wrote Capt. William Z. Clayton of the 1st Minnesota Battery. Stephen Pierson of the 33rd New Jersey was tickled

Fig. 9.1. Venting a Fieldpiece. The all-important task of closing the vent while spong-ing and ramming is illustrated in this image. Faithful performance of this duty on the part of the Number 3 of the gun detachment was literally a life-or-death issue for the Number 1, who performed the sponging and ramming duties. *Frank Leslie's Scenes and Portraits of the Civil War* (New York: Mrs. Frank Leslie, 1894), 247.

to see members of the 13th New York Battery stand by their guns after the Battle of Peach Tree Creek. An artillery sergeant "leaned against his piece, one arm thrown over it, patting it affectionately with his hand, as a mother might pat her child."[8]

Artillerymen learned to take care of their pieces. They manhandled them out of mud holes during marches and cleaned them up at the end of the day, sometimes clearing away the human blood and brains splattered over tubes and carriages after a battle. They learned to care for the ammunition too. "I have to open the caissons every day and dry the ammunition and sit right on the carriage myself and not trust it to any guard," wrote John W. Chase of the 1st Massachusetts Battery.[9]

Unit pride tended to be extremely high in the artillery, based on the inter-action of small, specialized groups of men. "Each of our Platoons, working a Gun, is a little Republic," concluded Thomas Christie of the 1st Minnesota Battery, "of which the Sergeant is chief Magistrate and the two Corporals his Assistants. Everything is done about the internal affairs of the Platoon without

Fig. 9.2. Members of Battery A, 1st Pennsylvania Light Artillery (Keystone Battery). The small group of men who manned a battery formed tightly knit relations because of their need to work as a team. Not only members of the gun detachments but also the drivers were part of that team. If this little community did not work smoothly, the battery's effectiveness was severely reduced. LC-DIG-ppmsca-33214.

consulting any commissioned Officer, the Sergeant and the Boys themselves being considered fully competent for all the various duties."[10]

CAMPAIGN AND BATTLE

A high level of pride was helpful when the hard realities of campaign and battle hit the men. Unless they served in batteries assigned to cavalry units, artillerists walked on the march; *"frogging it* as in Infantry" was the way Moses A. Cleveland put it. Only rarely were they allowed to ride on the carriages, but because the vehicles had no springs, doing so was "the hardest riding that a person ever was obliged to endure." The combination of heavy rain and dirt roads made "traveling mud heaps" of the carriages, splattering dirty water over anyone near the moving wheels. Some artillerymen used their tarpaulins as shelter from the rain if they had no tents, but Hunt forbade this practice, noting that these were issued to protect the special harness used by artillery horses. The men were allowed to transport their knapsacks on carriages but were severely restricted as to how much clothing and personal items they could carry.[11]

Firing a piece involved heavy labor, and fatigue became a common complaint among artillerists. At times they became too tired to serve the piece. Capt. Charles H. Lanphere reported that many men of Battery G, 1st Michigan Light Artillery "actually . . . fell from sheer exhaustion" at Chickasaw Bayou. Soft ground made it more difficult to move the gun forward after recoil, increasing their exertions. Losing comrades in action meant doubling duties for those remaining.[12]

Perhaps the weather more than any other factor led to exhaustion. Hot temperatures increased the physical strain on gun detachments. At times the men "stripped to the hide, with sweat and blood running down their bodies." At First Bull Run, half of the crew in John D. Imboden's battery "fell upon the ground completely exhausted" by the heat. For others, working the guns in hot weather became "*killing* labor." Federal gunners on the first day at the Battle of Corinth looked "more like coal-heavers than soldiers, with perspiration streaming down their faces blackened with gunpowder." For George Perkins of the 6th New York Battery, thirst caused by inhaling powder smoke and the concussion of the gun pounding on his chest weakened him considerably during firing at the Wilderness.[13]

SIGHTS

The experience of combat was highlighted by the senses. It was possible to actually see a projectile fly through the air "if the eye is almost exactly in the line of its flight," recalled Edward Porter Alexander. One man saw the fragments of a shell fly through the air when it exploded ten feet in front of him.[14]

In darkness, one could see the fuze burning in a projectile during flight. It produced a blue light, with sparks falling from the fuze hole. If in direct line the light seemed to hang stationary in the air as it approached. This visual experience always was accompanied by an aural experience, the shriek of the projectile as it passed through the air and the loud thud of its explosion.[15]

SOUNDS

"The music of such missiles is somewhat terrifying," admitted Charles Wellington Reed. For Frederick S. Daniel, it was startling to hear the near explosion of an enemy shell at First Bull Run because previously he had only heard them at a distance. This sound brought home the fact that someone was trying to kill him.[16]

Even so, many artillerists were thrilled to hear the guns in action. They could distinguish between the sounds made by different calibers and types and were excited to greater exertion by the stimulus of the noise. When Thomas Christie told his father about the effect that sound had on his level of enthusiasm, he assumed no one who was not an artillerist could understand his feelings.[17]

Of course, many artillerists found no comfort in the noise of battle. Some compared it to the explosion of a volcano, while others noted that the sound was amplified when firing at night. Men recalled the sounds made when projectiles hit something near them. Canister balls rattled "among the bushes like pebbles on the side of a house," wrote Henry Semple. "The sound of a tumbling Parrott shell in full flight, is the most horrible noise that ever was heard!" complained William Meade Dame of the Richmond Howitzers. It was "a wild, venomous, fiendish scream, that makes every fellow, in half a mile of it, feel that it is looking for *him particularly*."[18]

The effect of artillery sounds on the hearing depended largely on how far the guns happened to be from the hearer. It was possible to detect the sound from as far as twenty miles, according to some reports. At a distance artillery fire was a spectacle, nonthreatening and interesting. But up close many artillerists became temporarily deaf for several days after a heavy engagement, even though they put cotton in their ears. Philip D. Stephenson lived and worked in small enclosures of earthworks at Kennesaw Mountain in June 1864, and he was sure those confined spaces amplified the sound of firing pieces and bursting incoming rounds. "It was almost like a shell exploding in a room," he observed. August Bondi, a member of the 5th Kansas Cavalry who stood near two howitzers during an engagement, became deaf for life in his left ear because of it. Some artillerymen also suffered permanent hearing loss.[19] After the Battle of Port Republic in June 1862, Edward A. Moore went through an adjustment period. "My eardrums kept up the vibrations for hours. Sleep soon overcame me, but still the battle reverberated in my head." That adjustment period lasted three weeks for Patrick H. White of Battery B, 1st Illinois Light Artillery. He shivered all over every time he heard a loud noise after the Battle of Belmont in November 1861.[20]

CONCUSSION

Artillerymen had to contend with concussion, the forceful pressure of air against their bodies, far more than any other servicemen. The discharge of cannon produced terrible concussion, which individuals felt at differing levels of intensity. When Battery E, 1st Illinois Light Artillery fired a piece in the streets of Brandon, Mississippi, at retreating Confederates, the concussion broke all the window panes of the Shelton House hotel "with a magnificent crash" and caused civilians to flee in panic.[21] "It makes a fellow's head ring when the gun goes off," complained John Watkins. Leaning away from the piece, lifting one's heels off the ground, and keeping one's mouth open helped reduce the effect. Yet a member of the 1st Connecticut Battery "yelled with pain every time" a piece was discharged, complaining that it felt "like a sharp knife through the head from ear to ear."[22]

The explosion of incoming rounds also produced concussion. Augustus Buell was knocked down by a shell burst that led to "a queer numbness about my head and temporary deafness." William Meade Dame "distinctly felt the heat of the explosion on my skin, and grains of powder out of the bursting shell struck our faces, and drew blood. The concussion was terrific!" Many reported being moved several feet by the displacement of air produced by a projectile sailing within inches of their bodies, others of being knocked to their knees by the concussion. For some the "wind of a shell" produced delirium. For others it produced permanent damage. A sergeant of Battery A, 1st Illinois Light Artillery "injured his brain . . . in a critical condition" due to a close shell burst at Fort Donelson.[23]

BATTLE LOSSES

Batteries drew a lot of fire, but the casualty rate was about the same as for most infantry units. Loss ratios for various units ranged pretty widely. For Clark's Missouri Battery (CS), it was 4.2 percent at Iuka on September 19, 1862. But the 11th Ohio Battery lost 52.3 percent of all its personnel at Iuka while suffering a casualty rate of 85.1 percent among the men in its gun detachments.[24] But many men who were hit continued to perform duty. In Robertson's Florida Battery and Semple's Alabama Battery, about half the men injured by Union fire continued working the guns rather than seeking medical attention. During the Atlanta Campaign, the 5th Wisconsin Battery lost four men slightly wounded and a dozen others who were touched by spent bullets or pieces of shells but were not counted as casualties.[25]

To some extent the gun and carriage shielded members of the detachment from the effects of enemy fire. But in many cases incoming rounds splintered the carriage wood or broke off pieces of metal that in turn hit crewmembers. One man in Battery F, 1st Michigan Light Artillery was hurt by pieces of a bullet that splintered after smashing into the carriage.[26]

The nature of battlefield injuries ranged from slight to devastating. Men were burned when enemy fire exploded their ammunition boxes, and it was possible to lose both arms and both legs to a projectile. The latter tragedy happened when the individual sat on the ground, clasping his hands around his knees. Another man lost one leg and both arms while kneeling to cut a fuze.[27] And many artillerymen were killed when projectiles literally passed through their bodies.[28] The head became a gory, visible target of artillery fire. Many men were decapitated by incoming rounds or had only parts of their heads torn away, scattering bits of brain and fragments of skull around the site of instant death.[29] Other parts of the body were torn away, such as the chest of Capt. F. O. Claiborne, who commanded the 3rd Maryland Battery (CS). Oscar Legare, six feet tall and aged seventeen, was sighting a piece of the 5th Company, Washington Artillery at Peach Tree Creek when a Federal shell exploded "full into the face, head, and upper bodies" of himself and a comrade. The "two boys were torn to pieces from the waist up," wrote Philip D. Stephenson. "We found long strips of flesh high up on the trees behind them."[30]

These chilling examples were only part of the dangers attending battery service. Many artillerists were injured or killed when the process of serving the piece went wrong. Premature discharges were the most common accident. This happened most often in training before taking the field, but it could happen even in experienced units. Three premature discharges occurred in Battery A, 1st Ohio Light Artillery at Resaca in May 1864. In contrast, Battery H, 1st New York Light Artillery did not suffer an accident due to premature discharge until June 1864, three years after its organization.[31] Imperfect sponging was the most common cause of premature discharges, and that usually happened when Number 3 took his thumb off the vent too soon. Confusion accounted for some of these tragic accidents. A man mistakenly thought his piece had been fired and, when he advanced to the muzzle to sponge the tube, was caught by the discharge and lost an arm.[32]

Careless handling of rounds during firing led to a number of accidents. Members of the 6th Maine Battery at the Wilderness piled fixed rounds near breastworks that caught fire and set the charges off, wounding five cannoneers. Improper packing of rounds in the ammunition chests also led to trouble; they became unstable and could be set off by a jolt. A caisson moving over a railroad crossing near Huntsville, Alabama, exploded with "a flash of vivid light, a deafening boom, and a body-shaking jar," wrote Reuben Williams. The two men riding on it were "blown into fragments," the trunk of one ending up in a nearby tree. Two of the horses were dismembered by the blast, which killed a total of four men and four horses, with seven more men and horses injured.[33]

The carriages themselves became a source of danger. When Lumsden's Alabama Battery moved quickly at New Hope Church, one man fell as he was jumping onto a carriage. The wheels ran over his hips and crippled him for life. Other men suffered broken legs from similar circumstances. Handles were in place on limbers and caissons for men to hold, but none of the vehicles had springs. If they hit a rock or ditch, men could be thrown off. Robert Stiles was nearly killed when this happened to him.[34]

Carelessness accounted for many accidents to artillerymen. They were injured when pieces recoiled or were being moved about in position. Forgetting oneself and walking in the line of fire occurred as well. Charles Wainwright was nearly killed at Gettysburg when he forgot the position of one piece and almost walked into its line of fire, feeling the flash of powder on his face. While these accidents mostly resulted in survivable injuries, a member of the Charlottesville Virginia Battery at Second Winchester suffered an agonizing death when he tried to squeeze through a narrow gate at the same time that a piece was being driven through. The wheel came close enough so that the washer hook "caught and tore open his abdomen, dragging the poor wretch along by his intestines, which were literally pulled from his body in a long, gory ribbon."[35]

Finally, the horses proved to be a source of injury. Recalcitrant or frightened animals threw drivers, who sometimes were then run over by carriage wheels before they could get out of the way. Every battery, North and South, recorded at least a few injuries and some deaths due to horse-related incidents.[36]

COMBAT MORALE

It has become a trope among students of history to praise the bravery of all men in uniform. That tendency hides the fact that all soldiers are human; many of them are brave, but others fail the test of battle. Still others fall well within those two extremes, brave one day and ready to run the next. To do justice to history, we need to accept the fact that soldiers are as capable of good and bad conduct as anyone else.

The primary literature of the Civil War is filled with praise of soldiers written by their commanders.[37] But it also is filled with evidence of a lack of constancy under fire, and much of that resulted from a lack of commitment. There were some men who sought a place in the artillery because they thought it would be easier than infantry service. Hugh S. Gookin was afraid of being drafted and volunteered in "some good Artillery Corps" because he thought it "would be well enough to get as soft a place as possible." He wound up in the 2nd Company, Washington Artillery. We do not know how well he fared in that storied unit, but his attitude certainly did not fit the type of man most battery officers preferred.[38]

"I am obliged to accuse Privates Doolittle and Duff of cowardice," wrote Lt. Edward Brotzmann of Battery C, 1st Missouri Light Artillery after the Battle of Davis's Bridge on October 5, 1862; they "left their guns before the engagement commenced and never reported." At times the battery commander applied his own "severe punishment" for incidents such as this. Drivers sometimes lost their cool and fled a dangerous spot in panic, taking caissons and gun limbers with them.[39]

A major breakdown of combat morale took place at Williamsburg, when Wainwright sent in Capt. Charles H. Webber's Battery H, 1st US Artillery. Only one or two men were willing to man their pieces, while the drivers moved their vehicles so far to the rear as to be of little use. Webber, who was brand new to his unit, tried to exhort the men to better service but completely failed. Wainwright called on Battery D, 1st New York Light Artillery for volunteers to man Webber's guns, and many men responded. They kept the regular guns firing, which encouraged a few of Webber's men to come forward, though no more than about five for every piece in action.[40]

Hart's Arkansas Battery experienced a similar fate at Pea Ridge. It replaced Good's Texas Battery in a very dangerous spot and folded after ten minutes under fire. "They were literally cut to pieces and retired" without orders, wrote Capt. John J. Good. Hart's Battery was disbanded in disgrace, but Capt. William Hart personally redeemed himself when he volunteered to serve as a gunner for Provence's Arkansas Battery in a fight at Farmington, Mississippi, during the Corinth Campaign.[41]

Lt. George Norton's Battery H, 1st Ohio Light Artillery used deceit to escape heavy fire at Gettysburg. Positioned on the far left of Thomas Osborn's artillery line on Cemetery Hill, the men quietly dumped forty-eight rounds of ammunition into a nearby hole. Others saw them and reported to Osborn, who rode over and gave Norton a piece of his mind. Soon after, the battery raced away from its position. Osborn decided not to follow up on this dereliction of duty, which was a conspiracy between Norton and his men.[42]

Capt. Newit J. Drew led Company E, 1st Mississippi Light Artillery at Chickasaw Bayou but left the field on December 28, not showing up until the next morning. He was arrested that day but was never tried and eventually returned to duty. Lt. James C. Otey of Davidson's Virginia Battery abandoned his command during the Battle of the Crater. He was arrested and faced court-martial. When Capt. John B. Myers disappeared for two days at Shiloh, he was discharged from the service and his 13th Ohio Battery was disbanded. At Chickamauga Capt. Edward Grosskopff fired a few rounds that endangered friendly troops on the first day of the battle and "early disappeared from the field" on the second day.[43]

Crumbling under pressure was uncommon in the artillery arm of both armies, but it happened more often than students of the Civil War tend to realize. Dereliction of duty produced weak sectors unsupported by reliable artillery fire, and the incidents left a stain on the reputations of men that often never went away.

MAINTAINING MANPOWER

Artillery effectiveness demanded the maintenance of a minimum number and quality of men. For the most part it was possible to screen out poor material, but maintaining adequate numbers was more difficult. This was a more acute problem for artillery than for infantry or cavalry. Even if an infantry regiment dropped from an initial strength of 1,000 men to 300 (as many did by 1863) or even to 100 (as some did by 1864), it could still function in the field. But an artillery battery required an absolute minimum number of men to serve each gun. While it is difficult to fix that absolute number, we know that only two or three men were not enough. A piece needed nearly its full complement of nine men to work effectively. It also required at least two to six drivers to manage the limber and caisson for that piece.

Hunt stated that a six-gun battery needed at least 150 men to operate at a level of effectiveness. "The service of guns on the field requires a great amount of physical power. Under all circumstances the work is exceedingly exhausting, and when the number of men is much reduced it becomes too great for endurance." He pointed out that in the French army, a six-gun battery was allowed 234 enlisted men, and the British Army allowed about the same number. Congress only authorized 147 men for each Union battery, barely enough to man the unit. The inevitable drain on manpower, mostly due to disease, detailing to other duties, and combat losses, required a constant effort to find replacements. By November 1863 Hunt needed 1,945 new men for the volunteer batteries and 896 men for the regular batteries in the Army of the Potomac to bring their manpower up to standard.[44]

Dealing with manpower shortages by recruiting new men was haphazard at best. Neither army established an effective system of finding new enlistees; success depended entirely on how energetically the officers of a given unit pursued recruiting. Battery I, 2nd Illinois Light Artillery began the war with 102 volunteers in the fall of 1861, but only fifteen recruits joined the next year and sixteen in 1863. Eighty-one new men joined the battery in 1864, but they were on average two inches shorter and two years younger than the original enlistees, and almost all of them were foreign born. Wainwright received a heavy infusion of recruits into Fifth Corps batteries in the fall of 1864. It took a good deal of training to incorporate these men into his units.[45]

If sufficient recruits were not forthcoming, officers tried to conserve manpower by not exposing their men unnecessarily on the battlefield. They ordered them to take cover until time to return fire. This common-sense tactic worked to a degree, but at some point the gun crews would be exposed to incoming rounds just the same.[46]

To a certain degree, many men wanted to transfer permanently out of one branch of the army and into another (or even into the navy) for many different reasons. In some cases, this helped the artillery, while in others it simply increased the manpower shortage. Gen. Joseph E. Johnston tried to stop transfers within the Army of Tennessee, refusing to approve applications for men who wanted to leave Dent's Alabama Battery because he considered it "a confederate Battery" to be protected and nurtured, according to Capt. Stouten H. Dent. At the same time, Johnston refused to let men transfer from infantry regiments into artillery batteries, telling Capt. Thomas J. Key that all infantrymen "would go into cavalry and batteries if it were allowed, and that he would not transfer a soldier drilled in infantry to make a bad cannoneer."[47]

The Federal army did not hinder the transfer of artillerymen from or to batteries as did the Confederates. One sees examples of volunteer artillerymen wishing to transfer to regular batteries. Lt. Tully McCrea chose thirty-five volunteer artillerymen from a large batch of applications to enter his Battery I, 1st US Artillery in the fall of 1862. He assumed they wanted to get away from incompetent volunteer officers and found them to be "such good men."[48]

All methods of manpower maintenance noted thus far involved official recruitment or transfer of men. None of them alone sufficed; even all of them combined could not fully solve manpower shortages in batteries. So, for good reason, artillery officers relied heavily on temporary and informal means to acquire men for their guns. Often times during battle, officers asked nearby infantry regiments for help. Because of widespread illness, the 6th Massachusetts Battery could muster only forty men at the Battle of Baton Rouge on August 5, 1862. When Lt. William W. Carruth called on the 21st Indiana, that regiment supplied all the men he needed to get through the day. At the Battle of Champion Hill in May 1863, a couple of men from the 17th Ohio Battery implored troops of the 83rd Indiana for assistance. Isaac Jackson and five others of his company volunteered. They enjoyed the experience so much that five of the six decided to remain on duty with the battery for nearly a year.[49] Picking up on this theme, Rosecrans mandated after Stones River that each infantry regiment send ten men from every company to receive artillery instruction. This "proved of immense benefit," according to the historians of the 86th Indiana.[50]

A spirit of adventure and a willingness to help the common cause led thousands of infantrymen to lend a hand. When Pvt. John Marshall of the 24th Ohio fired all his cartridges on the second day at Shiloh, he "threw down his musket and served as a cannoneer." Even a citizen ambulance driver named Peter Carlin volunteered to serve a gun in Battery I, 1st US Artillery at the Battle of White Oak Swamp during the Seven Days Campaign. Men of the 39th Illinois left a sheltered spot to expose themselves while helping Battery E, 3rd US Artillery during Tenth Corps operations along the Richmond-Petersburg line in October 1864. At times generals even lent a hand at a battery during an engagement.[51]

Detailed Men

Battery commanders found a longer-term way to obtain infantrymen by securing authorization to detail them from their regiments for indefinite periods of time. This became the most important method of maintaining manpower. It avoided the finality of official transfer from one branch to another, bypassed the uncertainties of recruitment, and tapped into the spirit of interbranch cooperation that existed among some men in every arm of the service. This method relied heavily on the cooperation of officers in both the artillery and infantry. And if an artillery officer convinced his superiors to order it, even recalcitrant infantry officers had to obey.

The process of detailing men to temporarily serve in artillery units began early in the war. When Battery B, 4th US Artillery joined the Army of the Potomac in the fall of 1861, it had only 64 men. McClellan increased its strength by drawing a total of 117 men from half a dozen infantry regiments during the period October 1861 to June 1862. About 100 of them served the guns for the rest of their term of service while officially listed as on detached duty from their regiments.[52]

The staying power of Battery B's detached infantrymen was unusual, but the method of acquiring them was not. All batteries relied on detailed men from other units to maintain their manpower. They always drew a handful of men from each of several units so as not to drain one regiment of too many troops. Often they used these detailed infantrymen as drivers rather than placing them in gun detachments.[53] However utilized, these men underwent a crash course in how to handle artillery. If they were intelligent and sincere, this training proceeded quickly. But if they did not understand the importance of their job, trouble developed. Capt. Jacob Foster placed a detailed infantryman at the Number 3 post who simply did not understand why it was important to cover the vent while Number 1 sponged. The result was a premature discharge that took off Number 1's right hand and ruined one eye. Foster never assigned a detailed man to such an important job again.[54]

Judging by reports and personal accounts, however, most detailed men fulfilled their duties well and played key roles in the battery's success. This was especially so if they had volunteered rather than been ordered for temporary artillery service, indicating a prior interest in the work. "I like the Artillery much better than the Infantry," wrote Cyrus Morton Cutler of the 22nd Massachusetts after serving for a while with Battery C, 1st New York Light Artillery. He indicated that only twenty-five original enlistees still served the battery by August 1863; the rest were men detailed from many infantry regiments. An entire company of the 29th Iowa assumed artillery duty at Little Rock early in 1864. The men liked it because, said one, "we get rid of considerable hard duty."[55]

When there were no volunteers, infantry officers often chose their worst men for detail to batteries. Two such detailed men assigned to the 20th Ohio Battery "behaved very cowardly" at Chickamauga. Moreover, infantry officers often lobbied for the return of their detached troops. This produced "a continual struggle . . . between regimental and battery commanders for their possession," as Hunt put it.[56] Isaac Jackson became the pawn in such a struggle. He and several comrades shifted to Capt. Charles S. Rice's 17th Ohio Battery soon after the Battle of Champion Hill. A month later Col. Frederick W. Moore of the 83rd Indiana ordered all of them back to his regiment. They did not want to return and pleaded with Rice for help. The captain spoke with brigade leader Col. Stephen G. Burbridge, who supported the detailed men but was reluctant to issue an order concerning the matter. Moore became aggressive, sending troops to arrest the detailed men and to bring them back, but Rice stopped it. The result was a heated argument between the two officers. After that, Rice convinced Burbridge to issue an order allowing him to retain the detailed men. Moore "was quite mad when he found he was beat."[57]

Statistics indicate that detailed men made up a large proportion of artillery personnel. After examining reports, Wainwright found that 30 percent of First Corps artillerymen in the Army of the Potomac in February 1863 were detailed men. In Battery A and Battery F, 1st Rhode Island Light Artillery, nearly half the men were detailed from other units in June and December, respectively, in 1864.[58]

This heavy reliance on detailed men sustained many batteries for the long haul of their war service. In Battery A, 1st Rhode Island Light Artillery, 26.3 percent of all wartime personnel were detailed from infantry units. In Battery D, 1st Rhode Island Light Artillery, 34.5 percent were detailed. Interestingly, 53.2 percent of the detailed men in Battery D came from infantry units, while 46.8 percent came from other artillery units. In Battery F, 1st Rhode Island Light Artillery, 93 percent of the detailed men came from one infantry unit, the 5th Maryland, while the rest came from four artillery batteries.[59]

SOCIOECONOMIC BACKGROUND

It is interesting to ask what type of man was drawn to artillery service. Research has shown that those who volunteered to join batteries as regularly enrolled personnel rather than detailed from infantry units tended to have significantly different socioeconomic backgrounds compared to those who enlisted in the infantry and cavalry. Joseph Glatthaar's study of the Army of

Northern Virginia, based on a sample of 600 men, included 150 artillerymen, 150 cavalrymen, and 300 infantrymen. Glatthaar found that artillerymen were four times more likely than infantrymen and five times more likely than cavalrymen "to come from [the] top 100 cities" of the South. The proportion of farmers among them was half that of infantrymen; their occupational background tended to be linked to skilled trades, clerical roles, and professions. Artillerymen were less likely to be listed as absent without leave or to desert than their colleagues in the other arms. Their combat losses were higher than those of cavalrymen but lower than those of infantrymen.[60]

A study of 141 out of 258 men on the roster of Company G, 1st Mississippi Light Artillery tends to support Glatthaar's findings about the occupations of artillerists. Only 20.5 percent of them were farmers, while 26.9 percent were students and 7.8 percent were clerks. The rest ranged across the spectrum of craftsmen and artisans, tending to suggest city living. Of the original enlistees in the 1st Connecticut Battery, 34.2 percent were farmers. While higher than in other batteries, that proportion was still well below the average in the Union army.[61]

In contrast, a study of 220 men in the 9th Texas Battery based on census data, compiled service records, and county tax rolls indicates different trends than those of the Mississippi unit. Far more Texans were farmers, 56.7 percent, while the proportion of those engaged as skilled workers, in commerce, or in the professions was quite low. Only 6.7 percent were students. Much probably depended on where a particular battery was recruited. If it organized at or near a town, it likely drew more skilled men than farmers. Even infantry regiments organized at large towns or cities wound up with fewer rural men. The 12th Missouri (US) recruited largely from Saint Louis and the contiguous area across the Mississippi River in Illinois; only 28.5 percent of its men were farmers, a proportion only slightly more than half the national average.[62]

But the most likely factor that differentiated the socioeconomic background of artillerists from infantrymen and cavalrymen was the technical nature of the service. The "comparative mechanical elaboration and complexity, and the blending of scientific knowledge and manual and bodily dexterity" of artillery service was unique. Robert Stiles believed this drew "a broader-gauged man" to batteries.[63] The combination of technical or professional occupations with the nature of artillery service may account for the higher proportion of married men in batteries. Of 149 men who listed their marital status in the 1st Connecticut Battery, 36.9 percent were married. This was almost exactly the proportion of married men in Company A, 1st Mississippi Light Artillery. In contrast, of 791 men who indicated marital status in the 12th Missouri Infantry (US), only 9.3 percent were married.[64] Many artillerists mixed technical training or experience in civilian life with a taste for military matters. Jacob T. Foster attended an academy of science as a teenager. He did an apprenticeship with the state engineer of New York on the Erie Canal before moving to Wisconsin, where he worked as a surveyor, road builder, and railroad engineer. In Tennessee, Rutledge's Battery was re-cruited from among railroad workers by the chief engineer of the Nashville and Northwestern Railroad.[65]

The proportion of Confederate artillerymen who came from the slave-owning elite varied widely. In Company G, 1st Mississippi Light Artillery, 28.1 percent of 135 men were slaveowners. Adding them to those who belonged to a slaveowning family but did not personally own slaves, the proportion rises to 40 percent. That is much higher than average in the slave states. But in the 9th Texas Battery, the proportion was 20.9 percent, significantly below the average.[66]

OFFICERS

The role played by officers in maintaining artillery effectiveness was over-whelmingly important. In a small unit such as the battery, one man could exert enormous influence. He had an opportunity to establish personal re-lations with nearly every subordinate and create a good impression with ev-ery word. The men admired certain qualities in a battery captain, including courage, optimism, strong discipline without harshness, and a knowledge of his chosen branch.[67]

The artillery officer had to be a good military manager. Although small, the battery was a complex unit. Albert Ames pointed out that he was responsible for $80,000 worth of government property. "You little know how much one has to look after with a Battery," Lt. Marshall Miller complained to his wife when he temporarily took charge of Battery F, 1st Michigan Light Artillery. He superintended the feeding of men, horses, and mules while filling out half a dozen sets of reports and returns every month in addition to moving and fighting the battery. "I have gotten sick of being Captain," Miller admitted. "There is too much responsibility for me."[68]

While Miller recognized his limitations, other artillery officers did not. Field service weeded out those found wanting, and their men often were the severest judges. "The company is going to the dogs," complained Henry Robinson Berkeley of the Hanover Virginia Artillery. "Bravery alone will not keep up a battery. It requires a hard-working, industrious man of good executive ability; one who never tires, and is always on the lookout for his men and horses." The battery was broken up, and the incompetent captain, George Washington Nelson, secured a staff position.[69] Even when officers knew the technical side of their branch, they were not necessarily good commanders. Maj. Robert A. Hardaway was "an excellent artillerist, a good shot, and very fond of the scientific parts of the service, but not good at managing men, [and] hard on his horses," wrote Col. Stapleton Crutchfield. "He is rather indifferent to what he regards as the drudgery of the service." This crushing evaluation had no effect on Hardaway's career; he was promoted and continued to lead a battalion for the rest of the war, impairing efficiency the entire way, no doubt.[70]

No one was better at evaluating artillery officers than William N. Pendleton. He often suggested that certain men could perform better service in other branches. Pendleton found some of them lacking in energy or administrative skill, but because they were brave and did not impair effectiveness too much, he felt justified in retaining them. In both armies boards of examination evaluated artillery officers and recommended some be relieved or shifted to other duties.[71]

Bad captains ruined batteries and good captains rehabilitated them. Davidson's Virginia Battery collapsed at the Battle of the Crater. Capt. George S. Davidson had resigned a few days before the engagement, citing advancing age (he was forty-eight years old) and his inability to purchase a horse. Maj. Wade H. Gibbs, the battalion commander, wanted Lt. John H. Chamberlayne to replace him. Chamberlayne had already rehabilitated the Crenshaw Virginia Battery in time to perform well at Chancellorsville, but he was captured during the Pennsylvania Campaign and lost the opportunity to be assigned permanently to command that unit. He was serving on Gibbs's staff at the time, and orders for him to command Davidson's unit were issued on July 28, 1864.[72] But before Chamberlayne could assume command, the Federals blew the mine at Petersburg, and Davidson's battery was in a key position to fire at the follow-up attack. Davidson was gone already, so Lt. James C. Otey held command. He folded under the pressure, and the men mostly followed his example. Gibbs and a couple of staff officers served a gun in the battery for a while until the major was severely wounded, then its cannon fell silent again. His replacement rounded up enough volunteers from other batteries and infantry units to resume firing, but the battery failed to do its share in the battle.[73]

Chamberlayne took charge right after the engagement. Otey now was facing a court-martial, and the only other officer in the battery had already been found incompetent by a board of examination. Chamberlayne hoped to whip the unit into shape. "I have a difficult task," he told his mother. "To reorganize, furnish the men with many needful things, discipline them & all the time working in the trenches, & fighting a little every day. But the men are willing." He noticed a big improvement by early September; the most important sign of it was that, "I like them & they obey me & seem to like me." A month later Chamberlayne told his mother: "I found them a mob, they are now soldiers, in a month or two they will be good soldiers, in six months excellent. Of the peasant class they are ignorant slovenly & timid, but docile, obedient & capable of being made regular soldiers."[74]

Officers were the key to unit effectiveness. Of course, there was a danger that the necessary gulf between officer and enlisted man could be compromised. When Osborn became Howard's chief of artillery, he thought "a less feeling of equality between officers and men would add" to the already high level of efficiency in the Army of the Tennessee's artillery.[75]

In contrast to the artillery officer hungering for promotion outside his branch, just as many preferred to stay with the big guns. Edward Porter Alexander enjoyed the scientific and technical challenges of artillery service and recognized that "so very few educated & trained officers" could handle those challenges. "Mere rank" did not entice him to another branch. Alexander was never happier than when contemplating what his artillery battalion could do on the battlefield. "My spirits rose with a delicious sense of the wicked power of which I was in control, & which I was soon going to turn loose upon our enemy."[76]

In the Union forces Wainwright's "highest ambition . . . was to earn a solid name in the army as a first-class officer in my own arm of the service." He had "visions of some occasion on which I might gallop half a dozen batteries into position at the decisive moment" of a battle. While those visions never materialized, Wainwright devoted his skill and energy to making the Army of the Potomac's artillery as effective as possible.[77]

NONCOMMISSIONED OFFICERS

The noncommissioned officers also exerted influence in making batteries effective in the field. They were middle-level managers in charge of gun detachments and caissons, implementing orders from officers while keeping the privates in line. Battery commanders often praised them. Their duties were "by no means trifling," as Lt. Andrew T. Blodgett of Battery H, 1st Missouri Light Artillery put it. Chiefs of gun detachments received accolades for coolness under fire and accurate shooting when it counted. Because of a shortage of lieutenants, Orderly Sgt. J. J. Dengl commanded a section of the 3rd Iowa Battery at the Battle of Helena on July 4, 1863, and "showed himself to be emphatically an artillery officer."[78]

DRIVERS

About half of the privates in a battery served as drivers. Six of them handled the teams associated with every piece (three to drive the limber-piece combination and three to drive the limber-caisson). In addition, drivers managed the battery's wagon, forge, and baggage wagons. They were the most overlooked artillerists compared to the men who worked the cannons, but they played a vital role. The battery was immobile without them. The driver's role was nearly as complex and required drilling just as rigorously as that of the gun detachment.[79]

At first, it was natural for the rural recruits to become drivers because of their familiarity with horses, for they had to care for two animals each. But it was unwise to restrict anyone to only one role. With time the drivers were given instruction on the piece so they could replace members of the gun detachment as needed. And it always was a good idea for the gun crews to learn the rudiments of handling horses. In good batteries a tight bond developed between drivers and crewmen based on mutual respect and a willingness to help each other when necessary. Drivers suffered attrition due to illness and battle injury and had to be replaced quickly if the unit hoped to remain mobile. Once, a Federal battery received authorization to hire black drivers when it could not find replacements from any other source. These African Americans were paid at the same rate as teamsters.[80]

Not everyone could drive an artillery team. Thomas Penniwell tried his best when joining Battery I, 2nd Illinois Light Artillery but could not handle horses, so he became a gunner. Lewis F. Lake joined Battery B, 1st Illinois

Light Artillery early in 1864 and was assigned to be a driver. "Now as I never could manage one horse under a saddle, you can perhaps imagine the boy that never liked to ride a horse take the charge of two and manage in a battle. The very thought of it made my hair stand on end." He explained all this to his commander, who then shifted him to a gun detachment.[81]

That his commander so readily assented to Lake's viewpoint indicates how much officers wanted confident, reliable men to drive the horses. And yet they sometimes risked those valuable men when the situation demanded it. Lt. Samuel N. Benjamin dismounted a dozen of his drivers and set them to carry ammunition and serve his guns during a hot exchange at Second Bull Run. Other officers were compelled to give muskets to their drivers and send them to man trenches at Petersburg.[82] Even their normal duties exposed drivers to danger. They were wounded by shell fire. Horses became nervous when their familiar rider was gone and performed less assuredly under pressure. Adding to the strain of battle was the fact that drivers often had to move their carriages over ground littered with dead and wounded men and horses. They tried to avoid running over them, but sometimes it was impossible unless they had the time to stop and move the bodies to clear a passageway.[83]

Some drivers were found wanting in the stress of combat. For example, Capt. Felix H. Robertson threatened to shoot several drivers who were about to run away so that he could hitch up a few pieces when Breckinridge's Division was repulsed and in retreat at Stones River.[84] But those who failed the test of combat were in a minority. Most drivers, like the majority of their comrades in the artillery arm, managed to endure the experience of battle in ways acceptable to their superiors. Capt. Edward Bouton of Battery I, 1st Illinois Light Artillery recalled that Sherman confessed something to him one day in December 1862. "He had felt a great concern regarding what we should do for field artillery," Bouton wrote. It had been thought in the prewar army that three years' training and experience had been necessary to make a good artilleryman, and in Europe it had been posited that five to seven years were necessary. Sherman need not have worried, for most volunteer artillerymen in the United States managed to achieve a level of proficiency in a matter of months rather than years. There was no time, as there was in peace, to take one's leisure in learning the bloody trade.[85]

10

. . . .

ARTILLERY HORSES

A rtillery horses were animal combatants, although within the context of human experience they were draftees rather than volunteers. Most of them responded reasonably well to their specialized training and outfitting, becoming reliable warriors, but some never accepted their unrequested role as soldiers and fought back. Their war service was a story of human-animal interaction. It involved tragedy, as thousands of horses were killed in combat and many thousands more died of rampant diseases. But the story also is one of caring, even love, between many drivers and their horses. Equines often formed bonds with some of their human counterparts, while experiencing nothing but neglect or cruel treatment from others. To a limited degree, artillery horses could exercise agency, but mostly that was by fighting back against their drivers or escaping army service. Of all the unsung heroes of the war, horses rank high on the list of overlooked soldiers.

It has been estimated that seven and a half million horses lived in the United States on the eve of the Civil War. About three million equines (horses and mules) were used by the Union and Confederate armies from 1861 to 1865, and at least 261,672 of them were in the artillery. These animals were, as historian Ann N. Green has put it, "the most industrialized of the army's horses" because they pulled the heaviest loads.[1]

The weight of the artillery piece and their exposure to fire meant horses had to be carefully selected for their physical attributes and trained to endure the sounds of combat. They also had to work within a team of six horses, which was guided by three drivers, to maneuver the heavy gun and its accompanying limber over rugged terrain and often around the bodies of men and other horses littering the ground.

Because horses were "the main dependence of a light battery," *Instruc-*

tion for Field Artillery urged officers to become "thoroughly acquainted with the[ir] natural history." By this the authors meant knowing how to feed and care for them. The manual included a great deal of information about the animal. Its front was forty inches wide and its length ten feet. The travel time was on average four and a half minutes to walk for 400 yards, two minutes to trot the same distance, and one minute to gallop. Their "labor is excessive" compared to that of any other equine in army service. Therefore, the average daily march rates were slower. While infantry could move fifteen miles in six hours, artillery needed ten hours to cover the same distance.[2]

Artillery horses worked differently than did animals hitched to wagons. They used a specially designed harness because the mechanics of pulling the gun and limber were quite different from pulling a wagon or carriage. The animals worked with what the manual called "quick draught," pulling mostly through "the weight thrown into the collar than by muscular exertion." The authors believed that one artillery horse could not be expected to draw more than 600 pounds (compared to a draft horse, which could pull 1,600 pounds). John Gibbon, however, argued that the artillery horse was capable of pulling much more than the manual stated, up to 1,800 pounds "on a good smooth road." But he admitted that was unusual and should not be expected except under the right conditions.[3]

The manual spelled out the qualities of an ideal artillery horse. It should be from five to seven years old and fifteen hands, three inches tall. Its weight should be between 1,100 and 1,200 pounds. "Well broken to harness, free from vice, perfectly sound in every respect, full chested, . . . full barreled, with deep broad loins," and "solid hind quarters." Large hoofs and good feet were preferable. Gibbon devoted several pages of his handbook to discussing how to examine a horse, which included using its teeth as a guide to its age and general health. "Long-legged, loose-jointed, long-bodied, or narrow-chested horses should be at once rejected," cautioned the manual, "as also those which are restive, vicious, or *too free* in harness."[4]

The standard team for each combination of limber and piece, and for every combination of limber and caisson, was six horses arranged in three teams of two each. The forward team was known as the lead, next was the middle, and last (next to the limber) was the wheel team. A driver who rode on the left horse guided each team, controlling his mount plus the horse to his right. Of course, such a combination demanded a great deal of training to achieve concert of effort.[5]

Whether to add more horses to artillery teams became a point of discussion during the war. The manual allowed for additions if needed, up to eight horses for some pieces. Gibbon pointed out that the smaller the team, the more easily it was handled by the drivers, and he believed that more than ten horses were "very difficult to manage." Most officers settled on the regulation six horses per team no matter how heavy the gun. Even those in units assigned to accompany fast-moving cavalry felt that more than six horses per team failed to give them greater mobility. Battery commanders increased the size of their teams if they encountered rough roads or steep slopes, but they did not maintain that larger number as a rule.[6]

Counting the teams pulling limbers and caissons with those pulling the wagons and forges, batteries typically fielded about as many animals as men. When the 14th Massachusetts Battery began the Overland Campaign, it contained 120 horses compared to 132 men. The Army of the Potomac entered the 1864 campaign with a total of 24,492 horses; most were cavalry mounts, but 5,158 were artillery animals, constituting 21 percent of the army's horses.[7]

Battery commanders tended to not only select the right kind of horse but also assign them logically into teams. They placed the heavier horses in the wheel team, next to the limber or caisson, while lighter, smarter, and more agile horses wound up in the lead team. Average animals filled the ranks of the middle team. Drivers were selected on the same basis, with heavier men controlling the wheel team.[8] For some officers, teaming horses of the same color produced desired aesthetic appeal. "These teams were perfectly matched and any pair of them would be likely to attract attention if driven through any city attached to a carriage," wrote Capt. Edward Bouton of his horses. Frederick W. Wild of Alexander's Baltimore Battery (US) wanted to avoid drawing attention, arguing that light-colored animals were "too easily seen by the enemy" and became good targets.[9]

NATURE OF HORSES

Horses are among only a dozen or so species that have been domesticated out of some 4,000 species during the past 10,000 years. That process of domestication, which started about 6,000 years ago, has created a tight bond between horse and man. Both parties acquired something useful or important to them by agreeing to work with each other. Horses are natural bonding animals; they socialize a lot with each other, recognize a pecking order, understand the body

Fig. 10.1. Battery B, 2nd US Artillery. In this interesting photo the battery is in the formation Order in Line. The first echelon consists of the piece and limber, drivers are seated on the left horses of each six-horse team, and the six Napoleons are in an irregular line. The second echelon consists of the members of the gun detachments on horses, signifying that the battery has been converted to horse artillery to accompany cavalry forces. The third echelon consists of the limbers and caissons. The salient visual impression of this photograph is the large number of horses used by a cavalry battery. LC-DIG-ppmsca-33200.

language of that order, and respond to self-assurance and authority. They are apt pupils for training because they are sensitive to cues and respond to them readily, but they can be resistant if not treated properly.[10]

We should not think in terms of extremes when considering the horseman relationship. It is not dominance by man over a brute creature, nor does it consist of full independence by the animal. It is instead a working relationship between two sentient beings, a give-and-take that both have willingly engaged in. The relationship can run the gamut but far more often settles into a pattern somewhere in the middle of the spectrum that is comfortable for both horse and man. It has always been this way. Animal agency is often discussed in the literature of animal studies in a controversial manner. The extent to which it exists is the extent to which the relationship between animal and man is flexible enough to allow it at any given moment. Yet it is very real and must be taken into consideration. Man's agency within that relationship is also limited; there are only so many things he can coax a horse into doing.[11]

Perhaps the best model for understanding horses in war is the relationship between performance animals and the people who train them, ride them, or perform with them. Studies of race horses and sea mammals at water theme parks show that intense training regimens produce results, although it is not because man is compelling ignorant animals to perform by repetitive actions. Whether it is a racehorse or a dolphin, a great deal of intelligence and cooperation is offered by the animal. They learn quickly how to work with the trainer/performer. And within the performance, there is room for variation. Race horses often ignore the signals of their jockeys and run at the speed or pace of their own judgment. Variations within the canned performance of a dolphin at a theme park often take place because the sea mammal wishes to relieve boredom, forcing the human co-performer to adjust his or her own routine. The animal and the human, engaged in the same repetitive action, are largely in the same category. Both are doing the routine to make a living; both are cogs in the entertainment industry.[12]

The same could easily be said of artillery animals and soldiers in the military industry. There was a difference, of course, in the nature of their work. "Horses are not inherently afraid of battle the way humans might be," noted Ann Green, "because for them it does not exist until they experience it." But when confronted with evidence of combat, they were sensitive to its threat. Sights, sounds, and smells triggered warnings of unexpected and dangerous things to come. Training could help the horse deal with these things: "they listen for and trust the voice of rider or driver."[13]

Good Civil War artillerists understood the nature of the horse. One of them called it "a curious, shy, inquisitive animal" that needed "to be handled with great care and patience." Frederick Wild learned through experience not to appear excited while harnessing his team during a sudden alarm. If the horse sensed fear or anxiety, it did not cooperate. Like humans, horses differed in their temperament and personality. "Some were brave," continued Wild, "some were cowards, some were nervous and easily frightened, some were exceed-

ingly ambitious, others were indolent and lacked ambition, others were intelligent, [and] some were absolutely ignorant."[14]

Soldiers were more than willing to give brave horses their due, calling
many of them heroes. Edward A. Moore remembered one whose forefoot was
severed by a shell explosion. Even though its harness was taken off and put
on a replacement, the injured animal continued to move near the spot in the
team it was accustomed to filling when the battery moved off, trying to keep
up with its comrades. Someone had to stop and shoot it.[15]

But some horses refused to adjust to the military regimen and never became good warriors. Every battery had its share of animals who kicked, bit,
and balked every time someone tried to put on harness. One horse with Battery
B, 1st Illinois Light Artillery threw its driver, knocked over the other horse in
the team, and mixed "horses, drivers, limber and harnesses in an unmerciful
manner" while drilling. Unpredictable animals were the bane of many batteries. At times it was possible to solve the problem by placing an unruly animal from lead to middle team. According to John Billings, some refused duty
in any position and died of the strain imposed on them by military service.[16]
Many artillerists were injured by kicking, biting horses. During the Battle of
Williamsburg, a horse of Battery H, 1st New York Light Artillery suddenly
kicked Charles Wainwright, placing his hoof just below the officer's stomach
and, as he recalled, "throwing me halfway across the road; an inch higher or
lower would have ruined me for life if it did not prove fatal." But even a kick
to the head did not necessarily prove fatal for some fortunate artillerists.[17]

Training was the key to making horses reliable combatants. They underwent a drill regimen nearly as intense as that for men. It started with the
basics, accustoming the horse to the saddle, bridle, and harness. Then it proceeded to mounting and dismounting and pairing animals together in teams.
It gradually escalated to include simple and then complicated formations and
maneuvers and changing gait from one speed to another. This progressive
training did not always proceed quickly. Jacob Roemer recalled that it took
two weeks to break the horses into accepting saddles and to begin to respond
to drill instruction.[18]

On completing the first phase of training, man and horse were accustomed
to each other, the latter willing to accept harness and guiding equipment.
Both were ready to enter the second phase, which involved instruction in
formations and maneuvers. Here was where the best preparation for field

service took place. Most horses that had reached this stage were willing to learn, trusted their drivers, and were eager to cooperate with the other teams. "Horses enjoy the excitement, and they learn to know different commands of the bugle," wrote a man in the 24th New York Battery. The animals readily identified the short, pungent sounds of the bugle with certain things their drivers urged them to do. Firing blank charges while the team rested nearby presented the horse with an unusual and threatening sound. Many jumped instinctively when hearing cannon fire, but calm and confident handling by the driver taught them there was nothing to fear.[19]

As herding animals, horses usually were willing to go along with the flow. Recalcitrant animals often calmed down when they realized the other team horses were calm. It helped if drivers moved them around so they could become accustomed to wheel, middle, and lead positions and better understand team dynamics.[20]

In the process of training and serving together, man and beast often developed bonds of affection. Lewis Sykes treated his horses "as friends and cared for them as faithfully as he would have done for any human being," wrote an admiring comrade. John E. English of the same unit loved Ned so much that when the horse was shot in battle, he cradled his arms around its neck, "crying and trying to help the poor horse to his feet and get him away from the battle field." Drivers often named their charges. Old Saturn earned his name because at first he seemed disposed to take a bite out of anyone who came near but with time became calm and gentle. Hercules seemed to denote a pride in the strength of a horse. Moses became the name of an animal that was smart, faithful, and "responded to kind treatment by being willing to do all that I wished him to do," wrote Frederick Wild. "We soon learned to understand each other." Don C. Cameron of the 1st Wisconsin Battery felt that drivers benefited greatly from their intimate contact with horses. It "kept them more humanized and nearer to God."[21]

On many battlefields, just like their human counterparts, some artillery horses forgot their training and lost their nerve. They threw drivers and injured them or ran through lines of friendly infantrymen, hurting them as well. Horses became "perfectly ungovernable," as Lt. Harry C. Cushing of Battery H, 4th US Artillery wrote of their conduct on the second day at Chickamauga. When heavy fire descended on Fenner's Louisiana Battery during the North Anna phase of the Overland Campaign, the horses were the first to suffer. All

Fig. 10.2. 1st New York Battery. In this photo the battery also is in the formation Order in Line, but the drivers have dismounted and are standing beside their horses. The photographer lined up the image to emphasize the 20-pounder Parrotts. Horses and limbers are carrying the men's baggage. A two-wheeled battery wagon, identifiable by its curved top, is barely visible in the background. LC-DIG-cwpb-01029.

of the animals at one gun went down, and when three horses of another were shot, the rest "saved themselves by running away."[22] These instances of horse failure in combat probably can be explained by inadequate training. Not every driver was capable of properly nurturing his pair of horses to their full capacity. In this the animals mirrored the experience of soldiers, who also relied heavily on good examples and guidance from their officers.

Drivers not only prepared their horses for combat but also took care of them on a daily basis. The manual stipulated the daily ration as twelve pounds of grain (oats, corn, or barley) and fourteen pounds of hay. Four gallons of water also was part of the daily ration. The manual allowed for 100 pounds of straw per month to serve as bedding for the animals. The combination of grain and hay was important. "Corn alone will not keep horses in condition," wrote Capt. John B. Rowan. In fact, he thought a steady diet of grain alone left the animal vulnerable to disease. Corn certainly produced health problems when it was moldy and rotting, leading to scours, a form of diarrhea.[23]

Providing adequate amounts of hay proved to be the most difficult logistical problem of the war. Hay was a bulky item, often baled into compact bundles for easier transportation but more often shipped loose. Either way it took up more space on river steamers, coastal vessels, and railroad cars than any other supply item. Moreover, the demands of war led to periodic shortages, even for the agriculturally rich northern states. If hauling room was short, horse feed was the first item to be dropped on the assumption that it could be found in local areas wherever troops were stationed. But that assumption often proved to be false. "We will do what we can with buds, grass, & c.," wrote Pendleton at one point. Sometimes the animals were fussy about what they ingested. Horses raised in the mountains of southwest Virginia refused the water found in the tidewater of the state as impure. Philip D. Stephenson was grateful when quartermasters provided horse feed; when the men's rations fell short, they ate some of the animals' corn.[24]

Food shortages for horses occurred many times, although they tended to be worse among the Confederates. Hungry horses chewed the poles of their caissons after forty-eight hours without rations at Stones River. The Army of the Potomac reduced the ration to five pounds early in the Overland Campaign, and it affected the strength and stamina of the horses. Even when it was raised to ten pounds, that hardly sufficed to sustain them. "I feel very bad when I look at my horses," wrote Cushing at Chattanooga, "and see what wrecks they *are* and remember what splendid animals they *were*" as a result of food shortages.[25]

Beyond feed, horses required a great deal of attention to maintain their health. It was necessary to rub them down with straw to restore circulation to their body parts burdened by harness or saddle. Everything depended on the reliability of drivers; good soldiers took care of their horses, and bad soldiers neglected them. Lt. Jacob Federhen, "a lover of the animal," was put in charge of horses in the 1st Massachusetts Battery and "pursued a careful system of feeding, watering, and grooming." Wild took charge of a small mare that had sores on her legs and was ridden with lice. By careful washing with soap, he rehabilitated her health. She became "affectionate as a child" and was devoted to him.[26]

Good care became especially important when disease struck the artillery horse population. Gathering tens of thousands of animals together produced a prime breeding ground for communicable diseases, and the horses paid a heavy price. The first signs appeared in the fall of 1861, when a "distressing hoof disease" afflicted the Army of the Potomac. It quickly rendered unserviceable nearly 40 percent of the animals in Battery B, 1st Rhode Island Light Artillery. Glanders, a communicable disease that produced high fever and thick nasal mucus, appeared in the Army of Northern Virginia at the same time. It spread to become the worst of several horse diseases during the war, killing tens of thousands of animals North and South. Efforts to quarantine or kill horses failed to prevent its spread. Of 145 horse deaths recorded in the 10th Massachusetts Battery during the war, 53 of them perished because of glanders. That represented 36.5 percent of the total deaths in the battery and 75.7 percent of the deaths by disease.[27]

Neither army was prepared to deal with widespread horse diseases. There were very few trained veterinarians in the United States when the war broke out, and drivers relied on hearsay and folk remedies to deal with illnesses. One strategy was to establish recovery camps where ill horses could be separated from healthy animals. The success rate was pretty encouraging if the animal was only worn down by hard service but very poor if suffering from a deadly disease.[28]

WEAR AND TEAR OF CAMPAIGNING

Besides disease, the wear and tear of campaigning imposed a heavy strain on artillery horses. Short rations, long hours hauling heavy equipment over rough terrain, and presenting a large target to enemy fire combined to make campaigning and combat very dangerous enterprises.

Campaign and battle conditions often led drivers to keep their animals harnessed for days at a time, which proved a serious burden for the horses. The harness was large, heavy, and complicated. The *Ordnance Manual* devoted more than twenty pages to describing it. None of the drivers had worked with such a harness before. They learned to take almost as much care of this item, laying it out to prevent entanglement and oiling the leather, as they did with the horses.[29]

Worn for days at a time, the harness rubbed a horse's hide and produced sores. Combined with sweat, the problem worsened until hair and hide came off with the harness when it finally was taken off the animal. Afflicted horses in the 1st Connecticut Battery required two weeks to heal from such suffering; they were lucky. Battery A, 1st Ohio Light Artillery lost fifteen horses wounded during the Chickamauga Campaign, but its captain estimated he would lose twenty-five more due to harness sores.[30]

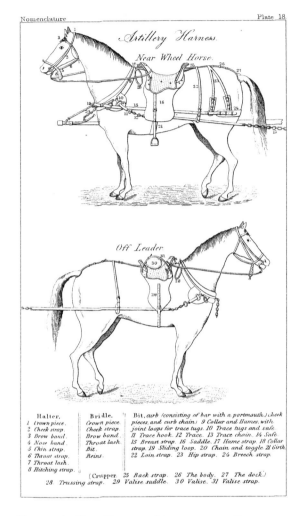

 Plate 18

Artillery Harness.

Near Wheel Horse.

Off Leader

Halter.	Bridle.	Bit, curb (consisting of bar with a portmouth,) cheek
1 Crown piece.	Crown piece.	pieces, and curb chain.) 9 Collar and Hames, with
2 Check strap.	Check strap.	joint loops for trace tugs. 10 Trace tugs and safe.
3 Brow band.	Brow band.	11 Trace hook. 12 Trace. 13 Trace chain. 14 Safe.
4 Nose band.	Throat lash.	15 Breast strap. 16 Saddle. 17 Hame strap. 18 Collar
5 Chin strap.	Bit.	strap. 19 Sliding loop. 20 Chain and toggle. 21 Girth.
6 Throat strap.	Reins.	22 Loin strap. 23 Hip strap. 24 Breech strap.
7 Throat lash.		
8 Hitching strap.		

(Crupper. 25 Back strap. 26 The body. 27 The dock.)
28 Trussing strap. 29 Valise saddle. 30 Valise. 31 Valise strap.

Fig. 10.3. Artillery Horses and Harnesses. Artillery horses used specially designed harnesses that were heavier and more complicated than that used for draft animals pulling army wagons. As this illustration shows, it was different even for different horses within the same team. On top is the harness for a member of the wheel team (the team closest to the limber), which is more elaborate than the harness for a member of the wheel team (the team closest to the limber). *Instruction for Field Artillery*, plate 18.

Hot weather greatly increased horse casualties during a campaign. While pursuing John Hunt Morgan's cavalry through Indiana and Ohio, traveling up to fifty miles per day, three Union batteries abandoned about as many horses as they lost in combat. The animals "suffered much from heat, dust, and want of water." Reports indicated that horses "dropped in harness" on severe marches due to "excessive labor." At the end of the Carolinas Campaign, at least half of the artillery horses in the Fifteenth Corps were unserviceable. They were "jaded, poor, diseased, lame, blind, with sore back, sore necks," reported Lt. Col. William H. Ross.[31]

Combat took out many horses; every battery lost some in every engagement. In some battles the losses were staggering. Marshall's Tennessee Battery lost forty-nine horses in its first ten minutes at Chickamauga. Percentage of loss was high in heavy engagements. The 9th Massachusetts Battery suffered a 77.2-percent loss among its horses at Gettysburg. It is true that many wounded animals, like wounded men, were not severely injured and could continue serving or return after a short recovery. Slightly more than half the horses wounded in Battery B, 1st Rhode Island Light Artillery were still serviceable, but one wonders if they really could pull their share of the load.[32] Horses presented far bigger targets on the battlefield than men, and their losses often exceeded manpower casualties. Battery A, 1st Illinois Light Artillery lost thirty men and forty-eight horses at Shiloh, while the 5th Company, Washington Artillery lost eighty-three men and ninety-three horses from Shiloh to Missionary Ridge.[33]

Total losses of animals during the entire war service of a battery revealed a comparison of combat versus other causes of fatalities. Roemer reported that 25.5 percent of the 395 horses he drew from the government during the war were lost to enemy fire. Based on culling information from morning reports, John D. Billings tabulated the death of 145 horses during the course of the war in the 10th Massachusetts Battery. The biggest killer was disease, which accounted for 48.3 percent of the total. Second was exhaustion, which took out 29.6 percent. The Appomattox Campaign accounted for nearly 80 percent of the deaths by exhaustion. The horses could not stand the rapid movement while chasing Lee's army after a winter of short rations. Combat accounted for only 22.1 percent of horse fatalities. Billings noted that of the 110 original animals when the battery organized in 1862, only 1 was alive and serviceable at the time of muster out three years later.[34]

We have scant information about the type of projectile that most accounted for horse casualties on the battlefield, but Capt. Milton A. Osborne provided a clue. His 20th Indiana Battery lost four horses to Confederate shellfire and ten to small-arms fire at the Battle of Nashville. While this small example should not be extrapolated too seriously for the entire war, it does indicate that small-arms fire was more important as a horse killer than return artillery fire.[35] But when horses were hit by artillery fire, the gory results were forever etched on the memory of all. Shells decapitated horses, tore off their legs, broke up their bodies, and sprayed blood, tissue, and body parts across a wide area. When a horse was hit by a shell fragment that tore off "one whole buttock" on the third day at Gettysburg, Edward Porter Alexander was stunned at how the green grass was painted red by the injury.[36]

"I have seen horses wounded and mutilated in every degree of severity," recalled Edward A. Moore. "Some partially disemboweled, but still on their feet, turning round and round in one spot, till they lay down to die; others with great furrows plowed along their backs or sides, others still, with a leg shot away, tossing the head up and down as they labored to follow on, but all too brave to utter other than a half-suppressed groan." On the battlefield of Port Republic, Moore counted eighty to ninety dead horses on "less than an acre" of ground. One was "standing almost upright, perfectly lifeless, supported by a fallen tree." A member of the Washington Artillery recalled a dying horse lying on the ground, rubbing "a smooth place . . . by the moving to and fro of his head and neck, or where he had thrown out convulsively his legs." When both horses and men were hit and became entangled in one big mess in Latimer's Battalion at Gettysburg, the animals plunged and kicked and in the process further injured or finally killed the helpless men near them. Other Confederates had to shoot stricken horses to save their wounded comrades.[37]

At times infantrymen deliberately targeted enemy horses to immobilize a battery. This occurred at the Battle of Atlanta on July 22, 1864, and the Battle of Reams Station on August 25, 1864. Billings saw what happened at the latter engagement. Hit by bullets, many horses fell and lay a while, then stood up only to be hit again. Sometimes the animal shook its head "as if pestered by a fly" when a bullet plunged into the flesh but continued to stand "in bold relief above the slight earthworks." A horse with a broken leg stood on the other three until further rounds brought it down. Billings could hear the hollow snapping sound when a bullet broke the lower leg of an animal, and he counted one horse who received seven balls before succumbing. The sharpshooters did their job with gruesome efficiency. Only four of fifty-seven horses belonging to the battery survived this deliberate destruction.[38]

"Words fail to convey an adequate idea of the fortitude displayed by our horses," Billings wrote. In fact, it was a warrior's fortitude typical of many human soldiers. In Billings's mind and heart, the artillery horse was elevated to the same level as his comrades. There was a natural tendency to be touched by the suffering of these animals because they had been forced into these horrible circumstances. Sensitivity toward their suffering among those soldiers who noticed and cared about it denotes an unstated realization that man and his logistical needs had been responsible for placing horses in mortal danger, and many soldiers revealed a bit of guilt about it.[39]

But many other soldiers only looked upon suffering animals as a worthless commodity. When a horse broke its leg, it could not be shot until two commissioned officers approved. As government property, it was placed on the same level as a piece of equipment that had to be condemned by a board.[40] But there was room in the military system to ignore the rules. When Roemer authorized the killing of "a beautiful gray horse" that had a bullet lodged in its shoulder, he could not carry through with it. "When we were about to do so he looked at me so pitifully that I had not the heart to give the order to fire." He allowed the horse twenty-four hours to improve, and it eventually recovered from the wound.[41]

Disposing of the remains of dead horses was difficult given the size of the carcasses. Ironically, it was made easier for members of the 1st Connecticut Battery after the Battle of Secessionville in June 1862 because Confederate artillery had dismembered four of their horses, distributing pieces across a wide area. For intact carcasses on other battlefields, the typical form of disposal was burial. But when time or energy failed to allow details to bury animal remains, they often burned the carcasses. In early June 1862, three days after the Battle of Seven Pines, soldiers prepared eighty dead horses by piling pine cordwood among them and setting it afire.[42]

REPLACING HORSES

The problem of finding replacement horses loomed large for all artillery officers. They employed several strategies. The manual advised either taking horses from the caisson teams and from the battery wagon and forge or consolidating teams and leaving a piece or section idle. It was not always possible to find suitable animals in the countryside. The main reliance for replacements rested on Quartermaster General Montgomery C. Meigs, who purchased 20,714 artillery horses from September 1, 1864, to May 9, 1865, at a cost of $161 to $185 each. In contrast, his officers paid $144 to $185 for cavalry mounts and $170 to $195 for mules. Earlier in the war, in the fall of 1862, the price for artillery animals was $99 each.[43]

The quality of government-issued horses varied widely. Wainwright received ninety replacements soon after Gettysburg, of which two-thirds were "really good" while twenty were "entirely worthless." He considered this a better-than-average ratio; usually half the horses were "totally unfit for artillery use." The loss rate and the infusion of new animals created a never-ending cycle. When the 9th Massachusetts Battery started the Overland Campaign, three-fourths of its horses were brand new.[44]

It was far more difficult to find replacement horses for Confederate units. The problem appeared in June 1862 and worsened with the passage of time. "I know how scarce they are," wrote the artillery chief of Jackson's Corps as he reduced his request from 204 to 128 animals after Antietam. "The destruction of horses in the army is so great that I fear it will be impossible to supply our wants," Lee told Pendleton in the spring of 1863. Many areas of the Confederacy were denuded of animals by April 1864. "The supply of horses on the present extended scale cannot possibly be kept up," admitted Bragg, now President Davis's military adviser.[45] In the early days of mobilization, some states allowed their batteries to rent horses from civilians at forty cents per day until the unit was transferred to Confederate service. But impressment was the only way the Confederate government could acquire more horses if owners were not willing to sell them. It of course compensated the owners, but the action raised a good deal of anger. Given that nearly one-third of his artillery horses were unserviceable, Bragg pressed horses at Atlanta in the spring of 1863 for his Army of Tennessee until Gov. Joseph E. Brown protested the action.[46]

Only on rare occasions did northern armies resort to impressing horses from northern citizens. In the wake of Gettysburg, Thomas W. Osborn pressed animals from local civilians. He issued receipts so the owners could apply for compensation and thus was able to move his guns. Osborn later discovered that the government paid a flat rate of $125 for each horse, "a good sale for some, a bad one for others."[47]

As the problem of replacing artillery animals worsened, officers were on their guard to save the ones they already possessed. "I find it quite a detriment to have fine battery horses," complained Capt. John A Grow of the 25th New York Battery. "I have to exercise the utmost vigilance to keep them from being stolen." The commander of Lumsden's Alabama Battery posted a sentinel twenty-four hours a day during the winter of 1863–64 to safeguard his animals.[48]

Mules might have substituted for horses but were considered unsuitable for artillery service. Still, every unit possessed a number of mules to pull the battery wagon and battery forge. Alexander's Baltimore Battery had 150 horses but only eighteen mules, while Battery D, 1st Ohio Light Artillery possessed fifty horses and thirty mules. Horses suffered a much higher rate of attrition than mules because they were more exposed to enemy fire and had to pull heavier loads.[49] Mules were too nervous under fire to pull guns and caissons. Nevertheless, a handful of batteries used them for short periods of time because horses simply were not available. When George W. Morgan's division evacuated Cumberland Gap in September 1862, the artillery gave up most of their horses to dismounted cavalrymen. Mules then pulled most of the twenty-eight pieces in Morgan's command.[50]

The Confederates more often were reduced to mule power than the Federals. Walker's Division relied heavily on them to pull guns during the summer of 1863 in Mississippi, although Walker wanted to replace them as soon as possible. At least one battery mixed horses and mules to haul the pieces. The 3rd Maryland Battery (CS) substituted mules for balky horses during the retreat from Missionary Ridge as a way to save its guns from capture.[51]

The instances cited thus far seem to show that mules could be relied on to pull artillery on occasion, but there were many instances when they failed the test of combat. Guibor's Missouri Battery used mules in the Battle of Carthage on July 5, 1861. A team panicked and started to pull a limber toward the Federals until someone managed to catch it. The battery substituted horses by the time of its next engagement a month later at Wilson's Creek. At Stones River a Confederate hitched two mules with four horses to haul away a captured Federal piece but found his "team" was utterly incapable of working together. Capt. William W. Buckley's Battery D, 1st Rhode Island Light Artillery used mules to negotiate muddy roads during the unit's retreat from Lenoir's Station toward Knoxville on November 16, 1863. When the Confederates caught up with the column at Campbell's Station and forced a battle, the mules became unmanageable: Half of one team tried to run while their partners stayed put, the former trying to climb over the latter and causing chaos.[52]

It was clear to everyone that mules could not be relied on under fire. Although some of them remained calm, many others bolted at the first round. Ironically, many mules seemed to have ignored nonlethal hits by small-arms fire. "We all laughed at the manner in which a mule would shake himself when struck by a bullet," recalled Napier Bartlett of the Washington Artillery, "as if divesting himself of some superfluous hornet or gadfly." But when danger became apparent through a sudden and unexpected noise, mules were more inclined than horses to panic.[53]

Oxen used to be the only way that field artillery had been moved to the battlefield before the end of the eighteenth century. Once there, manpower took over. Horses were far superior to oxen not only in the speed with which they moved carriages but also in their steadiness under fire. Yet there are a few instances where oxen became useful to Civil War artillerymen. Bradford's Mississippi Battery took the field in August 1861 with only one piece and four horses. The latter soon gave out negotiating muddy roads. Members of the unit found two oxen at a local farm and a slave to drive them. The two oxen could do what four horses could not. During the Siege of Vicksburg, Federal artillerymen used oxen from local plantations to pull heavy guns from a river landing to the siege lines, part of the way up the tall and steep slope of Chickasaw Bluffs. It took fifteen oxen to pull one piece, the only way to move the heavy guns up that incline.[54]

Nevertheless, the horse remained the supreme artillery animal, the only one capable of quickly moving carriages on and off the battlefield, the only one able to emotionally withstand the test of combat, and the only one to elicit feelings of love and devotion from drivers. It was fully capable of reciprocating those feelings too. As with human warriors, not all artillery horses were brave or dedicated, but most of them adapted to the military system and soldiered on despite threats from disease, overwork, and enemy fire. Receiving credit for this only in the memoirs of some artillerists, the horse has remained mostly an obscure figure in our understanding of field artillery. It is time it received its due.

11

. . . .

DEFENSIVE OPERATIONS IN THE FIELD

O f the three arms involved in Civil War military operations, infantry and cavalry were capable of independent action on the battlefield. Artillery, although an important support for both of them, could not survive alone in combat. It could deal out heavy damage to attacking infantry or cavalry under the right conditions but was highly vulnerable without support. When asked if artillery needed help, Charles Griffin, who commanded Battery D, 5th US Artillery at First Bull Run, replied in the affirmative. "Certainly, it is helpless by itself—perfectly helpless. Artillery must be supported or you better not have it on the field."[1]

This lack of independence compelled a special relationship with the other two arms. Artillery had a closer bond with infantry than with cavalry because it was more heavily invested in joint operations with foot soldiers. The big guns barely kept up with the fast-moving cavalry and often played only a slight role in mounted warfare. "The infantry and artillery felt closer together," wrote William Meade Dame, and often joined in pointed jabs aimed at the cavalry.[2]

The experience of field artillery on the battlefield more or less divides into defensive and offensive roles, although the line between those two modes of operation was not always well defined. The army and interested observers had crafted a modest artillery doctrine before the Civil War. John Gibbon argued that, when on the attack, fieldpieces should avoid broken, rocky, or soft ground, but when on the defense, that type of terrain represented an advantage. He also thought that cavalry should support the guns if the ground was level and open and should be placed on both flanks of the battery. If in broken ground, infantry was preferable.[3]

PLACEMENT OF FIELD ARTILLERY AND INFANTRY

The close relationship between artillery and infantry led to differing opinions about how to place them in relation to each other. Gibbon thought guns should be put either in front of the intervals between regiments and brigades or on the flanks of infantry lines. Both Gibbon and Joseph Roberts warned against placing artillery in front of infantry formations, as that would prevent the foot soldiers from firing forward. To place infantry in front of the guns would expose them to casualties from premature shell explosions.[4]

The actual placement of batteries on the battlefield only partially followed these recommendations. When Don Carlos Buell established a habitual formation of battle lines in the Army of the Ohio, it included placing batteries close to the intervals in the infantry line. But Civil War armies rarely deployed with intervals between infantry regiments. Batteries therefore created their own space between regiments in the line or in front of or behind the line. If placed behind an infantry line, arrangements had to be made for allowing the foot soldiers to retire between the guns or to let the guns advance by opening lanes in the infantry formation. But vegetation and the lay of the land often dictated the placement of batteries far more than did doctrine.[5]

ARTILLERY SUPPORTING FOOT SOLDIERS

Both infantry and artillery officers believed a major goal of the big guns was to divert enemy fire from the foot soldiers. Hooker expressed this idea dramatically during the Battle of Williamsburg when he told Capt. Thomas W. Osborn to advance his battery, perhaps "to sacrifice you, but it is necessary to save the infantry." Supporting fire bolstered morale among friendly troops and often led to requests to open the big guns even when there was no target.[6]

The support offered to infantrymen by the artillery was not confined to the battle line but extended to the picket and skirmish lines too. It may seem counterproductive to place a large weapon on a skirmish line, but it was done on many occasions. In fact Albert N. Ames referred to his battery's "usual tour of picket duty on our front" during the Peninsula Campaign.[7]

Artillerymen took their role as pickets and skirmishers seriously. Capt. W. Irving Hodgson of the 5th Company, Washington Artillery harassed Federal skirmishers, "often firing at a single man and with good effect." Some enterprising officers preplanned their fire when the skirmish lines remained static so they could quickly hit the thin enemy line with effective rounds. The old regular artillerist Griffin, when later commanding an infantry division, or-dered solid shot fired to hit the ground in front of Confederate skirmishers so as to ricochet toward them. Battery K, 4th US Artillery, fired not only solid shot but also shell and spherical case while on the skirmish line.[8]

INFANTRY SUPPORTING ARTILLERY

It was not easy for infantry to know exactly where they should be placed to properly support artillery. Mixing them with the guns always produced dif-ficulties. One frustrated artillery officer reported that infantry placed to the rear "generally . . . do nothing or worse than nothing." As Edward Porter Al-exander put it, each arm needed "its own fighting front."[9]

Alexander's rule was often violated because of ignorance or circumstance, but a smart officer could compensate for these difficulties. Col. John B. San-born placed his 4th Minnesota Infantry fifty feet behind the 11th Ohio Bat-tery at the Battle of Corinth. The guns masked the center six companies, but Sanborn advanced two companies to right and left of the pieces so the troops could fire at advancing Confederates.[10] In contrast, Maj. Stephen D. Carpenter, who led the 1st Battalion, 19th US Infantry, gave little thought to supporting a battery at Stones River. He also placed his troops directly behind the roaring guns. When Brig. Gen. Richard W. Johnson saw this, he spoke briefly with Carpenter, a prewar acquaintance, pointing out to him that he was losing men with every incoming round. "I was sent to support this battery, and must do it," the harried major said only a few minutes before he was hit.[11]

Close proximity to the guns at Champion Hill caused men of the 30th Il-linois to become dizzy and to vomit, even though they hugged the ground to avoid the worst of the passing shells. Pieces of sabots, red hot from leaving the tube, hit and scorched them. Repeated use produced a sloppy mix of powder residue and condensation that also was "scalding hot." When this splattered over the prone Illinois men, their discomfort was complete.[12] Members of the 141st New York were so close to a battery at the Battle of Kolb's Farm during the Atlanta Campaign that the artillery commander advised the troops "to stand on the balls of our feet and keep our teeth apart, so that the concus-sion would not jar us so much." Capt. William Merrill, out of curiosity, tried to stand solidly and closed his teeth tight. "It seemed as though the top of my head blew off with the first discharge of the gun." Other infantrymen found cotton to stuff into their ears when near artillery firing, often having to wait for several days until their hearing returned to normal. But Lt. L. B. Spaulding of the 52nd Illinois found that cotton was useless to shield him from the intense pain in his ears caused by nearby cannon fire, and he feared permanent hearing loss as a result.[13]

Friendly troops to the rear of the 5th Company, Washington Artillery fired through the battery's formation at advancing Federals at Shiloh. They produced "an unexpected and murderous fire, as deadly to men and horse [of the battery] as that which came from the front," and the company had to retreat. At the Battle of Glendale, supporting troops counterattacked but were driven back toward Battery E, 1st US Artillery, masking its fire and leading to the loss of its guns.[14]

Of course, there are many stories of proper placement and effective support of batteries by infantry units. Not only did officers position them smartly, but the troops also performed their duty with dedication. Battle reports are filled with instances of impromptu assistance offered by infantry officers that saved a battery from capture at the last minute. More than 100 men of the 48th Illinois "rushed out in front of the battery and opened fire, which for the moment checked [the attacking Rebels], and enabled us to get away," reported Lt. William H. Gay of the 1st Iowa Battery on July 22, 1864. It also was not unusual for infantry to reclaim a gun, caisson, or limber abandoned by retreating artillerymen between the lines.[15]

But many times infantry support fell back too soon, leaving gunners to continue firing until the last minute. Capt. Eli Lilly of the 18th Indiana Battery railed against "the miserable shoulder-strapped poltroons who allowed the support to run away from the pieces in the hour of danger" at Chickamauga. At times the infantry retreated in disorder, spreading panic among battery horses and forcing gun crews to pull their pieces back by hand. If friendly troops masked their cannon, battery commanders typically refrained from firing even if it resulted in the capture of their guns. But at other times artillerymen accepted the risk of killing and wounding their own infantry. "It was better to sacrifice a few of their lives than to allow the rebels to capture our battery," recalled Lt. Tully McCrea of Battery I, 1st US Artillery of an incident at Antietam.[16]

FRIENDLY FIRE

All artillerymen were aware that premature explosions endangered friendly troops in their front but it was often necessary to place a battery behind the battle line. In many units it was a standing order not to fire explosive ordnance in such situations. Batteries either remained silent or did not put fuzes in their shells, effectively utilizing them as solid shot. If forced to fire explosive ordnance over friendly troops, unintended casualties often led infantrymen to threaten to shoot back at their own gunners.[17]

While John D. Billings argued that firing over friendly troops occurred "only exceptionally," it actually was very common. Usually it occurred out of necessity, a skirmish line or main line suddenly hard pressed and the only battery nearby positioned to the rear of the defending troops. At times the infantry lay prone to lessen the danger.[18] When Osborn had to fire over the heads of Union troops at Chancellorsville, he instructed five batteries positioned 400 yards behind the infantry to begin their work. The target was a Confederate infantry line 200–300 yards farther away than the friendly troops. Each battery "fired very carefully and very deliberately. The elevation of the guns being as slight as possible passed the shells over our line, and the fuses were so cut that the shells exploded immediately after passing our line of infantry." Lt. Augustus N. Parsons of Battery A, New Jersey Light Artillery employed percussion shells while firing over friendly troops to lessen the danger, switching to time-fuze projectiles only when the Unionists moved away from his front. Some batteries even fired canister when friendly infantry was within range and distance but did so, at least according to artillery officers, with care.[19]

Infantrymen recorded many near misses from their own guns in situations such as these. Moreover, fragments of sabots often stripped off from projectiles and hit men in passing. During the bombardment preceding Pickett's Charge at Gettysburg, Oliver O. Howard instructed his men to pile empty hardtack boxes in rear of the infantry line to protect the men from these "strippings of the shells as they flew" overhead.[20]

It was easier for gunners to avoid hurting their infantry comrades when firing over a distant line of friendly troops, but that process also reduced the effectiveness of their fire. Relying on solid shot to lessen the danger also lessened the effect on the target, and many artillerists believed their accuracy lessened as well when they had to adjust to the presence of friendly troops in their line of fire. It helped if the infantry cooperated a little. At Perryville some troops waved regimental flags to show Stanford's Mississippi Battery that its rounds did not hit them, and Stanford waved the battery ensign as a signal that he understood the message. At Chickamauga Brig. Gen. William P.

Carlin had to post men of his brigade in an undulation in front of Union artillery but instructed the battery commanders to fire at a distance greater than that of his troops' position.[21]

Billings estimated that only 10 percent of all friendly casualties due to artillery fire resulted from inept gunnery, while 90 percent were caused by faulty fuzes. We can never know if that is correct because no one tabulated data on that issue. Moreover, injuries caused by flying sabot pieces were often cited as a major concern, but no one tabulated data on that question as well.[22] Judging by the reports, it is difficult to believe that only 10 percent of friendly casualties resulted from inept gunnery. Batteries posted to the rear of friendly troops often fired canister at long distance, which created a terrible danger to their infantry comrades while posing no threat to the enemy. The 4th New York Battery on one occasion fired canister 1,500 yards from the Confederates, three times more than the recommended distance, killing at least one Union officer and two enlisted men. Col. Charles G. Harker's brigade lost one killed and eleven wounded when the Chicago Board of Trade Battery fired canister at Confederate guns 2,200 yards away at Stones River. That fire also wounded five men in the 6th Ohio Battery before the Ohio unit moved out of the way.[23]

Maj. Henry L. Abbott complained that his 20th Massachusetts lost one killed and four wounded at Bristoe Station in October 1863. He suspected several of those casualties were caused by the same Union batteries that had exacted similar losses on friendly regiments in previous engagements. Abbott was certain those battery commanders had earlier been warned about the problem but had not taken it seriously. It was no small matter; half the men Abbott lost at Bristoe Station were due to friendly fire. It should be pointed out, however, that infantry officers often informed battery commanders they were shelling their own troops, leading to an immediate cease fire or change of position by the guns.[24]

The worst cases of friendly fire took place during the Siege of Vicksburg, when Union batteries were compelled to take position behind the infantry line. Unfortunately, much of the explosive ordnance used by the Army of the Tennessee came with faulty fuzes. This combination created repeated instances of loss among infantrymen posted in front of a battery. Constructing a parapet at the rear of the trench, a parados to use the technical term, would have helped a great deal, but no one seems to have been aware of this expedient.

"We were in more danger from our own guns than from those of the enemy," complained Edmund Newsome of the 81st Illinois.[25]

The losses continued despite awareness of the problem. Two or three men a day were lost in Brig. Gen. William P. Benton's brigade to friendly artillery fire. The most visible casualty was Sgt. C. U. Besse of the 33rd Illinois, who lost both arms when a Union shell fragment cut so deeply into them that amputation became the only recourse. Besse died a few days later of his horrible injuries. Losses due to friendly fire "did more to pull the regiment down" in spirit than anything else during the siege. Artillerists sent messages to infantrymen in their front to alert them as to when they planned to fire. Thirteenth Corps commander Maj. Gen. Edward O. C. Ord estimated that by June 27 at least 100 men in Grant's army were lost to friendly fire.[26]

It is safe to assume that several thousand men in both armies were killed or wounded unintentionally by the fire of their own batteries during the Civil War. There were several causes, and none of them were easy to eliminate. Civil War armies failed to create systems of evaluating performance and adopting best practices after each campaign. For example, a division-level chief of artillery requested an investigation into the wild firing done by the Chicago Board of Trade Battery at Stones River, but there is no indication that was ever done.[27]

ARTILLERY AND CAVALRY

A relatively small proportion of field artillery was devoted to supporting cavalry in both armies. Even though the guns had to move fast to keep up with the mounted arm, there was relatively little difference between cavalry batteries and infantry batteries. The biggest change was mounting all members of the unit. Horses were issued to the gun detachments and artificers (the drivers already were mounted). This necessitated slight alterations in the formations and maneuvers to account for the additional number of mounted men. Another change was to lighten the caissons by reducing the number of ammunition boxes from three to two. Batteries accompanying cavalry did not reduce to lighter pieces. These limited modifications made it easy to detail a battery to cavalry support.[28]

The terminology tended to be confusing. Long before the war, the term "mounted artillery" had been applied to batteries that converted from oxen or hand-drawn means to using horses to pull carriages. The men continued to

Fig. 11.1. Batteries B and L, 2nd US Artillery. Converted to a unit capable of keeping up with cavalry forces, the battery is in the formation Order in Line. Its six 3-Inch Ordnance Rifles and limbers are in the first echelon, the mounted members of the gun detachments in the second echelon, and the limbers and caissons behind. LC-DIG-cwpb-00292.

walk. That type of battery represented the majority throughout the Civil War and did not refer to batteries assigned to accompany cavalry units. By 1861 with "mounted artillery" already taken, the army used terms such as "light artillery" and "horse artillery" to designate fully mounted batteries assigned to cavalry service. To make things even more confusing, the term "foot artillery" was applied to detachments of garrison and siege guns. All three types of artillery (infantry, cavalry, and garrison) failed to receive readily distinctive names.[29]

When it came to firing on enemy cavalry, *Instruction for Field Artillery* provided information about the average speed of mounted formations at a walk, trot, and gallop, plus how many rounds could be fired at those formations as they closed in. Solid shot and canister, at the appropriate distances, were the recommended projectiles. If supporting infantry formed in squares to resist mounted attacks, the battery commander was advised to position his limbers and caissons inside the square, with the guns placed just outside a corner of the square so they could be taken inside if necessary. If limbers and caissons could not be secured inside the square, they should be placed in line with the pieces to prevent enemy cavalry from riding through the battery formation.[30]

The United States never had a consistent heritage of fielding horse batteries before the war, and even during the conflict, Union and Confederate armies created a sizeable force of artillery for cavalry only in the East. In the Army of the Potomac, four regular batteries converted to horse artillery early in 1862, each armed with six 3-inch rifle guns, and several more converted later that year. By August 1863 eleven of the sixty-eight batteries (16.1 percent) in that army supported cavalry units. The 6th New York Battery was the only volunteer unit among them.[31]

In the East regular batteries were preferred for the role of supporting cavalry. Five regiments of regular artillery served during the Civil War, boasting a total of sixty batteries. Four of those batteries were assigned to permanent defenses, and of the fifty-six remaining units, twenty-two of them, or 39.2 percent, supported cavalry forces.[32]

In the West the Federals were far behind their eastern comrades in fielding horse artillery. The Chicago Board of Trade Battery, the 18th Indiana Battery, the 25th Ohio Battery, and the 10th Wisconsin Battery were among those converted to units capable of supporting cavalry. Very few of these western horse artillery units fielded light guns, but the 2nd Massachusetts Battery was fully armed with 6-pounder rifles, making it a prime candidate for cavalry service.[33]

Confederate horse artillery in the East was well organized. The Army of Northern Virginia had five batteries, one assigned to each of four cavalry brigades with the fifth as a reserve, by November 1862. Many artillerists were eager to ride with the mounted arm, but a shortage of horses limited the expansion of units that supported cavalry. How well the batteries served Lee's cavalry is a matter of opinion. Historians and contemporaries eulogized John Pelham for his dash and courage in directing the guns, but after his death in March 1863, the quality of the arm deteriorated. "As a rule their Horse Art'y was so badly handled in battle that we Art'y officers paid but little attention to it," wrote Capt. Alanson M. Randol of Batteries E and G, 1st US Artillery after the war.[34]

Confederates in the West created horse artillery in the fall of 1862. Freeman's Tennessee Battery supported Col. Nathan Bedford Forrest's command, while Col. Joseph Wheeler's brigade acquired Wiggins's Arkansas Battery and White's Tennessee Battery. A section of artillery was attached to Col. John H. Morgan's Brigade as well. By early 1864 Forrest had four batteries organized in a battalion commanded by twenty-year old John W. Morton.[35]

Officers had their opinions about the proper ordnance to use for cavalry service. Some argued that mountain-howitzer carriages tended to break down under the strain of rapid marching. Others recommended Napoleons because they were lighter than old 12-pounders and fired heavier ordnance than 6-pounders. After the Carolinas Campaign Lt. Elbert W. Fowler of the 10th Wisconsin Battery suggested taking off the spare wheel and one ammunition chest from the caisson to lighten the load on horses.[36]

Given the nature of cavalry operations, which were highly mobile, there was no need to mass artillery to achieve a defined tactical objective. Thomas H. Carter claimed after the war that he declined taking charge of Lee's horse artillery after the death of Pelham "because it could not be *massed,* and had to be fought piecemeal practically, and it was most efficient only *in mass.*"[37] Some artillery officers complained that their mounted supports did not help them very much. John C. Tidball noted that the horse soldiers were skittish, tending to retire when the enemy opened fire and leaving the gunners to fend for themselves. He recommended that mounted infantry armed with infantry weapons rather than carbines support the horse batteries. That suggestion was never taken seriously—in fact, the Federals never created mounted infantry units in the East.[38]

The Confederates were a bit more innovative in the tactical use of horse artillery than their counterparts. Brig. Gen. Turner Ashby ordered his battery to charge along with his mounted command in a fight at Middletown on May 24, 1862. Pelham personally directed a single piece in a daring attempt to catch Maj. Gen. George G. Meade's advancing division in flank fire at the Battle of Fredericksburg.[39]

Artillery units strained to keep up with fast-moving cavalry in the field. The Chicago Board of Trade Battery moved on average thirty miles each day (up to forty-nine miles on some days) during Wilson's Raid through Alabama and Georgia. Fast traveling over rough roads took a heavy toll on horses. Many animals in the 10th Wisconsin Battery literally died because of overwork and exposure during the Carolinas Campaign.[40] Angered by a report that an infantry battery accompanying a cavalry patrol had broken down after traveling sixty miles in twenty-four hours, William F. Barry put his foot down. The brigadier general insisted that only horse artillery accompany mounted expeditions and suggested ways to modify an infantry battery for that purpose. He thought an artillery commander could leave his caissons behind and rely on the fifty rounds per piece that were on the limber. In addition, there was no need for more than two guns for every 1,500 cavalrymen.[41]

In battle, cavalry and artillery sometimes got in the way of each other. At Gaines's Mill retreating Union horsemen rode in front of and through friendly artillery units, preventing them from firing or limbering to the rear. "Men were ridden down and the horses stampeded by the rush of the cavalry," reported Capt. William B. Weeden. "The whole line of artillery was thrown into confusion." Failure on the part of cavalry supports led to the loss of guns and equipment as well as men and position.[42]

But according to Gibbon, there was no possibility of fielding cavalry without artillery support. Cavalry had "but little or no fire of its own, and acting simply by the shock of its charge" could not deliver destruction at a distance. He and most officers of horse batteries took that responsibility seriously. Gibbon recommended explosive ordnance against enemy cavalry, not only because horses were big targets but also because the projectile burst often unnerved the animals and created panic. Jacob Roemer observed Confederate horses jumping several feet into the air as his case shot burst among them at Cedar Mountain. Astute battery commanders diverted enemy fire onto their units to save friendly cavalry. And they stopped enemy mounted charges, at times waiting until the horsemen were only fifty yards away before opening fire.[43]

As with every command, the quality of a good horse battery depended on the man in charge. For some officers, however, the shift from supporting infantry to supporting cavalry involved a learning phase. Lt. George Browne Jr. thanked Brig. Gen. William W. Averell, commander of the cavalry division he was assigned to, for helping him during his adjustment to supporting the mounted arm with his 6th New York Battery at the Battle of Kelly's Ford on March 17, 1863. But not every artillery officer had what it took to perform cavalry duty. The faster pace and the intense demands on men and animals required a certain attitude, something Lt. Harry C. Cushing admitted he did not have. When given the chance to convert Battery H, 4th US Artillery into a horse unit, he declined. Cushing did not want to spend the war conducting patrols, raids, and expeditions; he preferred to fight in big infantry battles, "when one can set down comfortably and take it quietly in a good honest give and take stand up fight."[44]

COUNTERBATTERY ACTION

When artillery opened on enemy guns, they engaged in counterbattery fire. This was both defensive and offensive at the same time, for it was an attempt to neutralize the enemy's ability to inflict long-distance damage. If successful, such fire could eliminate a major threat to the security of a defensive line and at the same time prepare the way for offensive action.

At times batteries were faced with the difficult question of whether to fire at enemy guns or enemy infantry. Under the pressure of heavy attacks by foot soldiers on May 3 at Chancellorsville, many Union artillerists opted to concentrate their fire on supporting Rebel artillery and received intense criticism for it. "The only thing that could have enabled us to hold the ground was to have silenced the enemy's batteries," argued Lt. Col. Charles H. Morgan, artillery chief of the Second Corps. The 5th Maine Battery solved that dilemma by targeting enemy cannon with its right section and infantry with its left. The relative proportion of targeting for Battery H, 1st New York Light Artillery at Spotsylvania was to direct one-third of the rounds at enemy artillery and the rest, by Charles Griffin's order, at areas where Confederate infantry was forming.[45]

Augustus Buell was convinced it was a sterner test of courage on the part of gun detachments to engage in heavy counterbattery fire, especially if the target could not be clearly seen, than in firing on infantry at close distance. It resulted in more casualties as well. That is one reason why Gibbon recommended battery commanders increase the interval between their pieces when engaging enemy guns to lessen damage by incoming rounds. Spreading the battery formation also offered more chances of catching enemy pieces in converging fire. Gibbon argued that concentrating the fire of two or three pieces on one enemy piece would also increase chances of success. Edward Porter Alexander exulted in enfilade fire on enemy guns because "the shot finds something to hurt wherever it falls."[46]

Artillerists often tried to conceal their position, which elicited ploys by the other side to force them into revealing their spot. Exploratory fire, some-

Fig. 11.2. Gettysburg Gun. This Napoleon of Battery B, 1st Rhode Island Light Artillery became a unique relic of counterbattery fire in the Civil War. Known as the Gettysburg Gun, a shell hit "the face of the muzzle, left side of the bore and exploded," taking out two members of the gun detachment. The rest tried to reload, but their new round stuck partway in and could not be moved because the tube had cooled and shrunk a bit. See Rhodes, *Gettysburg Gun,* 1, 18–19, 29, 31–32, 56. LC-DIG-ppmsca-33224.

times with blank cartridges, often took place. The men on the receiving end of such fire often refused to return it and thus retained their concealment for a while longer.[47]

While some artillerists used solid shot in counterbattery fire, they overwhelmingly preferred explosive ordnance—shell and case shot—to take out enemy guns. Intensive counterbattery fire could reduce available supplies quickly. "We had no ammunition to expend in artillery duels," reported Col. William T. Withers of the engagement at Chickasaw Bayou. Instead, he ordered his batteries to withhold fire when Federal guns challenged them, cover their own men, and save their ammunition to repel infantry attacks. "We are not allowed to fire at the Yankee Batteries," wrote Stouten H. Dent at one point during the Atlanta Campaign, "ammunition too scarce."[48]

The distance at which counterbattery fire took place varied widely. Perhaps the longest was recorded by Andrew Jackson Neal when he placed the Marion Light Artillery atop Lookout Mountain and fired at Union guns he estimated were 4,000 yards away, receiving shots that fell very near his pieces in return. At Fredericksburg a Confederate Whitworth rifle engaged 3-inch rifles of the 2nd Maine Battery in a duel at 2,700 yards and lost. There are reports of counterbattery fire taking place as close as 200 yards, well within canister distance. But, as noted in a previous chapter, a survey of 336 examples of firing during the war revealed that, on average, artillery-versus-artillery firing took place at 1,122 yards.[49]

The effect of counterbattery fire depended heavily on the gun detachments. If they gauged the distance properly and set the fuzes accordingly, they had a good chance of beating the enemy. The Jefferson Mississippi Artillery at Shiloh faced a Union battery at 400 yards, but the incoming rounds sailed five to twenty feet over Confederate heads. The Federal gunners had the range exactly but not the distance. Lt. W. Butler Beck fired so heavily at Confederate batteries at Burgess's Mill on October 27, 1864, that he unnerved the opposing gunners into cutting their fuzes too long or too short. "But for the bad practice of their gunners I fear there would have been but little left of my battery," he confessed. Thomas W. Osborn relied mostly on the accuracy of return fire to gauge whether his own rounds were hitting home in counterbattery contests.[50]

There were many instances of effective shooting in counterbattery fire. Facing six 10-pounder Parrott guns at First Bull Run, Capt. John D. Imboden watched as the opposing gunners overshot his position, "but at every round improved their aim and shortened their fuse." The Federal fire crawled nearer his guns until striking a knoll in front of Imboden's position, sending rounds ricocheting over his pieces. The Unionists observed this and adjusted the distance until hitting the Rebel battery squarely.[51]

Many confrontations between opposing batteries became vicious slugfests. "Fire slow, boys. Keep cool," said a lieutenant of the 1st Wisconsin Battery at Port Gibson on May 1, 1863. "D— 'em, if we can't whip 'em we'll tire 'em out." In Battery G, 1st New York Light Artillery it was the enlisted men who were "determined to 'have the last word'" in a duel with Confederate guns at Cold Harbor. They returned fire until their opponent was silenced. Battle spirit produced terrible conditions on many fields. Stephen D. Lee won promotion to brigadier general by his role in directing an artillery battalion at Antietam. But when Alexander succeeded him in that command, Lee told him to "pray

Fig. 11.3. Artillery Casualties at Resaca. The tragic blending of human and animal casualties in a battery pummeled by enemy fire is illustrated in this sketch by Capt. Adolph Metzner of the 32nd Indiana. It depicts what was left of a Confederate battery after the Battle of Resaca, May 14–15, 1864, during the Atlanta Campaign. LC-DIG-ppmsca-51289.

that you may never have to fight another Sharpsburg! Sharpsburg was just Artillery-Hell!"[52]

How to dominate counterbattery fire became the key to success. Concentrating all fire on only one opposition piece could do that, but the other opposing pieces would be free to damage your own guns. Yet by diverting fire to several targets, the chances of overwhelming any one of them reduced dramatically.[53] When one side achieved dominance, it could simply wreck the opposing hardware. Robert Stiles was stunned by the splintered carriages, crushed wheels, exploded ammunition chests, and upturned limbers that marked the location of Maj. Joseph W. Latimer's battalion at Gettysburg. Every piece of equipment from sponge buckets to ramrods could be broken into fragments by projectiles. Horses suffered tremendously from counterbattery fire, with reports that nearly all animals in a team were put out of action by only one round.[54]

The stress of heavy gun-to-gun exchanges produced extreme emotions. Union artillery fire at Malvern Hill not only wrecked Graham's Virginia Battery but also "completely stampeded" members of the gun crews, who cut horses from their harness and rode away. At Stones River four Confederate batteries fired on three pieces of Battery B, 1st Ohio Light Artillery. "It seemed just as if they would sweep us from the ground," reported Thomas C. Potter. A shell that ricocheted and "filled our faces with mud" angered Lt. Norman A. Baldwin. "He sprang up with, 'come boys and give them . . . [hell].'" The Ohioans fired ten rounds from each piece and then Baldwin ordered everyone to fall back to save themselves further injury.[55]

Both sides chalked up victories in counterbattery fire, but Maj. Gen. Daniel Harvey Hill was convinced that at Antietam, at least, the Federals dominated. Rebel gunners "could not cope with the superior weight, caliber, range, and number of the Yankee guns," Hill reported. They should have concentrated on Union infantry instead of trying to engage opposing batteries. Confederate guns "were smashed up or withdrawn before they could be effectually turned against massive columns of attack. An artillery duel between the Washington Artillery and the Yankee batteries across the Antietam on the 16th was the most melancholy farce in the war."[56]

Many artillery officers kept track of the time it took for them to silence enemy batteries. The shortest time was fifteen minutes (at 600 yards distance) and the longest two hours (at 1,400 yards distance). Some officers counted the number of rounds needed to "shut them up," and it varied from three (at 1,600 yards distance) to fifty-two (at 1,000 yards distance). Silencing the enemy might mean only a temporary cessation of their fire. At Williamsburg Osborn noted that Confederate batteries fell quiet only to resume action half an hour later and had to be silenced again. In part this was because the opposing batteries ceased fire in order to shift position. Lt. Joseph L. Simpson of Battery A, 1st Pennsylvania Light Artillery noted that Confederate batteries at Antietam changed their positions four or five times. Battery G, 5th US Artillery changed position after every round during the attack on May 27, 1863, at Port Hudson.[57]

Roemer tricked the enemy at Cold Harbor when he ordered his gun detachments to slacken return fire and then stop altogether to give them the impression they had been silenced. He was then able to pound Rebel infantry as they advanced toward a redoubt constructed on the Ninth Corps line and force them to fall back. The Federals had used a similar ploy during the Confederate bombardment preceding Pickett's Charge at Gettysburg the year before.[58]

Coolness, precision of aim, determination to put up with punishment until the job was done, and a range of imponderables were the factors determining whether one side or the other dominated in counterbattery engagements. It was the most deadly job field artillery took on during the war. Damage inflicted by incoming artillery projectiles was more spectacular and burdened morale more than damage inflicted by small-arms fire. Capt. Hubert Dilger of Battery I, 1st Ohio Light Artillery did not take into account losses inflicted by what he called "dem leetle balls," only counting casualties among his men inflicted by enemy artillery rounds. That was, of course, an extreme view of the relative significance of small-arms fire versus artillery fire, but it represents the views of one of the best artillerists in the Union army.[59]

CONCLUSION

Field artillery claimed an intimate relationship with infantry and cavalry because of its position as a supporting arm with no possibility of independent action. It absolutely needed help to survive. In turn the fieldpieces provided much needed support for both infantry and cavalry units, more so for the former than the latter. Fast-moving mounted troops offered the guns little opportunity to have an important effect because artillery had to plant itself in advantageous positions and have time to damage opposing targets; that time often was denied it by the swift evolution of cavalry engagements.

It was possible for infantry to survive on the battlefield without the support of fieldpieces, but its chances were greatly increased if a battery was there to lend a hand. Still, the relationship between the guns and the foot soldiers involved difficulties that ranged from how to closely place one arm near the other to the devastating effect of friendly fire. While officers in both arms worked continually to solve these problems, they never entirely disappeared, limiting the effectiveness of the fieldpieces.

The deadliest foe of field artillery was enemy artillery. Counterbattery fire held the greatest potential to devastate equipment, manpower, and horses, literally wrecking material and tearing to shreds both humans and animals. But the second-most-deadly enemy, opposing infantry, also could immobilize and neutralize a battery as seen in the next chapter.

12

. . . .

ARTILLERY AGAINST INFANTRY

Apart from counterbattery action, artillery found its most dangerous opponent in enemy infantry. Whether trying to attack them
or defend against them, field guns never consistently dominated
their infantry opponents. Even when enemy troops conducted a frontal attack against artillery, they sometimes succeeded. Neither the big guns nor
the foot soldiers could guarantee victory in their never-ending struggle on
the battlefield.

SUPPORTING INFANTRY ATTACKS

Doctrine recognized that artillery played a role in offensive action by infantry, although there was no consensus on how it should do so. Some commentators advocated placing the supporting guns on the flanks of the attacking
formation or even at its head, advancing with the foot soldiers, while others
had little hope this could be done effectively. There were only a handful of
partial attempts to move field guns forward in concert with an infantry assault during the Civil War, and none of them succeeded due to difficulties of
timing and the highly mobile nature of an infantry attack. Artillery could not
be effective except when it had the opportunity to find a good position, form
into battery, and fire at its target for a while. The timing of artillery barrages
could have been more accurately set if officers synchronized their watches,
but that seems to have happened only rarely.[1]

Field artillery mostly supported an infantry attack by staying behind the
friendly line of battle and firing at the point of assault from a distance. One of
the most salient examples lay in the Federal crossing of the Rappahannock
River in the early stages of the Fredericksburg Campaign. Henry J. Hunt sup-

ported the laying of five bridges with a massive artillery force. He assembled thirty batteries with 147 pieces, organizing them into four temporary divisions of seven to nine batteries each. Hunt issued instructions on how to deliver fire. The first priority was to target Confederate batteries; the second, enemy infantry. Federal guns were then to cover the advance of Union troops and avoid firing over friendly formations except when necessary.[2]

This massive firepower proved to be of only partial help when the move was launched on December 11, 1862. Hunt suppressed Confederate artillery fire and prevented enemy infantry from advancing toward the crossing points, but he could not suppress the fire of several hundred sharpshooters lodged in the cellars of houses, in ditches, and behind stone walls. Even a heavy, broadcast firing into the town failed to stop this. Only when the infantry crossed some units to root out these sharpshooters could the laying of bridges continue.[3]

Hunt crossed forty-one batteries the next day to support further operations on December 13. He assembled 220 pieces (92 rifles and 128 smoothbores) for the discouraging events of that day. Charles Wainwright placed 21 pieces to bear on the crest of the high ground targeted by George G. Meade's division, with John Gibbon's supporting division on the Union left, and 14 other pieces to pound Confederate batteries at other locations. After thirty minutes of intense firing, Wainwright judged that he had silenced virtually all Confederate artillery fire, and the two divisions moved forward to nearly break the Rebel line. Gibbon, an old artillerist, ordered the 2nd Maine Battery to advance with his infantry command. Capt. James A. Hall tried to do so, getting to a point about 200 yards from the enemy position. When the attack failed, Union guns fired canister to keep Confederate infantry from following up the retirement.[4]

For the attack on January 2, 1863, at Stones River, Braxton Bragg charged Capt. Felix H. Robertson with supporting Maj. Gen. John C. Breckinridge's division. Bragg told Robertson to let the infantry capture the targeted high ground just east of the river and then move the guns up to hold it. But Robertson found that Breckinridge differed from his commander's opinion, wanting the guns to advance with his infantrymen as they tried to capture the ground. Breckinridge asked Robertson to place the guns between the two lines of his division. That was an unworkable arrangement, masking the fire of the pieces, and Robertson refused. Then Breckinridge asked him to place the guns immediately behind the second line; Robertson again refused, citing his orders from Bragg. The division therefore advanced without close artillery support and captured the high ground. It ultimately was repulsed by both a concentration of fifty-eight Union guns and a heavy counterattack by Federal infantry. Robertson's artillery helped slow that counterattack.[5]

Artillery played a significant role in Confederate attacks at Chancellorsville on May 3. Edward Porter Alexander found some places to position guns the night before in this heavily cluttered landscape. The main position was a clearing about 200 yards long and 25 yards wide that offered a view of twenty-seven Union guns planted in an opening called Hazel Grove. He placed one battery here and two batteries along Plank Road. There was room for four pieces in "a thin place in the woods" at a farm road and in another clear spot 100 feet in diameter. Alexander placed a total of seventeen pieces in these four positions. Whether they played a decisive role in the capture of Hazel Grove is not clear, but once Alexander could use the grove, he packed it with guns to offer fire support for further operations. Lt. Col. Thomas H. Carter recalled that Maj. Gen. James E. B. Stuart, who directed the infantry attacks on May 3, told him the guns had played a key role in his success. The forty pieces assembled after the capture of Hazel Grove pounded the Federals around the Chancellor House and "broke the lines which he had *in vain* tried repeatedly to carry, and that the victory was essentially an Artillery victory."[6]

Union artillery played an effective role in the capture of Marye's Heights at Fredericksburg that same day. Col. Charles H. Tompkins told Sixth Corps batteries to concentrate their fire on Confederate infantrymen behind the stone wall at the foot of the heights "until the assaulting column had nearly reached the wall, and then to direct their fire upon the batteries upon the crest." The infantry succeeded, and guns moved forward. Battery F, 5th US Artillery "followed closely on the infantry in its attack, and came into position on the crest only a few seconds after its capture."[7]

Confederate efforts to soften up Meade's position at Gettysburg on July 3 represented the hopes and limitations of artillery support for infantry assaults during the Civil War. Alexander was placed in charge of the effort to deliver "the most effective cannonade possible. It was not meant simply to make a noise, but to try & cripple him—to tear him limbless, as it were, if possible." Alexander's first objective was to neutralize the Federal artillery and then to advance his own pieces to support Pickett's Division and Pettigrew's Division as they advanced. But the only position for his guns was nothing more than open ground in full view of and exposed to Union artillery, firing at distances mostly over 1,200 yards. Alexander counted 135 pieces along the Confederate line, the largest concentration of Rebel artillery on any Civil War battlefield.[8]

Alexander warned corps commander Lt. Gen. James Longstreet that the only way to gauge the effectiveness of his fire was the rate and volume of return fire by the Union guns. Moreover, there was little ammunition left, and Alexander had to reserve some rounds to support the infantry advance. He estimated that the bombardment and support phases should not exceed one hour. Adding to the pressure, Longstreet charged Alexander with determining whether the preparatory fire had been effective enough to warrant the launching of the attack as well as the moment it was best to start the infantry if the answer was affirmative.[9]

Beginning at 1 P.M., the Confederate pieces delivered a heavy fire, but it was extremely difficult for Alexander to gauge the effect. Anxious to start the infantry as soon as possible to save rounds, he was encouraged when the Federal pieces began to stop firing. But, as noted in a previous chapter, this was a calculated ploy to deceive the Confederates. Alexander sent word that the infantry had better start.[10] He then tried to organize close support for the assault. Earlier he had been promised the use of nine 12-pounder howitzers and had positioned them in a hollow so they would be fresh for the advance. But after the infantry started, Alexander found the hollow empty. Some of the howitzers had been ordered away by William N. Pendleton, while others had moved to a safer location. Alexander quickly went down his artillery line and selected batteries that had at least fifteen rounds of long-distance ammunition for each piece and ordered them forward. All told, he tapped a couple of pieces from each of eighteen batteries. Those pieces failed to offer any appreciable support. They could not find a good position close to the Union line or keep pace with the advance of the infantry. Alexander kicked himself for the rest of his life for failing to keep better control over the nine howitzers. He felt he had missed the best opportunity of his career to show that close support of an infantry assault was possible, although he never explained how he intended to overcome the inherent problems of this operation.[11]

The failure of the Pickett-Pettigrew attack, with half the men participating shot down or captured, proved that the artillery preparation had been ineffective. All accounts indicate that most of the Confederate rounds sailed over the Union line rather than into it, demonstrating that frontal fire often was negated by poor gunnery.[12]

In short, the possibilities of close artillery support for an infantry attack varied from one battlefield to another. In the West a more aggressive attitude existed among Union gunners. During a Fourth Corps advance against Confederate works in heavily vegetated country on June 10, 1864, during the Atlanta Campaign, a rifle battery was placed at the head of each infantry column so it could try to batter down earthen parapets. Lt. Col. Charles F. Morse of the 2nd Massachusetts Infantry was impressed. "I will give the Western arm credit for their superior use of artillery," he wrote a few days later. "Wherever infantry goes, the batteries follow right in line, and in this way guns can be used continually at very short range, producing of course, deadly effect." There are several other examples of western artillerymen placing guns forward of friendly skirmish lines to obtain close-distance fire on Confederate targets.[13]

But we should not take the western Federals as typical of all Civil War artillerists. The problems of close artillery support for infantry attacks was not due to the long-distance firing capability of the rifle musket, as previous historians have argued, but due to terrain features and the inherent difficulty of wheeled carriages pushed by men keeping pace with swift-moving foot soldiers. One battlefield may have offered some advantages in this way, while others did not. Contingencies played a large role in every attempt to support infantry advances.

FOOT SOLDIERS VERSUS THE BIG GUNS

Those responsible for developing artillery doctrine paid a great deal of attention to firing on opposing infantry. The *Ordnance Manual* noted that foot soldiers could cross 70 yards of ground while marching at common time, 86 yards at quick time, and 109 yards at double quick. One infantryman occupied a space of twenty inches in the rank and a depth of thirteen inches; five men stood in a space of one square yard. Joseph Roberts provided a chart indicating how many rounds a battery might fire at a moving mass of foot soldiers in a given amount of time. In other words, the developers of doctrine tried to reduce the artillery fight against infantry to a science.[14]

Gibbon urged commanders to fire solid shot with a charge of canister in front of it and to dispense with sponging when the enemy came within 150 yards. At that point he urged the use of canister only and pointing the tube very low to cause the balls to ricochet and scatter. Everyone agreed that oblique or enfilade fire was best but not always possible. Gibbon thought the first discharge always had the greatest emotional impact on the target, while Hunt thought accuracy of fire had the greatest effect in depressing enemy morale.[15] Everyone seemed to agree that the proper role of field artillery was to hit infantry and cavalry rather than opposing guns. Henry Halleck was willing to see no more than one-third of the pieces fire at enemy artillery while the rest concentrated on opposing foot soldiers. In any case, they believed that the big guns contributed more to victory if they sought to punish personnel in the opposing ranks rather than artillery hardware.[16]

Most battery commanders followed this part of the doctrine. Confederate battalion officers at Fredericksburg ordered battery leaders "to reserve their fire for the enemy's infantry at close range." Federal and Confederate officers at Stones River received similar orders. "I did not think it proper to reply," wrote Lt. Charles C. Parsons when he drew Rebel artillery fire, "so long as our ammunition could be used with better effect upon his infantry." At Kolb's Farm Union battery officers paid no attention to artillery fire until after they contributed to repelling the Confederate infantry assault.[17]

While dealing with infantry attacks, battery commanders used shell and case shot at a distance, although some of them fired these types of projectiles at distances of only 150 yards. Canister was invariably used at short distances. Sometimes artillerists fired canister without sponging to save time and get in more rounds, doubling and even tripling the canister rounds in one fire.[18]

Infantrymen were divided on the question of whether long-distance ordnance or short-distance canister was the most difficult fire to face. David McKinney of the 77th Illinois proved that long-distance ordnance could mesmerize the victim. One day during the Siege of Vicksburg, he noticed a solid shot flying toward his location. "For a few seconds I gazed, unmovable, at its rapid approach, fascinating me as it were by its fearful approach." Only at the last moment did he step sideways as it landed six feet away.[19]

Most long-distance projectiles failed to hit anyone, but when they did, their emotional impact could be devastating. One Federal shell killed and wounded eighteen men in the 29th North Carolina and a neighboring regiment at Stones River. At times the gun crew could hear the cries of "pain, terror, and anguish" it caused with accurate fire. Bodies were decimated, torn into pieces by shell bursts. Henry Robinson Berkeley of the Amherst Virginia Battery described a Federal soldier who had been "cut in two. The head, arms and about one-half of his ribs had been thrown against a fence, and remained with his heart and

Fig. 12.1. Artillery Tree at Shiloh. Cannon fire often shredded vegetation in the area of its target, sparing human casualties but devastating the natural environment. Although the damage was limited in extent, it could last for decades. Environmental factors both hindered and facilitated artillery fire just as it simultaneously protected and exposed targets, depending on many various circumstances on any given battlefield. *Frank Leslie's Illustrated Newspaper,* May 17, 1862, 53.

entrails sticking to the top rail, while some 10 feet of the lower part of the body had been thrown into a mud hole in the road." Many men were decapitated by artillery rounds in a merciful act of instantaneous death.[20]

These gory facts of combat tend to hide the fact that, as noted above, most artillery fire fell harmlessly to the ground or scarred trees and uprooted underbrush on the battlefield. Infantrymen could note that, despite all the noise, their regiments came off surprisingly well after a bombardment. The 148th Pennsylvania lost only two men wounded after heavy artillery fire that lasted nearly one hour at Bristoe Station. Moreover, every soldier witnessed a miraculous escape from danger at one time or another. A Confederate shell exploded in the ranks of the 42nd Ohio at Chickasaw Bayou and enveloped Charlie Henry in a cloud of powder smoke. "No one hoped ever to see more than a small piece of him again," wrote Joe Rudolph, "but when the smoke cleared there he stood with a broad grin on his face, not in the least disturbed." Capt. John Reese of the 81st Illinois explained how he experienced a similar escape at Champion Hill by telling his correspondent that there was "a good many places for Bullets and Balls to strike without hitting me." Hosea Rood of the 12th Wisconsin commented that Confederate artillery fire "proved quite harmless to us" during the latter phases of the Atlanta Campaign. "It gave us a magnificent display of fireworks" but few casualties.[21]

Statistics support Rood's comment. Artillery accounted for a surprisingly small percentage of combat injuries during the Civil War. Based on 141,970 recorded cases of battlefield wounds, the *Medical and Surgical History of the Civil War* reported that 9 percent were inflicted by shell fragments, 1 percent by canister, and 0.3 percent by solid shot. That means a total of 14,032 of the cases were accounted for by artillery fire, amounting to only 12.9 percent of the total wounds. In contrast, small-arms fire accounted for 87.9 percent of the wounds.[22]

The percentage varied from battle to battle. At Chickasaw Bayou, according to Surgeon Edmund Andrews, only 8.3 percent of 730 recorded cases of wounds were caused by artillery, while 91 percent were caused by small arms. Surgeon Thomas S. Hawley maintained a small data set stemming from wounded he treated at the Third Division, Fifteenth Corps hospital in the early stages of the Vicksburg siege. Of thirty-one cases treated after the failed Union attack of May 19, 26.7 percent were caused by artillery and 73.3 percent by small arms; he noted that 87.5 percent of the artillery wounds had been caused by shells. The rates were slightly different three days later when Hawley supervised the care of 107 men after the failed attack of May 22. At that time artillery accounted for 12.2 percent and small arms for 87.8 percent of the wounds.[23]

Only on comparatively rare occasions could artillery inflict overwhelming casualty rates on the target. As Brig. Gen. J. Patton Anderson's brigade went "swinging across a field" at Stones River, Federal artillery fired at short distance. The 30th Mississippi lost 62 men killed and 139 wounded "all within a very short space of time, and upon an area not greater than an acre of ground."[24]

ARTILLERY STANDS FIRM

Long after the war, Thomas H. Carter boasted that field guns could hold their own against infantry as long as they were concentrated and had a clear field of fire for up to 400 yards. "My belief is that it would be as impregnable against front attack as the Rock of Gibralter [*sic*]." Many of Carter's colleagues in gray and his opponents in blue were willing to bet on the big guns when they had opportunity to use canister on advancing troops. "That is what rakes them down," John W. Chase of the 1st Massachusetts Battery told his brother about canister fire.[25]

Officers were willing to use this projectile, but it had its limits. Firing double charges of canister appears to have been relatively rare. "I was too old an artillery man to have indulged in that extravagance *beyond* or even *at* 300 yards," recalled Capt. James Chester of Batteries E and G, 1st US Artillery. Even the 5th Massachusetts Battery, a workhorse unit in the Army of the Potomac, fired triple canister only once in its war service—to help repel Pickett's Charge.[26]

There is always a danger of overemphasizing even the use of single rounds of canister in the Civil War. Short-distance fighting, for which canister was made, tended to be highly dramatic and awe-inspiring, but it did not represent the majority of combat situations. "The amount of canister fired was tremendous," Wainwright declared of First Corps artillery at Gettysburg. But he admitted that it came to only 392 rounds of 4,460 rounds fired, or only 8.7 percent. Three of his batteries fired more than the "usual supply carried with each battery," but Wainwright failed to note that the usual supply was quite low compared to the number of long-distance projectiles normally carried in the ammunition chests. Another example of heavy canister use that represented only a small proportion of total rounds fired is the 6th Ohio Battery at Chickamauga. The unit helped repel a Confederate attack, engaging for a time in close-distance firing. Yet the battery used only 20 rounds of canister out of 109 projectiles, or 18.3 percent of the rounds it fired that day.[27] In other words, a few dramatic moments did not represent average artillery practice during the Civil War.

In addition to canister, batteries employed long-distance projectiles against infantry advances. They adjusted according to distance, firing shells and case shot beyond 400 yards, shifting to canister at less than that distance, and reverting back to shells and case shot when the enemy retired beyond 400 yards.[28] There are many examples of artillery repelling an infantry attack at comparatively long distance, with the foot soldiers breaking and giving way at a point beyond 50 yards. This happened at Malvern Hill, Stones River, Kolb's Farm, and the Fourth Offensive at Petersburg. In many of those cases, it is clear that enfilading fire by other batteries or effective support by friendly infantry contributed to the repulse.[29]

Even within the short distance of fifty yards, there are many examples of batteries breaking infantry attacks with canister fire. Much has been made of the fact that one piece of Battery A, 1st Rhode Island Light Artillery fired one canister round into the 26th North Carolina during the Pickett-Pettigrew attack at Gettysburg at a distance of only twenty yards. In fact, a monument has been erected on the battlefield to memorialize the event. But the truth is that similarly short-distance canister fire took place on many other battlefields too. Fifty and sixty yards were recorded as canister firing distances at Fort Donelson and Shiloh and thirty yards at the Battle of Pilot Knob in September 1864. Battery B, Pennsylvania Light Artillery poured canister into packed infantry only fifteen yards away during heavy fighting at Stones River.[30]

Artillerists admitted that the most satisfying kind of combat was to fire at retreating infantrymen. "That was the part of artillery service that may be denominated 'pie,'" wrote Alexander, "to fire into swarming fugitives, who can't answer back. One has usually to pay for his pie before he gets it, so he has no compunctions of conscience or chivalry." He found it exhilarating to damage a fleeing enemy as much as possible. "There is no excitement on earth like it. It is far prettier shooting than at a compact, narrow line of battle, or at another battery."[31]

But gunners enjoyed their pie only on rare occasions. Alexander tasted it on May 3 at Chancellorsville and on July 2 at Gettysburg. Many Federals also tasted it on October 19, 1864, at Cedar Creek and on December 16 at Nashville. They were well advised to savor the moment, for those few instances represented a tiny proportion of their war service.[32]

INFANTRY GAINS THE UPPER HAND

The struggle between artillery and infantry was never dominated by either arm. Whether one or the other gained the upper hand depended on many factors in the tactical environment of every battlefield. But there is no doubt that infantry often succeeded in direct confrontations with the big guns.

Rifle fire could devastate a battery's complement of animals and men. At Iuka friendly infantry support fell back and left the 11th Ohio Battery isolated. The artillerists fought to the last, losing 55.8 percent of their total manpower and 85.1 percent of their gun detachments. What was left of the battery fell back, leaving the pieces behind, but the survivors managed to recover them after the Confederates evacuated the area.[33] Sharpshooters annoyed artillery mercilessly, and it was never easy to counter their fire, some of which was delivered from distances of 500 yards and more. Supporting infantry often were reluctant to advance far enough to deal effectively with them. Fortunately for the artillery, losses to distant sharpshooting tended to be much lighter than from close-distance firing by a line of battle.[34]

A handful of battery commanders reported how many of their men were taken down by rifle fire compared to artillery, but they usually included this data only when the ratio of small-arms fire was unusually high. At Shiloh the 5th Company, Washington Artillery suffered the loss of twenty-seven men and thirty horses all due to rifle fire, although one battery member admitted that some of it was friendly fire from supporting Confederate infantrymen. Of the nine men lost in the Washington Artillery of Georgia at that battle, 88.8 percent were due to small-arms fire. The Warren Light Artillery of Mississippi lost seven men at Stones River, 71.5 percent of them due to rifle fire. Half of the losses sustained by the 11th New York Battery on June 17 and 24 at Petersburg were due to the same cause, and the 6th Maine Battery lost two killed and six wounded, "all sharpshooters wounds," on June 17 at Petersburg.[35]

These statistics indicate that, given the right circumstances, infantrymen could significantly reduce a battery's manpower. When opposing troops then advanced and supporting infantry fell back, the battery officer was faced with the ultimate test of his ability to command. To retreat or to stand and fight became his choice. Many artillery officers decided that the better part of valor was to pull away. They often made that decision when the advancing infantry was fifty yards from the muzzles, although that was only a rule of thumb. The longer they waited the less chance of getting the pieces out of danger, but some men bravely waited until the enemy was only fifteen yards away before ordering their subordinates to pull out.[36]

The Confederates were so close to Battery G, 2nd US Artillery at Glendale that Capt. James Thompson placed double spherical case shot rounds in the tube and cut the fuze to explode "on leaving the gun." On several occasions cannoneers were bayonetted by the enemy, who swarmed in among the pieces. The left section of Battery F, 2nd Illinois Light Artillery, "acting as artillery always should do," continued firing to the last in the battle of July 22 east of Atlanta. It lost all equipment except the caissons because it waited "too late for them to get away."[37]

The outcome of any duel between artillery and infantry depended more on circumstances than on any inherent power either arm was able to employ. As Capt. Daniel Wait Howe of the 79th Indiana put it, if infantry could avoid being damaged by canister fire in a charge on a battery, it had a good chance of shooting the cannoneers or horses and either forcing the unit to retire or capturing it. "The general reader who sees accounts of men 'marching up to the cannon's mouth' is apt to believe that this is a poetic stretch of imagination. But it is not. Such scenes were often witnessed during the Civil War." Howe thought that attacking field fortifications required the greatest amount of courage, but attacking a battery required the next greatest measure.[38]

Infantry support was absolutely vital to the security of the guns. If attackers could compel that support to fall back, their chances of taking the enemy cannon increased dramatically. William Miller Owen of the 3rd Company, Washington Artillery recalled the Union infantry assaults against the stone wall at the foot of Marye's Heights at Fredericksburg. The Federals were not stopped by the heavy shelling of Confederate artillery "bursting in their ranks, making great gaps." The blue lines just kept moving "as though they would go straight through and over us." Even firing canister merely staggered but did not stop the infantry. Only when Cobb's Brigade stood up behind the stone wall and fired its small arms did the attackers finally stop and retire.[39]

The salient examples of batteries falling to an infantry attack occurred when support evaporated and the guns were left high and dry. Poor shooting—for example, firing canister that sailed over the heads of advancing infantrymen—increased the gunners' vulnerability. Fighting hand to hand, using handspikes and rammers, with the attacking infantry was no substitute for stopping the advance with short-distance ordnance before the situation ever came to close combat.[40]

The capture of artillery pieces became a hallmark of tactical success in the Civil War, along with the capture of flags and the destruction of large numbers of opposing troops. The Federals lost by their accounting twenty-two of sixty-two pieces engaged in the Battle of Gaines's Mill during the Seven Days Campaign. The Confederates captured twenty-nine Union pieces in their offensive on December 31 at Stones River and thirty-nine guns at Chickamauga. But two months after the latter engagement, the Federals captured forty-one pieces from the Confederates during the Battle of Chattanooga.[41]

Rebel loss of guns increased dramatically during the last year of the war. The Army of Tennessee left 20 pieces behind when it evacuated Atlanta in

September 1864, and Hood lost close to half of his 124 pieces while invading Union-held Tennessee in November and December. When important cities and their semipermanent fortifications fell, the haul included a mix of field-pieces and heavy artillery. Sherman's army group captured 97 cannon, about four-fifths of them fieldpieces, during the Carolinas Campaign. His artillery chief estimated that if he counted all the guns secured when Charleston, Wilmington, and Fort Fisher fell during the same time as the Carolinas drive, the total would come to 700 guns of all types and sizes. The surrender of Gen. Joseph E. Johnston's force in late April 1865 brought another 168 pieces into Federal control.[42] In Virginia during the last year of the war, the Army of the Potomac captured 32 pieces (most of them at Spotsylvania on May 12) while losing 25 guns from May 4 to October 31, 1864. The Army of the James's Eighteenth Corps captured 13 pieces on September 29 during the Fifth Offensive at Petersburg. When Lee's army left Petersburg on April 3, 1865, it carried with it 250 artillery pieces. A week later, when surrendering at Appomattox, it had only 61 left.[43]

There is no doubt that a certain percentage of guns listed as captured by either army on the battlefield were actually abandoned by their crews. Some of them were not considered valuable. The Federals found a 2-pounder piece left by the retreating Confederates at Williamsburg during the Peninsula Campaign; it had been made in Spain in 1778. At other engagements valuable ordnance was left behind for want of means to carry it off. The Confederates abandoned nine guns and thirty-five caissons at Shiloh "for want of horses," as Maj. Francis A. Shoup put it.[44]

Both sides made efforts to secure captured or abandoned artillery carriages and equipment as much as possible, for they usually could be repaired and put to use. In fact, the Confederate Adjutant and Inspector General's Office issued a general order in November 1862 requiring the chiefs of artillery in every field army to organize details with teams of horses before an engagement to haul away captured material as soon as possible. The Confederates often used these items to quickly fill the wants of their batteries before sending the rest to ordnance departments.[45]

CONCLUSION

The struggle between field artillery and opposing infantry never resolved it-self. Throughout the war, neither side gained the upper hand in any consistent or final way. The ability of gunners to deal decisively with foot soldiers was limited by imperfect fuzes for long-distance ordnance, by the relatively light weight of their bursting charges, and by the tendency of shells to fragment into large pieces that failed to cover much area when they exploded. Even short-distance ordnance, like double canister, did not necessarily cover all of the target area. It was possible for determined infantrymen to push forward through a hail of artillery fire and capture a battery, especially if supporting infantrymen abandoned the guns. From the beginning of the war to its end, infantry and artillery traded deadly blows, with no assurance that either side would win.

13

· · · · · · · · · · · · · · · · · ·

FIELD ARTILLERY AND FORTIFICATIONS

The creators of doctrine in the Civil War era knew that field fortifications played a significant role in artillery work. John Gibbon
provided details on how to construct fortified gun emplacements
and discussed the nature of different soils as they affected the digging of those
works. The parapet needed to be between ten and twelve feet thick, with an
interior crest at least eight feet high. The embrasures (the gap in the parapet through which an artillery piece fired) needed to be twenty inches wide
at the outer end and much more narrow at the inner end. The trick with the
embrasure was to make it small enough to protect the gun detachment but
wide enough to allow the piece proper range for firing. Wooden platforms
were necessary to prevent the wheels of the carriage from sinking into ruts,
which would alter its firing effectiveness. Sand or sandy soil, as noted by the
Ordnance Manual, resisted enemy artillery fire better than "the productive
earths, or clay, or earth that retains water."[1]

In the field artillerists improvised a good deal with material to create protection. They gathered cotton bales and hay bales to make a parapet, using
bushes or cornstalks to hide a full view of the emplacement from enemy eyes.
On the night of April 6, 1862, the Federals made a low parapet of earth and logs
for some heavy guns and Battery E, 2nd Illinois Light Artillery near Pittsburg
Landing after the first day of combat at Shiloh.[2] At Yorktown Henry J. Hunt
often detailed artillery officers to help infantry units plan and construct re-
doubts along the Union line so as to accommodate the needs of field batteries.
Sandbags often were used to revet artillery embrasures. George B. McClellan
wanted mantlets to close the embrasures for more complete protection when
the pieces were being reloaded. Two types were employed: One was made

of heavy rope, and the other consisted of half-inch wrought iron fastened to three-inch oak planks.[3]

Some artillerists chafed at the thought of cooping up their guns in an earthwork. Thomas H. Carter preferred to operate in the open, where he could change position every few rounds to throw off Union aim. On the Federal side, Lt. M. D. McAlester urged batteries to occupy open ground to "regain their important property of mobility."[4]

But the overwhelming majority of artillerists soon came to appreciate good earthworks. Both sides dug in their guns during the Fredericksburg Campaign. Some were planned by engineer officers, but the gunners always had their own ideas about how to improve the work. "We have to fight here, not you," members of the 3rd Company, Washington Artillery told engineers as they raised the parapet higher; "we will arrange them to suit ourselves." When a piece of the Donaldsonville Artillery left its work to gain a position in the open, it was disabled by Federal fire after only five rounds.[5] At Stones River Capt. Overton W. Barret was convinced that even "some small earthworks" saved his Confederate battery from much harm. Federal artillerists at Fairview during the Chancellorsville Campaign dug one-gun emplacements a foot and a half deep, placing the spoil in front. "It looked as far as could be seen in the open field like a row of horse-shoes lying inside of each other," commented an observer. Similarly light works sprouted up along the Union line at Gettysburg. "The protection they afforded was of course small," commented Capt. R. Bruce Ricketts.[6]

VICKSBURG

But the trend was toward deeper, more extensive protection. At Vicksburg the Federal siege line grew to be twelve miles long and sported eighty-nine fortified batteries holding 220 pieces. While most of them were fieldpieces, the Federals used some heavy guns, including 30-pounder Parrotts and 32-pounder and 42-pounder pieces. Naval vessels cooperating with Grant loaned a few guns too. The Confederates placed at least 102 pieces along the siege line plus another 70 heavy pieces in their batteries along the east bluff of the Mississippi River.[7]

In both armies the artillerists did most of the digging and repair of their emplacements. The Federals learned not to make their parapets more than eight feet thick after they established artillery dominance early in the siege. At some Union works the artillerists revetted the parapet with gabions and fascines and constructed good platforms for their pieces, while at others fence rails and cotton bales sufficed. They all scrounged lumber and timber from nearby buildings. Mantlets, normally made of tightly wound rope, hung inside the embrasure. On the Thirteenth Corps sector, engineers experimented with bags of tightly stuffed cotton, which proved to be effective against small-arms fire. They also devised heavy wooden collars and attached them to the breech of the piece to protect the crew.[8]

With constant practice on the same targets, Union gunners damaged the opposing earthworks and achieved artillery dominance at Vicksburg. William L. Brown of the Chicago Mercantile Battery boasted that two out of three rounds hit opposing embrasures, while William Christie of the 1st Minnesota Battery estimated his comrades could place three out of every five rounds in them. Union projectiles tore down segments of Confederate parapets or landed squarely in trenches to kill and mangle half a dozen men at one stroke. They also degraded traverses, "knocking off the top, foot by foot," in the words of a Mississippi soldier. Near the Jackson Road, a 9-inch piece was, in the words of one observer, "battering down our works" faster during the day than the Confederates could repair them during the night. The Federals unleashed 142,912 rounds of ammunition during forty-seven days of siege, amounting to more than 3,000 rounds per day.[9]

ATLANTA

The struggle for Atlanta compelled the fieldpieces to operate from behind earthworks repeatedly for four months rather than forty-seven days. Those works often were constructed by pioneers (infantrymen detailed to special work detachments) but always were finished by the battery members. Very often most of the work took place during the night, when it was safer to expose oneself. "'Spades to the front'" was the order in the 1st Iowa Battery after midnight of July 20, "and then it was dig, dig the night through," wrote Samuel Black. "A pile of dirt in front and a hole in which to work the gun looks good." Douglas's Texas Battery constructed nine forts at different locations during the first month of the campaign.[10]

Parapets from ten to fourteen feet thick and high enough to entirely cover a man while standing were ideal. For Lumsden's Alabama Battery, the em-

Fig. 13.1. Union Battery in Confederate Atlanta City Line. The protection afforded gun crews by well-made field fortifications is well illustrated by this photograph, exposed by George N. Barnard soon after the fall of Atlanta. Here, Union guns have replaced Confederate pieces in the forts of the City Line that ringed the city. This Napoleon has a cover over the vent. The photo likely was taken at Confederate Fort V, looking toward Fort W, on the northwestern segment of the line. LC-DIG-cwpb-03401.

brasures normally were eighteen inches wide at the near end and eight feet wide at the far end. Even so, shells and small-arms fire often sailed through to damage the piece or kill or wound crewmen. Mantlets would have helped, but there is no evidence of their use by either side during the Atlanta Campaign. The 1st Iowa Battery stuffed gunny sacks with cotton and placed them in the embrasure, but that would only have stopped prying eyes from observing what took place inside the work rather than an artillery round.[11]

Whenever gun crews took up a new position, the first requirement was to dig in, or sink the battery. They took off the ammunition chests from the limbers and placed them in holes in the ground, also digging holes for the wheels of the limbers so as to sink them as much as possible. Constructing casemates provided all around coverage, top as well as sides, but they were rarely used during the Atlanta Campaign. At times artillerists tried to mask their position by placing cut brush in front of the earthen parapets. To avert a surprise attack at night, Francis A. Shoup requested such things as fireballs made of cotton soaked with turpentine that could be used to light up an area.[12] "Where Batteries are as well protected as ours and the Yankee Batteries before us about as much is made of Artillery duels as the sledge hammer makes out of the anvil," concluded Andrew Jackson Neal of the Marion Light Artillery. Capt. James P. Douglas estimated the Federals fired 300 shells at one of his positions over several days, but he lost only one man wounded in the battery.[13]

Just as at Vicksburg, Federal gunners could achieve dominance over their opponents and degrade their protective earthworks, at least for a time. On July 5, 1864, infantry brigade leader Brig. Gen. Arthur M. Manigault watched as four Union batteries concentrated fire on the Confederate line near Smyrna Station. The Federals placed many rounds in and through the embrasures until the Rebel crews "lost their nerve, and almost abandoned their guns, seeking shelter close under the works. It was not the first instance in which I had seen evidence of our artillery giving up too easily, and they began about this time to show too great dread of the superiority which the enemy possessed over us in this arm, and to use a vulgar but very expressive phrase, were considerably 'under the hack.'"[14]

Union artillery tended to outshoot their opponents during the Atlanta Campaign and devastated Confederate infantry and artillery alike. Lt. Col. Alexander A. Greene recorded the damage inflicted on his 37th Alabama along the New Hope Church–Pickett's Mill–Dallas Line. A Federal battery of 20-pounder Parrotts opened "with terrible effect" from 300 yards at 4 P.M. on May 27. One shell hit the top of the parapet and fell into the trench, exploding and killing four Confederates. Greene lost fifty-six men out of four companies that fielded a total of only one hundred troops that evening. "Three men had their heads carried away," he revealed, "1 had his right shoulder torn off, 1 had both hands carried away, and many had painful wounds in the head." Only two of his men lost their nerve and ran away. Greene detailed sharpshooters, but their old Austrian rifles made no impression on the Federals. Only when his

brigade commander sent twenty men from other regiments armed with En-
field rifles did the sharpshooting have an effect. After that it caused wild firing
by the Federals and relieved his battered regiment of the worst punishment.[15]

Greene's regiment depended on inadequate earthworks, as did Andrew
Jackson Neal's Marion Light Artillery of Florida on June 19. Union skirmish
fire harassed Neal's battery near a sharp salient in the Confederate Mud Creek
Line, where the guns were pummeled by fire from three directions. Thirty-one
bullets pierced the flag, the staff was cut by an additional seven bullets, and
the trees nearby were riddled. "I counted about eighty balls on the body" of
one "little sapling," Neal informed his father. So much small-arms fire came
through the embrasures that the face of the pieces and the upper part of the
axles and wheels were punched by "hundreds of marks." Even the men's canteens and blankets inside the emplacement were riddled with bullets. Neal
lost four of his forty men before sending the survivors to the rear. The Confederates held the Mud Creek Line only one day, retiring that night to the
Kennesaw Mountain Line.[16]

Intense fighting on July 21 provided another example of Federal artillery
dominating inadequate fortifications. Brig. Gen. James A. Smith's Texas
brigade took position east of Atlanta behind slight works constructed by
the cavalry and did not have time to improve them. At 7 A.M. a Federal battery
opened fire from a position 800 yards to his left and enfiladed the Texan line,
"committing dreadful havoc in the ranks. I have never before witnessed such
accurate and destructive cannonading. In a few minutes 40 men were killed
and over 100 wounded by this battery alone." One round took out seventeen
of eighteen men in one company of the 18th Texas Cavalry (dismounted).[17]
"They have better artilleries than we have," wrote Maj. William A. Drennan
of the 27th Mississippi on another occasion, "or it may be in their guns—or
their ammunition; to say the least of it they do more execution with their
guns in the way of dismounting pieces and throwing shells in entrench-
ments than we do." But, as noted in the previous examples, Union artillery
expertise was greatly aided by Confederate inadequacy in digging earthwork protection.[18]

The Atlanta Campaign was a learning experience for the Army of Tennessee. Beginning with relatively little prior use of field fortifications, it was
caught flatfooted on more than one occasion. At Resaca light fieldworks proved
inadequate against enfilading Union artillery fire that devastated the infantry

units holding a sharp angle in the line. At Cassville the absence of traverses led to a decision by the army commander to abandon an otherwise strong defensive position when Union guns obtained enfilading fire on the line. The Confederates, however, learned their lessons the hard way. From Cassville south, they began to build increasingly effective fieldworks at each position until ringing Atlanta with one of the strongest systems of fortifications any city of the war could boast. Deep trenches, high and thick parapets, and numerous traverses were the best protection against artillery fire.[19]

OVERLAND CAMPAIGN

Henry J. Hunt thought the artillery of the Army of the Potomac was at its peak when the Overland Campaign began in early May 1864. From the beginning, earthworks played a significant role in its operations. The 6th Maine Battery lost relatively few men at the Wilderness because it was protected by "heavy breastworks." The earthworks grew in size and complexity at the next confrontation around Spotsylvania, forcing gunners to find ways of dropping rounds behind parapets and onto couching enemy troops. In Battery B, 4th US Artillery gunners learned how to graze the top of Rebel works so that the round would fall into the trench behind them. The absence of Confederate artillery support contributed to the crushing of the Mule Shoe Salient on May 12 because Lee thought Grant was moving away from Spotsylvania the previous night. When Union Second Corps troops conducted a massive assault at dawn the next day, there were few pieces available to defend the salient.[20]

At Cold Harbor Capt. Edwin B. Dow estimated that the addition of embrasures to his earthworks doubled the protection afforded his men in the 6th Maine Battery. During the general assault on June 3, Fifth Corps artillery fired 3,435 rounds, amounting to eighteen tons of iron. But Charles Wainwright guessed it had little effect on the Confederates because of their heavy earthworks. Even though the infantry failed to break Lee's line, many units dug in at their high-tide mark to advance the Union position. The artillery followed them. "All of the men that could be spared from the guns, together with the drivers of the limbers and caissons, were at once set to work to throw up [new] works," reported Lt. Augustin N. Parsons of Battery A, 1st New Jersey Light Artillery. "The ground being very loose and sandy, the men were soon well protected from the enemy's skirmishers and sharpshooters."[21]

Fig. 13.2. Coehorn Mortar. These small pieces could be carried through the trenches by four men, planted almost anywhere, and quickly go into action. Served well, they could be devastating to enemy troops despite well-made earthworks because of their high angle of fire. *Harper's Weekly,* July 30, 1864, 485.

The semisiege conditions at Cold Harbor called for more high-angle artillery fire such as that delivered by mortars. The Coehorn mortar was small enough to be carried by four men and could propel a seventeen-pound shell with one pound of powder up to 1,000 yards distance. Hunt had started the Overland Campaign with eight Coehorns and had used them briefly at Spotsylvania and at the North Anna. At Cold Harbor Battery D, 4th New York Heavy Artillery took charge of six Coehorns, initially planting two of them 800 yards from the Confederate line on June 3 but later that day moving them forward until only 150 yards away. The next day these weapons clearly damaged the Confederates. Rebel sharpshooters concentrated fire at them, but the mortar crews retaliated. They saw two sharpshooters "blown 10 feet into the air, with heads detached" as a result of their fire, and the rest ran away. Requests for more Coehorns flowed in to Hunt's headquarters after this, but it would take too long for more to reach the field at Cold Harbor.[22]

Even before the start of the Overland Campaign, Hunt had conducted experiments with using fieldpieces as mortars. He dug a hole for the trail of a Napoleon and tried various distances to see if the carriage would withstand the shock without the relief of recoil. At Fort Fletcher near Cold Harbor, Jacob Roemer did the same thing and found that it worked. He cut the powder charge down to six and then five ounces, obtained forty-five degrees elevation, and fired fifty-three rounds without breaking the carriage.[23] The Confederates also deployed several fieldpieces as mortars, choosing howitzers because of their arced angle of fire. The Federals suffered casualties because of this and constructed more sophisticated shelters, digging bombproofs five feet deep and twelve feet square at the 10th Massachusetts Battery position.[24]

Earthworks sprang up tall and strong at Cold Harbor, but in places they were not well made, exposing crews to skirmish fire. One piece in Manly's North Carolina Battery suffered, the spokes of its wheels riddled by small-arms fire until the men replaced them, only to see the new ones become riddled as well. Spent bullets rolled out of the tube when they tipped the gun forward. The battered carriage was sent to the arsenal at Richmond, where it was put on display to show "what musketry fire might be and do," as Robert Stiles put it. Pieces in other Confederate batteries were so battered that they "looked as if they had had smallpox, from the striking and splaying of leaden balls against them. Even the narrow lips of the pieces, about their muzzles, were indented in this way."[25]

Mantlets would have helped a great deal, but they were in short supply at Cold Harbor. There is no evidence the Confederates used any during the Overland Campaign, and only scant evidence that the Federals tried to improvise them. At Cold Harbor members of the 10th Massachusetts Battery filled hardtack boxes and gabions with dirt to close their embrasures when not in use. Hunt asked if the mantlets constructed for McClellan to use at Yorktown were in storage at Washington, but the confrontation at Cold Harbor ended before they could be located and shipped to the field.[26]

PETERSBURG CAMPAIGN

The use of fortifications during the Overland Campaign prepared the way for a smooth transition to their use during the long confrontation at Petersburg. Stuck in trenches for ten months, both sides perfected artillery protection to its highest degree. Battery officers called for infantry details to help their men dig in, using Black laborers at times as well. Roemer pushed for the construction of traverses for flank protection. At many locations along the Union and Confederate lines, bombproofs were constructed, usually shallow but

Fig. 13.3. Mantlet at Petersburg. Alfred R. Waud sketched this image of a piece on the Eighteenth Corps sector of the Richmond–Petersburg lines as it was being sighted. The embrasure is covered by a rope mantlet with a hole through it for the forward end of the tube. Waud included a Coehorn mortar in the foreground and indicated how members of the gun detachment worked during the process of sighting. LC-DIG-ppmsca-21048.

with layers of logs and several feet of earth to provide top cover. "There was no security of life and limb without them," wrote P. C. Hoy of Bradford's Mississippi Battery.[27]

Mantlets became available, many of them constructed at Fortress Monroe and shipped to the works. By July 16 the Federals were using thirty of these covers along the line. They consisted of rope tightly woven until four inches thick. Col. Henry L. Abbot, commander of the siege train attached to the Army of the Potomac, thought they provided adequate protection. In tests a Springfield rifle musket fired from a distance of twenty paces penetrated only three inches of the rope. Abbot also witnessed the effect when a Confederate 10-pounder rifle fired from a distance of 600 yards and hit the mantlet. It broke the lashing and tore down the poles that supported the covering, but by then the velocity was so reduced the projectile merely knocked down a Federal cannoneer without seriously hurting him. Small-arms fire penetrated these four-inch mantlets only if they happened to hit a spot where "the ropes were not closely lashed together." Rope mantlets six inches thick also appeared at some Union works later in the campaign. The Confederates tended to use wooden mantlets, but Abbot called them "a very poor device" after examining one following the campaign.[28]

Gunners found that if they concentrated fire at one spot, they could degrade enemy parapets. The Napoleons of Battery H, 1st New York Light Artillery fired 213 solid shot at one Rebel location, "cutting down their work around two of their guns in such a manner as to give our sharpshooters command of their pieces," wrote Capt. Charles E. Mink about action on June 18. It took 550 rounds to obliterate the embrasures in an earthwork fronting the 2nd Maine Battery, but such damage could be repaired under cover of darkness.[29]

Petersburg lent itself to the widespread use of mortars by both sides. These weapons came in varied sizes, from Coehorns up to a giant 13-inch piece mounted on a railroad car. Charles Wainwright trained his men how to use Coehorns because most of them had never seen one in action. After test firing a dozen rounds behind the line, they knew what to do. Abbot noted that some mortars tended to blow out friction primers "with great violence" when fired. The flying metal injured several men, so he suggested covering the vent with a metal shield.[30] The Confederates lagged behind the Federals in mortar use at Petersburg, initially fixing fieldpieces to simulate mortars. When genuine mortars arrived from Richmond, they tended to be 12-pounders, which were far outclassed by the heavier Union mortars in both weight and accuracy. The Confederates created two mortars made of "heart white oak" that provided more than a week of firing before they burst.[31]

The biggest artillery fight of the Petersburg Campaign was the Battle of the Crater on July 30. Hunt assembled 110 guns and fifty-four mortars to fire directly on the area. But more pieces than that number fired at other parts of the Confederate line. The bombardment, which began right after the mine went up, continued until 164 guns and mortars had unleashed 9,196 rounds.[32]

Hunt set priorities for the firing, which included smashing wooden obstructions in front of the Confederate line, silencing Rebel artillery, and bombarding the ground behind enemy works to impede reinforcements moving forward. The gunners already had accurate distance and range on their targets and were ready to open as soon as the mine exploded. "As a display of accurate firing, the affair reflected great credit on all the batteries engaged," concluded Wainwright. The Federals placed canister rounds in their 10-inch mortars, firing them off along with the 10-inch shells.[33]

The Confederates assembled far fewer pieces. At least twenty-five field

TABLE 13.1. Types and Sizes of Ordnance in Place to Support the
Mine Attack, July 30, 1864

Types and Sizes	Number of Pieces	Percentage of Total
4.5 Inch Siege Rifle	20	12.2
3-Inch Ordnance Rifle	52	31.7
Napoleon	38	23.2
10-Inch Mortar	10	6.1
8-Inch Mortar	16	9.7
Coehorn Mortar	28	17.1
Total	164	100

guns and about a dozen small mortars fired on Union troops who temporarily occupied the crater, concentrating on human targets rather than trying to silence Federal guns. Wainwright reported that his Fifth Corps emplacements received no more than forty rounds in counterbattery fire all day. Even though some Rebel emplacements received fifty rounds a minute at the height of the bombardment, the gun crews did not suffer much because of their earthwork protection. A few well-placed Confederate guns and mortars seriously damaged the packed and confused Union infantry position within and near the Crater for several hours. At least two 12-pounder mortars were manhandled within fifty yards of the Federals in the latter part of the battle, preparing the way for infantry attacks that ejected the Yankees.[34]

The Crater was an unusual event in the effectiveness of Confederate guns and mortars supporting Lee's infantry. Far more typical of the campaign was the long, dreary days of position warfare in deep trenches and behind heavy parapets. At the height of the campaign, the Ninth Corps sector stretched for five miles and sported ninety-one guns and forty mortars. The former consisted of forty-two Napoleons, thirty-four 3-inch rifles, eleven 30-pounder Parrotts, and four 4.5-inch guns. The latter consisted of twenty-two Coehorns, fourteen 8-inch mortars, and four 10-inch mortars. To oppose these 131 pieces, the Confederates deployed 126 pieces, including thirty-five mortars. With all of these pieces well dug in, the chances of seriously damaging targets remained slight.[35]

Over the long course of the campaign, artillery fire took place either as

TABLE **13.2.** Ordnance Positioned between Fort Sedgwick
and Hare House, August 25, 1864

Types and Sizes	Number of Pieces	Percentage of Total
Napoleon	36	35.7
4.5-Inch Siege Rifle	4	3.9
3-Inch Ordnance Rifle	36	35.7
10-Pounder Parrott	8	7.9
Coehorn Mortar	11	10.9
8-Inch Mortar	6	5.9
Total	101	100

retaliation for an unexpected pounding by the enemy or out of idleness and interference by infantry officers. On September 14 the Confederates fired on Union working parties, so Tenth Corps guns retaliated for several hours, with seventy-nine pieces unleashing 1,741 rounds. The Confederates stopped firing at working parties after this incident.[36] In other cases, there was no apparent reason for the onset of an artillery exchange. Confederate mortars fired on the Ninth Corps on December 19, and Union pieces responded. The firing continued for several hours, with only one infantryman on the Union side hit. "Local commanders along the line frequently direct or importune officers in charge of the guns, to try a shot or two, which invariably starts the whole line to firing," wrote John C. Tidball. At other times "some vagrant shot fired by one side or the other, more from curiosity than anything else," would start it. "An immense expenditure of ammunition thus takes place with but little result."[37]

On both sides of the Petersburg lines, artillery commanders constantly worked to maintain a high level of effectiveness. Pendleton listed maintenance of carriages, tubes, and earthworks high on the list of priorities. Hunt roamed the lines to inspect every piece and try to detect new Confederate emplacements. Rebel mortar crews test fired during the day and marked the range by nailing cleats on their wooden platforms. They numbered the cleats and kept a record of them so as to adjust the range of their fire to hit any target within their scope during the night.[38]

Petersburg witnessed the largest concentration of artillery in one place for the longest time during the Civil War. Although it cannot be said that the big guns played a role in determining the outcome of the campaign, they certainly played a large and decisive role in shaping its characteristics. Very often during the ten-month campaign, the most salient sound was artillery firing, and the heaviest losses among personnel on many days were due to the same cause. The depth and strength of fortifications, as well as the frequency of bomb-proofs, testified to the need for protection against artillery fire on both sides.

SIEGE TRAIN

The Army of the Potomac possessed the only siege train organized during the Civil War and used it widely during the Petersburg Campaign. The train had originally been created under McClellan in 1862 and saw service at Yorktown, where it consisted of 101 pieces ranging from 12-pounders to 200-pounder Parrotts. The Confederates evacuated their lines before the full weight of these guns could be brought to bear. Battery No. 1 opened fire on April 30, 1862, and fired 137 rounds of 100-pound and four rounds of 200-pound shells by the night of May 3–4, mostly on the wharf at Yorktown, from distances of 3,800–4,700 yards. William F. Barry, McClellan's artillery chief, considered it "a source of great professional disappointment" that the enemy did not stay longer so he could demonstrate "the superior power and efficiency of the un-usually heavy metal used in this siege."[39]

One can better understand Barry's disappointment when comparing his siege train with the most recent historical precedent of that time. Maj. Alexander Doull, an ordnance officer in the siege train, pointed out that the British planted 18-pounders and 13-inch mortars, while the French used 50-pounders and 32-pounders, at the Siege of Sebastopol, October 1854–September 1855. The heaviest was the 13-inch English mortar at 11,300 pounds. In contrast, the 13-inch American mortar of 1861 weighed 17,120 pounds. "The guns placed in position before Yorktown exceed, therefore, in weight by 50 per cent. any guns that have ever before been placed in siege batteries," wrote Doull. He also noted that the British siege train consisted of seventy-two pieces, while the 1st Connecticut Heavy Artillery, one of two regiments in charge of McClellan's siege train, alone placed seventy-one pieces at Yorktown.[40]

Hunt suggested strengthening the siege train, which had been inactive for two years, in April 1864. He recommended that Colonel Abbot of the 1st Connecticut Heavy Artillery take charge of it. At that time the train con-sisted of eighteen 4.5-inch pieces, ten 30-pounders, ten 10-inch mortars, six

TABLE **13.3.** Tenth Corps Artillery Firing, September 14–15, 1864

Types and Sizes	Number of Rounds	Percentage of Total
Napoleon	24	30.4
3-Inch Ordnance Rifle	18	22.7
10-Pounder Parrott	4	5.1
6-Pounder James	5	6.4
4.5-Inch Siege Rifle	2	2.5
30-Pounder Parrott	6	7.5
13-Inch Mortar	1	1.3
10-Inch Mortar	4	5.1
8-Inch Mortar	4	5.1
Coehorn Mortar	11	13.9
Total	79	100

100-pounders, and four 10-inch siege howitzers. Abbot acquired additional pieces and placed them aboard coastal transports for shipment to the Army of the Potomac. His guns were not needed until late June, just at the onset of the Petersburg Campaign. Abbot took charge of all heavy guns not only for the Army of the Potomac but also for the Army of the James at Petersburg. He mostly used men of the 1st Connecticut Heavy Artillery to man them.[41]

Abbot's subordinates fired a total of 3,833 rounds during the Battle of the Crater, and even in slack times they averaged 2,534 rounds per day, as in March 1865. The 1st Connecticut Heavy Artillery fielded six companies controlling forty-two pieces in August, but Abbot expanded the siege train by adding the 3rd Connecticut Heavy Artillery. He also had charge of the guns along the Bermuda Hundred Line. In all Abbot commanded eighteen companies with 199 pieces by the end of the campaign. Although still a colonel, he led 2,700 artillerists in the two regiments.[42]

Artillery officers in the West had access to heavy guns, but they never organized a special unit of them. They managed the advance on Corinth in 1862, the sieges of Vicksburg and Port Hudson in 1863, and the Atlanta Campaign in 1864 without a siege train. Barry, who served as artillery chief on Sherman's staff during the last operation, argued that 20-pounder Parrotts were "sufficiently heavy for such work as the operations of the campaign would be likely to render necessary." The 11th Indiana Battery, with four 20-pounder Parrott guns and two 24-pounder howitzers, "was designed to serve as a heavy field or also siege battery" during the campaign. Only when Sherman wanted to bombard Atlanta was it necessary to use heavier metal. At that time eight 4.5-inch rifled siege guns were moved by railroad to the army.[43]

CONCLUSION

The mix of fortifications and field artillery did not decisively alter the role of the big guns on Civil War battlefields. Protection certainly made it more difficult for one battery to knock out another and increased the ability of cannoneers to hold out against infantry attacks. But it was not impossible for artillery or infantry to contend with enemy guns, even if those pieces were protected by parapets. Fortified cannon fell to enemy attacks at Reams Station, Jonesboro, and the last fight at Petersburg on April 2, 1865. If well made, the earthworks affected operations more than if they were poorly planned and built.

What really changed was the nature of artillery combat. Gunners had to devise ways to compensate for the well-constructed earthworks of the enemy by learning how to graze the top of parapets with their rounds so as to deflect the projectile downward. Howitzer fire became more important, and guns with flat trajectories worked well when it came to battering down inadequately constructed parapets. These same cannoneers learned how to make their own earthworks better, paying special attention to the placement, size, and shape of the embrasures.

In many ways, those embrasures became the most important element of the artillery earthwork. It was not only the portal through which gunfire emitted but also the weakest part of the work. Enemy skirmishers and sharpshooters found their best chance of damaging the gun detachment by firing through it. In a heated infantry attack, the embrasure also represented the best door through which to gain entry into the gun emplacement. At the Battle of Franklin, members of the 6th Ohio Battery fought hand to hand in an effort to stop the Confederates from crawling through such an opening and into their works. The Rebels "several times got into the embrasure, pushing their guns through and fired upon the cannoneers," reported Lt. Aaron P. Baldwin. "They were so unpleasantly close that we had to resort to the use of sponge staves, axes, and picks to drive them back. Private Jacob Steinbaugh killed a daring rebel with an ax and disabled another with a pick."[44]

The Federal line at Franklin held despite the heavy press of infantry against the works. Herein lay the most important contribution of artillery fortification—it could constitute the chief difference between victory and defeat if the conditions happened to be right on any given battlefield.

14

. . . .

WORKING TOWARD EFFECTIVENESS

Contemporary assessments of artillery and its effectiveness varied widely. "I have heard and read opinions of army officers, stating that the artillery during the late war was overrated," wrote Capt. Alfred F. R. Arndt of Battery B, 1st Michigan Light Artillery. On the other hand, many praised it as "a most efficient arm." William S. Rosecrans tried to prove his artillery served well at Stones River. He estimated that 20,000 rounds of Union artillery fire accounted for 728 Confederate casualties while 2 million rounds of Federal small-arms fire accounted for 13,832 Rebel losses. That averaged 27.4 artillery rounds needed to hit one man in contrast to 145 bullets to accomplish the same effect. What Rosecrans based all this on was never disclosed, and thus his figures have to be taken with a healthy dose of skepticism.[1]

In contrast to Rosecrans's wishful thinking, some officers were brutally frank about the lack of artillery effectiveness. Antietam could have been a Confederate victory, according to Daniel Harvey Hill, except for three reasons. One of them was "the bad handling of our artillery. This could not cope with the superior weight, caliber, range, and number of the Yankee guns." Hill witnessed a duel between the Washington Artillery and some Union pieces that became, in his words, "the most melancholy farce in the war." Lee confessed that the Federals had "more experienced artillerists and better prepared ammunition" and mostly "better guns" than he did in the Maryland Campaign.[2] In fact, many Confederates admitted their inferiority in artillery. "The immense superiority of the enemy in artillery practice" was too evident to be ignored. Lt. Gen. William J. Hardee put it down to the northern superiority in industrial capacity. "Long-range cannon and improved projectiles can be made only by great mechanical skill, heavy machinery, and abundant resources," he wrote after Stones River. "The enemy is, therefore, superior in artillery."[3]

Now and then a Federal admitted that Confederate batteries fired well, but far more often they criticized Rebel performance when comparing it with their own. Lt. Charles R. Doane of the 4th New Jersey Battery wrote of "the oft-mentioned fact that the Confederate service can make no boast of her artillerists." Henry L. Abbot thought it was "beyond doubt" that Union guns were served in a superior way.[4] It is not surprising that Union officers normally thought they were doing a better job than the Confederates. Rebel guns at Antietam were "very active," admitted Capt. John C. Tidball of Battery A, 2nd US Artillery, "but with some exception his practice was bad." The two biggest failures of Confederate fire were that it sailed too high in the air and that the fuzed projectiles failed to explode. "Their range was good on us," commented John Merrilles of Battery E, 1st Illinois Light Artillery, "time just about right, but with too much elevation—the fragments whistling and screaming hideously enough overhead, but going a mile beyond."[5] Col. Armistead L. Long of Lee's staff had received artillery training from Hunt before the war. As he evaluated the Confederate bombardment preceding Pickett's Charge at Gettysburg, Hunt recalled that training and reminded Long of it when they chatted at Appomattox. "I remembered my lessons at the time," Long told him, "and when the fire became so scattered, wondered what you would think about it!"[6]

But accuracy was not the only component that needed to be evaluated when assessing the effect of artillery fire. The impact of the long arm on emotions had to be significant, Hunt concluded. "What is called the moral effect of artillery is proportional, not to the noise it makes, but to its actual destructive effects," he believed. "If they are great and sustained, artillery becomes a terror to the enemy, and a wonderful inspirer of confidence to its own troops." If not, then artillery became an object of "contempt with both friend and foe."[7]

Many soldiers on the receiving end of artillery fire agreed that it had an emotional effect, but one that could be dealt with by most men. Capt. Alexander Miller Ayers of the 125th Illinois thought the sound of incoming rounds gave the impression that "all the Demons were turned loose at once & were certain to kill every body any wheres near." But he also admitted that "they scare a great deal more than they kill. I am not so afraid of them as I am of musket balls." Many others echoed Ayers conclusion. "Artilery [sic] is not as effective as musketry," wrote Confederate Horace Park.[8]

LIMITATIONS ON EFFECTIVENESS

In short, extreme answers to the question of artillery effectiveness are counterproductive. In some ways the big guns worked well, and in other ways many factors limited their effect on the battlefield. Some factors were inevitable and difficult to overcome, while others resulted from limitations in technology, administration, and practice that could be corrected with time and experience. In some cases, these latter limitations needed more than four years of conflict to be worked out or had to await further developments over the span of decades rather than months.

The natural environment of the battlefield imposed some limitations on field artillery. Guns had to be placed within a certain distance of the target and within line of sight to have any hope of damaging it. As Tully McCrae put it, "position is the chief factor" in good artillery work. John Gibbon noted that if placed on higher ground than the target, accurate shooting could be enhanced if the height was not too great. He estimated that "the most advantageous command [or height] is 1/100 of the distance, which gives a grazing fire and numerous ricochets." Command of more than 7/100 should be avoided.[9] But many officers were forced to take position on ground too high for effective work. If the slope fell off abruptly, the pieces could not be depressed enough to cover approaches to the position. Open, gently sloping ground was considered the best for light-battery positions, and it allowed for long line of sight.[10]

Timbered ground offered concealment for the guns. Vegetation limited the enemy's ability to see them and, to a degree, shielded them physically from enemy fire. The down side, of course, was that heavy vegetation impeded opportunities to move around and cooperate with infantry. On fields such as Chickamauga, which was unusually cluttered, the want of effective artillery support was felt by infantry officers. Often the gunners had to make do with firing through the woods, aiming at puffs of smoke to gauge where the opposing batteries were located, a "very unsatisfactory mode of fighting," as one frustrated officer put it.[11]

Heavily vegetated landscapes led some observers to conclude that the United States was not a fit place for the "full development and legitimate use of artillery." After seeing service in both major theaters of war, William F. Barry thought this was especially so in the West, "where large tracts of uncleared land and dense forest materially circumscribe its field of usefulness and often force it into positions of hazard and risk." Charles Wainwright made the same comment about the country from the Wilderness to Petersburg. Wooded terrain especially nullified the usefulness of rifles, for their chief advantage was long-distance firing.[12]

Wet weather hampered the effectiveness of field artillery as well. Softened ground made it more difficult to move and to serve the pieces. Recoil drove the wheels deeper into the muck at every discharge. Trails also settled, affecting the distance settings. The only solution was to constantly move the gun to a fresh spot of soft ground. Sandy soil offered similar problems to gun crews.[13]

Moving artillery across cotton or corn rows was difficult. Pieces, limbers, and caissons bounced crazily over them. Ditches of any depth proved a worse obstacle to movement. Mountainous terrain affected cross-country movement to a high level of difficulty. Many roads in Appalachia were so steep that gun crews hitched a dozen horses to each carriage, locked the wheels, and used block and tackle (one end attached to a tree, the other to the carriage) to get them up or down. Fording streams became a problem only when the approaches to and from the crossing were bad or the water level was high. In the latter cases it was not uncommon for the entire piece to be submerged at the deepest part of the ford, the teams barely able to pull it through.[14]

Environmental factors affected artillery work in another way. Soft, spongy ground was bad for working a gun but good for nullifying incoming rounds. Many artillerists reported that enemy projectiles were smothered by mucky or plowed ground and did them little harm. Artillery fire shattered trees and underbrush, but those growths also, to a degree at least, tended to deflect a lot of it from its intended targets.[15] For all the trouble posed by environmental factors, artillerists learned to adjust their practice and take advantage of them. Rolling pieces forward, for example, to fire over crests and back to reload in greater safety was common. Using vegetation to screen a battery's position also was common. Overall, these features evened out in terms of advantages and disadvantages for field artillery.[16]

AMMUNITION SUPPLY

The question of ammunition supply was vital to combat effectiveness. How many rounds should be carried into the field, how fast should it be expended, and how should it be replenished became important issues in artillery practice.

Napoleon believed that artillery should carry a supply of 150 rounds per piece into the field, but in practice his batteries probably carried less. Expectations were higher in the Civil War. Gibbon argued that 400 rounds per piece should be carried, with half of them conveyed in the ammunition chests loaded on the limbers and caissons and the rest in divisional and general ammunition trains. Whether this number was enough depended entirely on firing practices—how fast battery commanders ordered their crews to pump rounds at targets. This practice varied widely.[17]

At the start of the Overland Campaign, 250 rounds per piece was the accepted ratio for transport into the field, but Hunt carried 270 rounds per piece to hedge his bets. At times expenditure was very heavy. At Spotsylvania on May 12, nearly half of the available 12-pounder ammunition was fired away. The next day Hunt requisitioned 14,000 rounds of Napoleon ammunition and placed a rush order on its delivery. The logistical system of the Union army during that campaign was superb—Hunt got his rounds.[18] During the Petersburg Campaign, Hunt often divided batteries into two temporary groups, one to remain in the forts along the line and another to accompany infantry columns in efforts to extend the Union position farther to the west. When pushes were planned, he arranged for 100 rounds of ammunition to remain with every piece left behind in a fort and 250 rounds to accompany every piece on the movement.[19]

Ammunition ratios varied from one field army to another. Grant supported a generous allowance of 500 rounds per piece during much of the campaign against Vicksburg. During the drive on Atlanta, Sherman's army group maintained an allowance of 400 rounds per piece. But with Lee's army, it was only 200 rounds per piece during the Gettysburg Campaign, with the nearest Confederate depot 150 miles away at Staunton, Virginia.[20]

The system of resupply also required a method of moving rounds to the gun detachments during battle. Ammunition chests on the limbers and caissons were the most immediate links in this logistical chain. Capt. Charles A. Phillips of the 5th Massachusetts Battery instructed his sergeant in charge of the caissons at Fredericksburg on how to do this: "When an empty limber comes back to you, send one of the caisson limbers to the front and fill up the empty limber from the middle and rear chests. When one of the two caissons is empty, have another full one sent up to you. Send the empty caisson to the Division Ordnance Train, probably across the river near our camp. It is denoted by an American Flag marked 1st Division 5th Army Corps, and Capt. Batchelder has charge of it. Put the caisson in charge of the most intelligent driver, and tell him to fill it up and keep account of the ammunition he gets and return without delay."[21] With such detailed instructions, any reliable sergeant could keep up the flow of ammunition. But unexpected breaks in the chain often occurred. Battery M, 5th US Artillery fired throughout nearly all of May 12 at Spotsylvania except for two hours when it fell silent because of "failure in supply of ammunition." On the second day of the Battle of Nashville, Capt. John W. Lowell reported "a great fault committed by some one" that caused two to four guns to remain "almost constantly idle" due to lack of ammunition.[22]

Even worse than idle guns was taking the battery out of position and moving to the rear in search of more rounds. The practice of withdrawing to replenish ammunition became widespread enough to draw from Hunt a circular forbidding it. He instructed his subordinates to set up an effective system of resupply and make sure it operated during engagements. Hunt also forbade the practice of piling up rounds next to the gun, arguing that rapid, careless firing was the cause of both problems. "Proper pointing gives ample time under all circumstances for procuring ammunition, one round at a time, from the limber chests; the only exception is in the case of canister at close range."[23]

On several occasions shortages on the strategic level affected the supply of ammunition on the tactical level. A nationwide shortage affected the Army of Tennessee in the late spring of 1863, with available rounds ranging from 66 to 171 per piece. These strategic-level shortages tended to be temporary. When higher-level shortages affected Union operations, they always were due to transportation difficulties rather than to systemic problems in production. These Union transportation difficulties affected the early phase of Grant's overland drive toward Vicksburg in the spring of 1863, Burnside's defense of Knoxville in the fall of 1863, and Sherman's drive toward Atlanta in the summer of 1864.[24]

Hunt proposed using caissons rather than wagons to haul ammunition into the field. He argued that ordnance trains tended to get mixed up with commissary and quartermaster trains, causing confusion when limber drivers went in search of more ammunition. This type of mix-up led to numerous complaints. Soon after the Battle of Shiloh, Maj. Francis A. Shoup suggested that ordnance stores be carefully segregated from all other baggage to avoid "great confusion." Various solutions were attempted. They included assigning a responsible officer to supervise resupply and painting distinctive marks on ordnance wagons so they could be seen at a distance.[25]

The Army of the Potomac convened a board in February 1863 to discuss the proposed use of caissons instead of wagons for ammunition supplies. Charles Griffin vigorously objected to it, and even Wainwright, who usually supported Hunt's ideas, criticized the proposal. Its implementation would have increased the number of caissons, horses, and drivers, and the army was short of the latter two at that time. Hunt persisted, writing a long and detailed proposal in late September 1863 that was rejected by higher authorities in Washington, DC.[26] But Hunt did not fully recognize that the problems limiting the effectiveness of supply arrangements failed to be crippling. The system generally worked well, and the issues that cropped up were dealt with or failed to seriously hamper operations. This was one reason his caisson idea was so flatly rejected by fellow officers and higher-level administrators alike.

ASSESSING THE EFFECT OF FIRING

Artillerists placed a great deal of emphasis on evaluating the effectiveness of their fire. Their corporate identity was wrapped up in mathematic calculation and a high sense of professionalism. Officers required that battery commanders report how many rounds were fired, how well the projectiles and fuzes operated, and what effect they had on the enemy.

Battery commanders and gunners placed themselves in position to observe the effect of their rounds, especially at the start of firing. That often meant moving 100 yards from the guns to be clear of the smoke. Capt. William H. McCartney could clearly see the effect of two volleys fired by his 1st Massachusetts Battery as they tore apart a Confederate battery at Fredericksburg. Union skirmishers brought to him a piece of wood shattered from a Confederate gun carriage that flew into their line.[27]

Many officers could see the effect of their rounds on opposing infantry lines as men fell and formations broke apart. Based on his experience, Jacob Roemer believed that overshooting was a major problem. He advised aiming at the feet of enemy infantry lines and at the feet of charging horsemen to lessen this effect. Only when accumulating battle smoke or trees, brush, and undulations in the ground intervened were they unable to observe the effect. That is why some officers instructed their men to fire no more than half a dozen rounds from each gun, pause to gauge the effect, and then continue.

But this did not always solve the visibility problem. Because higher authorities required the inclusion of this information in their reports, many artillery officers admitted they could not tell what effect their fire had on the target.[28]

If they could not see the effect, officers found other means of information. If opposing guns fell silent in counterbattery action, they counted it as proof of accuracy. Another method was to wait until the fight ended and examine the enemy position. Counting bodies and observing the wreckage of carriages provided evidence of fire effectiveness. Another method was to question prisoners, many of whom provided gripping testimony.[29]

Many artillery officers evaluated enemy rounds that sailed into their position to decide how to counter them. Some officers picked up unexploded projectiles. They could tell the type, caliber, and weight of opposing pieces from this hard evidence, which was better than simply guessing. Roemer used his watch to gauge Rebel fire directed at his battery at Second Bull Run. He estimated his opponent used eight-second fuzes and found that they burst half a mile to the rear of his position. So he told his gunners to cut five-second fuzes in response; after only two rounds they forced the enemy guns to retire.[30]

BATTERY MAINTENANCE

Artillery demanded constant care to maintain its level of effectiveness in the field. Most of this burden fell on the shoulders of a battery's commissioned and noncommissioned officers, who had to manage the men, horses, and equipment. After the Battle of Williamsburg, Wainwright immersed himself in maintenance duties for three days. "Fighting a battle, I find, is the smallest part of a campaign. The repairing of damages, writing reports, and getting ready to go at it again is infinitely more fatiguing. Another's day's work and I am only just beginning to see daylight."[31]

Wainwright's unit experienced ordinary battle damage at Williamsburg. In other engagements artillery commands suffered far more. Rosecrans's artillery was devastated at Stones River. Entire batteries were wrecked or captured, with the Federals losing twenty-eight guns in this terrible fight. Rebuilding, then, was the order of the day. Surviving men were temporarily assigned elsewhere (to help garrison the forts protecting Nashville, for example) until replacement cannon and equipment could reach the army. It was rare for even the most devastated battery to simply disappear as long as there was a chance of replacing lost men and material.[32]

For some batteries, rebuilding was necessary even without the devastation of combat. Some units were so ill managed that they could not be relied upon. Normally, a change of officers became necessary. Lt. William T. Ratliff was ordered to leave Company A, 1st Mississippi Light Artillery and take over Company C early in May 1863. The latter had been allowed to decline during the past winter. Its commander, Capt. William B. Turner, had resigned, and its lieutenants were inexperienced. "I never saw a more ragged, dirty set of men," Ratliff recalled. They lacked discipline and were discouraged and angry that a stranger had taken command. But Ratliff was equal to the challenge. He persuaded a paymaster to issue four months' pay; found clothes, harness, and other needed articles; and endeared himself to the good soldiers in the unit; the others eventually came over to his side as well.[33]

The keys to battery maintenance were the quality of officers and the availability of resources. Vibrant military systems that could provide both had a good chance to maintain an effective artillery arm. The 10th Massachusetts Battery lost nearly all its equipment except the caissons and twenty-nine out of seventy men at the Battle of Reams Station on August 25, 1864. By September 11 it had replaced the horses, harness, and other material. Nine days later four new pieces arrived. We do not know how long it took to replace the twenty-nine men, but in material terms the battery went from near oblivion to fully functional in less than a month.[34]

Some commanders possessed a near mania for improving their batteries. Roemer requested time to trim up Battery L, 2nd New York Light Artillery just after reaching Kentucky from the East in April 1863. He replaced damaged wheels, polished metal, and repainted wood to overhaul his command in eighteen days. The subsequent campaign into East Tennessee was difficult, but sixty-nine out of seventy-one men in his unit reenlisted that winter. At about the same time, authorities decided to separate Battery L from the 2nd New York Light Artillery and make it an independent unit, redesignated the 34th New York Battery. In January 1864 Roemer gave all his guns and equipment to Battery D, 1st Rhode Island Light Artillery and took his men to New York on thirty-day veteran furloughs. Then he recruited more volunteers, obtained new pieces and equipment, and essentially created a new command around the veterans from Battery L. By April 22, 1864, the 34th New York Battery was ready for the Overland Campaign. In October 1864, protected by the heavy earthworks at Petersburg, he thoroughly cleaned, repaired, and painted all his carriages.[35]

While Roemer demonstrated what could be done by a good officer with resources at his disposal, good officers with few resources had to scramble for whatever they could find. Cannibalizing equipment from less effective or more poorly maintained batteries was "the best thing that could be done at the time," according to the Third Corps artillery chief after Chancellorsville. Consolidating two understrength batteries on a temporary basis occurred quite often. Batteries A and B, 1st Rhode Island Light Artillery, for example, were consolidated after Gettysburg. The Battery B men took charge of the left section of the new organization, and the whole was known as Battery A. With the arrival of more recruits and replacement cannon, the two units were separated again after only a month. Next year, after the devastation of Reams Station, they were consolidated again, with the new unit designated as Battery B.[36]

Another method of consolidation was to retain the organizational structure of both batteries but simply place one commander over them. Batteries H and M, 4th US Artillery operated as one unit under Lt. Charles C. Parsons at Stones River. After the battle they were separated for a while but reunited in the same way at the insistence of several officers. They remained so for some time, "preserving the companies distinct except for action on the field," as Harry C. Cushing put it.[37]

The story of three units in the battle of July 22 east of Atlanta offers instructive detail about whether damaged artillery units could be resurrected. Battery H, 1st Illinois Light Artillery was torn apart by a Confederate attack that day, but Capt. Francis De Gress managed to unspike his guns after they were recaptured and obtained horses and harness from what was left of Battery A, 1st Illinois Light Artillery, which also had been decimated in the fight. De Gress got Battery H ready for action by 9 A.M. on July 23. The next day Lt. George Echte was assigned to command the residue of Battery A, only to learn that De Gress had already stripped it of horses and equipment. Ironically, Battery A had been consolidated with Battery B, 1st Illinois Light Artillery on July 10, and the new unit had been designated as Battery A. Battery F, 2nd US Artillery, had lost most of its men and horses and all of its guns on July 22. It was not reconstituted, but the remaining personnel reinforced three other batteries.[38]

Hunt disapproved of breaking up batteries as a result of reduced personnel and equipment because it created bad feeling among the men. He suggested the creation of special recruiting stations for the artillery of each state with depot batteries, so that these recruits could be trained before taking the field as ready replacements. This would have mimicked traditional practice in the armies of Europe. But as with so many of Hunt's suggestions, this one fell by the wayside.[39]

The Confederates consolidated batteries more extensively than did their opponents. Lee overhauled his artillery after Antietam due to shortages of manpower and horses. In some cases, "neglect and the inefficiency of the officers" justified the move. He began to implement this policy, "to make the artillery of the army more efficient," on October 4, 1862. Lee broke up twenty batteries and transferred their personnel and equipment to other units. He dismissed superfluous officers, which "mortified" some of them but "pleased" many others who wanted an excuse to leave the service.[40]

Lee's overhaul set up his artillery arm for the rest of the war, but the Army of Tennessee was not so fortunate. When Joseph E. Johnston took command in January 1864, he found there were enough guns, but the arm was deficient in "discipline & instruction, especially in firing. The horses are not in good condition. It about two hundred rounds of ammunition. Its organization is very imperfect." Sixty-four of the 112 pieces had too few horses to maneuver effectively. Johnston requested that Edward Porter Alexander be assigned to whip it into shape, but that was never approved. This poor condition was not new to the army. In the fall of 1862, following the Kentucky Campaign, the artillery arm hit a low point due to severe shortages of animals and forage.[41]

The stress of the Atlanta Campaign severely compromised this already weak arm. By August 1864 the artillery had only 125 rounds per gun compared to 400 for the Federals. It had an average of fifty-one horses per battery, which dropped to forty-four horses a month later. Teams had to be reduced from six to four horses per carriage, and two caissons from each battery were turned over to the quartermaster's depot. With this, the artillery arm of the Army of Tennessee was "permanently crippled," as Larry Daniel has put it.[42]

Deterioration continued after Atlanta fell. By November the army began using mules to pull guns; even oxen and officer horses were pressed into service. Hood's march against Sherman's supply lines in October and his invasion of Tennessee in November sealed the fate of his long-suffering artillery. Lack of forage and hard marching devastated the horse supply. Abject defeat at Nashville coupled with a desperate retreat to Alabama then completed its near-destruction. Hood lost most of his guns and sent the few that were left to Columbus, Mississippi, where they were reorganized into serviceable batteries and sent to different garrisons in the Deep South.[43]

ADMINISTRATIVE EFFECTIVENESS

Capacity for fighting on the battlefield may have been the ultimate aim of maintaining and rehabilitating batteries, but administrative effectiveness between battles was important in reaching that goal. Recordkeeping, inspection reports, courts of inquiry, discipline, and esprit de corps underlay combat effectiveness, no matter how much veterans bragged about the man who was a good fighter but not a good soldier. Combat performance far more often was influenced by more general conditions such as morale, respect for and obedience to officers, and proper food, clothing, and pay than it was by spontaneous heroics that could just as easily become abject fear. A battery had to be in good shape before battle if it hoped to do well under fire. "The captain of a battery has a very independent position," argued William Wheeler of the 13th New York Battery, "and it lies with him almost entirely whether his battery is a good and serviceable one or not."[44]

The battery commander relied on several administrative aids in his work. Even though Hunt bemoaned the "want of a code of regulations" for the artillery, which threatened its efficiency and led to "a misapplication of its powers," there is no reason to believe this was a serious problem. The military system did provide guidelines for administrative effectiveness. The *Revised United States Army Regulations of 1861* included a change promulgated in 1863 in its reprinting that required artillery commanders to maintain detailed records of all rounds fired. Highly placed officers issued instructions of their own as well. Brig. Gen. John M. Brannan, chief of artillery, Department of the Cumberland, guided his subordinates about how to fill out and process monthly inspection reports. Barry, artillery chief on Sherman's staff during the last year of the war, "was devoted heart and soul to this branch of the service." He also displayed the type of thorough professionalism that underlay effectiveness in administrative matters.[45]

Thomas W. Osborn became artillery chief of the Eleventh Corps when it had the worst batteries in the Army of the Potomac. He began by riding from one camp to the next, making it clear to each that he would tolerate no resistance to his orders. Osborn broke up one battery as hopelessly inept, condemned any material that was not serviceable, and told officers to requisition replacements. He changed the camps of most batteries because the grounds had become absolutely filthy. "I have directed the officers to comply strictly with the requirements of the artillery tactics," he reported. "I have ordered them to drill certain hours of the day, and most assuredly they needed it."[46]

Regular inspection reports were a mechanism to keep artillerists on their toes. The best kind of report covered all aspects of a battery's life. The results of these inspections alerted higher authorities to developing problems, measured a battery commander's effectiveness, and served as ammunition in an effort to force an officer to change his ways.[47]

Wainwright, artillery chief of the First Corps, provided information on the inspection process in late September 1862. Of a dozen batteries reviewed, all needed additional manpower and nearly all had some detached infantry serving in them. All the units were "sadly" in need of horses, and only half the animals already serving had horseshoes. Wainwright did a thorough job, managing to inspect two batteries each day and looking through battery records. "I was surprised to find how loosely and inaccurately almost all the books were kept," he admitted, discovering that the best-kept books were those in units that rated the poorest in other areas of his inspection. "Not one of the batteries was what it ought to be and most of them very far off from it."[48]

Wainwright specifically commented on two units in his journal. Capt. Edwin B. Dow's 6th Maine Battery was "about as bad as any I have come across lately. Captain Dow addresses also his men as mister; asks in place of ordering; has no idea what public property he has on hand; his horses are wretched, carriages shoddy, and harness in wretched condition." Capt. Rufus D. Pettit's Battery B, 1st New York Light Artillery kept its guns "in superb order, and he had made pendulum hausses long enough to get fifteen degrees of elevation. But his horses were wretched, uncleaned and uncared for; his camp dirty, and the men's tents stuck down just wherever suited the occupants to put them."[49]

Inspections forced officers to clean up their equipment and encourage their men to make a good appearance. It was customary for inspecting officers to ask questions of the men to gauge how well they knew the equipment and their duties. The resulting reports could bear significantly, leading superior officers to deny leaves or furloughs to substandard batteries, as happened in the Army of the Potomac in March 1863.[50]

Inspection reports among the Confederates ranged widely in quality. Some of them consisted only of brief statements such as "Good, but needs drilling."

Other reports were more insightful. After reading one about Hart's South Carolina Battery, Lee lectured his cavalry commander, Maj. Gen. James E. B. Stuart. He pointed out that Hart failed to keep property records or morning reports; the memory of orderly sergeants was the only source of information concerning such topics. His horses were in bad shape, the cannon had not been cleaned or the harness greased, and the ground around his camp was filthy. We do not know what resulted from Lee's message to Stuart, but it is extraordinary that the commander of a field army had to intervene in such matters as this.[51]

Another administrative tool was the court of inquiry, although really only a blunt weapon rather than a finely honed tool. It also was rarely called into action because a group of officers had to be detached from their duties, conduct a thorough investigation, and make an official judgment that affected an officer's career and reputation. Courts of inquiry tended to become political affairs, with officers trying to avert mortal damage to their sense of honor, and rarely resulted in genuine good for the service.

But some courts of inquiry could be useful in regulating conduct. A court convened to investigate the actions of Lt. Pardon S. Jastram of Battery E, 1st Rhode Island Light Artillery at the Battle of Glendale during the Seven Days Campaign. He spiked one of his pieces before evacuating the position. Division leader Brig. Gen. Philip Kearney called for a court of inquiry. The officers comprising the court heard the evidence and concluded that the enemy was 200 yards away when Jastram gave the order to spike the piece. They criticized him for abandoning it too hastily and for not trying later that evening to retrieve it. McClellan, in reviewing the findings, agreed with the court but considered its reprimand to be enough censure and disapproved of any further proceedings.[52]

Jastram's court of inquiry, however, dealt with a comparatively minor issue. It involved a lieutenant and not a higher-ranking, more politically connected officer and was conducted quickly after the questionable conduct took place. Courts of this nature probably exerted a good influence on conduct, but with more serious charges involving more prominent officers, courts took on an entirely different character.

PAPERWORK

Regular paperwork also was important in effectiveness but placed a heavy burden on the battery commander. It included not only documents concerning his men but also documents concerning the cannon, equipment, and horses—all of the latter were government property, and he was personally responsible for it. "There is no one here who will do the business of the Battery but myself," complained Marshall M. Miller of Battery F, 1st Michigan Light Artillery to his wife. "I have had and have got to make out more than 30 different reports and papers and a great many I know but little about."[53]

Jacob Roemer attacked paperwork with thoroughness. When receiving any government property, the issuing officer gave duplicate invoices to the receiving officer, who in turn gave another set of duplicate receipts back to him; that way both men documented their actions. The battery commander filled out returns of property "monthly, bi-monthly, or quarterly, as required by Army Regulations," along with copies of vouchers to indicate what if anything happened to the property. At the end of his service, the battery commander hoped this paper trail would please the auditors in Washington, DC; only then could he be mustered out of service with a clean slate. If the paperwork failed him, the officer could be charged for the value of property for which he had not accounted.[54]

The fiscal year ended on June 30, and in 1863 that happened to be just before the Battle of Gettysburg. James Stewart rushed to complete his paperwork all that night, "making out muster and pay-rolls and comparing them. Then there were the quartermaster, commissary, ordnance, and regimental returns to be made out and mailed by the morning of the 1st of July. I was extremely anxious to have these returns off my hands" because it looked as if his battery would be in action the next day.[55]

Artillerymen were required to report how many rounds they fired in each engagement so officers could gauge their resupply needs. The battery commander relied on his ordnance officer for this information, but sometimes that man lost track. Lt. Augustus N. Parsons could only estimate his battery fired between 1,400 and 1,500 rounds at Chancellorsville because he lacked a precise counting of expenditure.[56]

Examining boards held the potential to play a role in maintaining field effectiveness, but they do not seem to have been uniformly organized. Moreover, boards worked only when the officers appointed to them performed their duty conscientiously. Wainwright demonstrated their potential for improving the artillery arm when appointed to a board in December 1861. Various battery officers were examined to reveal their level of intelligence and knowledge of tactics. One man seemed to have the intellectual ability to understand his duties but had not devoted much effort to learning them; he was given a second chance. Another obviously worked very hard to prepare for his examination but "made wretched work of it" due to a very poor education in civil life. "He can hardly write at all, and cannot spell." Yet another man "did not know the first thing; could not tell the proper intervals and distance in line; nor where the different cannoneers should sit on the boxes." This one admitted that "he had never studied the tactics" and ultimately was dismissed from the service. More than one officer resigned rather than present himself for examination.[57]

If all boards worked as conscientiously as the one Wainwright described, and if they had been uniformly spread across the army, they could have tremendously increased the efficiency of Union artillery. But good boards seem to have been as spotty in their appearance among the Confederates as among the Federals.[58]

EXPERIMENTS

Both armies engaged, to an extent far greater in the artillery arm than in the infantry or cavalry, in conducting experiments to test equipment and supplies. Most of these tests concerned projectiles and fuzes, the area of most new developments, and Hunt was the most important impetus behind them. They took place in the last year of the war, and while not producing revolutionary results, often confirmed new techniques to make projectiles and fuzes work better.

Hunt pushed through with experiments concerning projectiles for 10-inch mortars and 10-pounder shells in May 1864. His objective was to combine paper fuzes with Bormann fuzes to obtain longer time frames, up to thirty seconds, for explosive projectiles. Abbot tested a new shell devised by a Mr. Pevey that consisted of "two concentric shells thinner than usual and connected firmly by studs." The space between the two was filled either with "small iron balls or [an] incendiary composition." The tests were encouraging, Abbot estimating that the design resulted in over 100 percent more fragments.[59]

A handful of Confederate artillerists also pursued experiments. On more than one occasion, Edward Porter Alexander conducted tests of ordnance, projectiles, and fuzes. As with the Federals, none of these efforts resulted in earth-shattering revelations, but they promoted small advances in understanding elements of the artillery arsenal.[60]

USING CAPTURED EQUIPMENT

The Confederates often commented on how frequently they relied on capturing artillery to replenish their stock of guns. But it was common for both sides, not just the Confederates, to reuse captured equipment. In fact, taking captured and abandoned cannon, limbers, caissons, and ammunition into their own stockpile was simply using common sense. The captor often used such items immediately, turning the guns around and firing them at the retreating foe. Reusing enemy material was an element of efficiency in managing the artillery arm.

Artillerists used any captured cannon in working order. It was not unusual for a battery to lose some guns, only to have the enemy use them, and then to see them recaptured by the original owners in a counterattack that same day. Often the captured material was unofficially retained by batteries that needed it, but more often the captor turned it in to the Ordnance Department for official distribution. Ironically, three Confederate cannon captured late in the war participated in a fifteen-gun salute to honor Union victory a few weeks later.[61]

One of those Union victories, the last assault at Petersburg on April 2, 1865, saw a unique effort to work captured guns. Lt. William H. Rogers of the 1st Connecticut Heavy Artillery was given 100 men and an infantry support to enter the captured earthworks, turn around any cannon found, and fire them at the enemy. Rogers divided his contingent into three platoons, each with three gun detachments. The men left their own works in company with Union infantrymen and got into the opposing fortifications almost simultaneously with them. During the course of the day, they put six Confederate pieces into action for the Union cause, firing 400 rounds of Rebel ammunition plus another 400 rounds brought up from the Federal line.[62]

Rogers's effort was unique only in that it was organized beforehand and therefore was highly successful. Far more often the immediate use of captured ordnance was an ad hoc affair that sometimes worked but often failed to produce results. Yet when it worked, the satisfaction was immense. Charles Phillips wrote of the excitement in using enemy weapons when discussing the battle of April 2. "We rather enjoyed it. There was a great sense of freedom in firing the rebel guns as we did not care whether we burst them or not. We dismounted one gun by the recoil, and split the reinforce on the breech of another."[63]

Using captured cannon was easy, but it is surprising how often artillerists dug up unexploded enemy projectiles, perhaps adjusting them a bit, and fired them back. John Merrilles reported that many Confederate shells failed to explode during heavy artillery exchanges in the Jackson Campaign of July 1863. They were collected and fired back at the Rebels as solid shot. Many Confederates were particularly keen on collecting unexploded Union ordnance because they recognized that it was of a higher quality than their own ammunition. In fact, Rebel authorities paid cash to their soldiers for unexploded projectiles collected at Petersburg; some men were killed and wounded while seeking to claim such bounties.[64]

CONCLUSION

Civil War armies largely consisted of men who had no training or experience in military matters before the firing on Fort Sumter. They had to learn the complicated art of war from scratch under great pressure. It can be said that the artillery arm took that job more seriously than the other two arms because of the highly technical nature of artillery service. That nature tended to draw men with a bent toward mathematics, order, and professionalism. Most of the officers and many of the noncommissioned officers, even many of the privates, took an unusual pride in doing their work well. It cannot be said, however, that they always succeeded in their effort to reach effectiveness, but they probably did so more often than their comrades in the infantry or cavalry. At the end of the war, artillerists could look back on four years of strenuous effort to make their arm work well.

15

. . . .

AFTER THE CIVIL WAR

Four long years of war created a deep well of experience and practical wisdom among the better artillery officers. Jacob Roemer's command (Battery L, 2nd New York Light Artillery, which was converted into the 34th New York Battery) participated in fifty-seven battles, marched 18,758 miles, and fired fifty-six tons of iron during the war. Battery I, 1st Illinois Light Artillery participated in seventeen large battles and forty-six "important skirmishes." In addition, it engaged in "probably a hundred minor skirmishers that were never reported."[1]

It seemed a shame to waste all this practical experience after Appomattox. John Gibbon urged Grant to establish a board for the examination of all volunteer and regular artillery officers with a view of retaining the best ones in service. "This should be a practical rather than a theoretical examination, and the officer's services and standing in the field should be largely inquired into and weigh heavily with the boards in coming to a decision."[2]

But Gibbon's suggestion was not acted upon. Instead the volunteer artillery arm was demobilized pretty quickly, and the regular artillery arm reduced to save money. Federal batteries turned in their horses and equipment to the government. Confederate batteries not involved in a formal surrender (during which their horses and equipment largely became property of the Federal government), disposed of their animals and equipment in a very different way. Maj. Charles W. Squires allowed each man in his battalion to take home an artillery horse. He wanted to give the equipment to the Federal army, but no one showed up at his location near Corsicana, Texas, to receive it. Consequently, Squires allowed the citizens of the county to take wagons, axes, spades, and other equipment. He did not indicate what he did with his guns.[3]

Henry J. Hunt continued working to improve the artillery arm after the war. He had lost as many struggles for improvement as he had won during the conflict, and now his success rate would fall even more. Hunt's biggest struggle began when he was assigned to a board with the object of revising the army's regulations. The board members began their work in July 1871 and continued for ten months. Among other things, Hunt revived the recommendation he had supported during the war for the creation of an artillery chief for the entire US Army. Congress failed to approve this and many other things the board recommended.[4]

But Hunt's work on this board also revived the battle he had fought with Winfield S. Hancock over his actions at Gettysburg on July 3. Hancock wrote to the House Military Committee in January 1872 referring to Hunt's order to cease fire as an example of how dangerous it was to allow artillery officers too much authority in battle. His correspondence was published. When Hunt fought back in self-defense, Hancock responded with more attacks. The tussle continued for many years, with Hunt becoming frustrated by his failure to find allies willing to oppose Hancock. Sherman and Meade supported the infantry in this interservice struggle. Hunt continued to argue that Hancock had endangered the Union position by interfering with his careful plan to cease firing; but because the Federals prevailed anyway, he had not tried to push the issue. Hancock acted very badly in attacking Hunt's reputation, and his brother officers abetted him in this sordid effort. By 1881, after Hancock had lost his bid for the presidency on the Democratic ticket, Hunt told a correspondent that his long-running dispute with him had been "unfortunate[,] at any rate regrettable."[5]

At some point Sherman had suggested to Hunt that he follow the example of British officers and publish his viewpoints on artillery organization in the public press. Hunt replied that it would do no good. There was a receptive audience for professional opinion in British political culture but not in the United States. Such a publication would fall on deaf ears. To prove the point, Hunt gave a talk on "Our Experience in Artillery Administration" to the Massachusetts Historical Society in 1888, which was published in the *Journal of the Military Service Institution of the United States* three years later. It included many points he had worked on during and after the war but failed to influence the right people.

"With proper organization and administration our artillery in the Civil War, good as it was, might have been more serviceable and produced greater results," Hunt argued. "Its pressing need was, as it still is, a responsible chief for the whole arm, with a competent staff, military and administrative." Each battery in the field relied on different bureaus of the War Department for supply, equipment, and personnel, but all could be centralized by the creation of an artillery chief for the entire army. Hunt still believed that the Union guns had been from one-third to one-half less efficient during the war than they could have been if a proper administrative structure had been created. It also cost from one-third to one-half more money than was necessary because of that omission. Hunt's *Journal of the Military Service Institution* article made no headway, nor did his widely read article on the third day at Gettysburg published in *Century* magazine.[6]

If Congress and the infantry generals had no interest in enlarging the administration of the artillery arm during the war, they had even less interest in the days of peace. The one thing that hurt his cause the most was not Hancock's callous opposition, but the fact that the Union artillery worked surprisingly well given the problem Hunt persisted in discussing. For the infantry generals, the motive was retention of command and control in their own hands; for the congressmen and the public, the motive was to save money and not meddle with a system that seemed to work.

It should be kept in mind that Americans had created the largest artillery arm ever raised in Western Hemispheric history during the war of 1861–65. With 752 batteries North and South, it also was one of the largest, most powerful artillery arms to be seen in world history. The Civil War occurred at the cusp of a transition period in artillery technology and introduced some new themes in the history of gunnery. But most of the old technology still applied as well. While Civil War armies employed the largest accumulation of rifled field guns to be seen, the tubes were overwhelmingly made of familiar metals (bronze, brass, wrought iron, and cast iron) as opposed to a truly revolutionary metal such as steel. Gunpowder, the oldest propellant known to man, had not been replaced. Fuzes to ignite long-distance projectiles either were old ones or newer devices that did not work with the reliability necessary to ensure success. And the creation of northern artillery brigades and southern artillery battalions represented little more than a slight improvement in the management of artillery in the field.

In other words, it would be difficult to mount an effective argument that the Civil War was a watershed in artillery history. In this area, as in virtually every other, the Civil War was mostly an old-fashioned war tinged with slight indications of the future.

The Americans did try to advance their artillery arm after Appomattox, attempting to learn from their experience and push further toward whatever they thought was the future. Just after the war ended, the army looked into replacing wooden carriages with wrought-iron devices, believing the metal carriages would be more durable and less expensive. They made and tested a few of them, only to find metal carriages inadequate. Not until the 1880s did steel carriages become popular in Europe. On another front, pieces that worked well during the conflict did not survive it. The 10-pounder Parrott rifle had been one of the three mainstays of the Federal and Confederate armies, but it soon dropped out of favor after the war.[7]

Louis-Philippe d'Orléans, comte de Paris, who had been a French observer during the war, was keen to study the conflict after Appomattox. He wrote to Hunt requesting information about experiments in rifled artillery conducted by the Army of the Potomac, indicating an awareness that the war was the first real test of the rifle. But the count did not find anything extraordinary in rifled gunnery during the American conflict. Results were inconclusive, to say the least, robbing the Civil War of its potential significance as a major event in the development of field artillery.[8]

EUROPEAN DEVELOPMENTS

To see the cutting edge of new artillery technology, one must focus on Europe, not the United States. By 1867 the concept of using hydraulic buffers or brakes to deal with recoil was developed in Europe, even though a workable device did not appear until about 1890. During the 1870s, the concept of indirect fire became a subject of concentrated study as European artillerists worked out a viable process for it.[9]

European wars that immediately followed the Civil War are given high marks for effective use of field artillery. Using 12-and 24-pounders, as did the Federals and Confederates, Prussian gunners supported their infantry in the Danish War of 1864. These were largely smoothbore pieces, however, and the change to rifles proceeded slowly. Even during the much larger Austro-Prussian War of 1866, 54 of 144 Prussian batteries fielded smoothbore pieces. Historians believe the Austrian artillery outperformed the Prussians during that short conflict. Using muzzle-loading bronze pieces, the Austrians were able to assemble concentrations of up to sixty guns on certain sectors of the battlefield. Stung by their poor performance, the Germans adopted significant reforms after they won that war. Arming themselves with steel breech-loading rifles, they improved training and target practice. The Prussians assigned a battalion of guns to each division and grouped the rest as a corps reserve.[10]

The Prussians dominated the artillery struggle during their war with France in 1870–71. They aimed at accumulating large numbers of pieces, catching the enemy in crossfires, and taking advantage of their longer distance to overcome the largely smoothbore pieces in the French army. On several occasions Prussian artillery saved the day when its infantry failed to deliver victory. The German triumph was in part due to superior technology, more aggressive handling of the artillery arm, and a generally low level of operational effectiveness that plagued not only the French artillery but its infantry and cavalry as well. If the French guns had been modernized and commanded effectively, one wonders if the Prussian artillery would have been so successful. The Franco-Prussian War demonstrates what can happen if one side enters a conflict significantly ill-prepared.[11]

Developments in the United States proceeded much more slowly than in Europe. By 1868 the army settled on an artillery system built around the 3-Inch Ordnance Rifle, the Napoleon, the mountain howitzer, and the Gatling gun. Only the Napoleon predated the Civil War, which was a mark of some forward thinking. The 3-Inch Ordnance Rifle remained the mainstay of US service for at least a quarter of a century. The artillery system was enlarged a bit by 1880 with the addition of pieces made of steel. In organization the northern artillery brigade and southern artillery battalion reflected concurrent European practices that predated the Civil War and continued afterward. The American artillery manual changed only slightly, with small alterations in semantics.[12]

In Europe important technical developments proceeded steadily during the remaining decades of the nineteenth century. Nearly every nation shifted to steel breechloaders after the Prussian success of 1870–71. Work on a recoil device had begun in the 1860s but took some time to reach its apogee. Initially the hydraulic cylinder merely arrested recoil without returning the tube to its original position. During the 1870s, a device appeared that could not only arrest recoil but also return the tube in a rough way, but it still required the gun detachment to readjust elevation and range. By 1897 the French developed a system that mixed air pressure in combination with water to return the tube to its exact original setting, allowing the gun detachment to fire the piece rapidly, up to thirty rounds per minute. During the first decade of the twentieth century, all nations developed a similar quick-firing fieldpiece of their own.[13]

By 1886 the world entered a new age with the introduction of high explosives to replace gunpowder. Mixing picric acid with nitrocellulose, the French developed an explosive force that could break a metal casing into splinters rather than fragments. Calling it melinite, they sparked the development of many other types of high explosives in other countries that added far more destructive power to fuzed projectiles. The first usable smokeless powder appeared by 1884 in France, soon to be followed by variants in other countries. In Britain, for example, cordite was developed by the late 1880s. Based generally on some mixture of nitrocellulose with other components, smokeless powder not only eliminated the heavy smoke pall typical of Civil War artillery exchanges but also propelled the projectile much more effectively. The old gunpowder had "produced high breech pressures, burned rapidly, and drove the projectile only a short distance down the cannon tube," noted historian Boyd Dastrup. But the new smokeless powder "burned more slowly and propelled the rounds longer in the tube to generate greater muzzle velocity, range, and power." It also allowed designers to make the tube thinner and longer, enhancing artillery mobility. Smokeless powder became widespread by the 1890s.[14]

The newly unified German state probably led the world in taking advantage of these developments by creating a sophisticated system of training and preparation for war in peacetime. Roemer, now a first lieutenant in the 5th US Artillery, observed one of a dozen artillery schools in Germany in the mid-1880s and was impressed by what he saw. German batteries endured a four-week training course in target practice, recording every round fired at man-sized targets, some of which popped up unexpectedly and moved. Battery maneuvers took place over ditches, through woods, and among other natural obstacles. Long marches took place to build up endurance. Officers learned how to use silent signals, such as moving their swords, to give orders. Roemer also inspected the horse stables, which consisted of brick or masonry buildings with "perfect" ventilation. "In this respect the horses are as well provided for as the men," he wrote.[15]

The Germans greatly increased the number of their pieces. In 1866 they fielded 72 guns for each corps, raising this to 144 by 1905 and 160 by 1914. German doctrine recognized that with increased distance, it was not so vital to mass artillery hub to hub to concentrate fire on a single target as had been necessary in the past. Dispersed artillery now could concentrate its fire. This allowed German guns to both support local units and join in a bigger fire plan. Doctrine therefore stressed closer artillery-infantry cooperation and lessened the tedious arguments over concentration that had occurred during the Civil War.[16]

Indirect artillery fire became important as well. The longer distance of field-artillery fire meant the guns were capable of hitting targets far beyond the line of sight. Indirect firing also allowed the guns to seek cover in the landscape and better avoid return fire. The first significant use of indirect fire took place during the Russo-Japanese War of 1904–5, and other nations studied the concept intently after that conflict. In the United States indirect firing was codified in official regulations by 1907. The process required a forward observer and a reliable means of communication but, once worked out, offered field artillery an important new operational method.[17]

WORLD WAR I

All the technical and operational developments in field artillery that took place after the Civil War came together in World War I to produce pieces capable of long-distance, accurate, and amazingly repeated firing. Union and Confederate soldiers would hardly have comprehended these dramatic changes that had mostly developed during the thirty or so years before 1914. And yet the extensive fronts of World War I, two of which stretched for 500 miles and more in France and Russia, did not give full play to field artillery. The western front soon settled into massive trench systems on both sides of a no-man's-land that decisively shaped the contours of operations. The static nature of this positional warfare allowed both sides to deploy large numbers of heavy artillery alongside their field guns. These heavy pieces came to dominate the battlefield, collapsing trenches and churning the landscape into a barren waste of shattered vegetation, pockmarked with millions of shell craters. Artillery dominated the battlefield like it had never done before, but that was mostly by guns that had been designed to operate against fixed assets in siege-like conditions rather than in a long line of earthworks in the open country.[18]

Numbers tell the tale. In 1915 the French army fielded forty-seven heavy guns per mile of its sector in the Champagne. In 1917 the British deployed one heavy gun for every twenty-one yards of its front near Arras and one for every twenty yards at Messines Ridge. By the end of the war, up to 40 percent of the British Army on the western front consisted of artillery of some type, and more than one-third of that massive arm consisted of heavy or medium guns. The batteries along the western front alone packed more destructive power by artillery into those narrow confines than in all previous wars in world history combined.[19]

The demands of combat produced innovative and sophisticated ways of using artillery in the field. World War I led to the introduction of moving guns by motor-powered trucks and by mounting tubes on motorized tank chasses, although neither method became common before the end of the conflict. The guns were adapted to gas warfare, firing projectiles to deliver harmful chemicals into enemy lines, and the creeping barrage was developed to more closely support advancing infantry. The latter involved moving the distance of firing according to a prearranged schedule so friendly troops could move forward as close to the landing shells as possible and be covered in advancing across no-man's-land. More sensitive detonators exploded projectiles so as to break up massive belts of barbed wire placed to obstruct the infantry's advance.[20]

Indirect fire was required, given the long distance of heavy and even field guns, but previous methods of working it out with forward observers had serious limitations in World War I. Countershelling often tore up telephone lines, and it was not always possible for the observer to find a place from which he could properly see where the projectiles landed. It was obviously impossible for him to see if the heavy guns were firing at distances of several thousand yards in front of him. The French preferred to obtain accurate information of enemy targets by aerial observation, plot them precisely on a map, and register their artillery on those points. This was the most sophisticated form of indirect firing and came to be common practice among all belligerents. Another method involved sound ranging with microphones to detect enemy artillery pieces when they fired. This proved quite successful but could only be used in counterbattery fire.[21]

By 1918 heavy use had caused wear and tear among the big guns, so much so that their accuracy was compromised. The Germans compensated for this by conducting minute examinations of their pieces, taking them to the rear and test firing with exacting care to chart the peculiarities of each individual piece. Assisted by professional mathematicians, fire tables were constructed for each piece. These tables took into account "such factors as wind speed, barometric pressure, moisture content of the air," and, in some cases, even the "rotation of the earth."[22]

Artillery operations in World War I, in short, were a far cry from those of the Civil War, once again giving pause to anyone who thinks that the conflict of 1861–65 was in any real sense a modern war as far as field and heavy artillery was concerned. Neither the armies nor the societies that created them in the Civil War would have been technically or intellectually capable of fielding and handling an artillery arm in the ways that armies and societies did in the Great War. When the US Army entered the conflict in 1917, it was very far behind the curve set by the British, French, and Germans and never caught up with their standard. American field guns usually saturated a given area with shells rather than closely supporting advancing infantry or precisely locating targets. This was in part due to the relatively short time during which US forces engaged in large-scale operations, only the last six months of the war. If they had experienced a longer greening time, American artillery practice would have had a chance to catch up with the Allies.[23]

Artillery came to play a far bigger, far more complicated role in military operations in World War I. Its effect was striking. Artillery accounted for about 20 percent of losses in the Russo-Japanese War (with the ratio increasing to 50 percent in the siege of Port Arthur). During World War I, the percentage is not easy to pin down. A study of 15,452 deaths (among 1.9 million) in the German army revealed that 54.7 percent were caused by artillery fire and 39 percent by rifle fire. Another study of German soldiers who suffered nonlethal wounds indicated that 43 percent were caused by artillery fire and 50.6 percent by rifle fire. These statistics should probably be seen as the minimum level of destructiveness caused by artillery rather than the maximum. It is quite possible that more comprehensive data would raise artillery wounds and deaths even higher. But these minimum statistics indicate that the big guns were at the very least more than doubly effective as killers on World War I battlefields compared to past conflicts.[24]

WORLD WAR II AND AFTER

Future wars never duplicated the western front, at least not in terms of its immensity and long duration, and thus heavy artillery rarely had an opportunity to intrude in the arena where field artillery normally operated. Technical developments between the two world wars moved swiftly. The push to motorize armies led to the fulfillment of beginnings oriented toward producing self-propelled artillery by World War II. The use of rockets was rejuvenated in the 1930s, and this variant of field artillery, with effective distances up to 6,000 yards, was widely used by the major belligerents in World War II. Heavier-caliber field guns came into play as well. The French 75-millimeter had been a standard in World War I, but by the time of World War II, it had been replaced by the German 88-millimeter (10,300-yard distance) and the American 105-millimeter (12,500-yard distance). The British replaced their 18-pounder of World War I with a 25-pounder in World War II (13,400-yard distance). Firing at a target a couple of miles away had been considered long distance in the Civil War; now the guns were capable of firing six or seven miles with some degree of accuracy.[25]

Aerial observation continued to be the best way to locate targets at such long distances, and the American army developed planes and control methods so it did not have to rely on the US Army Air Forces to perform this essential task. The Americans also developed an integrated fire-control center to direct the firing of a battalion's guns using radio. Field artillery took on antitank and antiaircraft roles to meet the changing nature of combat. The army also developed a variable time fuze designed to detonate the projectile by reflected radio waves, which reportedly increased effectiveness by 50 percent.[26]

It may well be that the Americans led the world in developing field artillery during World War II. They certainly achieved great strides not only in the hardware but also in deployment and management in the field. With the creation of the famous triangular infantry division in 1940, they assigned forty-eight fieldpieces to support the 5,211 riflemen in the division. That amounted to one gun for every 108 infantrymen compared to theoretical ratios of two to three pieces for every 1,000 men during the Civil War. That 1860s ratio was very much in line with Napoleonic ratios and widely at variance with World War II standards.[27]

But in terms of management, in a sense, little had changed. Artillery attached to a division was still under the command of the division leader, not the artillery chief. But the major difference was that the army had developed a much more effective doctrine for cooperation between the two arms than existed in the Civil War. Combined-arms concepts had been growing for some time and came into full-blown form during World War II. Training emphasized ever-closer cooperation of all assets available to the division. In some ways the artillery arm hit closer to the heart of combined-arms doctrine than other elements because it proved so vital to success on the battlefield. "The best performer in the combined arms team was the field artillery," historian Michael Doubler has written of the American First Army during the Normandy Campaign. "Infantry commanders understood artillery doctrine and knew how to employ their fire support." There were no unseemly arguments between infantry officers who sought to protect their turf and ambitious artillery officers who saw a better way to employ their guns like the never-ending fight between Hunt and Hancock.[28]

Field artillery continued to develop after 1945. The Korean War indicated the need for improving self-propelled guns until it became possible to endow them with as much as 75-degrees elevation and 360-degrees traversing. Cold War pressures led to the development of rocket technology, both guided and ballistic, which conceptually is often folded into the field of artillery. The Corporal and Redstone guided missiles of the 1950s could hit targets 80–200 miles away and were capable of delivering tactical nuclear weapons. Ballistic missiles like the Honest John could target areas 24 miles away. Atomic Annie, a 280-millimeter piece, could fire a nuclear projectile by 1953 and was followed in the early 1960s by nuclear devices deliverable by an 8-inch howitzer and a 105-millimeter howitzer. The 1970s and 1980s saw the introduction of computer technology into field artillery management in addition to laser-guided munitions to pinpoint small, highly mobile targets such as tanks. Unmanned aircraft could now locate targets without risking a pilot, and computers increasingly were employed to aid fire control on all levels.[29]

Interestingly, even though modern technology has largely solved the many problems inherent in indirect fire, the kind of direct fire that prevailed during the Civil War remained an element in field artillery practice. In fact, one historian has argued that direct fire reached its zenith in the twentieth century. He points out that all antitank firing, at least during World War II, had to be done directly. Most antiaircraft firing also had to be done by direct sighting. Sophisticated methods for indirect firing simply made that method possible, it did not replace direct firing any more than small-unit infantry combat ceased to exist because of the atomic bomb.[30]

If Civil War artillerists would not have recognized the artillery used in World War I, they would have been completely bewildered by what was to come after that conflict. We can accurately locate the war of 1861–65 as taking place in the final period of a long historical era that began in the fifteenth century and improved during the next 400 years to a threshold in the mid-nineteenth century. The Civil War occurred at the beginning of that threshold. Its field artillery represented only slight improvements over the guns used in the Napoleonic Wars of a half century before and would be completely out-classed by developments beginning only a handful of years after Appomattox. Once started, those new developments took field artillery into worlds not dreamed of by the men who stood by their cannon in the Civil War.

CONCLUSION

The Civil War dwarfed all previous conflicts in the Western Hemisphere in terms of its size and scale of combat, ranking among the major wars of European history in those ways as well. Although European officers flocked to observe the American conflict, the lessons they derived from it were mixed, to say the least. In fact, many of them tended to dismiss the Civil War as providing little in the way of relevant lessons for professional armies. Blinded by the fact that both sides raised massive volunteer armies from among the general populace, European theorists ignored an equally significant fact: that highly effective soldiers could be made from scratch through the right combination of existing doctrine, productive training, and a willingness to learn from hard experience on the battlefield. Even professional soldiers had to relearn a great deal when faced with a long, demanding war such as the one that broke out in North America in 1861. In short, there is much that the historian, at least, can glean from the Civil War even if European contemporaries tended to shortchange the conflict.

We should begin without preconceptions of any kind. Playing away from any assumptions that a weapon such as the rifle musket or the rifled artillery piece inevitably dominated the course of events is a healthy way to approach the Civil War. Many factors came to play roles in shaping the combat environment as well as the shape of campaigning between battles. But after considering the major factors, one must conclude that the Civil War failed to witness any kind of a revolution in artillery practice. The long arm was important as a support for infantry and cavalry, but it did not dominate the battlefield consistently or clearly, nor were any new weapons, doctrine, or practices introduced to significantly alter the traditional role of artillery in field operations.

MANAGING THE ARTILLERY ARM

Historians have always seen the dispersal system of the early war period as a mistake in artillery management, arguing that it inhibited ad hoc concentration of the guns to target a specific part of the opposing line and prepare the way for infantry attacks. This is an overly simplistic view of a complex topic. L. Van Loan Naisawald, for example, overstated the case by arguing, "in this war seldom would a battery commander or a division artillery chief have the right even to select his own firing position."[1]

As we have seen, a careful search of battle reports and personal accounts reveals a wide variance in how infantry commanders handled the batteries assigned to their brigade, which intimately affected the opportunities artillery commanders enjoyed. It is true that some infantry officers were quite ignorant of artillery practice, threw their weight around callously, and impeded the artillery officer in his duties. But an equal number knew how to handle artillery and did a very good job of it. The rest were smart enough to let their battery commanders do as they pleased. In probably two-thirds of the cases, artillery officers had either cooperation from their infantry commander or a free hand in managing their batteries in combat.

Historians also bemoan the dispersal system as preventing ad hoc concentration of the guns. "This was a bad system," declared Jack Coggins, "dispersing the guns through the army, and preventing concentration of fire." Yet at the same time, Coggins praised the concentration that took place at Malvern Hill on July 1, 1862, which occurred during the dispersal phase in the history of artillery in the Army of the Potomac.[2] It is obvious that dispersal did not prevent ad hoc concentration. As we have argued in this book, dispersal was not a leather-bound system of artillery management. It was flexible enough to allow for ad hoc concentration as long as ranking infantry officers supported it. Sterling examples of this occurred not only at Malvern Hill but also at Shiloh and Stones River in field armies that were practicing the dispersal system at the time. Moreover, one can point to relatively few ad hoc concentrations of field artillery during the last half of the war after dispersal had been replaced by the consolidation system.

Some historians make the argument that ad hoc concentrations were not possible during this stage due to the heavily vegetated battlefields encountered by the armies in 1864, but that, too, is an exaggeration.[3] Only on a handful of battlefields, such as the Wilderness and some areas during the Atlanta Campaign, did the armies find woods and brush impeding their use of artillery. This was not the case at Petersburg, Franklin, Nashville, and most of the other battles fought in the last year of the war. In fact, more engagements took place on relatively open fields of battle than within crowded woods during the last year of the conflict.

The true importance of the consolidation system lay in administration, not battlefield management. Grouping batteries into artillery brigades (in the Army of the Potomac) and artillery battalions (in the Army of Northern Virginia) placed them in the administrative hands of artillery officers rather than infantry commanders and infantry brigade staff. The artillery officers who commanded those artillery brigades and artillery battalions knew full well what the batteries needed in the way of specialized ordnance stores. Just as importantly, they were highly capable of inspecting the batteries with an eye toward improving their field readiness. This was the most important benefit of the consolidation system. It also to a degree satisfied a deep and abiding desire for promotion opportunities and enhanced respect in the table of organization felt by ambitious artillery officers.

But the consolidation system failed to give those artillery officers the opportunity to command and control their batteries in combat. That right was specifically retained by infantry officers, who were jealous of their command prerogative. Those men also had a reasonable argument in their assertion that in battle, one person needed to accept full responsibility for all resources within his sector, including artillery power. They felt it was impossible to coordinate battle plans between the two arms if artillery officers had the right to do as they pleased without the approval of the infantry commander.

Ad hoc concentration has almost assumed a mantra among historians when they discuss artillery management in the Civil War. But, truthfully, field guns played a very important role in direct support of infantry units as well as in concentrated firepower on a single target. They had to be dispersed as a general rule in order to properly support infantry units. Concentration could only sometimes be attempted for limited and specific tasks before dispersal would have to be implemented once again in any given battle. There is no doubt that dispersed placement of the guns occurred overwhelmingly more often than ad hoc concentrations, but that was not a managerial or tactical error. Batteries performed their greatest good by offering immediate fire support to infantry units, not in the relatively rare opportunities given them for concentrated barrages that failed as often as they succeeded.

RIFLE MUSKET

The previous standard interpretation of the rifle musket's role in Civil War history began even before the firing on Fort Sumter. When the process of rifling became possible on a widespread scale in the 1850s, observers predicted the increased distance of the new weapon would revolutionize military operations. Many Civil War soldiers continued to believe this, even though they preferred to fire the new weapon at short distances, and the mystique of long-distance rifle fire simply increased after Appomattox. Until the onset of World War I, most observers assumed that rifled small arms would dominate the battlefield as the smoothbore had done before the middle of the nineteenth century.[4]

Naisawald reflected this interpretation as it related to the role of field artillery in the Civil War when he penned his history of the Army of the Potomac's long arm. The rifle musket neutralized the offensive capability of field guns, he asserted, and "relegated the artillery to a defensive role." Naisawald believed, as did every other historian, that the increased distance of small arms made it too dangerous for artillery to plant itself close to enemy infantry. Larry Daniel asserted that any spot within 200 yards of the rifle musket was now out of consideration for a battery, terming close-distance positions as "an outdated Napoleonic tactic."[5]

Paddy Griffith was the first historian to break away from this interpretation of the rifle musket as dominating Civil War battlefields. He also discussed the relationship between rifled small arms and field guns. Griffith admitted that Civil War artillery was more effective on the defensive than on the offensive, but then the same was true of Napoleonic artillery as well. "Most of Napoleon's attempted central break-ins with artillery fell short of the desired effect," Griffith has stated, "whereas most of the defences stiffened with properly concentrated mass fires were outstandingly successful." He considered the massing of guns close to the enemy in order to "blow a hole" in their position a complicated and risky tactic that even Napoleon could not fully master. The reason it rarely was attempted and never succeeded in the Civil War was due to "doctrinal ignorance." A lack of training for it, rather than the presence of the rifle musket, was the reason. "No large-scale artillery charge ever took place in the Civil War, despite a number of close approximations."[6]

Continuity with the past, rather than a decisive break from it, character-ized artillery work in the Civil War. If the rifle musket was not generally used for long-distance fire, if previous armies had rarely made close-distance artil-lery bombardment work on the battlefield, then there is little else in the way of evidence to support an argument that improved small arms significantly influenced combat in the Civil War. The truth is that the improvement was only slight, felt entirely in the area of potential distance of fire. The rifle mus-ket was still a muzzleloader, capable of firing about as fast as a smoothbore, and it was very soon superseded by magazine-fed small arms that could more readily affect battlefield operations with their increased rate of fire. Ironically, advances in the technical capabilities of field artillery increased at a more rapid rate during the late nineteenth century so that the big guns truly could dominate the battlefield much more readily than small arms. The introduc-tion of machine guns during the same period also outstripped the rifle in its ability to shape battle tactics and performance.

RIFLED ARTILLERY

The performance of new rifled artillery in the Civil War has drawn widely divergent conclusions from historians. Edward McCaul, whose focus was the fuzes that ignited long-distance projectiles, placed himself on one end of the spectrum by asserting that the technical problems with those fuzes were worked out during the course of the conflict. As a result, "the combination of rifled artillery and new fuzes made the Civil War a much deadlier war, one in which there was no safe place on the battlefield." McCaul went on to conclude, "Long range artillery fire was so deadly during the Civil War that it was the first war in which anyone who could be seen could be killed." Brent Nosworthy has also stressed the accuracy of artillery, or at least its "potential accuracy."[7]

As we have seen in the preceding chapters, McCaul's conclusions are not supported by the volume of evidence emerging from the conflict. The prob-lems with long-distance fuzes were not solved during the war, and many ar-tillerists were severely disappointed by the performance of their rifled guns. The fact that they preferred an arsenal of mixed pieces, with about half of it consisting of smoothbores, is another indication of their attitude toward the value of rifled artillery.

On the other end of the spectrum from McCaul there is Griffith, who erred a bit in the other direction. Griffith devalued rifled artillery, terming it "the unwelcome *prima donna* of the artillery arm." He overvalued the Napoleon for its effective short-distance capabilities, calling it "the much-loved maid of all work—the close- and medium-range crusher which achieved the big results." If that were literally true, Civil War artillerists would not likely have opted for rifles to fill half their arsenal. Griffith was on firm ground when he stated that the most effective artillery fire occurred at about 1,000 yards or less, well within the effective distance of the Napoleon. But the 3-Inch Ordnance Rifle and the 10-pounder Parrott also could deliver effective fire at that distance, even though it was far short of their theoretical capability for long-distance fire.[8]

As Nosworthy has correctly observed, the "continued reliance" on the Napoleon "was thoroughly grounded in pragmatic considerations, rather than symptomatic of widespread resistance to change."[9] But the other side of the coin is equally true. Civil War artillerists valued rifled artillery equally as much as the smoothbore and for equally pragmatic reasons.

There is no doubt that rifled artillery failed to live up to expectations during the Civil War, and it failed to supplant smoothbore technology. This was not only due to faulty fuzes. The difficulty of accurately sighting a target at long distances on battlefields cluttered with trees, brush, and hills played a significant role as well. The relatively light power of long-distance projectiles, fragmenting into large pieces that could easily miss a man even if exploding close to him, was another factor. It was impossible to shift to indirect fire, the only way to compensate for the difficulties of seeing a target at a distance. The few cases of its improvisation on the battlefield were not overwhelmingly successful and had no influence on doctrine or methods.

Just as a handful of naturally adept infantrymen could use the rifle musket to sharp shoot at long distances, so could a handful of especially good gun detachments fire a rifled piece accurately at long distances now and then. But that did not mean anything in terms of affecting the course of battles. To do that, it was necessary for *most* of the rifle muskets and rifled artillery to be used effectively at long distances, rather than the odd exception to the rule. The rule was that most infantrymen could not use the rifle musket for long-distance fire, while the average gun detachment could not make full use of their rifled pieces to deliver fire on distant targets in a consistent and meaningful way.

Civil War artillerists were wise to hedge their bets by choosing the best smoothbore and the two best rifles as their standby during the latter half of the Civil War. In this way they secured flexible assets that could be used to cover nearly all possible targets they could expect to encounter on the battlefield. Rifled artillery needed further technical advances to come into its own, but these would take place only after the Civil War ended.

ARTILLERY EFFECTIVENESS

How far Civil War artillery managed to achieve a level of effectiveness, whether it worked well or influenced military operations, begs the question of comparison. How did it do in reference to the Napoleonic Wars, the last set of great conflicts in the past, and in reference to World War I, the next great conflict to come?

Rory Muir has written what is probably the most thoughtful evaluation of field artillery in the Napoleonic era, and his conclusions were tentative at best. "There seems to be little reliable evidence on which to base firm conclusions" about how effectively artillerists of many nations worked their guns on the numerous battlefields of that time. Theorists of the day ascribed great potential to the arm by assuming that every piece, if handled well, could produce 60–120 losses among opposing units every hour. That would amount to one casualty produced by one to one and a half projectiles every sixty minutes. "But not even the bloodiest battles produced enough casualties to support these estimates," Muir conceded.[10]

Muir found no statistics that broke down the cause of battle wounds (in contrast, several exist for the Civil War), but information arising from the admission of veterans at the Invalides in Paris offers some help. In 1762, quite a few years before the Napoleonic era, those numbers indicate that 13.4 percent of those admitted had been wounded by artillery fire. Extrapolating generously from this very imperfect data, Muir guessed that up to 20–25 percent of losses on Napoleonic battlefields might have been caused by artillery fire. He found an estimate of 5.5-percent losses in the Civil War due to artillery and, extrapolating in an equally generous fashion, guessed that, in contrast, 12–15 percent of Union and Confederate casualties might have been the result of artillery work.[11]

More reliable statistics exist for artillery casualties in the Civil War than for the Napoleonic era. While those Civil War numbers vary according to the source one uses, one thing is clear—they all fall within a relatively narrow range at the lower end of the spectrum. We may not know exactly what percentage of losses occurred because of artillery, but we do know that it was quite low. The same, we can safely assume, was true for the Napoleonic conflicts.

Muir believed that artillerists tended to open fire at long distances, too far to be truly effective, based on reports provided by participants of Napoleon's battles. He also provided evidence about results of practice firing during the era. Setting up a large piece of canvas and testing their skill, Napoleonic artillerists could hardly brag about the results. They hit the target well at short distances but not at long. While striking it 100 percent of the time at 600 yards, that rate fell to 26 percent at 950 yards and only 15 percent at 1,300 yards. Opening fire at anything more than about 700 yards resulted in quickly falling rates of accuracy.[12]

Another factor to consider is steadiness, a willingness to stay and fight it out in difficult circumstances. Muir concluded that Napoleonic artillerists had a tendency to evacuate a position before the enemy closed in on it, which he identified as a trait shared by all artillery officers of all nations involved in the Napoleonic Wars. It is quite possible, he believed, that relatively little artillery fire was delivered at distances of less than 300 yards.[13]

Contrasting Civil War artillery to Muir's findings supports the notion that the past, rather than the future, is the true comparison. The Civil War represented an incremental advance compared to fifty years before, but that fell far short of truly significant change over time. Expectations were high in 1861, but those mainly rested on what enthusiasts believed would happen when rifled artillery took the field. As we have seen, those expectations for long-distance fire were at best only partially fulfilled. The loss ratio caused by artillery fire in the Civil War can be reliably placed at about 10 percent, hardly an improvement, if any, over the Napoleonic Wars. There were, however, differences in distance of fire. If Muir was correct, Napoleonic artillery failed to explore the full range of distance firing it was capable of producing. This was certainly not true of Civil War artillery. The reports are very firm in showing that Union and Confederate guns fired at a very wide spectrum of distances from very close to very far. Allied with very-short-distance firing was a strong willingness among Civil War artillerists to stand firm and continue fighting as long as they possibly could, even if the enemy were only a few yards away.

We can argue that Civil War artillery fulfilled its combat mission more fully than did Napoleonic artillery, but that was a matter of increments, creeping a bit farther along the way toward increased effectiveness. There was no revolutionary turn in the 1860s. In contrast, Civil War artillery bore little resemblance to the long arm of World War I. Truly revolutionary developments in technology tremendously altered the potential for destruction beginning in the 1880s and extending to the outbreak of the Great War in 1914. Those developments, sketched in the previous chapter, tremendously increased artillery power on the battlefield.

But the western front is not a truly accurate indication of field artillery power because it represented such unusual conditions. Millions of troops locked in static and heavily entrenched positions allowed the introduction of massive amounts of heavy artillery not usually employed in field campaigns. This heavy artillery thoroughly dominated the zone of operations, overwhelmed the contributions of field guns, and turned the front into a hellish environment.

The use of field guns in the mobile operations of World War I—on the eastern front, in Romania, in Salonika, and in the Middle East—was the true gauge of developments in the artillery arm since the days of the Civil War. In those mobile operations field artillery contributed a higher degree of support for infantry operations than one can see in the 1860s. That trend continued into World War II and Korea. As long as armies had enough modern guns, and as long as they were organized effectively with sound doctrine, good training, and experienced management, artillery and infantry operated as a cohesive team. The guns often made the difference in infantry assault and defense. Combined-arms doctrine, a phrase unknown to Civil War officers even though they tried to practice the concept, ruled thinking by this stage of military history. The better armies made it work well, and that made a difference in their rate of success on the battlefield.

We are compelled to see the Civil War as not only a mostly old-fashioned war as far as its artillery was concerned but also achieving at best only limited improvement over the past performance of the long arm. Historians have mostly recognized this conclusion, even if they have not explicitly stated it. Naisawald acknowledged that Civil War artillery "was a potent force—but only defensively. No offensive operation of either side was decisively affected by the offensive use of artillery; it was beyond the capabilities of the matériel and fire control systems of that era." But Naisawald and his colleagues strongly tended to blame the rifle musket as the root cause for this situation, although Spencer Jones believed that shortages of horses accounted for some of it as well. Confederate artillerists were shy about placing their guns too close to opposing infantry armed with long-distance muskets for fear of losing more animals than they could afford, Jones contended.[14]

The assumption among historians is that offensive action by field artillery was not possible without placing the guns close to the enemy, and close placement became impossible once rifle muskets were widely distributed. But Griffith, who did not ascribe to the rifle musket thesis, argued that there was "a certain failure to make the most of . . . field artillery" in the Civil War. In other words, it was more due to a failure of doctrine and practice than to the rifle musket. He believed artillerists and infantry commanders alike should have tried to concentrate the guns more often as a regular method of fighting. The fire could then "be carefully co-ordinated at points where the battle as a whole could best be influenced. This often meant that enfilading crossfires could be arranged, giving much more destructive effect than direct front fire at the same time as they relieved the gunners from fears of being personally overrun." While Griffith too readily dismissed the practical benefits of dispersing guns to support brigades, his point that Civil War artillerists failed to try concentrating their pieces more often and for purposes other than to soften up a target for an infantry attack is well taken.[15]

Griffith also argued that field artillery "had a shock power and a deterrent effect which is beyond the statistical reckoning. It could break enemy units and disperse attacks even when it did not hit enemy soldiers." In essence, this could be achieved better at short distance and in defensive actions. All the factors that lessened the effectiveness of long-distance firing, discussed in the preceding chapters, meant that field artillery had less chance of achieving this effect on enemy morale at long distances than short.[16]

Whether Civil War field artillery was capable of supporting infantry attacks is a matter of opinion. It certainly failed to achieve a record of doing so, but that was not due to the rifle musket. After all, half the pieces were rifled and thus capable of delivering fire from positions far beyond the potential distance (500 yards) even of rifle musket fire. Griffith was right to pinpoint doctrine as a more important cause, and it is obvious that faulty fuzes, the limited bursting power of projectiles, and the difficulties of delivering fire at distances greater than about 1,000 yards contributed to its failure in that regard. But on the defensive, especially at distances of 1,000 yards or less, Civil War field artillery still exerted impressive power on the battlefield.

MEMORY AND COMMEMORATION

Civil War artillerists probably had a higher degree of regard for their branch of the service than was common in the infantry or cavalry. Edward Porter Alexander wrote of "the arm which I loved & believed in," expressing the gunner's devotion to the branch that demanded of him more in the way of dedication, learning, and stamina than was typical of either the infantry or cavalry.[17]

A great deal of this devotion was centered on the equipment artillerists came to know so intimately. Cannons and other pieces of materiel became objects expressive of their feelings toward the military art. During the Petersburg Campaign, when Jacob Roemer's men had some spare time, they picked up fifteen pounds of Confederate bullets, "melted and cast [them] into the form of a miniature 10-inch mortar," and presented it to him. Roemer liked it very much and kept the little piece for the rest of his life, firing it to celebrate Independence Day every year.[18]

During the Bermuda Hundred Campaign, a Confederate projectile hit the hub of a piece in the 1st Connecticut Battery. It disabled the gun and flung the hub band into Curtis Bacon, who later died of gangrene caused by the injury. Capt. Alfred P. Rockwell arranged for the wrecked wheel to be sent to Connecticut, where it was placed in Battle Flag Corridor of the state capitol in Hartford. The names and dates of the engagements fought by the battery were painted on what was left of the rim. The wheel remains on display at the capitol today.[19]

Dan Webster and Don C. Cameron of the 1st Wisconsin Battery vividly expressed the feelings of artillery veterans about their pieces even long after the war had ended. "None but a soldier can 'sense' the affection with which a cannoneer regarded his gun," they wrote in their unit history. If he saw an old Civil War gun, sensory memories flooded his consciousness. "The pungent scent of battle lingers in muzzle, vent and equipments. He is not satisfied until he raises the limber lid, when, lo, what a host of emotions and memories float through his brain as the old, old intimate odors of primer, fuze, cartridge, wood, and iron shell penetrates his nostrils. If the chest has been empty a quarter of a century, like the nose, the scent remains there still."[20]

Artillery veterans had many opportunities to see old cannon because those

Fig. C.1. DeGolyer Battery Site, Vicksburg National Military Park. Located in the center of the Union siege line, the sector held by Maj. Gen. John A. Logan's division of the Seventeenth Corps, Capt. Samuel DeGolyer's 8th Michigan Battery site is commemorated by the park service with this line of original Civil War tubes mounted on reproduction carriages. From front to back, the six pieces are a Napoleon, a 12-pounder howitzer, two Napoleons, and finally two 12-pounder howitzers. This is possibly the only site on a Civil War battlefield where an entire battery of six pieces is represented by that number of cannon; normally, only one or two pieces represent a battery site. The earthworks are reproduced because most of the Union siege line was demolished soon after the fall of Vicksburg. Photograph by Earl J. Hess.

pieces became objects of public display after the war. They graced the lawns of many courthouses across the country and speckled the landscape of preserved Civil War battlefields. When a veteran of the 1st Wisconsin Battery visited the Grand Army of the Republic Post at Marshalltown, Iowa, he discovered four 20-pounder Parrotts arrayed across the courthouse lawn. With his GAR comrades, he examined the pieces. The man kept a memorandum book with information about the guns used by the 1st Wisconsin during the war and thus was armed with enough information to find that one of the pieces had actually been used by his battery (based on the serial number etched on the rim of the muzzle). "I was kneeling, facing the gun and my forehead went down on to the iron face," the unnamed veteran reported. "The tears jumped to my eyes and I thought more in a minute than I can write in an hour. I dashed away the tears and jumped up ashamed. Those grizzled veterans had their hats off. They would have respected me had I blubbered like a baby; that is true comradeship."[21]

When the Federal government began to create national parks of Civil War battlefields, it naturally turned to the ordnance that remained in government warehouses. For example, the chief of ordnance in the Department of the South transferred eighteen Civil War guns to the Gettysburg Battlefield Monument in May 1891. This lot included four 3-Inch Ordnance Rifles, ten 12-pounder bronze howitzers, two 24-pounder howitzers, and two 3-inch Whitworth breechloaders. All of them except for six of the 12-pounder bronze howitzers were unserviceable. This represented but one shipment of Civil War ordnance to one battlefield park during the era.[22]

Interested people have maintained records of surviving Civil War cannon, and the result is surprising. The total number of known survivals amounted to 5,761 tubes by 2012, with half a dozen added to the register that year. A small number are privately owned, but the majority reside in public parks maintained not only by the Federal government but also by state and local governments. No one has counted the number of reproduction pieces and equipment as opposed to original cannon, but that number must be pretty sizeable as well.[23]

Interest in Civil War field artillery continues. It not only springs from general public interest in the war but also is inspired by the thousands of original artillery tubes one can see and touch on most preserved battlefields of the conflict. Those tubes, which burned red hot for four years of deadly struggle, helping shape the future of the United States, now stand as silent monuments to the men and animals who served them.

NOTES

ABBREVIATIONS

ADAH	Alabama Department of Archives and History, Montgomery
ALPL	Abraham Lincoln Presidential Library, Springfield, IL
CHM	Chicago History Museum, Chicago, IL
DU	Duke University, Rubenstein Rare Book and Manuscript Library, Durham, NC
EU	Emory University, Manuscripts, Archives, and Rare Books Library, Atlanta, GA
LC	Library of Congress, Manuscripts Division, Washington, DC
LSU	Louisiana State University, Louisiana and Lower Mississippi Valley Collection, Baton Rouge
MHM	Missouri History Museum, St. Louis
MHS	Massachusetts Historical Society, Boston
MinnHS	Minnesota Historical Society, St. Paul
NARA	National Archives and Records Administration, Washington, DC
NC	Navarro College, Pearce Civil War Collection, Corsicana, TX
NYSL	New York State Library, Albany
OHS	Ohio Historical Society, Columbus
OCHM	Old Court House Museum, Vicksburg, MS
OR	*The War of the Rebellion: A Compilation of the Official Records of the Union and Confederate Armies,* 70 vols. in 128 pts. (Washington, DC: Government Printing Office, 1880–1901); all citations are to series 1 unless otherwise stated
SIU	Southern Illinois University, Special Collections Research Center, Carbondale
SOR	*Supplement to the Official Records of the Union and Confederate Armies,* 100 vols. (Wilmington, NC: Broadfoot, 1993–2000)
SRNB	Stones River National Battlefield, Murfreesboro, TN
TSLA	Tennessee State Library and Archives, Nashville
TU	Tulane University, Special Collections, New Orleans, LA

UM   University of Mississippi, Archives and Special Collections, Oxford

UNC   University of North Carolina, Southern History Collection, Chapel Hill

UTK   University of Tennessee, Special Collections, Knoxville

VHS   Virginia Historical Society, Richmond

VNMP   Vicksburg National Military Park, Vicksburg, MS

WHS   Wisconsin Historical Society, Madison

WLC-UM   University of Michigan, William L. Clements Library, Ann Arbor

WRHS   Western Reserve Historical Society, Cleveland, OH

PREFACE

1. *Instruction for Field Artillery,* 1 (all citations are to the 1860 edition unless otherwise indicated); *OR,* ser. 3, 1:746.

2. *Instruction for Field Artillery,* 1.

3. Birkhimer, *Historical Sketch,* 54n.

4. Hogg, *Artillery,* 183. For examples of contemporary and current use of "fuze," see *Instruction for Field Artillery,* 13; Roberts, *Hand-Book,* 122; Broun, *Notes on Artillery,* 45; Gibbon, *Artillerist's Manual,* 257; and McCaul, *Mechanical Fuze,* 9. For examples of contemporary and current use of "fuse," see *OR,* 25(2):151; *History of the Fifth Massachusetts Battery,* 114 (hereafter *Fifth Massachusetts Battery*); Jones, *Artillery Fuses,* 161–62; and McKee and Mason, *Civil War Projectiles,* 161–72.

5. *Instruction for Field Artillery,* 38, 41; Roberts, *Hand-Book,* 54–55.

6. *Instruction for Field Artillery,* 1–2; Gibbon, *Artillerist's Manual,* 343.

7. *Instruction for Field Artillery,* 2.

8. Hunt, "Our Experience in Artillery Administration," 200.

9. Naisawald, *Grape and Canister,* 60; Coggins, *Arms and Equipment,* 63.

10. McWhiney and Jamieson, *Attack and Die,* 123; Naisawald, *Grape and Canister,* 179; Daniel, *Cannoneers in Gray,* 44, 158–59; Griffith, *Battle Tactics of the Civil War,* 166, 171, 173–74; Hess, *Rifle Musket,* 197–215; Hess, *Civil War Infantry Tactics,* xv–xix.

11. McCaul, *Mechanical Fuze,* 9, 77; Griffith, *Battle Tactics of the Civil War,* 169–70.

12. I agree with Robert Epstein's assertion that the introduction of new weapons technology did not alter the operational or tactical situation of Civil War battlefields. See Epstein, "Patterns of Change and Continuity," 375, 387.

1. THE EUROPEAN ARTILLERY HERITAGE

1. Dastrup, *Field Artillery,* 6–9; Hogg, *Artillery,* 100; Rogers, *History of Artillery,* 15, 19, 24, 27.

2. Dastrup, *Field Artillery,* 7, 10; Hogg, *Artillery,* 238–39.

3. Dastrup, *Field Artillery,* 10; Hogg, *Artillery,* 156–60.

4. Dastrup, *Field Artillery,* 11; Rogers, *History of Artillery,* 39.

5. Bull, *"Furie of the Ordnance,"* xix–xx, 155, 157, 159–63.

6. Bull, *"Furie of the Ordnance,"* 161–64.

7. Hogg, *Artillery,* 94, 101, 106; Lynn, *Giant of the Grand Siècle,* 508; Dastrup, *Field Artillery,* 12–13.

8. Lynn, *Giant of the Grand Siècle,* 501–3; Lynn, "Forging the Western Army," 41–42, 44.

9. Dastrup, *Field Artillery,* 14, 21.

10. Hogg, *Artillery,* 147, 149–50.

11. Hogg, *Artillery,* 142–43.

12. Hogg, *Artillery,* 104; Birkhimer, *Historical Sketch,* 238.

13. Rogers, *History of Artillery,* 72; Nosworthy, *With Musket,* 362; Duffy, *Military Experience,* 217; Dastrup, *Field Artillery,* 27.

14. Dastrup, *Field Artillery,* 13.

15. Dastrup, *Field Artillery,* 21–22; Lynn, *Bayonets of the Republic,* 205–6.

16. Nosworthy, *With Musket,* 393–94.

17. Bailey, *Field Artillery,* 151; Hogg, *Artillery,* 101–2; Showalter, *Wars of Frederick the Great,* 70; Nosworthy, *With Musket,* 370–72, 396–97; Lynn, *Bayonets of the Republic,* 203, 205; Quimby, *Background of Napoleonic Warfare,* 158, 164–65; Hogg, *Artillery,* 104.

18. Nosworthy, *With Musket,* 382–83.

19. Nosworthy, *With Musket,* 384, 390; Bailey, *Field Artillery,* 49–50, 151–52.

20. Quimby, *Background of Napoleonic Warfare,* 106, 146–48, 150–52.

21. Quimby, *Background of Napoleonic Warfare,* 152–54.

22. Dastrup, *Field Artillery,* 23.

23. Duffy, *Military Experience,* 231–32; Nosworthy, *Anatomy of Victory,* 315, 318; Lynn, *Bayonets of the Republic,* 210, 214.

24. Bailey, *Field Artillery,* 179; Nosworthy, *With Musket,* 381; Muir, *Tactics,* 30; Duffy, *Austerlitz,* 87, 92.

25. Hogg, *Artillery,* 240; Rogers, *History of Artillery,* 88.

26. Nosworthy, *With Musket,* 359–60; Muir, *Tactics,* 31; Bailey, *Field Artillery,* 186.

27. Muir, *Tactics,* 32–33, 38.

28. Quimby, *Background of Napoleonic Warfare,* 291, 296–98; Bailey, *Field Artillery,* 183, 185; Hamilton-Williams, *Waterloo,* 287, 342.

29. Nosworthy, *Bloody Crucible,* 471.

30. Birkhimer, *Historical Sketch,* 252.

31. Birkhimer, *Historical Sketch,* 257, 260–61, 263, 265; Dastrup, *Field Artillery,* 24, 31–32, 319; Showalter, *Railroads and Rifles,* 150–51, 159, 173–74, 177, 179.

32. Dastrup, *Field Artillery,* 30; Rogers, *History of Artillery,* 93–97.

33. Gibbon, *Artillerist's Manual,* 37–40.

34. Hogg, *Artillery,* 189–90; Dastrup, *Field Artillery,* 29.

35. Dastrup, *Field Artillery,* 29; Hogg, *Artillery,* 190.

36. Hogg, *Artillery,* 150–51.

37. Dastrup, *Field Artillery,* 32.

38. Dastrup, *Field Artillery,* 30.

39. Straith, *Treatise on Fortification and Artillery,* 173–77; Dastrup, *Field Artillery,* 32.

40. Showalter, *Railroads and Rifles,* 176–77.

41. Rogers, *History of Artillery,* 76, 79; Dastrup, *Field Artillery,* 26; Showalter, *Railroads and Rifles,* 147–49. Early in the Civil War, Col. Henry J. Hunt argued that the term "company"

"properly refers to infantry soldiers" and should not be used when referring to a battery. *OR,* ser. 3, 1:746.

42. Dastrup, *Field Artillery,* 27; Hogg, *Artillery,* 246–48, 250; Rogers, *History of Artillery,* 195, 197.

43. Dastrup, *Field Artillery,* 28; Bailey, *Field Artillery,* 176–77; Rogers, *History of Artillery,* 197–98.

44. Hogg, *Artillery,* 250–51; Rogers, *History of Artillery,* 206–9.

45. Hogg, *Artillery,* 254.

2. THE AMERICAN ARTILLERY HERITAGE

1. Birkhimer, *Historical Sketch,* 276.

2. Birkhimer, *Historical Sketch,* 223–24, 227, 276.

3. Birkhimer, *Historical Sketch,* 77, 183–84, 186, 208–9.

4. Spring, *With Zeal and with Bayonets,* 194–95; Birkhimer, *Historical Sketch,* 76–77, 96.

5. Birkhimer, *Historical Sketch,* 312–13.

6. Spring, *With Zeal and with Bayonets,* 195, 197.

7. Birkhimer, *Historical Sketch,* 36–37, 40–41; Longacre, *Man behind the Guns,* 32.

8. Birkhimer, *Historical Sketch,* 277–79, 281–83; Hazlett, Olmstead, and Parks, *Field Artillery Weapons,* 191.

9. Birkhimer, *Historical Sketch,* 78.

10. Longacre, *Man behind the Guns,* 47; Birkhimer, *Historical Sketch,* 201.

11. Murphy, *Two Armies,* 193–206; McWhiney and Jamieson, *Attack and Die,* 36–38.

12. Birkhimer, *Historical Sketch,* 79, 97; Longacre, *Man behind the Guns,* 30; Hunt, "Our Experience in Artillery Administration," 217.

13. Birkhimer, *Historical Sketch,* 77, 299, 302.

14. Birkhimer, *Historical Sketch,* 301–2, 316.

15. Birkhimer, *Historical Sketch,* 314–15.

16. Birkhimer, *Historical Sketch,* 303, 317–18.

17. Birkhimer, *Historical Sketch,* 303–5.

18. Birkhimer, *Historical Sketch,* 59–60, 305–6; McWhiney and Jamieson, *Attack and Die,* 36–37; Hsieh, *West Pointers,* 47–50; Hunt, "Our Experience in Artillery Administration," 207.

19. Birkhimer, *Historical Sketch,* 320–21; Anderson, *Instruction,* 109.

20. Birkhimer, *Historical Sketch,* 306–7; Longacre, *Man behind the Guns,* 66–69; *Instruction for Field Artillery,* v.

21. Birkhimer, *Historical Sketch,* 307, 323–24; Lord, "Army and Navy Textbooks," 101; *Instruction for Field Artillery* (1968); *1864 Field Artillery Tactics.*

22. *Instruction for Field Artillery,* 79.

23. Lord, "Army and Navy Textbooks," 101.

24. Gibbon, *Artillerist's Manual,* preface, 9–37, 41–47, 62–103, 109–57; Lord, "Army and Navy Textbooks," 101; Roberts, *Hand-Book,* 4.

25. Broun, *Notes on Artillery,* preface; cards, William Leroy Brown Service Record, 1st Virginia Artillery, M324, NARA.

26. *Ordnance Manual for the Use of the Officers of the United States Army,* 1; *Ordnance Manual for the Use of the Officers of the Confederate States Army,* preface. For references to other artillery books, see Baker, *Ninth Mass. Battery,* 31; Birkhimer, *Historical Sketch,* 306–7; and *Complete Cannoneer,* 6–168. For Civil War officers requesting copies of various artillery books, see Manning F. Force to Mr. Kebler, August 1, 1863, M. F. Force Papers, University of Washington, Special Collections, Seattle; *OR,* 19(1):155; Henry L. Abbot to Hunt, May 7, 1864, Box 10, Henry Jackson Hunt Papers, LC; "Regulations for the Care of the Field Works and the Government of their Garrisons," n.d., Box 13, ibid.; and Charles A. Phillips to Dear Sir, August 5, 1863, Unit 14, Federal Soldiers' Letters, UNC.

27. *Instruction for Field Artillery,* 2; Hazlett, Olmstead, and Parks, *Field Artillery Weapons,* 30, 51.

28. *Instruction for Field Artillery,* 8; Hazlett, Olmstead, and Parks, *Field Artillery Weapons,* 220.

29. Roberts, *Hand-Book,* 10; *OR,* 20(2):400; Hazlett, Olmstead, and Parks, *Field Artillery Weapons,* 109, 220; Trepal, "Gun Foundry," 73, 76.

30. Hazlett, Olmstead, and Parks, *Field Artillery Weapons,* 109; Johnson and Anderson, *Artillery Hell,* 24–25.

31. Hazlett, Olmstead, and Parks, *Field Artillery Weapons,* 88–89, 91–92.

32. Johnson and Anderson, *Artillery Hell,* 21.

33. *Instruction for Field Artillery,* 2, 3n.

34. Hazlett, Olmstead, and Parks, *Field Artillery Weapons,* 147–48, 221.

35. Hazlett, Olmstead, and Parks, *Field Artillery Weapons,* 147–48, 154; Beecher, *First Light Battery Connecticut,* 100; Dastrup, *Field Artillery,* 31; *Fifth Massachusetts Battery,* 127.

36. Hazlett, Olmstead, and Parks, *Field Artillery Weapons,* 206–7, 209, 211–12.

37. Hazlett, Olmstead, and Parks, *Field Artillery Weapons,* 163, 165, 167; record of events, 14th Ohio Battery, *SOR,* pt. 2, 50:465, 469.

38. *Instruction for Field Artillery,* 8; Roberts, *Hand-Book,* 30; Nesmith, "Stagnation and Change," 8–9.

39. Nesmith, "Stagnation and Change," 17.

40. Nesmith, "Stagnation and Change," 18.

41. McCaul, *Mechanical Fuze,* 181–82; Kerksis and Dickey, *Heavy Artillery Projectiles,* 7.

42. Kerksis and Dickey, *Heavy Artillery Projectiles,* 7–8.

43. Hazlett, Olmstead, and Parks, *Field Artillery Weapons,* 161–62; McCaul, *Mechanical Fuze,* 92.

44. Hazlett, Olmstead, and Parks, *Field Artillery Weapons,* 161–62; McCaul, *Mechanical Fuze,* 92; Billings, *Tenth Massachusetts Battery,* 222n.

45. McCaul, *Mechanical Fuze,* 13–14, 16–17.

46. McCaul, *Mechanical Fuze,* 19–20, 23.

47. McCaul, *Mechanical Fuze,* 28–29, 179.

48. McCaul, *Mechanical Fuze,* 30–31, 40, 96, 99–100.

49. McCaul, *Mechanical Fuze,* 41, 85, 103–4.

50. Longacre, *Man behind the Guns,* 59, 61, 63–65; Birkhimer, *Historical Sketch,* 134.

51. Hunt, "First Day at Gettysburg," 259; Birkhimer, *Historical Sketch,* 63–68.

52. Hazlett, Olmstead, and Parks, *Field Artillery Weapons,* 220.

53. Dastrup, *Field Artillery,* 32.

3. WAR FOOTING

1. *Instruction for Field Artillery,* 5–6.

2. Grandchamp, *Boys of Adams' Battery G,* 9–11, 13–14.

3. Hughes, *Pride of the Confederate Artillery,* 2, 4, 9, 12; [Bartlett], *Soldier's Story,* 8–9, 11–12; W. I. Hodgson, "History of the 5th Company Battalion Washington Artillery from April 1861 to June 6, 1862," 1, 3, 7, 12, Box 14, Folder 1, Civil War Papers, Battalion Washington Artillery Collection, TU.

4. Bergeron, *Guide to Louisiana Confederate Military Units,* 29.

5. Walton, *Behind the Guns,* vii.

6. Grandchamp, *Boys of Adams' Battery G,* 40; *Fifth Massachusetts Battery,* 53; *SOR,* pt. 2, 70:440; Williams, "Company C—Light Battery," 537; *Historical Sketch of the Chicago Board of Trade Battery,* 17–18.

7. *Instruction for Field Artillery,* 3, 69.

8. Merrill, *24th Independent Battery,* 207–8; Bennett, *First Massachusetts Light Battery,* 13–14. The cannoneers and the drivers who served the piece were also known as a platoon, with two platoons constituting a section. *Instruction for Field Artillery,* 67–68, 75.

9. Billings, *Tenth Massachusetts Battery,* 41–42.

10. Rhodes, *History of Battery B,* 181.

11. Billings, *Tenth Massachusetts Battery,* 40; *Instruction for Field Artillery,* 110–11, 114–17; Maxwell, *Autobiography,* 215.

12. Anderson, *Instruction,* 14; Smith, *Brother of Mine,* 139.

13. *OR,* 40(1):433; Bennett, *First Massachusetts Light Battery,* 99; Baker, *Ninth Mass. Battery,* 13; Chamberlayne, *Ham Chamberlayne,* 172; *Fifth Massachusetts Battery,* 115.

14. Hess, *Civil War Infantry Tactics,* xiii–xxi.

15. *Instruction for Field Artillery,* 73–74.

16. *Instruction for Field Artillery,* 275–77.

17. *Instruction for Field Artillery,* 72–73.

18. *Instruction for Field Artillery,* 278; Scott, *Military Dictionary,* 62; Gibbon, *Artillerist's Manual,* 354.

19. *Instruction for Field Artillery,* 206–26, 247–48, 274–75; Anderson, *Instruction,* 118; Gibbon, *Artillerist's Manual,* 355.

20. *Instruction for Field Artillery,* 74, 247; "Battery F," Box 3, Folder 26, James Barnett Papers, WRHS.

21. *Instruction for Field Artillery,* 73, 78, 249.

22. *Instruction for Field Artillery,* 306–7, 309–11; Anderson, *Instruction,* 124n.

23. *Instruction for Field Artillery,* 107.

24. *Instruction for Field Artillery,* 71–72; Anderson, *Instruction,* 108.

25. *Instruction for Field Artillery,* 282–83, 288–91, 298–99, 302, 304.

26. *Instruction for Field Artillery,* 252–53, 292–96, 297–98, 300–302, 306.

27. *Instruction for Field Artillery,* 77, 259, 311–12; Anderson, *Instruction,* 119.

28. Anderson, *Instruction,* 180–81; *Instruction for Field Artillery,* 336–39, 341; Gibbon, *Artillerist's Manuel,* 355.

29. *Instruction for Field Artillery,* 76–78, 238, 287, Plate 33; Anderson, *Instruction,* 88n, 119.

30. *Instruction for Field Artillery,* 268–70, 285–86.

31. *Instruction for Field Artillery,* 63, 331–34.

32. Hoy, *Bradford's Battery,* 256; Collier and Collier, *Yours for the Union,* 60.

33. Tracie, *Annals of the Nineteenth Ohio Battery,* 53; Billings, *Hardtack and Coffee,* 181–83.

34. Griffin, *Three Years a Soldier,* 188; Billings, *Hardtack and Coffee,* 184; Merrill, *24th Independent Battery,* 192; Rhodes, *History of Battery B,* 20; Furney, *Reminiscences,* 16–21; Fitzhugh, *Cannon Smoke,* 68–69; [Daniel], *Richmond Howitzers,* 19.

35. Hackemer, *To Rescue My Native Land,* 62; *SOR,* pt. 2, 42:380, 385–86; *History of the Organization,* 18.

36. *Instruction for Field Artillery,* 250–52; Bradford Nichol Memoirs, August 9, 1861, TSLA.

37. *Instruction for Field Artillery,* 134–37; Hackemer, *To Rescue My Native Land,* 16; Baker, *Ninth Mass. Battery,* 25.

38. *Instruction for Field Artillery,* 107, 118–19, 124–25; Anderson, *Instruction,* 46–47; Rhodes, *History of Battery B,* 181–82; Maxwell, *Autobiography,* 216.

39. Rhodes, *History of Battery B,* 182; *Instruction for Field Artillery,* 127–31; Nichol Memoirs, February 11, 1862, TSLA.

40. *Fifth Massachusetts Battery,* 145.

41. Billings, *Hardtack and Coffee,* 186; Rhodes, *History of Battery B,* 51; Joseph William Eggleston Autobiography, 24, VHS.

42. Moore, *Story of a Cannoneer,* 37; Nevins, *Diary of Battle,* 18, 168; Baker, *Ninth Mass. Battery,* 30; Furney, *Reminiscences,* 17; Beecher, *First Light Battery Connecticut,* 98–99.

43. Eggleston Autobiography, 9, VHS.

44. Reichardt, *Diary of Battery A,* 27; Hackemer, *To Rescue My Native Land,* 216.

45. Nevins, *Diary of Battle,* 8; Aldrich, *Battery A,* 50; *Fifth Massachusetts Battery,* 700–701; Billings, *Hardtack and Coffee,* 185; Furney, *Reminiscences,* 25; Bauer, *Soldiering,* 12; Eby, *Observations,* 73; Copp, *Reminiscences,* 439; Douglas, *Douglas's Texas Battery,* 171; Fitzhugh, *Cannon Smoke,* 79–81.

46. Naisawald, *Grape and Canister,* 34, 534.

47. Furney, *Reminiscences,* 25; Crumb and Dhalle, *No Middle Ground,* 97–98; Fitzhugh, *Cannon Smoke,* 2; Griffin, *Three Years a Soldier,* 218; John Reiley to friends at home, October 19, 1862, Francis and John Reiley Papers, WRHS; Webster and Cameron, *First Wisconsin Battery,* 192.

48. *OR,* 10(1):276, 52(1):24, 26.

49. [Davidson], *Battery A,* 19; Nevins, *Diary of Battle,* 244.

50. *Revised United States Army Regulations,* 17; [Daniel], *Richmond Howitzers,* 19.

51. Lewis, *Battery E,* 24; Otto, *11th Indiana Battery,* 8; [Jones], *Under the Stars and Bars,* 19–20; Rowell, *Yankee Artillerymen,* 27; Kimbell, *Battery "A,"* 34; Smith, *Richard Snowden Andrews,* 43.

52. Gallagher, *Fighting for the Confederacy*, 65–66; *Fifth Massachusetts Battery*, 140–41.

53. Beecher, *First Light Battery Connecticut*, 100; Furney, *Reminiscences*, 35; *Fifth Massachusetts Battery*, 146; Rowell, *Yankee Artillerymen*, 27; Nichol Memoirs, July 30, 1861, TSLA.

54. *Fifth Massachusetts Battery*, 139–40.

55. Watkins to John, December 5, 1862, John Watkins Papers, UTK.

56. Webster and Cameron, *First Wisconsin Battery*, 22–23, 36.

57. Baker, *Ninth Mass. Battery*, 149; Lewis, *Battery E*, 399.

58. Collier and Collier, *Yours for the Union*, 124; *SOR*, pt. 2, 70:459–60; Webster and Cameron, *First Wisconsin Battery*, 96; Cushing to Lieutenant Atwater, February 18, 1863, Harry C. Cushing Letters, UTK; Nevins, *Diary of Battle*, 176, 317; *History of the Fourth Maine Battery*, 63; Rhodes, *History of Battery B*, 180; Cate, *Two Soldiers*, 66, 68, 73; Douglas, *Douglas's Texas Battery*, 64–65.

59. Albert G. Grammer Diary, August 6, 13, 1863, OCHM; Rhodes, *History of Battery B*, 267; Walton, *Behind the Guns*, 85; Edwin B. Dow to Albert Merrill, April 13, 1864, Box 10, Henry Jackson Hunt Papers, LC; Report of Target Practice, late April 1864, ibid.; John C. Tidball to John Craig, April 30, 1864, ibid.; *OR*, 33:676; *Fifth Massachusetts Battery*, 706, 800.

60. *OR*, 11(2):437, 25(1):276; *SOR*, pt. 1, 3:756, 787; Eby, *Observations*, 73; Stiles, *Four Years*, 95–96.

61. *OR*, 17(1):319, 38(3):362; *SOR*, pt. 1, 4:626; .

62. *OR*, 10(1):373, 11(2):249, 12(2):486, 21:267, 25(1):54, 36(1):645.

63. *OR*, 11(2):172, 20(1):524, 36(1):650, 658; Boos, "Civil War Diary of Patrick H. White," 659; Moore, *Story of a Cannoneer*, 97.

64. Aldrich, *Battery A*, 251; *OR*, 11(2):207, 40(1):728.

65. *OR*, 25(1):487; Govan and Livingood, *Haskell Memoirs*, 67.

66. Crumb, *Eleventh Corps Artillery*, 31–32; Ladd and Ladd, *Bachelder Papers*, 2:1146, 3:1381–83; *OR*, 36(1):650; Eggleston Autobiography, 17, VHS; W. W. Carnes to Quintard, February 13, 1895, Charles Todd Quintard Papers, DU.

67. *OR*, 11(2):356, 38(1):496, 42(1):790; *SOR*, pt. 1, 2:497.

68. *OR*, 11(2):52, 22(1):123–24.

69. *OR*, 17(1):642.

70. *Instruction for Field Artillery*, 204.

71. McCrea, "Light Artillery," 523; *OR*, 30(1):588, 30(2):186, 38(3):471, 40(1):490; Fout, *Dark Days*, 288; Douglas, *Douglas's Texas Battery*, 197; *SOR*, pt. 1, 4:652–53; Wiley, *Reminiscences of Confederate Service*, 48.

72. *OR*, 30(1):799, 31(2):453, 36(1):939, 38(3):472; Ladd and Ladd, *Bachelder Papers*, 1:281; Eggleston Autobiography, 15, VHS; *Historical Sketch of the Chicago Board of Trade Battery*, 23.

73. *OR*, 38(1):495, 45(1):489.

74. *OR*, 11(2):255, 472, 19(1):325, 20(1):523, 22(1):124, 38(3):469; *SOR*, pt. 1, 3:780; Ladd and Ladd, *Bachelder Papers*, 1:385–86; Stewart, "Battery B," 185.

75. Ladd and Ladd, *Bachelder Papers*, 3:1453; *OR*, 13:295, 36(1):657, 47(1):854.

76. *OR*, 17(1):310–11, 19(1):308, 20(1):824.

77. *OR*, 20(1):580, 895, 30(1):882, 45(1):471; Moore, *Story of a Cannoneer*, 151; Ladd and Ladd, *Bachelder Papers*, 1:281.

78. *OR,* 8:237, 19(1):325.

79. Wheeler, *Letters,* 409; Fout, *Dark Days,* 288.

80. *OR,* 10(1):527, 12(2):569, 576, 22(1):519, 25(1):594, 613, 34(1):631; *SOR,* pt. 1, 3:525, 4:370–71, 661, 6:601; Ladd and Ladd, *Bachelder Papers,* 3:1633; Chalaron, "Battle Echoes from Shiloh," 219; Hughes, *Civil War Memoir of Philip Daingerfield Stephenson,* 299.

81. *OR,* 10(1):147, 38(3):361.

82. Cowan, "Cowan's New York Battery"; Rhodes, *History of Battery B,* 289; Furney, *Reminiscences,* 78–79.

83. Buell, *"Cannoneer,"* 209–10; Malone, *Memoir,* 148.

84. *Instruction for Field Artillery,* 335; Anderson, *Instruction,* 45–46; *OR,* 21:514; Sears, "11th Ohio Battery at Iuka."

85. *OR,* 17(1):130, 646, 20(1):413–14, 31(2):640, 40(1):486, 490; Don C. Cameron to William T. Rigby, May 13, 1903, 1st Wisconsin Battery Folder, VNMP; Morton, *Artillery of Nathan Bedford Forrest's Cavalry,* 209–10; Chalaron, "Battle Echoes from Shiloh," 222; *SOR,* pt. 1, 3:516.

86. Roberts, *Hand-Book,* 50; George W. Sledge Diary, April 29, 1864, Mississippi State University, Special Collections, Starkville; *OR,* 25(1):486–87, 41(1):458; "Order Book, 5th Company, B.W.A.," 173, Box 12, Folder 1, Civil War Papers, Battalion Washington Artillery Collection, TU; Hughes, *Pride of the Confederate Artillery,* 94; Lee, *Memoirs of William Nelson Pendleton,* 145; Rhodes, *History of Battery B,* 52; Tracie, *Annals of the Nineteenth Ohio Battery,* 85; *SOR,* pt. 1, 4:652; Ames to Home Circle, May 4, 1863, Albert N. Ames Papers, NYSL.

87. Gibbon, *Artillerist's Manual,* 348–50.

88. *Instruction for Field Artillery,* 52–55; Gibbon, *Artillerist's Manual,* 350.

89. Anderson, *Instruction,* 110.

90. *SOR,* pt. 1, 6:354; *OR,* 10(1):64–67, 47(1):579.

91. Wheeler, *Letters,* 408.

92. Nevins, *Diary of Battle,* 297–98.

93. *Instruction for Field Artillery,* 58; Haupt, *Military Bridges,* 188–91.

94. *SOR,* pt. 2, 50:515.

95. *OR,* 11(2):258, 284, 36(1):754, 768; John Merrilles Diary, July 18, 1863, CHM.

96. Anderson, *Instruction,* 104–5.

97. Gibbon, *Artillerist's Manual,* 353.

98. *Instruction for Field Artillery,* 65–66; Buell, *"Cannoneer,"* 27–29.

99. Moses A. Cleveland Journal, March 3, 1864, MHS; *History of the Organization,* 248.

100. Cleveland Journal, March 4, 1864, MHS; Billings, *Hardtack and Coffee,* 190; Moore, *Story of a Cannoneer,* 214.

4. HARDWARE

1. Hazlett, Olmstead, and Parks, *Field Artillery Weapons,* passim.

2. Longacre, *Man behind the Guns,* 191; Cushing to mother, October 4, 1863, Harry C. Cushing Letters, UTK; John Merrilles Diary, June 20, 1863, CMH.

3. Gorgas, "Contributions to the History," 93.

4. Hughes, *Civil War Memoir of Philip Daingerfield Stephenson,* 164–65.

5. Dent to wife, May 1, June 22, 1864, Stouten Hubert Dent Papers, ADAH; *SOR,* pt. 1, 5:368; Little and Maxwell, *Lumsden's Battery,* 50; White, "Diary of the War," 154; Hazlett, Olmstead, and Parks, *Field Artillery Weapons,* 93–94.

6. Hazlett, Olmstead, and Parks, *Field Artillery Weapons,* 121; Johnson and Anderson, *Artillery Hell,* 24; Hazlett, "3-Inch Ordnance Rifle," 33, 35.

7. *Fifth Massachusetts Battery,* 125; Hazlett, "3-Inch Ordnance Rifle," 35; Johnson and Anderson, *Artillery Hell,* 24.

8. Kaplan, *Artillery Service,* 4; Johnson and Anderson, *Artillery Hell,* 24; *OR,* 13:296; Nevins, *Diary of Battle,* 237; Hazlett, "3-Inch Ordnance Rifle," 34.

9. Little and Maxwell, *Lumsden's Battery,* 49–50; Moore, *Story of a Cannoneer,* 109; White, "Diary of the War," 189; Williams, "Company C—Light Battery," 542–43.

10. Buell, *"Cannoneer,"* 22; *OR,* 21:195, 38(1):825, 827, 38(3):176, 47(1):907; Nevins, *Diary of Battle,* 32, 145–46, 351–52.

11. Hunt, "Our Experience," 216; Birkhimer, *Historical Sketch,* 294; *Fifth Massachusetts Battery,* 327.

12. Watkins to Friend John, March 23, [1864], John Watkins Papers, UTK; *OR,* 38(3):365–66; *SOR,* pt. 1, 4:388; "Rebel Bull Session," 26; Ramsay, "Light Batteries A, D, F and I," 563–64.

13. A. C. Waterhouse to William T. Rigby, June 16, 1902, Battery E, 1st Illinois Artillery Folder, VNMP; Hazlett, Olmstead, and Parks, *Field Artillery Weapons,* 116–17; Hoy, *Bradford's Battery,* 271.

14. *OR,* 21:189–90.

15. *OR,* ser. 3, 1:919–20; *SOR,* pt. 1, 4:388.

16. Thomas, *Cannons,* 45–46; *OR,* 11(2):538, 11(3):686–87, 38(1):121; Kaplan, *Artillery Service,* 5; Kerksis and Dickey, *Heavy Artillery Projectiles,* 1.

17. Ramsay, "Light Batteries A, D, F and I," 554, 556; "Rebel Bull Session," 26.

18. Brown to father, July 4, 1863, William L. Brown Collection, CHM; *OR,* ser. 3, 1:274–75; Thomas, *Cannons,* 43; *OR,* 26(1):691.

19. Nevins, *Diary of Battle,* 18–21, 22; Webster and Cameron, *First Wisconsin Battery,* 150–51.

20. *SOR,* pt. 1, 2:375; *OR,* 11(2):903; Hazlett, Olmstead, and Parks, *Field Artillery Weapons,* 157; account by Marcus D. Elliott, in *Portrait Biographical Album,* 820; *OR,* ser. 3, 4:469.

21. *OR,* 5:29.

22. *OR,* 38(1):121, 46(1):1010.

23. Melton, "Cannon Sights," www.civilwarartillery.com/equipment/cannonsights.htm; Thomas, *Cannons,* 64–65; *Instruction for Field Artillery,* 39–40.

24. *OR,* 20(1):723, 741, 753, 762, 768.

25. Ritter, "Sketch of Third Battery," pt. 5, 190.

26. *OR,* 46(1):362.

27. Roberts, *Hand-Book,* 15, 26; Gibbon, *Artillerist's Manual,* 51–52.

28. *OR,* 11(2):288, 19(1):437; Bennett, *First Massachusetts Light Battery,* 61; *SOR,* pt. 1, 2:756.

29. *OR,* 12(2):653; Ladd and Ladd, *Bachelder Papers,* 2:844.

30. *OR,* 11(2):167, 12(2):571, 46(1):187; John C. Tidball to Hunt, March 25, 1865, Box 11, Henry Jackson Hunt Papers, LC.

31. Moore, *Story of a Cannoneer,* 99; *OR,* 17(1):643; *SOR,* pt. 1, 4:388, 391.

32. John C. Tidball to Hunt, March 25, 1865, and J. H. Parkes endorsement, March 25, 1865, Box 11, Hunt Papers, LC; *OR,* 20(1):579; Gibbon, *Artillerist's Manual,* 238; Maxwell, *Autobiography,* 245.

33. Anderson, *Instruction,* 31–32; Moore, *Story of a Cannoneer,* 264.

34. Receipt, November 26, 1863, Charles R. Grandy Service Record, Norfolk Virginia Artillery, M324, NARA.

35. Roberts, *Hand-Book,* 125; *Instruction for Field Artillery,* 7, 14–15; Maxwell, *Autobiography,* 215.

36. *OR,* 20(1):770, 45(1):327–28.

37. Angst, "Archaeological Investigations at Morgan Hill," 99; Reeves, *Dropped and Fired,* 39, 69–70, 73–74.

38. *OR,* 20(1):753, 30(2):202, 34(1):632; *SOR,* pt. 1, 5:682, 686.

39. Gibbon, *Artillerist's Manual,* 296; *SOR,* pt. 1, 4:72; *SOR,* pt. 3, 1:258; *OR,* 34(1):632; Gordon, "Battle of Big Bethel," 30.

40. Gibbon, *Artillerist's Manual,* 296; *OR,* 36(2):62, 42(1):421.

41. *Instruction for Field Artillery,* 64; John Merrilles Diary, July 17, 1863, CHM; Collier and Collier, *Yours for the Union,* 262; Griffin, *Three Years a Soldier,* 123–24.

42. Nevins, *Diary of Battle,* 52; *OR,* 12(2):575, 21:566, 587, 31(1):478; *SOR,* pt. 1, 6:781, 2:755–56; Gallagher, *Fighting for the Confederacy,* 316; "Military reminiscences of the war as participated in by the Army of Tennessee," Llewellyn Griffin Hoxton Manuscripts, UVA.

43. Nevins, *Diary of Battle,* 52; *OR,* 10(1):245–46, 11(2):267, 17(1):241, 20(1):413–14, 456, 871, 24(2):411; *SOR,* pt. 1, 5:281; Griffin, *Three Years a Soldier,* 217.

44. *OR,* 11(1):538, 25(2):749; Moore, *Story of a Cannoneer,* 57.

45. *OR,* 20(1):956; Furney, *Reminiscences,* 46.

46. *SOR,* pt. 1, 2:752–53, 7:521; Gibbon, *Artillerist's Manual,* 359; *OR,* 12(2):306, 17(1):342; Reichardt, *Diary of Battery A,* 61.

47. Morton, *Artillery,* 219–20. This is the only reliable evidence of hiding an artillery piece by burying it in the ground that I have seen.

48. *OR,* 47(1):852.

49. *Instruction for Field Artillery,* 11; *Ordnance Manual for the Use of the Officers of the United States Army,* 30; Gibbon, *Artillerist's Manual,* 301; *OR,* 21:516–17.

50. Barlow, "Light Battery Service in 1861."

51. Semple to wife, March 15, 1863, Henry C. Semple Papers, ADAH; Gibbon, *Artillerist's Manual,* 239; Buell, *"Cannoneer,"* 20, 22.

52. *OR,* 20(1):768; Robert H. Fitzhugh to John N. Craig, April 22, 1864, Box 10, Hunt Papers, LC.

53. *Instruction for Field Artillery,* 11; Buell, *"Cannoneer,"* 20.

54. *Fifth Massachusetts Battery,* 125–26; McCaul, *Mechanical Fuze,* 112, 183; Robert H. Fitzhugh to John N. Craig, April 22, 1864, Box 10, Hunt Papers, LC.

55. Reeves, *Dropped and Fired,* 107, 109.

56. Roberts, *Hand-Book,* 134.

57. *Instruction for Field Artillery*, 16; Roberts, *Hand-Book*, 134; Hewitt, Schott, and Kunis, *To Succeed or Perish*, 10, 131n26.

58. Gibbon, *Artillerist's Manual*, 158–61; Hazlett, Olmstead, and Parks, *Field Artillery Weapons*, 213.

59. Gibbon, *Artillerist's Manual*, 103–4; Hazlett, Olmstead, and Parks, *Field Artillery Weapons*, 218; *Instruction for Field Artillery*, 34.

60. Hazlett, Olmstead, and Parks, *Field Artillery Weapons*, 213.

61. *OR*, 11(2):86.

62. *OR*, 11(1):538, 11(2):860, 903, 12(2):485, 20(1):455, 21:266–67; *SOR*, pt. 1, 2:752, 3:746; Benjamin F. Nourse Diary, December 31, 1862, DU.

63. *OR*, 17(1):342, 20(1):842, 873, 21:195, 216, 460, 637; *SOR*, pt. 1, 2:726.

64. *OR*, 10(1):277, 11(2):355, 20(1):355, 21:467, 517; *SOR*, pt. 1, 3:746.

65. Nevins, *Diary of Battle*, 265; *OR*, 22(1):404, 30(1):282, 472, 31(2):560; Ladd and Ladd, *Bachelder Papers*, 1:569.

66. *OR*, 31(2):388, 42(1):821, 43(1):275–76, 45(1):328, 51(1):1271; *SOR*, pt. 1, 6:597, 7:335, 5:286; Rhodes, *History of Battery B*, 281; Baker, *Ninth Mass. Battery*, 31; Clark, *Hampton Battery F*, 31.

67. *OR*, 7:208, 11(2):247, 21:182, 197–98, 36(1):643, 651; *SOR*, pt. 1, 2:726; *SOR*, pt. 2, 31:650; Daniel, *Cannoneers in Gray*, 103.

68. *OR*, 47(1):1041, 52(1):85; *Fifth Massachusetts Battery*, 196–97, 200, 202–3.

69. *SOR*, pt. 2, 50:387; *Report of the Joint Committee*, 2:243; Crumb, *Eleventh Corps Artillery*, 13; *Instruction for Field Artillery*, 132–33.

70. *SOR*, pt. 1, 2:754, 4:389.

71. *OR*, 5:67–68.

72. *OR*, 20(1):456, 21:182, 189–90, 197–98, 30(1):282, 472; Daniel, *Cannoneers in Gray*, 103.

73. Krause, "French Battle for Vimy Ridge," 98–99.

74. Roberts, *Hand-Book*, 136, 152–53.

75. Stiles, *Four Years*, 194–95; Hazlett, Olmstead, and Parks, *Field Artillery Weapons*, 218–219; *Fifth Massachusetts Battery*, 114.

76. *OR*, 34(1):412; Scates to father, November 13, 1861, Walter Scates Papers, NC.

77. Hazlett, Olmstead, and Parks, *Field Artillery Weapons*, 219; Morton, *Artillery*, 209; Ladd and Ladd, *Bachelder Papers*, 1:387; *OR*, 33:582.

78. *Instruction for Field Artillery*, 63.

79. *OR*, 20(1):479, 30(1):414; *SOR*, pt. 1, 3:801.

80. Joseph William Eggleston Autobiography, 16, VHS; *OR*, 20(1):522, 30(1):426, 801.

81. *OR*, 11(2):85, 12(2):467, 19(1):326; Lewis, *Battery E*, 209.

82. Wheeler, *Letters*, 390.

83. *Instruction for Field Artillery*, 14.

84. *Fifth Massachusetts Battery*, 114; Gibbon, *Artillerist's Manual*, 170; *SOR*, pt. 1, 5:687; *Instruction for Field Artillery*, 17–21; *OR*, 29(2):413–14.

85. Bradford Nichol Memoirs, November 12, 1861, TSLA.

86. Douglas, *Douglas's Texas Battery,* 10; White, "Diary of the War," 199; *OR,* 40(1):442; "Journal of Siege Operations," 129, Box 1, Hunt Papers, LC; *SOR,* pt. 1, 5:284.

87. Watkins to Friend John, March 23, [1864], John Watkins Papers, UTK; *OR,* 19(1):963.

88. *OR,* 24(3):588; *SOR,* pt. 2, 19:441, 50:389; Jacob T. Foster Memoirs, 56, WHS; Webster and Cameron, *First Wisconsin Battery,* 166.

89. *SOR,* pt. 1, 4:388.

90. *Instruction for Field Artillery,* 3, 23; Hazlett, Olmstead, and Parks, *Field Artillery Weapons,* 219; Thomas, *Cannons,* 13; Furney, *Reminiscences,* 147; Wild, *Alexander's Baltimore Battery,* 131; Lewis, *Battery E,* 216, 311.

91. Receipt, April 16, 1862, Francis A. Shoup Service Record, M331, NARA; receipt, April 18, 1863, and special requisition received, June 30, 1864, Overton W. Barret Service Record, Barret's Missouri Battery (CS), M322, ibid.; receipt, March 5, 1864, Robert A. Hardaway Service Record, M331, ibid.; special requisitions, March 9, 25, 1864, Thomas J. Stanford Service Record, Stanford's Mississippi Battery, M269, ibid.; *Fifth Massachusetts Battery,* 94.

92. *Ordnance Manual for the Use of the Officers of the United States Army,* 135–36; Griffin, *Three Years a Soldier,* 128; Thomas, *Cannons,* 67–68.

93. Wild, *Alexander's Baltimore Battery,* 13; Billings, *Hardtack and Coffee,* 184, 278.

94. Kaplan, *Artillery Service,* 395–96; "Correspondence of Ira Butterfield," 138; Buell, "*Cannoneer,*" 58–59.

95. Gibbon, *Artillerist's Manual,* 355–56; Jacob T. Foster Memoirs, 41, WHS; *SOR,* pt. 1, 7:452.

5. FIRING THE BIG GUNS

1. *Instruction for Field Artillery,* 108.

2. *Instruction for Field Artillery,* 272; Dame, *From the Rapidan to Richmond,* 115–16.

3. Gibbon, *Artillerist's Manual,* 250; *Instruction for Field Artillery,* 118; Maxwell, *Autobiography,* 216.

4. Dame, *From the Rapidan to Richmond,* 124–25; Buell, "*Cannoneer,*" 213.

5. *Instruction for Field Artillery,* 41.

6. Anderson, *Instruction,* 62n; Birkhimer, *Historical Sketch,* 323; *Ordnance Manual for the Use of the Officers of the United States Army,* 134, 426; Gibbon, *Artillerist's Manual,* 297–98; Beecher, *First Light Battery Connecticut,* 352.

7. *Instruction for Field Artillery,* 64, 270–71, 331; Gibbon, *Artillerist's Manual,* 356.

8. *OR,* 8:265, 10(1):301, 20(1):579, 30(1):649, 38(2):667–68; Crumb, *Eleventh Corps Artillery,* 24; *SOR,* pt. 1, 5:226, 7:620; Ladd and Ladd, *Bachelder Papers,* 3:1633–34.

9. *SOR,* pt. 1, 7:620; *OR,* 38(2):667–68.

10. Wiley, *Norfolk Blues,* 57; Baker, *Ninth Mass. Battery,* 162.

11. Gibbon, *Artillerist's Manual,* 234; Naisawald, *Grape and Canister,* 550; Broun, *Notes on Artillery,* 54.

12. Gibbon, *Artillerist's Manual,* 343; Halleck, *Elements,* 128; Roberts, *Hand-Book,* 80; *OR,* 24(2):560.

13. *Instruction for Field Artillery,* 330; Ramsay, "Light Batteries A, D, F and I," 554; *History of the Organization,* 197; *OR,* 20(1):965, 24(2):229–30.

14. Gibbon, *Artillerist's Manual,* 343; Roberts, *Hand-Book,* 49; *SOR,* pt. 1, 3:783; *OR,* 30(1):883, 38(1):498–99.

15. *OR,* 38(3):410–11.

16. Gibbon, *Artillerist's Manual,* 250; Roberts, *Hand-Book,* 49–50; Muir, *Tactics,* 34.

17. Crumb, *Eleventh Corps Artillery,* 32; Buell, *"Cannoneer,"* 58; Billings, *Hardtack and Coffee,* 183; Maxwell, *Autobiography,* 216; Gallagher, *Fighting for the Confederacy,* 246; Bouton, *Events of the Civil War,* 87.

18. *OR,* 11(2):107, 36(1):657, 38(2):484; John Merrilles Diary, July 19, 1863, CHM.

19. Smith, *Brother of Mine,* 240; Dudley, *Autobiography,* 27; *Fifth Massachusetts Battery,* 374; Jackson, *"Some of the Boys,"* 98; *OR,* 11(2):105.

20. *History of the Fourth Maine Battery,* 54; Crary, *Dear Belle,* 209.

21. Crumb, *Eleventh Corps Artillery,* 32.

22. Tobias Charles Miller Letter, CHM; White, "Diary of the War," 261–62. For reports of rounds fired in a given amount of time by the entire battery rather than by the piece, see *OR,* 19(1):326, 20(1):742, 25(1):303, 30(1):883, 30(2):105, 36(1):763, 984, 42(1):603, 785, 45(1):489–90, 47(1):418; Kimbell, *Battery "A,"* 45; and Billings, *Tenth Massachusetts Battery,* 184.

23. Reminiscences, 54, Emerson Rood Calkins Family Papers, WHS; Ramsay, "Light Batteries A, D, F and I," 572; *OR,* 11(2):860; Smith, *Brother of Mine,* 77–78.

24. Broun, *Notes on Artillery,* 57; Roberts, *Hand-Book,* 51.

25. Nevins, *Diary of Battle,* 152; Hinman, *Sherman Brigade,* 535; *OR,* 20(1):241, 580, 46(1):191.

26. *OR,* 21:827–28.

27. *OR,* 21:827–28.

28. *OR,* 21:828; Nevins, *Diary of Battle,* 134.

29. *OR,* 27(3):600.

30. *SOR,* pt. 1, 3:756, 773, 801, 7:225.

31. *OR,* 38(3):61–62.

32. Gibbon, *Artillerist's Manual,* 236–37; Roberts, *Hand-Book,* 57n.

33. *Instruction for Field Artillery,* 38, 41; Roberts, *Hand-Book,* 54–55; *OR,* 25(1):722; Billings, *Tenth Massachusetts Battery,* 358.

34. Handwritten "Table of Ranges," Richmond Arsenal, October 17, 1862, Henry C. Semple Papers, ADAH; handwritten table of ranges in diary, n.d., John Watkins Papers, UTK; Buell, *"Cannoneer,"* 22.

35. Hazlett, Olmstead, and Parks, *Field Artillery Weapons,* 104. This Napoleon is currently displayed at Fort Frederick, Maryland.

36. *SOR,* pt. 1, 3:488, 490.

37. Gibbon, *Artillerist's Manual,* 251; *OR,* 20(1):753.

38. J. B. Moore to Longstreet, June 28, 1886, James Longstreet Papers, DU; Carnes, "Artillery at the Battle of Perryville," 8; *SOR,* pt. 1, 2:727.

39. Furney, *Reminiscences,* 162–63; *OR,* 31(2):728.

40. Baker, *Ninth Mass. Battery,* 79; Smith, *Seventh Iowa,* 167; *OR,* 7:208, 11(1):350; Smith, *Brother of Mine,* 239–40.

41. Malone, *Memoir,* 148–49.

42. *OR,* 11(2):205; Wheeler, *Letters,* 392; Stiles, *Four Years,* 193–94; *SOR,* pt. 1, 7:653–54.

43. Roberts, *Hand-Book,* 174; *OR,* 21:211.

44. *OR,* 38(1):484; Ritter, "Sketch of Third Battery," pt. 5, 191.

45. *OR,* 22(1):543.

46. *OR,* 11(2):119, 22(1):519, 31(2):559, 42(1):790; *SOR,* pt. 1, 3:782; John Merrilles Diary, July 19, 1863, CHM; Blodgett, "Tenth Indiana Battery at Moccasion Point"; Black, *Soldier's Recollections,* 78.

47. *OR,* 19(1):326; *Fifth Massachusetts Battery,* 310; *SOR,* pt. 1, 3:552–53. For more reports of distance and elevation, see *OR,* 7:208, 11(2):119, 207, 17(1):753, 19(1):405, 21:201.

48. *SOR,* pt. 1, 3:786; *OR,* 25(1):303–4, 42(1):788.

49. *OR,* 11(2):199, 21:203, 31(2):558, 33:761, 40(1):430–31; Furney, *Reminiscences,* 25.

50. Hess, *Knoxville Campaign,* 86; Poe, *Personal Recollections,* 27.

51. *OR,* 21:460, 25(1):882.

52. Nesmith, "Stagnation and Change," 44.

53. Nesmith, "Stagnation and Change," 52; Ehlen and Abrahart, "Terrain and Its Affect," 157–58, 160–61, 163, 165–67, 170.

54. *OR,* 11(2):288, 39(1):195.

55. *OR,* 3:73, 25(1):303, 32(1):444, 38(3):264, 468, 39(1):194; Gallagher, *Fighting for the Confederacy,* 179.

56. *OR,* 17(1):224, 19(1):310, 36(1):651, 38(1):831, 42(1):428, 542.

57. Roberts, *Hand-Book,* 59; *SOR,* pt. 1, 3:784; *OR,* 25(1):487, 821; Wise, *Long Arm of Lee,* 2:539.

58. Gallagher, *Fighting for the Confederacy,* 251, 443.

59. *Fifth Massachusetts Battery,* 821; *OR,* 11(2):56.

60. Crumb and Dhalle, *No Middle Ground,* 55; *OR,* 11(2):118; O'Brien, "Telegraphing in Battle," 479.

61. *OR,* 38(5):728–29, 753.

62. *OR,* 38(2):487–88.

63. *OR,* 11(2):903, 20(1):522, 36(1):653.

64. *OR,* 19(1):309.

65. *OR,* 10(1):247, 30(1):563; Ramsay, "Light Batteries A, D, F and I," 568; Lewis, *Battery E,* 310; Runge, *Four Years in the Confederate Artillery,* 97.

66. *OR,* 17(1):225–26, 20(1):723, 43(1):418, 45(1):440, 462; Krick, *Parker's Virginia Battery,* 184.

67. *OR,* 20(1):242.

68. Fitch, *Annals of the Army of the Cumberland,* 297–98.

69. Naisawald, *Grape and Canister,* 443–44; Daniel, *Cannoneers in Gray,* 103.

70. *OR,* 17(1):641, 692.

71. Naisawald, *Grape and Canister,* 545; Furney, *Reminiscences,* 317.

6. PROJECTILES AND FUZES

1. McKee and Mason, *Civil War Projectiles,* 99–160.

2. Broun, *Notes on Artillery,* 54; Gibbon, *Artillerist's Manual,* 232.

3. Broun, *Notes on Artillery,* 54; McCaul, *Mechanical Fuze,* 103; *OR,* 45(1):398–99.

4. McCaul, *Mechanical Fuze,* 126; Gibbon, *Artillerist's Manual,* 232, 247.

5. Mallet, "Work of the Ordnance Bureau," 12; receipts, August 31, September 17, 28, 1863, Henry C. Semple Service Record, M331, NARA; receipt, December 31, 1863, Richard W. Goldthwaite Service Record, Goldthwaite's Alabama Battery, M311, ibid.; "Journal of Siege Operations," 158, Box 1, Henry Jackson Hunt Papers, LC.

6. *Instruction for Field Artillery,* 12–13; Broun, *Notes on Artillery,* 55; *Fifth Massachusetts Battery,* 126.

7. Roberts, *Hand-Book,* 98–99; Broun, *Notes on Artillery,* 56; McCaul, *Mechanical Fuze,* 26, 103; *Instruction for Field Artillery,* 41.

8. Gibbon, *Artillerist's Manual,* 250; *Instruction for Field Artillery,* 43.

9. Broun, *Notes on Artillery,* 55; N. M. Osborne to Doctor, May 15, 1863, Edward George Washington Butler Papers, DU; Watkins to John, December 5, 1862, John Watkins Papers, UTK.

10. White, "Diary of the War," 256.

11. *OR,* 20(1):723, 29(2):413–14; Gallagher, *Fighting for the Confederacy,* 248.

12. Roberts, *Hand-Book,* 99; *Fifth Massachusetts Battery,* 126; *Instruction for Field Artillery,* 11; Broun, *Notes on Artillery,* 54; Eskildson, "Grape and Canister."

13. Gibbon, *Artillerist's Manual,* 236, 249.

14. White, "Diary of the War," 261; *Instruction for Field Artillery,* 43; Roberts, *Hand-Book,* 99; Semple to wife, February 5, 1863, Henry C. Semple Papers, ADAH.

15. *Instruction for Field Artillery,* 11; *OR,* 29(2):391; *OR,* 33:676.

16. Hazlett, Olmstead, and Parks, *Field Artillery Weapons,* 125; McCaul, *Mechanical Fuze,* 44.

17. *Fifth Massachusetts Battery,* 235, 303, 311; *OR,* 11(3):242, 36(1):658, 40(1):611; *SOR,* pt. 1, 5:279, 283, 293.

18. *SOR,* pt. 1, 5:296.

19. *OR,* 36(3):720, 46(1):667.

20. *OR,* 21:209, 25(1):303, 26(1):691, 47(1):179; *SOR,* pt. 1, 5:279; *Fifth Massachusetts Battery,* 126.

21. *OR,* 47(1):179, 373.

22. *OR,* ser. 3, 1:296; *Fifth Massachusetts Battery,* 235–36; *OR,* 19(1):326, 21:209, 38(1):487.

23. *OR,* 38(1):487, 47(1):179, 373.

24. Hazlett, Olmstead, and Parks, *Field Artillery Weapons,* 113.

25. Tate, *Col. Frank Huger,* 56.

26. Rowland, *Jefferson Davis,* 8:329; Mallet, "Work of the Ordnance Bureau," 4.

27. Hasegawa, "Proposals for Chemical Weapons," 499–500, 502–3.

28. *OR,* 36(3):888–89.

29. Roberts, *Hand-Book,* 101; receipt, September 6, 1863, Charles Swett Service Record, Swett's Mississippi Battery, M269, NARA.

30. Roberts, *Hand-Book*, 101; receipt, September 6, 1863, Swett Service Record; Farr, "Grape in Field Artillery"; *Ordnance Manual for the Use of the Officers of the United States Army*, 317–19.

31. Kerksis and Dickey, *Heavy Artillery Projectiles,* 47; Barlow, "Light Battery Service in 1861"; Scott, "Civil War Archaeology," 17–18.

32. Tapert, *Brothers' War,* 125; Gould and Kennedy, *Memoirs of a Dutch Mudsill,* 92; Wild, *Alexander's Baltimore Battery,* 63.

33. Dudley, *Autobiography,* 47; *OR,* 38(2):473, 481; Pierson, "From Chattanooga to Atlanta," 352; George Carrington Diary, June 10, 1863, CHM.

34. *Ordnance Manual for the Use of the Officers of the United States Army,* 308, 314.

35. Donnelly, "Rocket Batteries," 79–81; Merrill, *24th Independent Battery,* 141–42, 146, 148–50.

36. Hunt to G. H. Snelling, February 19, 1863, Box 2, Hunt Papers, LC.

37. Gallagher, *Fighting for the Confederacy,* 61.

38. Blackford, *War Years,* 84–85; *OR,* 11(2):245.

39. Donnelly, "Rocket Batteries," 82–85; *History of the Eleventh Pennsylvania Volunteer Cavalry,* 50, 54; *OR,* 18:35–36.

40. Donnelly, "Rocket Batteries," 85–87, 89–90.

41. *SOR,* pt. 1, 3:712–13; McKee and Mason, *Civil War Projectiles,* 93–96.

42. McKee and Mason, *Civil War Projectiles,* 161–72; McCaul, *Mechanical Fuze,* 9.

43. Gibbon, *Artillerist's Manual,* 256–57; Roberts, *Hand-Book,* 118–19; Broun, *Notes on Artillery,* 45; Jones, *Artillery Fuses,* 2, 4.

44. Gibbon, *Artillerist's Manual,* 257; Jones, *Artillery Fuses,* 161–67.

45. Gibbon, *Artillerist's Manual,* 257; *OR,* 20(1):768; Kerksis and Dickey, *Heavy Artillery Projectiles,* 20.

46. *OR,* 11(2):118, 11(3):242.

47. Nevins, *Diary of Battle,* 58; *SOR,* pt. 1, 3:786; *OR,* 31(2):555.

48. *SOR,* pt. 1, 3:488; *OR,* 20(1):741, 761–62.

49. *OR,* 45(1):327.

50. Gibbon, *Artillerist's Manual,* 257, 259; *Instruction for Field Artillery,* 13; Buell, "Cannoneer," 22; Roberts, *Hand-Book,* 122–23; Broun, *Notes on Artillery,* 45; Farr, "Grape in Field Artillery." The tool used to cut the powder train of the Bormann fuze was variously called a chisel, an awl, a gouge, or a punch. See *Instruction for Field Artillery,* 14; *Fifth Massachusetts Battery,* 114; McKee and Mason, *Civil War Projectiles,* 167–68; and Jones, *Artillery Fuses,* 155.

51. *OR,* 11(3):242, 20(1):723, 741, 768, 31(2):555.

52. Broun, *Notes on Artillery,* 45–46; *OR,* 25(2):151, 47(1):179.

53. Jones, *Artillery Fuses,* 28.

54. McCaul, *Mechanical Fuze,* 100; Broun, *Notes on Artillery,* 46; *OR,* 33:676.

55. Jones, *Artillery Fuses,* 76–80, 83; Tate, *Col. Frank Huger,* 78.

56. Jones, *Artillery Fuses,* 30–31, 65–66, 68, 72–75; Broun, *Notes on Artillery,* 46–47.

57. Griffin, *Three Years a Soldier,* 16; Smith, *Brother of Mine,* 233; *OR,* 11(2):105, 118, 33:676.

58. McCaul, *Mechanical Fuze,* 101–2; Jones, *Artillery Fuses,* 33–34.

59. Rowell, *Yankee Artillerymen,* 51; *OR,* 25(1):275.

60. *SOR,* pt. 1, 5:297. Referring to 3-Inch Ordnance Rifles, Capt. James M. Robertson wrote, "No time or combination fuses that I have yet tried have worked satisfactorily with these guns." *SOR,* pt. 1, 5:279.

61. "Memorandum of orders recd by C Alger from Brig Gen Ripley, chf of Bureau of Ordnance," n.d., Box 9, Hunt Papers, LC.

62. Jones, *Artillery Fuses,* 36, 38–40.

63. Jones, *Artillery Fuses,* 63–64; Mallet, "Work of the Ordnance Bureau," 12.

64. *OR,* 25(1):845, 881; receipt, November 26, 1863, Charles R. Grandy Service Record, Norfolk Virginia Light Artillery, M324, NARA.

65. McCaul, *Mechanical Fuze,* 84–85, 91–92.

66. McCaul, *Mechanical Fuze,* 8–9, 107.

67. Dozier, *Gunner in Lee's Army,* 78; Gallagher, *Fighting for the Confederacy,* 62; Shoup to William D. Pickett, February 5, 1862, Francis A. Shoup Service Record, M331, NARA.

68. *OR,* 11(2):83, 120, 247, 11(3):242, 19(1):34, 20(1):7694, 21:192, 198, 201–3, 207, 211, 466–67, 637–40; Nevins, *Diary of Battle,* 58–59; *Fifth Massachusetts Battery,* 409; *OR,*; John Donnell Smith to Brown, February 25, 1862, William Leroy Brown Service Record, 1st Virginia Artillery, M324, NARA; Beecher, *First Light Battery Connecticut,* 100; *SOR,* pt. 1, 3:532, 766, 768, 770, 772, 786–87, 801.

69. *OR,* 21:200–201, 207, 211, 216.

70. *OR,* 21:211, 31(2):553, 555, 558; Tate, *Col. Frank Huger,* 79; Underwood to Mary, May 25, 1863, Benjamin W. Underwood Letters, OCHM.

71. William A. Ewing to John A. Craig, April 21, 1864, Box 10, Hunt Papers, LC.

72. John E. Burton to Albert Merrill, April 11, 1864, and Hunt endorsement, April 12, 1864: "Report of Target Practice in Batt. F, 1st Pa Artill. April 19th 1864," Box 10, Hunt Papers, LC; *OR,* 25(1):50, 34(1):630, 38(3):176, 40(1):609, 611, 47(1):907.

73. Walton, *Behind the Guns,* 85–86.

74. *OR,* 38(1):490.

75. *OR,* 21:195, 207, 25(1):594, 40(1):611; *SOR,* pt. 1, 3:780, 5:686.

76. Gallagher, *Fighting for the Confederacy,* 62, 304; Dozier, *Gunner in Lee's Army,* 78; Alexander, "Great Charge," 358.

77. *Fifth Massachusetts Battery,* 231, 236; John Donnell Smith to Brown, February 25, 1862, William Leroy Brown Service Record, 1st Virginia Artillery, M324, NARA; William J. Hardee endorsement on Shoup to William D. Pickett, February 5, 1862, Francis A. Shoup Service Record, M331, ibid.

78. *Instruction for Field Artillery,* 8; *SOR,* pt. 1, 4:385; *OR,* 47(3):131.

79. *Instruction for Field Artillery,* 7.

80. *OR,* 7:191, 10(1):375; *SOR,* pt. 2, 50:395.

81. *OR,* 33:675.

82. *OR,* 31(1):347.

83. *OR,* 11(2):104, 17(1):774, 20(1):580, 30(1):594.

84. *OR,* 38(1):497–98.

85. *OR,* 36(1):656.

86. *OR,* 45(1):322, 324, 47(1):847.

87. Tracie, *Annals of the Nineteenth Ohio Battery,* 470.

88. *OR,* 10(1):301, 44:358.

7. BATTERIES, BATTALIONS, AND REGIMENTS

1. *OR,* ser. 3, 1:497, 2:519.

2. *Reminiscences of the Cleveland Light Artillery,* 77–78.

3. Birkhimer, *Historical Sketch,* 69.

4. Nevins, *Diary of Battle,* 314; *Reminiscences of the Cleveland Light Artillery,* 77–78.

5. *Fifth Massachusetts Battery,* 52–54.

6. Muir, *Tactics,* 29; *Instruction for Field Artillery,* 4; Gibbon, *Artillerist's Manual,* 341.

7. *OR,* ser., 3, 1:295; *OR,* 5:580.

8. *OR,* 17(2):843–44, 678, 24(2):411.

9. *OR,* ser., 4, 3:293–94; *OR,* 33:1285.

10. Kaplan, *Artillery Service,* 7; *OR,* 38(1):120, 46(2):86, 47(1):177; Sherman, *Memoirs,* 2:396.

11. *SOR,* pt. 1, 4:368; *OR,* 20(2):501, 24(2):13; Daniel, *Cannoneers in Gray,* 92.

12. *OR,* 20(2):399, 499, 24(2):381.

13. Birkhimer, *Historical Sketch,* 103–4; *OR,* 11(3):686, 25(2):837–38; Gallagher, *Fighting for the Confederacy,* 260.

14. Daniel, *Cannoneers in Gray,* 88.

15. Birkhimer, *Historical Sketch,* 103.

16. *OR,* 38(1):121; Kaplan, *Artillery Service,* 337.

17. *OR,* 11(2):239–40.

18. "Journal of Siege Operations," 26, Box 1, Henry Jackson Hunt Papers, LC; Birkhimer, *Historical Sketch,* 97–99.

19. "Journal of Siege Operations," 26, Box 1, Hunt Papers, LC.

20. Kaplan, *Artillery Service,* 61; Crumb and Dhalle, *No Middle Ground,* 89; *OR,* 29(2):239, 383–83.

21. Birkhimer, *Historical Sketch,* 97; McCrae, "Light Artillery," 521–22; Gallagher, *Fighting for the Confederacy,* 105; Kaplan, *Artillery Service,* 11.

22. Birkhimer, *Historical Sketch,* 100; *OR,* 33:583–84; Nevins, *Diary of Battle,* 374; "Journal of Siege Operations," 21, Box 1, Hunt Papers, LC; Longacre, *Man behind the Guns,* 197.

23. "Journal of Siege Operations," 21, Box 1, Hunt Papers, LC.

24. Nevins, *Diary of Battle,* 374–75; *OR,* 36(1):520, 756, 767, 985, 51(1):1166; Collier and Collier, *Yours for the Union,* 335; Birkhimer, *Historical Sketch,* 87; Fenner, *Battery H,* 47–48, 51.

25. Birkhimer, *Historical Sketch,* 101.

26. "Journal of Siege Operations," 91, 93, Box 1, Hunt Papers, LC; Nevins, *Diary of Battle,* 474, 476; *OR,* 36(1):288, 46(2):86; *History of the Fourth Maine Battery,* 97.

27. *Instruction for Field Artillery,* 2–3; *Fifth Massachusetts Battery,* 595, 599; *OR,* 20(2):128, 25(1):788.

28. *OR,* 17(1):268, 31(2):556, 38(1):825, 38(2):667, 38(3):58, 38(5):519–21, 44:354, 45(1):322.

29. General Orders No. 10, Headquarters, Army of the Mississippi, April 10, 1862, Francis A. Shoup Service Record, M331, NARA; Shoup to Braxton Bragg, April 14, 1862, ibid.; Daniel, *Cannoneers in Gray,* 46, 92, 94; Douglas, *Douglas's Texas Battery,* 193.

30. *OR,* 36(1):1036–39.

31. W. O. Conner to William T. Rigby, August 15, 1903, Cherokee Georgia Artillery Folder, VNMP; Laboda, *From Selma to Appomattox,* 7, 15; Trout, *Memoirs of the Stuart Horse Artillery,* 181, 183; *OR,* 19(2):282.

32. Tuthill, "Artilleryman's Recollections," 293; Reichardt, *Diary of Battery A,* 54, 67; *OR,* 19(1):309; J. C. Haddock, "Historical Sketch of the 4th Indiana Battery," 20, 4th Indiana Battery Regimental File, SRNB.

33. Walton, *Behind the Guns,* xix–xx.

34. *SOR,* pt. 2, 70:454–59, 466.

35. *Instruction for Field Artillery,* 3–4; *OR,* 5:580; *OR,* ser. 4, 3:293.

36. Rhodes, *History of Battery B,* 49–50, 109; *OR,* 36(1):284–86, 288–89, 42(1):410, 543; Twitchell, *Seventh Maine,* 20.

37. *OR,* 10(1):301, 20(1):235–41, 31(2):556, 38(1):487, 45(1):322; Kaplan, *Artillery Service,* 236.

38. *OR,* 12(3):494, 23(2):969, 38(1):120; *History of the Organization,* 56; McCaul, *Mechanical Fuze,* 79.

39. Laboda, *From Selma to Appomattox,* 2, 7, 86; Trout, *Memoirs of the Stuart Horse Artillery,* 181, 183; Mallet, "Work of the Ordnance Bureau," 8; *OR,* 19(1):835, 25(2):838.

40. Johnson and Anderson, *Artillery Hell,* 5–6; *SOR,* pt. 1, 3:484, 7:329; *OR,* 12(2):570–71, 21:573, 25(2):634–38, 838–39; Rowland, *Jefferson Davis,* 8:556–58, 564–65; Gallagher, *Fighting for the Confederacy,* 300; Buell, *"Cannoneer,"* 382.

41. *OR,* 8:237–38.

42. *OR,* 21:1046–47; Lee, *Memoirs of William Nelson Pendleton,* 231.

43. *OR,* 21:1047, 25(1):849, 25(2):618, 749, 828, 29(2):839; Gallagher, *Fighting for the Confederacy,* 172; Wiley, *Norfolk Blues,* 67.

44. Daniel, *Cannoneers in Gray,* 30–31, 56, 75–76, 109, 128; *OR,* 10(1):513, 831, 10(2):451–52, 20(1):768, 20(2):399; Little and Maxwell, *Lumsden's Battery,* 66; Hughes, *Pride of the Confederate Artillery,* 22; Felix H. Robertson to Dent, April 25, 1909, Stouten Hubert Dent Papers, ADAH; *SOR,* pt. 2, 32:574.

45. *OR,* 11(1):156.

46. *OR,* 20(2):297, 299; Bloomfield to father, February10, 1863, A. S. Bloomfield Papers, OHS.

47. Hunt, "Our Experience in Artillery Administration," 216; *OR,* 4:344.

48. Cox, *Military Reminiscences,* 1:182–83.

49. Tate, *Col. Frank Huger,* 97; Ritter to Rowan, October 4, 1863, William Louis Ritter Papers, NC; Arndt, *Reminiscences,* 5; Cushing to mother, February 21, March 1, 1863, Harry C. Cushing Letters, UTK; Imboden, "Incidents of the First Bull Run," 233–34n.

50. W. Irving Hodgson to William G. Barth, April 22, 1862, "Order Book, 5th Company, B.W.A.," Box 12, Folder 1, Civil War Papers, Battalion Washington Artillery Collection, TU; Crumb and Dhalle, *No Middle Ground,* 71.

51. Daniel, *Cannoneers in Gray,* 30–31; *OR,* 30(2):148, 159, 201, 38(3):873.

52. *OR,* 19(1):847–48, 20(1):525, 771, 855–56, 40(1):519, 45(1):458–59; *SOR,* pt. 2, 70:417; Wheeler, *Letters,* 348–49.

53. Hunt, "Our Experience in Artillery Administration," 216.

54. *OR,* 38(3):61.

55. *OR,* 36(1):756, 45(1):323.

8. UNION ARTILLERY BRIGADES AND CONFEDERATE ARTILLERY BATTALIONS

1. Hunt, "Our Experience in Artillery Administration," 197.

2. Halleck, *Elements,* 128; Mahan, *Elementary Treatise,* 24.

3. *Instruction for Field Artillery,* 2.

4. Lippitt, *Treatise on the Tactical Use of the Three Arms,* 63–64, 69; Roberts, *Hand-Book,* 49; *Revised United States Army Regulations,* 105.

5. Kaplan, *Artillery Service,* 66–67, 86, 386, 391; Stiles, *Four Years,* 53.

6. Birkhimer, *Historical Sketch,* 79–80, 90; Wise, *Long Arm of Lee,* 1:141, 208; Naisawald, *Grape and Canister,* 24; Griffith, *Battle Tactics of the Civil War,* 167; Nosworthy, *Bloody Crucible,* 461; Daniel, *Cannoneers in Gray,* 21, 44, 52, 86, 102.

7. *OR,* 10(1):472, 478, 20(1):455–56; Daniel *Cannoneers in Gray,* 37–39; Sears, *To the Gates of Richmond,* 311–12; Daniel, *Stones River,* 189–90. Lesser-known artillery concentrations took place at Pea Ridge, where the Federals massed twenty-one guns to prepare for a successful infantry attack on March 8, 1862 (Shea and Hess, *Pea Ridge,* 231–32, 236, 238); at Antietam, where the Federals massed thirty guns on their right flank by the end of the day (*OR,* 19[1]:226); and at Stones River, where the Confederates massed twenty-two guns on their main line west of the stream on January 2, 1863 (Daniel, *Cannoneers in Gray,* 63).

8. *OR,* 25(1):249–50.

9. Hess, *Pickett's Charge,* 113–17.

10. Kaplan, *Artillery Service,* 155–56; Naisawald, *Grape and Canister,* 444–45; *OR,* 36(1):1046, 1087–88, 42(1):405, 410, 45(1):497.

11. Kaplan, *Artillery Service,* 12, 14.

12. Birkhimer, *Historical Sketch,* 92; Owen, "Hot Day on Marye's Heights," 97.

13. *OR,* 10(1):513–14.

14. *OR,* 10(1):528, 20(1):751, 26(1):198; *SOR,* pt. 1, 2:754; Nevins, *Diary of Battle,* 244–45; Walton, *Behind the Guns,* 64.

15. Harwell and Racine, *Fiery Trail,* 27.

16. Furney, *Reminiscences,* 66–67; *SOR,* pt. 1, 3:764.

17. *OR,* 25(1):938; Beecher, *First Light Battery Connecticut,* 429.

18. *OR,* 11(2):171.

19. *OR,* 38(3):265, 361, 363; Furney, *Reminiscences,* 71–73.

20. Cockrell, *Gunner with Stonewall,* 87–88, 96–97, 99; *OR* 36(1):1050.

21. "Journal of Siege Operations," 17–18, Box 1, Henry Jackson Hunt Papers, LC; Nevins, *Diary of Battle,* 363, 365.

22. Nevins, *Diary of Battle,* 377, 396, 407, 428.

23. "Journal of Siege Operations," 13–15, Box 1, Hunt Papers, LC.

24. Kross, "'I Do Not Believe,'" 287–89, 293–94; Ladd and Ladd, *Bachelder Papers,* 1:426–27.

25. Hunt, "Third Day at Gettysburg," 372; Ladd and Ladd, *Bachelder Papers,* 1:228–29, 428–30; Nevins, *Diary of Battle,* 248–49; Longacre, *Man behind the Guns,* 171, 174.

26. Hunt, "Third Day at Gettysburg," 374; Crumb., *Eleventh Corps Artillery,* 39–40, 75–76; Ladd and Ladd, *Bachelder Papers,* 1:430–31; Nevins, *Diary of Battle,* 249; Hess, *Pickett's Charge,* 150.

27. Ladd and Ladd, *Bachelder Papers,* 1:432–33.

28. Ladd and Ladd, *Bachelder Papers,* 1:608; Hess, *Pickett's Charge,* 146–47, 149.

29. Nevins, *Diary of Battle,* 252–53; Ladd and Ladd, *Bachelder Papers,* 1:431–32; Hunt, "Third Day at Gettysburg," 375.

30. Hunt, "Third Day at Gettysburg," 375.

31. Tidball to Hunt, April 29, 1864, Box 10; "Journal of Siege Operations," 30, 89–90, 121–22, 142–43, Box 1; and copies of Hancock to Hunt, September 9, 17, 1864, and Hunt endorsement, September 9, 1864, Box 2, Hunt Papers, LC.

32. "Journal of Siege Operations," 144–45, Box 1, Hunt Papers, LC; Nevins, *Diary of Battle,* 525.

33. Wise, *Long Arm of Lee,* 2:822.

34. *OR,* 10(1):496, 924; Bradford Nichol Memoirs, April 6, 1862, TSLA; Nevins, *Diary of Battle,* 49.

35. Ramsay, "Light Batteries A, D, F and I," 575.

36. Ramsay, "Light Batteries A, D, F and I," 553; *OR,* 24(2):14–16.

37. *OR,* 20(1):580; Nevins, *Diary of Battle,* 237–38, 247; Crumb, *Eleventh Corps Artillery,* 16; Furney, *Reminiscences,* 195–96.

38. *OR,* ser. 3, 1:745.

39. Nevins, *Diary of Battle,* 39, 104.

40. Nevins, *Diary of Battle,* 104, 114.

41. Nevins, *Diary of Battle,* 107, 114, 144–45.

42. Nevins, *Diary of Battle,* 129, 131, 148.

43. Nevins, *Diary of Battle,* 164; *Report of the Joint Committee,* 4:92; Kaplan, *Artillery Service,* 87.

44. Nevins, *Diary of Battle,* 182.

45. Nevins, *Diary of Battle,* 193–94.

46. Nevins, *Diary of Battle,* 195, 198, 201.

47. Nevins, *Diary of Battle,* 204, 206; Naisawald, *Grape and Canister,* 332; Hunt, "First Day at Gettysburg," 259.

48. Collier and Collier, *Yours for the Union,* 239.

49. Nevins, *Diary of Battle,* 285; "Journal of Siege Operations," 15, Box 1; and Wainwright to Lorenzo Thomas, April 11, 1864, and Hunt endorsement April 13, 1864, and Meade endorsement, April 13, 1864, Box 10, Hunt Papers, LC.

50. Nevins, *Diary of Battle,* 501.

51. Harwell and Racine, *Fiery Trail,* 25, 27; *OR,* 38(1):484, 503, 825.

52. *OR,* 38(1):184–85, 486.

53. Harwell and Racine, *Fiery Trail,* 25–27.

54. *OR,* 45(2):603, 47(1):371–72.

55. *OR,* 25(2):614–15.

56. Daniel, *Cannoneers in Gray,* 87; Chamberlayne, *Memoirs of the Civil War,* 35; *OR,* 25(2):694.

57. Carter to Pendleton, March 19, 1863, Thomas H. Carter Service Record, M331, NARA; Dozier, *Gunner in Lee's Army,* 182.

58. *OR,* 25(2):694.

59. *OR,* 51(2):1049–50, 1052.

60. Daniel, *Cannoneers in Gray,* 87, 130–32; circular, Headquarters, Army of Tennessee, October 17, 1863, Henry C. Semple Papers, ADAH; *SOR,* pt. 1, 7:74, 76.

61. *OR,* 45(1):683–84; Daniel, *Cannoneers in Gray,* 168.

62. Squires, "My Artillery Fire," 25.

63. Birkhimer, *Historical Sketch,* 84, 86, 94; Daniel, *Cannoneers in Gray,* 21.

64. Longacre, *Man behind the Guns,* 91–92, 97, 119, 121, 124; Birkhimer, *Historical Sketch,* 212–13; Naisawald, *Grape and Canister,* 30, 440; *Report of the Joint Committee,* 4:92; Kross, "'I Do Not Believe,'" 285; McClellan to Hunt, July 30, 1863, Box 2, Hunt Papers, LC.

65. *Report of the Joint Committee,* 4:92–93.

66. Hunt to Burnside, April 15, 1863, Box 2, Hunt Papers, LC.

67. *OR,* 25(1):252; Hunt, "First Day at Gettysburg," 259; *Report of the Joint Committee,* 4:89–91.

68. *Report of the Joint Committee,* 4:447–48; Hunt to Humphreys, July 26, 1863, Box 2, Hunt Papers, LC; Humphreys to Hunt, July 27, 1863, ibid.; Hunt to Humphreys, July [30, 1863], Box 13, ibid.; Nevins, *Diary of Battle,* 271.

69. *OR,* 29(2):84–85.

70. Nevins, *Diary of Battle,* 276–77; Birkhimer, *Historical Sketch,* 216–17.

71. *OR,* 33:581.

72. Nevins, *Diary of Battle,* 525–26.

73. Kaplan, *Artillery Service,* 235–36; *OR,* 20(2):235–36, 23(2):133, 39(2):498–99.

74. Cutrer, *Longstreet's Aide,* 159, 229n27.

75. Gallagher, *Fighting for the Confederacy,* 112, 336; Dozier, *Gunner in Lee's Army,* 207.

76. Lee, *Memoirs of William Nelson Pendleton,* 184–85, 189, 198–99, 235, 272, 276–77, 365.

77. Wise, *Long Arm of Lee,* 1:77, 200, 2:743; Carmichael, "'Every Map,'" 272–73; Lee, *Memoirs of William Nelson Pendleton,* 156, 190–91, 237, 274, 314, 316–17, 320; Crist, *Papers of Jefferson Davis,* 11:410.

78. Wise, *Long Arm of Lee,* 2:747; Lee, *Memoirs of William Nelson Pendleton,* 142, 191, 381, 394; Runge, *Four Years in the Confederate Artillery,* 60.

79. Lee, *Memoirs of William Nelson Pendleton,* 274, 376.

80. *OR,* 10(1):413.

81. *OR,* 10(1):390–91, 469, 16(1):1088–94, 20(1):671, 30(2):36, 31(2):666.

82. Johnston to Bragg, March 16, 1864, Joseph E. Johnston Papers, DU; Lee, *Memoirs of William Nelson Pendleton,* 317; *OR,* 38(3):910, 45(1):687, 683.

83. *OR,* 33:742.

84. Nevins, *Diary of Battle,* 336.

85. Nevins, *Diary of Battle,* 336.

86. Nevins, *Diary of Battle,* 336–37, 339, 341, 413; *OR,* 33:742.

87. Birkhimer, *Historical Sketch,* 186–87n; Nevins, *Diary of Battle,* 94–95, 104; Rhodes, *History of Battery B,* 176.

88. Hunt to Seth Williams, March 17, 1863, Box 2, Hunt Papers, LC; Barry to Hunt, April 12, 1863, ibid.

89. "A Bill for the Better Organization of the Artillery of the U.S. Army," n.d., Box 13, Hunt Papers, LC; "Memoir to Accompany Project of Bill 'To Promote the Efficiency of the Artillery of the Army of the United States,'" n.d., ibid.; handwritten draft of "An Act for the reorganization of the Artillery of the Army of the United States," n.d., ibid.

90. Truman Seymour to Hunt, December 27, 1863, Box 13, Hunt Papers, LC.

91. *OR,* 46(2):83–86, 88; Nevins, *Diary of Battle,* 501.

92. *OR,* 25(2):651, 29(2):840, 842, 36(3):881–82; Pendleton to Lee, August 14, 1863, William N. Pendleton Service Record, M331, NARA; Lee, *Memoirs of William Nelson Pendleton,* 395.

93. *OR,* 33:1193; Smith to E. Barksdale, January 3, 1864, Melancthon Smith Service Record, M331, NARA; Smith to E. Surget, April 15, 1865, ibid.

94. Naisawald, *Grape and Canister,* 31–32; *OR,* 5:69, 33:581–82.

95. *OR,* 40(1):483, 46(1):662, 47(1):180.

96. Warner, *Generals in Blue,* passim; Warner, *Generals in Gray,* passim.

97. Buell, *"Cannoneer,"* 222.

9. SOLDIERING WITH THE BIG GUNS

1. This estimate of the number of artillerists is derived from reports of total enrollment in three Union batteries, extrapolated to all other Union and Confederate batteries. See Bennett, *First Massachusetts Light Battery,* 185–86; Chase, *Battery F,* 249–84; and Furney, *Reminiscences,* 317. See also *Instruction for Field Artillery,* 4; and *OR,* 29(2):410.

2. Gibbon, *Artillerist's Manual,* 345–46; Roberts, *Hand-Book,* 52.

3. Ames to father, September 21, 1864, Albert N. Ames Papers, NYSL; Rhodes, *History of Battery B,* 181; Buell, *"Cannoneer,"* 72.

4. Stiles, *Four Years,* 55–57.

5. *OR,* 38(1):122.

6. *OR,* 10(1):376, 11(2):53, 17(1):753, 25(1):843, 849, 30(1):414, 466; Stiles, *Four Years,* 81. For another example of a man covering the vent while injured, see Jacob T. Foster Memoirs, 44, WHS.

7. Hoy, *Bradford's Battery,* 255; Cate, *Two Soldiers,* 101; John Merrilles Diary, May 24, 1863, CHM; Smith, *Brother of Mine,* 233; Ritter to Rowan, October 4, 1863, William Louis Ritter Papers, NC; Douglas, *Douglas's Texas Battery,* 3; Bearss, "Diary of Captain John N. Bell," 221; Hess, "Material Culture of Weapons," 112–14.

8. Clayton to mother, May 24, 1863, William Z. Clayton Papers, MinnHS; Pierson, "From Chattanooga to Atlanta," 352.

9. *SOR*, pt. 1, 4:672; [Daniel], *Richmond Howitzers*, 13; Laboda, *From Selma to Appomattox*, 15–16; Collier and Collier, *Yours for the Union*, 3.

10. Smith, *Brother of Mine*, 251.

11. *OR*, 23(2):133; Williams, "Company C—Light Battery," 541; Moses A. Cleveland Journal, March 3, 1864, MHS; Hackemer, *To Rescue My Native Land*, 55; Campbell, *"Grand Terrible Dramma,"* 41; Fitzhugh, *Cannon Smoke*, 180; Special Orders No. 153, Headquarters, Army of the Potomac, June 5, 1863, Box 9, Henry Jackson Hunt Papers, LC.

12. *OR*, 10(1):611, 11(2):59, 17(1):641; Tracie, *Annals of the Nineteenth Ohio Battery*, 349; Nevins, *Diary of Battle*, 52.

13. Barlow, "Light Battery Service in 1861"; "Diary of Jacob Adams," 641–42; *SOR*, pt. 3, 1:258; Maxwell, *Autobiography*, 245; John Merrilles Diary, July 19, 1863, CHM; *OR*, 17(1):255; Griffin, *Three Years a Soldier*, 218.

14. Gallagher, *Fighting for the Confederacy*, 208; Benjamin T. Smith Reminiscences, 155, 162–63, ALPL; N. M. Osborne to Doctor, May 15, 1863, Edward George Washington Butler Papers, DU.

15. Ladd and Ladd, *Bachelder Papers*, 2:844; Moore, *Story of a Cannoneer*, 149–50; Smith, *Brother of Mine*, 131, 255; Griffin, *Three Years a Soldier*, 18.

16. Campbell, *"Grand Terrible Dramma,"* 225; [Daniel], *Richmond Howitzers*, 30–31.

17. *OR*, 17(1):217; Smith, *Brother of Mine*, 78.

18. *OR*, 20(1):856; Semple to wife, February 5, 1863, Henry C. Semple Papers, ADAH; Dame, *From the Rapidan to Richmond*, 152; Buell, *"Cannoneer,"* 212.

19. Isaac Roseberry Diary, January 2, 1863, EU; Hamilton, *Papers of Thomas Ruffin*, 3:448; Tracie, *Annals of the Nineteenth Ohio Battery*, 375; Ames to Home Circle, May 7, 1863, Albert N. Ames Papers, NYSL; Hughes, *Civil War Memoir of Philip Daingerfield Stephenson*, 199; Woodruff, *Fifteen Years Ago*, 400; reminiscences, April 8, 1864, August Bondi Papers, Kansas Historical Society, Topeka.

20. Moore, *Story of a Cannoneer*, 77; Boos, "Civil War Diary of Patrick H. White," 649.

21. John Merrilles Diary, July 19, 1863, CHM.

22. Watkins to John, December 5, 1862, John Watkins Papers, UTK; Twitchell, *Seventh Maine*, 50; Beecher, *First Light Battery Connecticut*, 152.

23. Buell, *"Cannoneer,"* 180; Dame, *From the Rapidan to Richmond*, 208; *Fifth Massachusetts Battery*, 657; *OR*, 7:192, 17(1):643; Joseph William Eggleston Autobiography, 18, VHS; Moore, *Story of a Cannoneer*, 30–31.

24. Barlow, "Light Battery Service in 1861"; Daniel, *Cannoneers in Gray*, 43; *OR*, 17(1):130–31; Sears, "11th Ohio Battery at Iuka." For other reports of ratio of losses, see *OR*, 20(1):909, 25(1):490, 30(1):806, 821; Naisawald, *Grape and Canister*, 446; Otto, *11th Indiana Battery*, 43; and Ritter, "Sketch of Third Battery," pt. 5, 186.

25. *OR*, 20(1):762, 30(2):175. See also *OR*, 8:265–66, 38(1):827–28.

26. Maxwell, *Autobiography*, 250–51; Black, *Soldier's Recollections*, 50; Miller to wife, July 22, 1864, Marshall Mortimer Miller Papers, LC.

27. *OR,* 24(2):30, 45(1):472; Smith, *Brother of Mine,* 246; Crumb and Dhalle, *No Middle Ground,* 73; Nevins, *Diary of Battle,* 188; J. N. Daniell to Leslie Battle Clark, July 5, 1906, Box 1, Folder 4, McEntire Family Papers, Texas Tech University, Southwest Collection / Special Collections Library, Lubbock; Gallagher, *Fighting for the Confederacy,* 316.

28. Roberts to wife, [January] 7, 1863, Charles Roberts Collection, UM; *OR,* 36(1):654, 38(2):475; Ames to Home Circle, May 8, 1862, Albert N. Ames Papers, NYSL.

29. Moore, *Story of a Cannoneer,* 93; Wiley, *Norfolk Blues,* 44; Rowell, *Yankee Artillerymen,* 161; *OR,* 20(1):856.

30. Francis G. Obenchain to William Rigby, September 12, 1903, Botetourt Virginia Artillery Folder, VNMP; Campbell, *"Grand Terrible Dramma,"* 225; Nevins, *Diary of Battle,* 243; *OR,* 38(1):827; Tapert, *Brothers' War,* 124; Hughes, *Civil War Memoir of Philip Daingerfield Stephenson,* 214–15.

31. Fout, *Dark Days,* 133; *OR,* 38(1):498, 40(1):488. For more examples of premature discharges, see *OR,* 20(1):520, 580, 34(1):631, 36(1):538, 40(1):485, 45(1):459; Gould D. Molineaux Diaries, May 19, 1863, Augustana College, Special Collections, Rock Island, IL; Butterfield, "Correspondence," 136; Hackemer, *To Rescue My Native Land,* 71; Webster and Cameron, *First Wisconsin Battery,* 96–97; and *SOR,* pt. 2, 50:436.

32. Hackemer, *To Rescue My Native Land,* 73, 101; Boos, "Civil War Diary of Patrick H. White," 648; Lewis, *Battery E,* 328; Robertson, *Civil War Letters of General Robert McAllister,* 358; Baker, *Ninth Mass. Battery,* 138.

33. *OR,* 36(1):514; Little and Maxwell, *Lumsden's Battery,* 43–44; *Military Record of Battery D,* 25; *Military History and Reminiscences of the Thirteenth Regiment of Illinois Volunteer Infantry,* 347; *History of the Organization,* 23–24; Hogan, *General Reub Williams's Memoirs,* 139–40.

34. Maxwell, *Autobiography,* 229; Aldrich, *Battery A,* 50; Stiles, *Four Years,* 194–95; Dame, *From the Rapidan to Richmond,* 78; John D. Toomey Reminiscences, CHM; Hewitt, Schott, and Kunis, *To Succeed or Perish,* 47; Deane, *"My Dear Wife,"* 73.

35. *OR,* 38(3):468; Sumner, *Battery D,* 161; Nevins, *Diary of Battle,* 244; Moore, *Story of a Cannoneer,* 76; *OR,* 20(1):751; "Battery C," 91, Box 3, Folder 25, James Barnett Papers, WRHS; Stiles, *Four Years,* 197.

36. Billings, *Tenth Massachusetts Battery,* 305; *OR,* 24(2):30; Sumner, *Battery D,* 178; *Military Record of Battery D,* 13.

37. *OR,* 11(1):354, 17(1):107, 20(1):956, 21:650, 25(1):310, 849, 34(1):413, 38(3):469; Douglas, *Douglas's Texas Battery,* 198.

38. Hugh S. Gookin to friend, December 3, 1863, Washington Artillery Letter, Historic New Orleans Collection, New Orleans, LA.

39. *OR,* 17(1):318, 26(1):198–99, 30(1):467, 504, 650.

40. Nevins, *Diary of Battle,* 50–51; Crumb and Dhalle, *No Middle Ground,* 24–25; Ames to Home Circle, May 8, 1862, Albert N. Ames Papers, NYSL.

41. Fitzhugh, *Cannon Smoke,* 164; Shea and Hess, *Pea Ridge,* 233, 373; *OR,* 10(1):924.

42. Shultz, *"Double Canister,"* 37; Crumb, *Eleventh Corps Artillery,* 37–38, 83–84; Collier and Collier, *Yours for the Union,* 267.

43. *OR,* 10(1):208–9, 17(1):107–8, 691–92, 20(1):477, 30(1):538, 40(1):760; cards, Newit J.

Drew Service Record, Battery E, 1st Mississippi Light Artillery, NARA; Hess, *Into the Crater,* 73, 112, 215.

44. *OR,* 21:188, 29(2):410, 46(2):83.

45. Walton, *Behind the Guns,* ix, xv–xvii; Hughes, *Pride of the Confederate Artillery,* 55n; Nevins, *Diary of Battle,* 171, 195.

46. *OR,* 20(2):400; *SOR,* pt. 1, 4:200.

47. Dent to wife, May 1, 1864, Stouten Hubert Dent Papers, ADAH; Cate, *Two Soldiers,* 28–30, 64, 66, 69, 73.

48. *OR,* 33:898–99; Crary, *Dear Belle,* 162–63.

49. *OR,* 15:64–65, 24(2):116–17; Jackson, *"Some of the Boys,"* 93–94.

50. Barnes, Carnahan, and McCain, *Eighty-Sixth Regiment,* 126.

51. *OR,* 10(1):322, 11(2):59, 86, 42(1):784–85.

52. Buell, *"Cannoneer,"* 17–19.

53. Ritter, "Sketch of the Third Battery," pt. 4, 115; Tourgée, *Story of a Thousand,* 137; *Fifth Massachusetts Battery,* 561–62.

54. *OR,* 15:62, 21:188–89; Ritter, "Sketch of the Third Battery," pt. 4, 117; Jacob T. Foster Memoirs, 42, WHS.

55. *OR,* 19(1):436–37, 30(2):175; pension application, August 3, 1881, John Riddermann Pension Record, Hewitt's Battery B, Kentucky Light Artillery Regimental File, SRNB; *SOR,* pt. 1, 3:801, 7:55; Cutler, *Letters from the Front,* 32; Popchock, *Soldier Boy,* 103.

56. Nevins, *Diary of Battle,* 286; *OR,* 30(1):563, 46(2):83; Walton, *Behind the Guns,* xiv; John C. Tidball to Hunt, March 1, 1865, Box 11, Henry Jackson Hunt Papers, LC.

57. Jackson, *"Some of the Boys,"* 106–7.

58. Nevins, *Diary of Battle,* 167; *OR,* 40(1):438–39; Chase, *Battery F,* 240.

59. Aldrich, *Battery A,* 407; Sumner, *Battery D,* 157–92; Chase, *Battery F,* 280–84.

60. Glatthaar, *Soldiering in the Army of Northern Virginia,* ix–x, 13, 46, 51–52, 54.

61. Hewitt, Schott, and Kunis, *To Succeed or Perish,* 98–123; Beecher, *First Light Battery Connecticut,* 20–22.

62. Perkins, *Daniel's Battery,* 28, 30, 44; Hess, "Twelfth Missouri Infantry," 151.

63. Stiles, *Four Years,* 54.

64. Beecher, *First Light Battery Connecticut,* 20–22; copy of descriptive roll, Company A, 1st Mississippi Light Artillery Folder, VNMP; Hess, "Twelfth Missouri Infantry," 151.

65. Jacob T. Foster Memoirs, 1–3, 12, 15–21, WHS; Squires, "Boy Officer," 11; Carmichael, *Lee's Young Artillerist,* 10, 19, 21; Bradford Nichol Memoirs, 1–2, TSLA.

66. Hewitt, Schott, and Kunis, *To Succeed or Perish,* 98–123; Perkins, *Daniel's Battery,* 47, 50.

67. Hughes, *Civil War Memoir of Philip Daingerfield Stephenson,* 235; Buell, *"Cannoneer,"* 24; *SOR,* pt. 1, 6:361.

68. *Report of the Joint Committee,* 2:242; Ames to father, September 12, 1864, Albert N. Ames Papers, NYSL; Miller to wife, August 13, September 18, 1864, Marshall Mortimer Miller Papers, LC.

69. Runge, *Four Years in the Confederate Artillery,* 23, 30–31.

70. *OR,* 25(2):634.

71. *OR*, 29(2):840; "Schedule of Assignment of Arty. Field Officers as proposed, Brig. Gen. W. N. Pendleton General Chief," August 14, 1863, William N. Pendleton Service Record, M331, NARA; Furney, *Reminiscences*, 28–29; Landis to West, January 10, 1865, John C. Landis Service Record, Landis's Missouri Battery, M322, NARA.

72. *SOR*, pt. 1, 6:694–95; Chamberlayne, *Ham Chamberlayne*, 169, 233–37, 245.

73. Hess, *Into the Crater*, 12–113.

74. Chamberlayne, *Ham Chamberlayne*, 233, 249, 251–52, 258, 261, 268, 276.

75. Bakewell, "Luck of the War Game," 18; *OR*, 11(2):59, 545, 19(1):344, 38(3):61; Barlow, "Light Battery Service in 1861".

76. Gallagher, *Fighting for the Confederacy*, 3, 16, 193, 196.

77. Nevins, *Diary of Battle*, 471–72.

78. Brown to father, July 28, 1863, William L. Brown Collection, CHM; *OR*, 11(2):59, 22(1):405, 38(3):366, 469, 46(1):1091.

79. Cameron, "Bravest of 'Em All."

80. Wild, *Alexander's Baltimore Battery*, 11; Trout, *Memoirs of the Stuart Horse Artillery*, 181; Templeton to father and mother, January 9, 1863, John A. Templeton Papers, University of Texas, Dolph Briscoe Center for American History, Austin; Hughes, *Civil War Memoir of Philip Daingerfield Stephenson*, 167; *OR*, 26(1):780.

81. Walton, *Behind the Guns*, 97; Lewis F. Lake Reminiscences, 5, ALPL.

82. *SOR*, pt. 1, 2:755; Hewitt, Schott, and Kunis, *To Succeed or Perish*, 57; William Miller Owen Diary, October 12–13, 1864, LSU.

83. Rhodes, *History of Battery B*, 212; [Bartlett], *Soldier's Story*, 126; Fleming to parents, January 9, 1863, John C. Fleming Papers, Newberry Library, Chicago, IL; "History of the Chicago Board of Trade Battery," 20, John A. Nourse Papers, CHM; Tapert, *Brothers' War*, 126.

84. *OR*, 17(1):268, 20(1):759, 43(1):419.

85. Bouton, *Events of the Civil War*, 85.

10. ARTILLERY HORSES

1. Heiss, *Veterinary Service*, 9; Armistead, *Horses and Mules*, 3; Green, *Horses at Work*, 124. There are no readily available statistics on the number of artillery horses used by either side during the war. I arrived at this figure by counting the number of batteries in both armies and using Jacob Roemer's statement that his battery used about 400 horses during the war. I also assumed that most Union batteries had six pieces and most Confederate batteries had four pieces. This formula (460 Union batteries with 400 horses each and 292 Confederate batteries with 266 horses each) resulted in 184,000 Union artillery horses and 77,672 Confederate artillery horses. Furney, *Reminiscences*, 300, 317.

2. *OR*, 20(1):300; *Instruction for Field Artillery*, 46–48.

3. *Instruction for Field Artillery*, 46–47; Gibbon, *Artillerist's Manual*, 167.

4. *Instruction for Field Artillery*, 46; Gibbon, *Artillerist's Manual*, 363–70.

5. *Instruction for Field Artillery*, 227.

6. *Instruction for Field Artillery*, 3–4; Gibbon, *Artillerist's Manual*, 347; *SOR*, pt. 1, 5:297; Crary, *Dear Belle*, 189; *OR*, 11(2):104; Loosley to wife, June 1, 1863, Edwin A. Loosley Papers, SIU.

7. *OR,* 36(1):922, 36(2):355, 38(3):677, 38(4):634; "Horses," Folder 23, John G. Devereux Papers, UNC; Wiley, *Norfolk Blues,* 174; *SOR,* pt. 1, 7:452.

8. Wild, *Alexander's Baltimore Battery,* 24–25; *OR,* 32(3):446, 49(1):649–50; Chamberlayne, *Ham Chamberlayne,* 169.

9. Bouton, *Events of the Civil War,* 85–86; Moore, *Story of a Cannoneer,* 153; Tuthill, "Artilleryman's Recollections," 293; Wild, *Alexander's Baltimore Battery,* 207.

10. Budiansky, *Nature of Horses,* 9, 18, 20, 40–41, 81–85, 147–67, 263.

11. Pooley-Ebert, "Species Agency," 150–52; Waran and Casey, "Horse Training," 186; McGreevy and McLean, "Behavioural Problems with the Ridden Horse," 198–99.

12. Scott, "Racehorse as Protagonist," 45–65.

13. Green, *Horses at Work,* 153.

14. Rhodes, *History of Battery B,* 21; Wild, *Alexander's Baltimore Battery,* 18, 207.

15. Billings, *Hardtack and Coffee,* 324; Moore, *Story of a Cannoneer,* 150.

16. Beecher, *First Light Battery Connecticut,* 154; Hackemer, *To Rescue My Native Land,* 55; Boos, "Civil War Diary of Patrick H. White," 642–43; *Fifth Massachusetts Battery,* 152; Billings, *Tenth Massachusetts Battery,* 42.

17. Nevins, *Diary of Battle,* 55; Lewis, *Battery E,* 359; John Reiley to friends at home, October 19, 1862, Francis and John Reiley Papers, WRHS.

18. *Instruction for Field Artillery,* 141–52, 193–205, 227–43; Chase, *Battery F,* 10; Miller to wife, August 19, 1862, Marshall Mortimer Miller Papers, LC; Furney, *Reminiscences,* 24.

19. Merrill, *24th Independent Battery,* 193; William Terry Moore Reminiscences, UM; *Fifth Massachusetts Battery,* 151.

20. *Fifth Massachusetts Battery,* 151–52; Rhodes, *History of Battery B,* 20.

21. Beecher, *First Light Battery Connecticut,* 420, 423; Sumner, *Battery D,* 74; Wild, *Alexander's Baltimore Battery,* 209; Cameron, "Bravest of 'Em All."

22. Baker, *Ninth Mass. Battery,* 22; *OR,* 17(1):259, 20(1):476, 30(1):800; Griffin, *Three Years a Soldier,* 97; Beers, *Memories,* 237.

23. *Instruction for Field Artillery,* 47–48; Ritter, "Sketches of the Third Maryland Artillery," 436–37; *OR,* 33:1169; Nevins, *Diary of Battle,* 500.

24. Hess, *Civil War Logistics,* 164; Gibson, "Hay," 51–53; *OR,* ser. 4, 3:293; *OR,* 25(2):695, 46(2):1305; Hughes, *Civil War Memoir of Philip Daingerfield Stephenson,* 342.

25. Little and Maxwell, *Lumsden's Battery,* 15; *OR,* 20(1):583, 36(1):643–44, 755; Ames to Home Circle, May 16, 1864, Albert N. Ames Papers, NYSL; *SOR,* pt. 2, 31:652; Hodgson to not stated, May 23, 1862, "Order Book, 5th Company, B.W.A.," Box 12, Folder 1, Civil War Papers, Battalion Washington Artillery Collection, TU; Cushing to mother, November 8, 1863, Harry C. Cushing Letters, UTK.

26. Gibbon, *Artillerist's Manual,* 351; *OR,* 19(2):642–43; Wise, *Long Arm of Lee,* 1:330–31; General Orders, Headquarters, Loring's Division, November 9, 1863, Winfield Scott Featherston Collection, UM; *Instruction for Field Artillery,* 193; Bennett, *First Massachusetts Light Battery,* 98; Wild, *Alexander's Baltimore Battery,* 207–8.

27. Rhodes, *History of Battery B,* 132; Dozier, *Gunner in Lee's Army,* 78; Sumner, *Battery D,* 38; John Merrilles Diary, July 10, 1863, CHM; *OR,* 33:1188; Nevins, *Diary of Battle,* 124, 169; Sharrer,

"Great Glanders Epizootic," 79–97; Billings, *Tenth Massachusetts Battery*, 47–49, 147–50, 152, 183–85, 242, 272, 288, 302–5, 348–51, 398–401, 404–9, 426, 431, 439–41.

28. Heiss, *Veterinary Service*, 9; *OR*, 33:1182–83; Jones, *Artilleryman's Diary*, 152.

29. *Ordnance Manual for the Use of the Officers of the United States Army*, 142–68; *History of the Fourth Maine Battery*, 13; *Instruction for Field Artillery*, 60–61; *OR*, 20(1):298; William Augustus Spaulding Diaries, January 4, 1863, MinnHS.

30. Beecher, *First Light Battery Connecticut*, 126; *OR*, 30(1):554.

31. *SOR*, pt. 1, 3:782; *OR*, 11(2):106, 120, 36(1):651, 939, 38(2):669, 47(3):77, 52(1):71; *SOR*, pt. 2, 50:387; Collier and Collier, *Yours for the Union*, 261.

32. Lucius G. Marshall to Hood, December 4, 1866, John B. Hood Papers, NARA; *OR*, 20(1):354; Lewis, *Battery E*, 210; Ladd and Ladd, *Bachelder Papers*, 1:177; Rhodes, *History of Battery B*, 214, 216.

33. *OR*, 20(1):804, 52(1):24; Slocomb to not stated, March 12, 1864, "Order Book, 5th Company, B.W.A.," Box 12, Folder 1, Civil War Papers, Battalion Washington Artillery Collection, TU; "Purcell Battery," 365.

34. Moore, *Story of a Cannoneer*, 331; Furney, *Reminiscences*, 317; Billings, *Tenth Massachusetts Battery*, 47–49, 147–50, 152, 183–85, 242, 272, 288, 302–5, 348–51, 398–401, 404–9, 426, 431, 439–41; *OR*, 46(1):795.

35. Gallagher, *Fighting for the Confederacy*, 248; *OR*, 45(1):532.

36. Stiles, *Four Years*, 196; Runge, *Four Years in the Confederate Artillery*, 98; Gallagher, *Fighting for the Confederacy*, 253.

37. Moore, *Story of a Cannoneer*, 77, 258; [Bartlett], *Soldier's Story*, 74; Stiles, *Four Years*, 218.

38. *SOR*, pt. 1, 7:123; *OR*, 19(1):255, 20(1):302; Billings, *Tenth Massachusetts Battery*, 315–16.

39. Billings, *Tenth Massachusetts Battery*, 315.

40. *Fifth Massachusetts Battery*, 143.

41. Wild, *Alexander's Baltimore Battery*, 61; Dame, *From the Rapidan to Richmond*, 121; Furney, *Reminiscences*, 260–61.

42. Beecher, *First Light Battery Connecticut*, 154; *OR*, 42(1):787; Furney, *Reminiscences*, 56; Crumb and Dhalle, *No Middle Ground*, 48.

43. *Instruction for Field Artillery*, 65; *OR*, 20(1):414, 20(2):327, 44:807; Wainwright to Hunt, August 21, 1864, Box 1, Henry Jackson Hunt Papers, LC; "Journal of Siege Operations," 86–87, ibid.; *SOR*, pt. 1, 7:614; Special Orders No. 41, Headquarters, Army of the Mississippi, April 26, 1862, P. G. T. Beauregard Papers, LC; "Special Orders Jan. 2, 1862 to Aug. 27, 1862," ibid.; *OR*, ser. 3, 5:220, 256.

44. Campbell, *"Grand Terrible Drama,"* 172; Nevins, *Diary of Battle*, 269; Baker, *Ninth Mass. Battery*, 117.

45. *OR*, 11(3):687, 19(1):963, 25(2):749; Johnston to Bragg, March 16, 1864, Joseph E. Johnston Papers, DU; *OR*, ser. 4, 3:293.

46. Receipt, December 19, 1861, Thomas J. Stanford Service Record, Stanford's Mississippi Battery, M269, NARA; Hamilton, *Papers of Thomas Ruffin*, 3:398; Daniel, *Cannoneers in Gray*, 71.

47. Crumb, *Eleventh Corps Artillery*, 44–45.

48. *OR,* 26(1):200; Albert G. Grammer Diary, December 19, 1863, OCHM; Maxwell, *Autobiography,* 217.

49. Wild, *Alexander's Baltimore Battery,* 207; *OR,* 39(3):468–69.

50. Billings, *Hardtack and Coffee,* 281; *OR,* 52(1):49.

51. *OR,* 24(3):965, 1050; Ritter, "Sketch of Third Battery," pt. 4, 116–17.

52. Barlow, "Light Battery Service in 1861"; Williams and Wooster, "With Terry's Texas Rangers," 312; Sumner, *Battery D,* 93–94.

53. Henry Bryan to George W. Brent, February 2, 1865, "Letter Book from November 30th 1864 to March 9th 1865 of Major H. Y. Bryan Asst. Insp. Gen. of Mil. Div. of the West," Reel 7, Container 40, P. G. T. Beauregard Papers, LC; [Bartlett], *Soldier's Story,* 74.

54. Hoy, *Bradford's Battery,* 255–56; Randall to mother, June 13, 1863, Cyrus W. Randall Correspondence, ALPL.

11. DEFENSIVE OPERATIONS IN THE FIELD

1. *Report of the Joint Committee,* 2:168–71.

2. Crary, *Dear Belle,* 152; Dame, *From the Rapidan to Richmond,* 102.

3. *Instruction for Field Artillery,* 2; Gibbon, *Artillerist's Manual,* 356–58; Halleck, *Elements,* 129.

4. *OR,* 10(1):486, 30(1):352; Gibbon, *Artillerist's Manual,* 356; Roberts, *Hand-Book,* 47–48; Mahan, *Elementary Treatise,* 23.

5. *OR,* 3:74, 17(1):790, 20(1):871, 21:636–637, 30(2):94–95, 52(1):238; Ladd and Ladd, *Bachelder Papers,* 3:1788–89; *SOR,* pt. 1, 6:170, 187.

6. Crumb and Dhalle, *No Middle Ground,* 27; Ladd and Ladd, *Bachelder Papers,* 1:306; *SOR,* pt. 1, 4:737; *OR,* 15:356, 19(1):436, 20(1):722, 40(1):430, 42(1):784.

7. Aldrich, *Battery A,* 50; Ames to Home Circle, June 22, 1862, Albert N. Ames Papers, NYSL; *OR,* 17(1):693, 20(1):299, 36(1):656; *SOR,* pt. 2, 31:650; *SOR,* pt. 1, 7:327; "The Atlanta Campaign," n.d., John Watkins Papers, UTK.

8. *OR,* 10(1):819–20, 20(1):478, 21:515, 36(1):534, 650–51.

9. *OR,* 11(2):237, 325, 25(1):505; Robert B. Beck Reminiscences, 23–24, Mrs. Douglas W. Clark Collection, LC; Chalaron, "Vivid Experiences at Chickamauga," 278; Gallagher, *Fighting for the Confederacy,* 248.

10. *OR,* 17(1):222.

11. Johnson, *Soldier's Reminiscences,* 79–80.

12. Hight, *History of the Fifty-Eighth,* 123; Boring, "Fighting for Vicksburg."

13. William Merrell, "Personal Memoirs of the Civil War," Lincoln Memorial University, Abraham Lincoln Library and Museum, Harrogate, TN; Bauer, *Soldiering,* 151; Smith, *Seventh Iowa,* 169–70.

14. Chalaron, "Battle Echoes from Shiloh," 218–19; *OR,* 11(2):255–56.

15. *OR,* 10(1):323, 12(2):469, 21:679, 36(2):61, 38(3):368.

16. *OR,* 25(1):597, 30(1):282, 467, 52(1):23; Crary, *Dear Belle,* 152.

17. *History of the Organization,* 201; *OR,* 17(1):628, 20(1):894; Gallagher, *Fighting for the Confederacy,* 248.

18. Billings, *Tenth Massachusetts Battery*, 286; *OR*, 11(2):249, 17(1):242, 259, 22(1):100, 124; Gardner, "First Kansas Battery," 250; Montgomery to not stated, January 17, 1863, McClain Montgomery Letters, 33rd Ohio Regimental File, SRNB; Jacob Van Zwaluevenburg Journal, 26,, WLC-UM.

19. Crumb and Dhalle, *No Middle Ground*, 131; *OR*, 25(1):484, 595, 675, 30(1):471.

20. Ellison, *On to Atlanta*, 48–50; *OR*, 38(2):484; Howard, *Autobiography*, 1:437.

21. *OR*, 12(2):420, 22(1):406, 30(1):504; *SOR*, pt. 1, 3:285, 765.

22. Billings, *Tenth Massachusetts Battery*, 286n; *OR*, 11(2):362, 17(1):260, 21:339.

23. *OR*, 11(2):355, 20(1):455, 474, 504.

24. *OR*, 29(1):286, 30(2):95; *SOR*, pt. 1, 4:656–57.

25. *SOR*, pt. 2, 31:650; John Merrilles Diary, May 30, 1863, CHM; *OR*, 24(1):620; Wood to wife, June 14, 1863, Edward Jesup Wood Papers, Indiana Historical Society, Indianapolis; diary, June 15, 1863, John Alexander Griffen Papers, ALPL; diary, June 2, 1863, Hugh Boyd Ewing Papers, OHS; [Newsome], *Experience in the War*, 33.

26. Erickson, "With Grant at Vicksburg," 478, 482, 485; Way, *Thirty-Third Regiment Illinois Veteran Volunteer Infantry*, 45; Edward to aunt, May 29, 1863, Edward H. Ingraham and Duncan G. Ingraham Letters, ALPL; Ord to wife, June 27, 1863, Edward Otho Cresap Ord Letters, Stanford University, Special Collections and University Archives, Palo Alto, CA.

27. *OR*, 20(1):474.

28. *Instruction for Field Artillery*, 152–92; Collier and Collier, *Yours for the Union*, 259.

29. "Correspondence," 278.

30. *Instruction for Field Artillery*, 42; Halleck, *Elements*, 129; Roberts, *Hand-Book*, 53.

31. "Correspondence," 278; Kaplan, *Artillery Service*, 88–89; *OR*, 29(2):130–31, 410.

32. Birkhimer, *Historical Sketch*, 206.

33. Kaplan, *Artillery Service*, 236; *OR*, 26(1):721, 38(1):121, 185; *SOR*, pt. 2, 50:513.

34. Trout, *Memoirs of the Stuart Horse Artillery*, 191; Maxwell, *Perfect Lion*, 235; Wiley, *Norfolk Blues*, 45; *OR*, 25(1):694; Ladd and Ladd, *Bachelder Papers*, 2:1252.

35. Daniel, *Cannoneers in Gray*, 89; Morton, *Artillery of Nathan Bedford Forrest's Cavalry*, 161–62.

36. *OR*, 16(2):757, 47(1):907; "Correspondence," 279; *SOR*, pt. 1, 3:490.

37. Kaplan, *Artillery Service*, 90; Thomas H. Carter to Daniel, October 11, 1904, John Warwick Daniel Papers, DU.

38. *SOR*, pt. 1, 3:518.

39. Wise, *Long Arm of Lee*, 1:166; Maxwell, *Perfect Lion*, 250–55; Griffin, *Three Years a Soldier*, 114.

40. *OR*, 47(1):907, 49(1):471.

41. *OR*, 19(2):472.

42. Roberts, *Hand-Book*, 52; *OR*, 11(2):282, 51(1):1271.

43. Gibbon, *Artillerist's Manual*, 343–44, 359; *OR*, 11(2):196, 47(1):907; Furney, *Reminiscences*, 43–44.

44. *OR*, 25(1):55; Cushing to father, February 16, 1863, Harry C. Cushing Letters, UTK.

45. *OR*, 25(1):285, 310, 36(1):655; *SOR*, pt. 1, 3:553.

46. Buell, *"Cannoneer,"* 181–82; Gibbon, *Artillerist's Manual,* 358; Gallagher, *Fighting for the Confederacy,* 251.

47. Hewitt, Schott, and Kunis, *To Succeed or Perish,* 57–58; *OR,* 17(1):629, 20(1):769, 22(1):123, 36(1):653.

48. *OR,* 11(2):542, 17(1):690–91, 20(1):411, 909, 46(1):189; Dent to wife, July 9, 1864, Stouten Hubert Dent Papers, ADAH.

49. Neal to Pa, October 12, 1863, Andrew Jackson Neal Letters, EU; *OR,* 19(1):435, 21:187, 30(1):553.

50. *OR,* 10(1):610, 42(1):427; Crumb, *Eleventh Corps Artillery,* 66–67.

51. *OR,* 21:318; Robertson, "'Boy Artillerist,'" 233; *SOR,* pt. 3, 1:256–57.

52. Cameron, "'Standing Up to It'"; *OR,* 36(1):524; Gallagher, *Fighting for the Confederacy,* 159.

53. *SOR,* pt. 1, 3:783.

54. Stiles, *Four Years,* 218; Bradford Nichol Memoirs, April 7, 1862, TSLA; Carnes, "Artillery at the Battle of Perryville," 9; Ramsay, "Light Batteries A, D, F and I," 559; Crary, *Dear Belle,* 206; *OR,* 8:265, 20(1):412–13, 770, 21:266, 45(1):337, 52(1):97; Miller to wife, June 10, 1864, Marshall Mortimer Miller Papers, LC; *SOR,* pt. 1, 2:725.

55. *OR,* 11(2):910–11; Thomas C. Potter to brother and sister, January 12, 1863, Battery B, 1st Ohio Light Artillery Regimental File, SRNB.

56. *OR,* 19(1):1026.

57. *OR,* 17(1):319, 26(1):198, 40(1):431; Nevins, *Diary of Battle,* 242–43; Crumb and Dhalle, *No Middle Ground,* 28; *SOR,* pt. 1, 3:544–45, 4:733.

58. Furney, *Reminiscences,* 214–15.

59. Johnson, *A Soldier's Reminiscences,* 281.

12. ARTILLERY AGAINST INFANTRY

1. Halleck, *Elements,* 128; Gibbon, *Artillerist's Manual,* 342, 357; Mahan, *Elementary Treatise,* 36–37; Daniel, *Cannoneers in Gray,* 34–35; Furney, *Reminiscences,* 220.

2. *OR,* 21:180–82.

3. *OR,* 21:182–83.

4. *OR,* 21:183–84, 459, 484, 515–16.

5. *OR,* 20(1):759–60.

6. *OR,* 25(1):822–23, 998–99; Gallagher, *Fighting for the Confederacy,* 204, 207; Thomas H. Carter to Daniel, October 11, 1904, John Warwick Daniel Papers, DU.

7. *OR,* 25(1):564, 614; *SOR,* pt. 1, 4:629.

8. Gallagher, *Fighting for the Confederacy,* 245–46; Hess, *Pickett's Charge,* 75–76.

9. Ladd and Ladd, *Bachelder Papers,* 1:485; Gallagher, *Fighting for the Confederacy,* 254–55.

10. Gallagher, *Fighting for the Confederacy,* 255, 258–59; Hess, *Pickett's Charge,* 158–65; Ladd and Ladd, *Bachelder Papers,* 1:489.

11. Gallagher, *Fighting for the Confederacy,* 247–48, 262; Alexander, "Great Charge," 363, 365; Ladd and Ladd, *Bachelder Papers,* 1:488.

12. Gallagher, *Fighting for the Confederacy,* 249, 251; Carmichael, "'Every Map,'" 270–71, 273–75; Hess, *Pickett's Charge,* 126–41.

13. *OR*, 38(1):880, 38(4):445, 45(1):471; Morse, *Letters*, 173; Watkins to not stated, August 24, 1864, John Watkins Papers, UTK; *SOR*, pt. 1, 7:224; Stiles, *Four Years*, 110.

14. *Ordnance Manual for the Use of the Officers of the United States Army*, 455; Roberts, *Hand-Book*, 51.

15. Gibbon, *Artillerist's Manual*, 251, 358–59; Roberts, *Hand-Book*, 48; Halleck, *Elements*, 129; "Instructions for firing," n.d., Box 13, Henry Jackson Hunt Papers, LC.

16. Roberts, *Hand-Book*, 50; Gibbon, *Artillerist's Manual*, 358; *Revised United States Army Regulations*, 105; Halleck, *Elements*, 129.

17. *OR*, 20(1):524, 763, 20(2):292, 21:586, 637, 38(2):470.

18. *OR*, 11(2):171, 17(1):241, 271, 20(1):476.

19. James T. Embree to father, January 9, 1863, Lucius C. Embree Papers, Indiana State Library, Indianapolis; Butler, *Letters Home*, 144; McKinney to sister, June 25, 1863, David McKinney Papers, WLC-UM.

20. Diary, December 30, 1862, George O. Pratt Papers, ALPL; Vance, "Twenty-Ninth Regiment," 490; Davidson to wife, January 4, 1863, James Innes Davidson Papers, ADAH; Lot Dudley Young Reminiscences, 29, State Historical Society of Missouri, Research Center, Columbia; Loosley to wife, June 1, 1863, Edwin A. Loosley Papers, SIU; Ackley to wife, June 28, 1864, Charles Thomas Ackley Civil War Letters, University of Iowa, Special Collections, Iowa City; Benjamin F. Nourse Diary, December 31, 1862, DU; *OR*, 20(1):288; E. R. Calkins, "Three and One-Half Years in the Civil War," 17, 8th Wisconsin Battery Regimental File, SRNB; Roberts to wife [January] 7, 1863, Charles Roberts Collection, UM; Runge, *Four Years in the Confederate Artillery*, 50–51; E. John Ellis to mother, January 12, 1863, E. John and Thomas C. Ellis Family Papers, LSU; Blackford, *War Years*, 90; L. E. D., "Part taken by 1st Tenn Regt at Battle Murfreesboro," Charles Todd Quintard Papers, DU; Wiley, *Confederate Letters of John W. Hagan*, 23.

21. *OR*, 29(1):270, 34(1):981; Bauer, *Soldiering*, 111; George Gresham Sinclair to Frank, January 6, 1863, 89th Illinois Regimental File, SRNB; Joe Rudolph to Crete, January 12, 1863, Lucretia Rudolph Garfield Papers, LC; Reese to Tissee, May 25, 1863, John Reese Papers, SIU; [Rood], *Service of Company E*, 325–26.

22. *Medical and Surgical History*, 3:696.

23. Andrews, *Complete Record*, 10–31; "Tabular Statement of the wounded in the Hospital 3rd Divis 15th AC Dept of the Tennessee from the Battle of Vicksburg May 19th 1863," Thomas S. Hawley Papers, MHM; "Tabular Statement of the wounded in Hospital 3rd Divis 15th A. C. Collated by Dr. Gill 95th Ohio from the Assault on Vicksburg May 22nd 1863," ibid.

24. Sykes, *Walthall's Brigade*, 497–98.

25. Thomas H. Carter to Daniel, October 11, 1904, John Warwick Daniel Papers, DU; Collier and Collier, *Yours for the Union*, 60.

26. Ladd and Ladd, *Bachelder Papers*, 1:655; *Fifth Massachusetts Battery*, 644.

27. Nevins, *Diary of Battle*, 264–65; *OR*, 30(1):649.

28. *OR*, 16(2):1157, 19(1):284.

29. *OR,* 11(2):747, 17(1):204, 36(1):653, 42(1):542; *SOR,* pt. 2, 70:303; Texas to editor, May 30, 1864, *Memphis Daily Appeal,* June 2, 1864.

30. Aldrich, *Battery A,* 216; Hess, *Pickett's Charge,* 252; *SOR,* pt. 2, 8:312–13; *OR,* 10(1):376, 437, 20(1):580, 41(1):459.

31. Gallagher, *Fighting for the Confederacy,* 210; Alexander, "Great Charge," 360.

32. *OR,* 43(1):415, 45(1):459.

33. Neil, *Battery at Close Quarters,* 2, 4, 6–7.

34. Selden Spencer, "Reminiscences of the Battle of Fort Donelson," MHM; Lathrop, "Confederate Artilleryman," 377; Nevins, *Diary of Battle,* 54; *OR,* 11(2):267; *Proceedings of the Eighth Annual Session of the Survivors of the Battle of Stone's River,* 46; Cleburne to Kinloch Falconer, May 27, 1864, "Records Cleburne's Div Hardees Corps A of Tenn," chap. 2, no. 265, RG 109, NARA; *OR,* 38(2):469.

35. Chalaron, "Battle Echoes from Shiloh," 218–19; *OR,* 10(1):565, 20(1):871–72; *SOR,* pt. 1, 7:224–26.

36. *OR,* 10(1):277, 611, 11(1):539, 25(1):614, 30(2):287; Lathrop, "Confederate Artilleryman," 380; Daniel H. Chandler, "History," 33, 5th Indiana Battery Regimental File, SRNB; reminiscences, 57–58, Emerson Rood Calkins Family Papers, WHS; *Fifth Massachusetts Battery,* 347.

37. *OR,* 11(2):173, 20(1):302, 24(2):95–96, 36(1):640, 38(3):576.

38. Howe, *Civil War Times,* 79–80.

39. Owen, "Hot Day on Marye's Heights," 98–99.

40. *SOR,* pt. 1, 2:781; Ladd and Ladd, *Bachelder Papers,* 2:980; *OR,* 10(1):146, 30(1):588, 45(1):326.

41. *SOR,* pt. 1, 2:418; Fitch, *Annals of the Army of the Cumberland,* 298; Daniel, *Cannoneers in Gray,* 103–4, 118.

42. *OR,* 38(2):471–72, 47(1):179, 185–86; Daniel, *Cannoneers in Gray,* 180–81.

43. OR, 40(1):282, 666; Rowland, *Jefferson Davis,* 8:573.

44. Lewis, *Battery E,* 43; Shoup to Bragg, April 15, 1862, Francis A. Shoup Service Record, M331, NARA.

45. *OR,* ser. 4, 2:194; *OR,* 20(1):850; Bradford Nichol Memoirs, 214, TSLA; Benjamin F. Nourse Diary, January 21, 1863, DU; *Fifth Massachusetts Battery,* 371.

13. FIELD ARTILLERY AND FORTIFICATIONS

1. Gibbon, *Artillerist's Manual,* 362, 385–415; *Ordnance Manual for the Use of the Officers of the United States Army,* 398; Roberts, *Hand-Book,* 179.

2. *OR,* 10(1):147, 22(1):489; Bradford Nichol Memoirs, May 26, 1862, TSLA; account of Kentucky campaign, 12–13, Box 156, Folder 2, Joseph Wheeler Family Papers, ADAH; Felix H. Robertson to Dent, April 25, 1909, Stouten Hubert Dent Papers, ADAH; Bouton, *Events of the Civil War,* 27–28.

3. *OR,* 11(1):351–52, 51(1):579–80; Hess, *Field Armies and Fortifications,* 78–84.

4. Dozier, *Gunner in Lee's Army,* 119; *OR,* 51(1):678–79.

5. *OR,* 21:209, 563–64, 575–76; Owen, "Hot Day on Marye's Heights," 97; Landry, "Donaldsonville Artillery," 198–201; Hess, *Field Armies and Fortifications,* 154–71.

6. *OR,* 20(1):768, 25(1):487, 726; Aldrich, *Battery A,* 176; Hess, *Field Armies and Fortifications,* 183–87; Ladd and Ladd, *Bachelder Papers,* 2:1172–73.

7. *OR,* 24(2):176, 178, 285; *SOR,* pt. 2, 36:34–35; *SOR,* pt. 1, 4:385; "Report of Field and Siege Guns and Ammunition on Rear Line of Defense, Vicksburg," July 4, 1863, Frederick M. Dearborn Collection, Harvard University, Houghton Library, Cambridge, MA.

8. *SOR,* pt. 2, 38:358; *OR,* 24(2):176, 182; William G. Christie to brother, June 23, 1863, Christie Family Letters, MinnHS.

9. Brown to father, June 14, 1863, William L. Brown Collection, CHM; Jones, "Rank and File at Vicksburg," 24; *OR,* 24(2):367; Lockett to Memminger, June 16, 1863, Box 4, Folder 124, Samuel H. Lockett Papers, UNC; R. M. Aiken to Rigby, April 12, 1903, including information from *Memphis Bulletin,* October 6, 1863, 33rd Illinois Folder, VNMP.

10. *OR,* 38(1):491, 504; Black, *Soldier's Recollections,* 80; Miller to wife, July 10, 1864, Marshall Mortimer Miller Papers, LC; Douglas, *Douglas's Texas Battery,* 99.

11. Maxwell, *Autobiography,* 236, 247, 249–50; Dent to wife, July 9, 1864, Stouten Hubert Dent Papers, ADAH; Little and Maxwell, *Lumsden's Battery,* 49; Black, *Soldier's Recollections,* 77.

12. Miller to wife, August 9, 1864, Marshall Mortimer Miller Papers, LC; Little and Maxwell, *Lumsden's Battery,* 42; Maxwell, *Autobiography,* 231–32; *OR,* 38(1):836, 38(3):175; *SOR,* pt. 1, 7:78; Shoup to Hypolite Oladowski, July 4, 1864, Francis A. Shoup Service Record, M331, NARA.

13. Neal to Ella, August 4, 1864, Andrew Jackson Neal Letters, EU; Douglas, *Douglas's Texas Battery,* 93.

14. Tower, *Carolinian Goes to War,* 196.

15. *OR,* 38(3):848–49.

16. Neal to Pa, June 20, 1864, Andrew Jackson Neal Letters, EU.

17. *OR,* 38(3):746.

18. "Diary," 30, William A. Drennan Papers, MDAH.

19. Hess, *Fighting for Atlanta,* 39, 41–43, 55, 222–25, 288–89.

20. *OR,* 36(1):286, 1044, 1086; *SOR,* pt. 1, 6:616; Buell, *"Cannoneer,"* 178; Thomas H. Carter to Daniel, October 11, 1904, John Warwick Daniel Papers, DU.

21. *OR,* 36(1):516, 761, 764; Nevins, *Diary of Battle,* 404; Hess, *Trench Warfare,* 155–68.

22. Kaplan, *Artillery Service,* 225; Lord, "Coehorn Mortar," 18; *OR,* 33:935, 36(1):527–28, 36(2):373, 36(3):533; Hess, *Trench Warfare,* 79, 190–91; "Journal of Siege Operations," 30, Box 1, Henry Jackson Hunt Papers, LC.

23. *OR,* 36(2):373; Abbot to Hunt, May 7, 1864, Box 10, Hunt Papers, LC; Furney, *Reminiscences,* 217–18.

24. *OR,* 36(1):1050–51, 36(3):749; *SOR,* pt. 1, 6:666; Billings, *Tenth Massachusetts Battery,* 268.

25. Stiles, *Four Years,* 302–3.

26. Billings, *Tenth Massachusetts Battery,* 267; *OR,* 36(3):741.

27. *OR,* 40(1):513, 516, 668; Furney, *Reminiscences,* 236; Lapham, *My Recollections,* 142–43; Hoy, *Bradford's Battery,* 273–74; "Journal of Siege Operations," 82, Box 1, Hunt Papers, LC.

28. "Journal of Siege Operations," 58, Box 1, Hunt Papers, LC; *OR,* 40(1):667–68, 46(1):664; Billings, *Tenth Massachusetts Battery,* 341.

29. *OR,* 40(1):488, 601.

30. Hess, *In the Trenches,* 75; *OR,* 40(1):604, 666–68; Chase, *Battery F,* 207; Nevins, *Diary of Battle,* 430.

31. *SOR,* pt. 1, 7:329; Gallagher, *Fighting for the Confederacy,* 436; Joseph William Eggleston Autobiography, 37, VHS.

32. Hess, *Into the Crater,* 63–64, 87, 218–19; *OR,* 40(1):280; "Journal of Siege Operations," 73, Box 1, Hunt Papers, LC.

33. *OR,* 40(1):279–80, 484–85, 600, 605, 658; Nevins, *Diary of Battle,* 443, 445.

34. Hess, *Into the Crater,* 219; Flanner, "Flanner's Battery," 617–18; *OR,* 40(1):485, 759.

35. *OR,* 46(1):1070–72.

36. "Journal of Siege Operations," 127, Box 1, Hunt Papers, LC.

37. "Journal of Siege Operations," 141–42, Box 1, Hunt Papers, LC.

38. *OR,* 42(2):1263; "Journal of Siege Operations," 89–90, 143–45, Box 1, Hunt Papers, LC; Eggleston Autobiography, 37–38, VHS.

39. *OR,* 11(1):339–40, 345, 348, 356–57.

40. *OR,* 11(1):356–58.

41. *OR,* 33:880–81, 40(1):655–56, 672; Abbot to Hunt, May 7, 17, 1864, Box 10, Henry Jackson Hunt Papers, LC.

42. *OR,* 40(1):673, 46(1):172–73, 659–60; "Journal of Siege Operations," 121, Box 1, Hunt Papers, LC.

43. *OR,* 38(1):121, 38(2):488.

44. *OR,* 45(1):334.

14. WORKING TOWARD EFFECTIVENESS

1. Arndt, *Reminiscences,* 4; *OR,* 17(1):262, 20(1):197.

2. *OR,* 19(1):858, 1026, 21:1046.

3. *OR,* 20(1):778–79, 24(2):390.

4. *OR,* 40(1):665–66, 42(1):785; *SOR,* pt. 1, 3:554; Wilkeson, *Turned Inside Out,* 130; *Fifth Massachusetts Battery,* 306–7.

5. *SOR,* pt. 1, 3:516; *OR,* 15:63, 25(1):594; John Merrilles Diary, July 12, 1863, CHM.

6. Hunt, "Third Day at Gettysburg," 373–74.

7. Hunt, "Our Experience in Artillery Administration," 200.

8. Ayers to wife, August 7, 1864, Alexander Miller Ayers Papers, EU; Horace Park to J. S. McBeth, August 2, 1864, University of Georgia, Hargrett Rare Book and Manuscript Library, Athens; Smith, *Seventh Iowa,* 169–70.

9. Gibbon, *Artillerist's Manual,* 357–58; McCrae, "Light Artillery," 521.

10. *OR,* 21:585, 40(1):483; *SOR,* pt. 1, 6:186, 359–60; Gallagher, *Fighting for the Confederacy,* 316, 400.

11. *OR,* 10(1):373, 20(1):935–36, 30(2):518, 38(2):469; *SOR,* pt. 1, 7:653; Boos, "Civil War Diary of Patrick H. White," 656.

12. *OR,* 21:199, 38(1):122, 40(1):483; Wheeler, *Letters,* 395; Gallagher, *Fighting for the Confederacy,* 304.

13. *OR,* 20(1):926, 36(1):652; *SOR,* pt. 1, 3:783, 6:557; Bakewell, "Luck of the War Game," 19; Crumb and Dhalle, *No Middle Ground,* 25; Moore, *Story of a Cannoneer,* 76.

14. Beecher, *First Light Battery Connecticut,* 150–51; *OR,* 25(1):1096, 32(1):302; Webster and Cameron, *First Wisconsin Battery,* 52, 55; Jacob T. Foster Memoirs, 28, 37, WHS.

15. Nevins, *Diary of Battle,* 55; *OR,* 20(1):443, 23(1):579.

16. *OR,* 7:208, 11(2):573; *SOR,* pt. 1, 5:295; Dame, *From the Rapidan to Richmond,* 114.

17. Muir, *Tactics,* 34; Gibbon, *Artillerist's Manual,* 345; *History of the Organization,* 190.

18. *OR,* 36(1):286; "Journal of Siege Operations," 20, Box 1, Henry Jackson Hunt Papers, LC; *OR,* 36(2):701.

19. "Journal of Siege Operations," 139–40, Box 1, Hunt Papers, LC.

20. *SOR,* pt. 1, 4:384–85; *OR,* 38(1):121; Gallagher, *Fighting for the Confederacy,* 246.

21. *OR,* 17(1):310, 20(1):722; *Fifth Massachusetts Battery,* 503.

22. *OR,* 36(1):772, 45(1):498; Walton, *Behind the Guns,* 107.

23. *OR,* 17(1):744, 21:460, 466, 27(3):600; Ramsay, "Light Batteries A, D, F and I," 555; Kaplan, *Artillery Service,* 19.

24. Daniel, *Cannoneers in Gray,* 74; F. A. Shoup to M. D. L. Stephens, ca. July 30, 1864, Featherston Order Book, Winfield Scott Featherston Collection, UM; *OR,* 24(1):592, 31(1):348, 38(1):483.

25. *OR,* 17(1):269, 29(2):237, 36(1):985; Shoup to Thomas Jordan, April 15, 1862, Francis A. Shoup Service Record, M331, NARA.

26. Nevins, *Diary of Battle,* 167; *OR,* 29(2):237–38; Naisawald, *Grape and Canister,* 459–60.

27. *OR,* 17(1):310; *SOR,* pt. 1, 3:783.

28. *OR,* 20(1):843, 21:194, 34(1):630, 38(1):504, 45(1):325, 47(1):877–78; *SOR,* pt. 1, 7:327; Furney, *Reminiscences,* 295; W. W. Carnes to Quintard, February 13, 1895, Charles Todd Quintard Papers, DU.

29. *OR,* 10(1):376, 19(1):326, 30(2):187, 38(2):468, 46(1):1011; Buell, *"Cannoneer,"* 213; John Merrilles Diary, July 17, 1863, CHM; *History of the Organization,* 174 .

30. *OR,* 11(1):418, 11(2):58, 39(1):706; Crumb and Dhalle, *No Middle Ground,* 28; Furney, *Reminiscences,* 74.

31. Nevins, *Diary of Battle,* 59.

32. "Battery A," 36–37, 41–42, Box 2, Folder 23, James Barnett Papers, WRHS; Philander B. Gardner diary, December 31, 1862–January 4, 1863, Box 2, Folder 17, ibid.; *OR,* 20(1):242.

33. William T. Ratliff to J. L. Power, November 5, 1900, Company C, 1st Mississippi Light Artillery Folder, VNMP.

34. Billings, *Tenth Massachusetts Battery,* 324, 340.

35. Furney, *Reminiscences,* 109, 177–78, 190–94, 254–56; *SOR,* pt. 2, 42:383, 388–90.

36. *OR,* 25(1):406; Ladd and Ladd, *Bachelder Papers,* 1:573; Rhodes, *History of Battery B,* 221, 231–33, 236, 332–33, 335.

37. Cushing to mother, January 31, 1863, Harry C. Cushing Letters, UTK.

38. *OR,* 38(3):262–63, 265, 538, 539; *SOR,* pt. 1, 7:47–48, 50.

39. *OR*, 21:189.

40. *OR*, 19(2):632–33, 647–55, 662; Dozier, *Gunner in Lee's Army,* 144.

41. Johnston to Davis, January 2, 1864: memo for Col. Brown, February 8, 1864, "Letters Sent, Aug. 8, 1863–October 20, 1863," [Letter Book, August 8, 1863–October 20, 1864], Box 5, vol. 4, Joseph E. Johnston Papers, Special Collections, College of William and Mary, Williamsburg, VA; copy of Semple to Sir, November 28, 1862, Henry C. Semple Papers, ADAH.

42. Daniel, *Cannoneers in Gray,* 163, 166, 171.

43. Bryan to Brent, February 2, 1865, "Letter Book from November 30th 1864 to March 9th 1865 of Major H. y Bryan Asst. Insp. Gen. of Mil. Div. of the West," P. G. T. Beauregard Papers, LC; *OR*, 45(1):325; Smith to E. Surget, April 15, 1865, Melancthon Smith Service Record, M331, NARA.

44. Wheeler, *Letters,* 405.

45. *OR*, 36(1):286–87, 49(1):742–43; *Revised United States Army Regulations,* 17; Hunt, "Our Experience in Artillery Administration," 215–16.

46. Crumb and Dhalle, *No Middle Ground,* 143–44.

47. "Report of Inspection of Capt. M. Welfley's Battery, second Brigade, first Division at Camp near Keetsville, Mo. March 27th 1862," erroneously filed in folder marked March 13–31, 1864, Ambrose E. Burnside Papers, RG 94, NARA.

48. Nevins, *Diary of Battle,* 105–6, 113–14.

49. Nevins, *Diary of Battle,* 131, 296–97.

50. Cushing to mother, January 31, 1863, Harry C. Cushing Letters, UTK; Collier and Collier, *Yours for the Union,* 229; *OR*, 25(2):120.

51. *OR*, 11(2):912, 29(2):820–21.

52. *OR*, 11(2):168–70.

53. Miller to wife, September 6, 1864, Marshall Mortimer Miller Papers, LC.

54. Furney, *Reminiscences,* 298–99.

55. Stewart, "Battery B," 183.

56. *OR*, 25(1):595, 27(3):600, 40(1):443.

57. Nevins, *Diary of Battle,* 4–5, 7.

58. Wise, *Long Arm of Lee,* 2:564–65.

59. Abbot to Hunt, May 7, 1864, Box 10, Henry Jackson Hunt Papers, LC; J. G. Benton to Hunt, June 15, 23, 1864, Box 2, ibid.; *OR*, 40(1):667.

60. Gallagher, *Fighting for the Confederacy,* 194; William Palfrey to M. H. Wright, June 29, 1864, Francis A. Shoup Service Record, M331, NARA.

61. *OR*, 11(2):511, 30(1):578, 47(1):852, 1041.

62. *OR*, 46(1):668–69, 672.

63. *Fifth Massachusetts Battery,* 947.

64. Smith, *Brother of Mine,* 142; John Merrilles Diary, July 13, 1863, CHM; Blodgett, "Tenth Indiana Battery at Moccasin Point"; Holzhueter, "William Wallace's Civil War Letters," 103; *OR*, 36(1):985, 10(1):565, 20(1):911; Stiles, *Four Years,* 52; Tate, *Col. Frank Huger,* 98; General Order, Headquarters, Artillery, Army of Northern Virginia, September 21, 1864, William N. Pendleton Papers, Museum of the Confederacy, Richmond, VA.

15. AFTER THE CIVIL WAR

1. Furney, *Reminiscences,* 303; Bouton, *Events of the Civil War,* 86.

2. *OR,* 46(3):1238.

3. Squires, "'My Artillery Fire,'" 28.

4. Longacre, *Man behind the Guns,* 231–32.

5. Longacre, *Man behind the Guns,* 232–33; George G. Meade to Sherman, April 1, 1871, William T. Sherman Papers, LC; Ladd and Ladd, *Bachelder Papers,* 1:444, 2:752.

6. Hunt, "Our Experience in Artillery Administration," 198, 202, 217, 220–24; Hunt, "First Day at Gettysburg," 259–60.

7. Birkhimer, *Historical Sketch,* 249–51; Hazlett, Olmsted, and Parks, *Field Artillery Weapons,* 109.

8. Louis Philippe D'Orleans to Hunt, May 20, 1865, Box 2, Henry Jackson Hunt Papers, LC.

9. Hogg, *Artillery,* 107–8, 138; Bailey, *Field Artillery,* 208–9, 211–13.

10. Showalter, *Railroads and Rifles,* 184–85, 187, 191–94, 217–20; Wawro, *Franco-Prussian War,* 57–58; Wawro, *Austro-Prussian War,* 290.

11. Wawro, *Franco-Prussian War,* 29–30, 54–59, 129–30, 158–59, 161–62, 174, 224, 226, 307; Echevarria, *After Clausewitz,* 48; Gudmundsson, *On Artillery,* 1–2, 4.

12. Birkhimer, *Historical Sketch,* 104, 217, 266, 297–98, 321, 326, 328–30.

13. Dastrup, *Field Artillery,* 38–40; Rogers, *History of Artillery,* 127–29, 131–34.

14. Dastrup, *Field Artillery,* 40–41.

15. "Correspondence," 414–15.

16. Wawro, *Austro-Prussian War,* 290; Echevarria, *After Clausewitz,* 141–42, 144, 146, 152–53.

17. Wellons, "Direct Fire," 2, 7; Dastrup, *Field Artillery,* 42–44.

18. Rogers, *History of Artillery,* 156, 161; Gudmundsson, *On Artillery,* 107.

19. Rogers, *History of Artillery,* 162–163.

20. Griffith, *Battle Tactics of the Western Front,* 140, 142, 147–48; Dastrup, *Field Artillery,* 48–49; Stevenson, *To Win the Battle,* 176.

21. Dastrup, *Field Artillery,* 46–47.

22. Gudmundsson, *Stormtroop Tactics,* 161.

23. Neninger, "American Military Effectiveness," 145.

24. Echevarria, *After Clausewitz,* 143; Saunders, *Trench Warfare,* 91; Duménil, "Soldiers' Suffering," 45.

25. Dastrup, *Field Artillery,* 55–58, 62; Rogers, *History of Artillery,* 209.

26. Dastrup, *Field Artillery,* 59–62.

27. Dastrup, *Field Artillery,* 63; Doubler, *Closing with the Enemy,* 301.

28. Doubler, *Closing with the Enemy,* 41, 304, 306.

29. Dastrup, *Field Artillery,* 64–66, 68, 70–72.

30. Bailey, *Field Artillery,* 49–50.

CONCLUSION

1. Naisawald, *Grape and Canister,* 60.

2. Coggins, *Arms and Equipment,* 63.

3. Naisawald, *Grape and Canister,* 445.

4. Hess, *Rifle Musket,* 217–27; Hess, *Civil War Infantry Tactics,* 202–25.

5. Naisawald, *Grape and Canister,* 179; Daniel, *Cannoneers in Gray,* 44, 158.

6. Griffith, *Battle Tactics of the Civil War,* 171, 176–77.

7. McCaul, *Mechanical Fuze,* 9, 77; Nosworthy, *Bloody Crucible,* 428.

8. Griffith, *Battle Tactics of the Civil War,* 169–70.

9. Nosworthy, *Bloody Crucible,* 467.

10. Muir, *Tactics,* 41–42.

11. Muir, *Tactics,* 46–47.

12. Muir, *Tactics,* 42–43.

13. Muir, *Tactics,* 44–46.

14. Naisawald, *Grape and Canister,* viii; Dastrup, *Field Artillery,* 32–33; Jones, "Horse Supply," 374.

15. Griffith, *Battle Tactics of the Civil War,* 166, 179.

16. Griffith, *Battle Tactics of the Civil War,* 170–71.

17. Gallagher, *Fighting for the Confederacy,* 336.

18. Furney, *Reminiscences,* 258.

19. Beecher, *First Light Battery Connecticut,* 433–34, 436–37.

20. Webster and Cameron, *First Wisconsin Battery,* 257–58.

21. Webster and Cameron, *First Wisconsin Battery,* 171.

22. Ladd and Ladd, *Bachelder Papers,* 3:1813–14.

23. Hazlett, Olmstead, and Parks, *Field Artillery Weapons,* 231–302; Bender, "Surviving Artillery List Grows by Six," 9.

BIBLIOGRAPHY

ARCHIVES

Abraham Lincoln Presidential Library, Springfield, IL
> John Alexander Griffen Papers
> Edward H. Ingraham and Duncan G. Ingraham Letters
> Lewis F. Lake Reminiscences
> George O. Pratt Papers
> Cyrus W. Randall Correspondence
> Benjamin T. Smith Reminiscences

Alabama Department of Archives and History, Montgomery
> James Innes Davidson Papers
> Stouten Hubert Dent Papers
> Henry C. Semple Papers
> Joseph Wheeler Family Papers

Augustana College, Special Collections, Rock Island, IL
> Gould D. Molineaux Diaries

Chicago History Museum, Chicago, IL
> William L. Brown Collection
> George Carrington Diary
> John Merrilles Diary
> Tobias Charles Miller Letter
> John A. Nourse Papers
> John D. Toomey Reminiscences

College of William and Mary, Special Collections, Williamsburg, VA
> Joseph E. Johnston Papers

Duke University, Rubenstein Rare Book and Manuscript Library, Durham, NC
> Edward George Washington Butler Papers
> John Warwick Daniel Papers
> Joseph E. Johnston Papers
> J. B. Moore Letter, James Longstreet Papers
> Benjamin F. Nourse Diary
> Charles Todd Quintard Papers

Emory University, Manuscripts, Archives, and Rare Books, Atlanta, GA
  Alexander Miller Ayers Papers
  Andrew Jackson Neal Letters
  Isaac Roseberry Diary
Harvard University, Houghton Library, Cambridge, MA
  Frederick M. Dearborn Collection
Historic New Orleans Collection, New Orleans, LA
  Washington Artillery Letter
Indiana Historical Society, Indianapolis
  Edward Jesup Wood Papers
  Indiana State Library, Indianapolis
  Lucius C. Embree Papers
Kansas Historical Society, Topeka
  August Bondi Papers
Library of Congress, Manuscript Division, Washington, DC
  P. G. T. Beauregard Papers
  Mrs. Douglas W. Clark Collection
  Lucretia Rudolph Garfield Papers
  Henry Jackson Hunt Papers
  Marshall Mortimer Miller Papers
  William T. Sherman Papers
Lincoln Memorial University, Abraham Lincoln Library and Museum, Harrogate, TN
  William Merrell, "Personal Memoirs of the Civil War"
Louisiana State University, Louisiana and Lower Mississippi Valley Collections, Special Collections, Baton Rouge
  E. John and Thomas C. Ellis Family Papers
  William Miller Owen Diary
Massachusetts Historical Society, Boston
  Moses A. Cleveland Journal
Minnesota Historical Society, St. Paul
  Christie Family Letters
  William Z. Clayton Papers
  William Augustus Spaulding Diaries
Mississippi Department of Archives and History, Jackson
  William A. Drennan Papers
Mississippi State University, Special Collections, Starkville
  George W. Sledge Diary
Missouri History Museum, St. Louis
  Thomas S. Hawley Papers

Selden Spencer, "Reminiscences of the Battle of Fort Donelson"
Museum of the Confederacy, Richmond, VA
    William N. Pendleton Papers
National Archives and Records Administration, Washington, DC
    Overton W. Barret Service Record, Barret's Missouri Battery
    William Leroy Brown Service Record, 1st Virginia Artillery
    Ambrose Burnside Papers, RG 94
    Thomas H. Carter Service Record, Officers
    Newit J. Drew Service Record, Battery E, 1st Mississippi Light Artillery
    Richard W. Goldthwaite Service Record, Goldthwaite's Alabama Battery
    Charles R. Grandy Service Record, Norfolk Virginia Light Artillery
    Robert A. Hardaway Service Record, Officers
    John B. Hood Papers, RG 109
    John C. Landis Service Record, Landis's Missouri Battery
    William N. Pendleton Service Record, Officers
    "Records Cleburne's Div. Hardees Corps A of Tenn." Chap. 2, No. 265, RG 109
    Henry C. Semple Service Record, Officers
    Francis A. Shoup Service Record, Officers
    Cuthbert H. Slocomb Service Record, Washington Louisiana Artillery
    Melancthon Smith Service Record, Officers
    Thomas J. Stanford Service Record, Stanford Mississippi Battery
    Charles Swett Service Record, Swett's Mississippi Battery
Navarro College, Pearce Civil War Collection, Corsicana, TX
    William Louis Ritter Papers
    Walter Scates Papers
New York State Library, Albany
    Albert N. Ames Papers
Newberry Library, Chicago, IL
    John C. Fleming Papers
Ohio Historical Society, Columbus
    A. S. Bloomfield Papers
    Hugh Boyd Ewing Papers
Old Court House Museum, Vicksburg, MS
    Albert G. Grammer Diary
    Benjamin W. Underwood Letters
Southern Illinois University, Special Collections Research Center, Carbondale
    Edwin A. Loosley Papers
    John Reese Papers
Stanford University, Special Collections and University Archives, Palo Alto, CA

Edward Otho Cresap Ord Letters

State Historical Society of Missouri, Columbia Research Center, Columbia

Lot Dudley Young Reminiscences

Stones River National Battlefield, Murfreesboro, TN

E. R. Calkins, "Three and One-Half Years in the Civil War," 8th Wisconsin Battery Regimental File

Daniel H. Chandler History, 5th Indiana Battery Regimental File

J. C. Haddock, "Historical Sketch of the 4th Indiana Battery," 4th Indiana Battery Regimental File

McClain Montgomery Letters, 33rd Ohio Regimental File

Thomas C. Potter Letter, Battery B, 1st Ohio Light Artillery Regimental File

John Riddermann Pension Record, Hewitt's Battery B, Kentucky Light Artillery Regimental File

George Gresham Sinclair Letter, 89th Illinois Regimental File

Tennessee State Library and Archives, Nashville

Bradford Nichol Memoirs

Texas Tech University, Southwest Collection / Special Collections Library, Lubbock

J. N. Daniell Letter, McEntire Family Papers

Tulane University, Special Collections, New Orleans, LA

Civil War Papers, Battalion Washington Artillery Collection, Louisiana Research Collection

University of Georgia, Hargrett Rare Book and Manuscript Library, Athens

Horace Park Letters

University of Iowa, Special Collections, Iowa City

Charles Thomas Ackley Civil War Letters

University of Michigan, William L. Clements Library, Ann Arbor

David McKinney Papers

Jacob Van Zwaluevenburg Journal, James M. Schoff Civil War Collections

University of Mississippi, Special Collections, Oxford

Winfield Scott Featherston Collection

William Terry Moore Reminiscences

Charles Roberts Collection

University of North Carolina, Southern History Collection, Chapel Hill

John G. Devereux Papers

Samuel H. Lockett Papers

Charles A. Phillips Letters, Unit 14, Federal Soldiers' Letters

University of Tennessee, Special Collections, Knoxville

Harry C. Cushing Letters

John Watkins Papers

University of Texas, Dolph Briscoe Center for American History, Austin
    John A. Templeton Papers
University of Virginia, Albert and Shirley Small Special Collections, Charlottesville
    Llewellyn Griffin Hoxton Manuscripts
University of Washington, Special Collections, Seattle
    M. F. Force Papers
Vicksburg National Military Park, Vicksburg, MS
    1st Wisconsin Battery Folder
    33rd Illinois Folder
    Battery E, 1st Illinois Artillery folder
    Botetourt Virginia Artillery Folder
    Cherokee Georgia Artillery Folder
    Company A, 1st Mississippi Light Artillery Folder
    Company C, 1st Mississippi Light Artillery Folder
Virginia Historical Society, Richmond
    Joseph William Eggleston Autobiography
Western Reserve Historical Society, Cleveland, OH
    James Barnett Papers
    Francis and John Reiley Papers
Wisconsin Historical Society, Madison
    Emerson Rood Calkins Family Papers
    Jacob T. Foster Memoirs

NEWSPAPER

Memphis Daily Appeal

WEBSITE

Melton, Jack W., Jr. "Cannon Sights." Civil War Artillery Projectiles and Cannon. www.
    civilwarartillery.com/equipment/cannonsights.htm.

ARTICLES AND BOOKS

Aldrich, Thomas M. *The History of Battery A, First Regiment Rhode Island Light Ar-
    tillery in the War to Preserve the Union, 1861–1865.* Providence, RI: Snow and
    Farnham, 1904.
Alexander, E. Porter. "The Great Charge and Artillery Fighting at Gettysburg." In *Bat-
    tles and Leaders of the Civil War,* 4 vols., edited by Robert Underwood Johnson
    and Clarence Clough Buel, 3:357–68. Reprint. New York: Thomas Yoseloff, 1956.
Anderson, Robert. *Instruction for Field Artillery, Horse & Foot, Translated from the*

French and Arranged for the Service of the United States. Philadelphia: R. P. De Silver, 1839.

Andrews, E. *Complete Record of the Surgery of the Battles Fought Near Vicksburg, December 27, 28, 29, & 30, 1862.* Chicago: George H. Fergus, 1863.

Angst, Michael G. "Archaeological Investigations at Morgan Hill, Site 40KN298, University of Tennessee, Knox County, Tennessee." Knoxville: Archaeological Research Laboratory, University of Tennessee, 2012.

Armistead, Gene C. *Horses and Mules in the Civil War: A Complete History with a Roster of More than 700 War Horses.* Jefferson, NC: McFarland, 2013.

Arndt, A. F. R. *Reminiscences of an Artillery Officer: A Paper Read Before the Michigan Commandery of the Military Order of the Loyal Legion of the U.S.* Detroit: Winn and Hammond, 1890.

Bailey, J. B. A. *Field Artillery and Firepower.* Annapolis, MD: Naval Institute Press, 2004.

Baker, Levi. *History of the Ninth Mass. Battery.* South Framingham, MA: J. C. Clark, 1888.

Bakewell, A. Gordon. "The Luck of the War Game Sometimes Makes Heroes." *Illinois Central Magazine* 4, no. 4 (October 1915): 18–20.

Barlow, W. P. "Light Battery Service in 1862." *St. Louis Daily Missouri Republican,* August 1, 1885.

Barnes, James A., James R. Carnahan, and Thomas H. B. McCain. *The Eighty-Sixth Regiment, Indiana Volunteer Infantry.* Crawfordsville, IN: Journal, 1895.

[Bartlett, Napier]. *A Soldier's Story of the War: Including the Marches and Battles of the Washington Artillery, and of Other Louisiana Troops.* New Orleans: Clark and Hofeline, 1874.

Bauer, K. Jack, ed. *Soldiering: The Civil War Diary of Rice C. Bull, 123rd New York Volunteer Infantry.* San Rafael, CA: Presidio, 1977.

Bearss, Edwin C., ed. "Diary of Captain John N. Bell of Co. E, 25th Iowa Infantry, at Vicksburg." *Iowa Journal of History* 59, no. 2 (April 1961): 181–221.

Beecher, Herbert W. *History of the First Light Battery Connecticut Volunteers, 1861–1865.* Vol. 1. New York: A. T. De La Mare, [1901].

Beers, Fannie A. *Memories: A Record of Personal Experience and Adventure during Four Years of War.* Philadelphia: J. B. Lippincott, 1888.

Bender, Jim. "Surviving Artillery List Grows by Six." *Artilleryman* 34, no. 2 (Spring 2013): 9.

Bennett, A. J. *The Story of the First Massachusetts Light Battery.* Boston: Deland and Barta, 1886.

Bergeron, Arthur W., Jr. *Guide to Louisiana Confederate Military Units, 1861–1865.* Baton Rouge: Louisiana State University Press, 1989.

Billings, John D. *Hardtack and Coffee; or, The Unwritten Story of Army Life.* Boston: George M. Smith, 1887.

——. *The History of the Tenth Massachusetts Battery of Light Artillery in the War of the Rebellion, 1862–1865.* Boston: Hall and Whiting, 1909.

Birkhimer, William E. *Historical Sketch of the Organization, Administration, Matériel, and Tactics of the Artillery, United States Army.* Washington, DC: Thomas McGill, 1884.

Black, Samuel. *A Soldier's Recollections of the Civil War.* Minco, OK: Minco Minstrel, 1912.

Blackford, W. W. *War Years with Jeb Stuart.* New York: Charles Scribner's Sons, 1945.

Blodgett, D. G. "The Tenth Indiana Battery at Moccasin Point." *National Tribune,* August 9, 1883.

Boos, J. E., ed. "Civil War Diary of Patrick H. White." *Journal of the Illinois State Historical Society* 15, no. 3–4 (October 1922–January 1923): 640–63.

Boring, B. F. "Fighting for Vicksburg." Pt. 2. *National Tribune,* August 16, 1894.

Bouton, Edward. *Events of the Civil War* [Los Angeles: Kingsley, Moles, & Collins, 1906].

Broun, W. Leroy. *Notes on Artillery: From Robins, Hutton, Chesney, Mordecai, Dahlgreen, Jacob, Greener, Gibbon, and Benton.* Richmond: West and Johnston, 1862.

Budiansky, Stephen. *The Nature of Horses: Exploring Equine Evolution, Intelligence, and Behavior.* New York: Free Press, 1997.

Buell, Augustus. *"The Cannoneer": Recollections of Service in the Army of the Potomac.* Washington, DC: National Tribune, 1890.

Bull, Stephen. *"The Furie of the Ordnance": Artillery in the English Civil Wars.* Woodbridge, Suffolk, UK: Boydell, 2008.

Butler, Watson Hubbard, [ed.]. *Letters Home: Jay Caldwell Butler, Captain, 101st Ohio Volunteer Infantry.* N.p, 1930.

Cameron, Don C. "Bravest of 'Em All: The Artillery Driver, Who Encountered All the Danger, but Got Neither Glory nor Promotion." *National Tribune,* June 18, 1903.

——. "'Standing Up to It': The 1st Wis. Battery Had a Lively Time at Thompson's Hill." *National Tribune,* August 1, 1895.

Campbell, Eric A., ed. *"A Grand Terrible Dramma" from Gettysburg to Petersburg: The Civil War Letters of Charles Wellington Reed.* New York: Fordham University Press, 2000.

Carmichael, Peter S. "'Every Map of the Field Cries Out about It': The Failure of Confederate Artillery at Pickett's Charge." *Three Days at Gettysburg: Essays on Confederate and Union Leadership.* Edited by Gary W. Gallagher, 270–83. Kent, OH: Kent State University Press, 1999.

——. *Lee's Young Artillerist: William R. J. Pegram.* Charlottesville: University Press of Virginia, 1995.

Carnes, W. W. "Artillery at the Battle of Perryville, Ky." *Confederate Veteran* 33 (1925): 8–9.

Cate, Wirt Armistead, ed. *Two Soldiers: The Campaign Diaries of Thomas J. Key, C.S.A. and Robert J. Campbell, U.S.A.* Chapel Hill: University of North Carolina Press, 1938.

Chalaron, J. A. "Battle Echoes from Shiloh." *Southern Historical Society Papers* 21. (1893): 215–24.

———. "Vivid Experiences at Chickamauga." *Confederate Veteran* 3 (1895): 278–79.

Chamberlaine, William W. *Memoirs of the Civil War between the Northern and Southern Sections of the United States of America 1861 to 1865.* Tuscaloosa: University of Alabama Press, 2010.

Chamberlayne, C. G., [ed.]. *Ham Chamberlayne—Virginian: Letters and Papers of an Artillery officer in the War for Southern Independence, 1861–1865.* Richmond: Dietz, 1932.

Chase, Philip S. *Battery F, First Regiment Rhode Island Light Artillery, in the Civil War, 1861–1865.* Providence, RI: Snow and Farnham, 1892.

Clark, William. Comp. *History of Hampton Battery F, Independent Pennsylvania Light Artillery.* Akron, OH: Werner, 1909.

Cockrell, Monroe F., ed. *Gunner with Stonewall: Reminiscences of William Thomas Poague.* Jackson, TN: McCowat-Mercer, 1957.

Coggins, Jack. *Arms and Equipment of the Civil War.* Garden City, NY: Doubleday, 1962.

Collier, John S., and Bonnie B. Collier, eds. *Yours for the Union: The Civil War Letters of John W. Chase, First Massachusetts Light Artillery.* New York: Fordham University Press, 2004.

The Complete Cannoneer: Compiled Agreeably to the Regulations of the War Department as Published in Artillery Drill by Geo. Patten, 1861. 2nd ed. Rochester, MI: Ray Russell Books, 1979.

Copp, Elbridge J. *Reminiscences of the War of the Rebellion, 1861–1865.* Nashua, NJ: Telegraph, 1911.

"Correspondence." *Journal of the Military Service Institution of the United States* 6. (1885): 185, 277–80, 413–15.

"The Correspondence of Ira Butterfield: A Group of Manuscript Letters in the Possession of the State Historical Society of North Dakota." *North Dakota Historical Quarterly* 3, no. 2 (January 1929): 129–44.

Cowan, Andrew. "Cowan's New York Battery." *National Tribune,* November 12, 1908.

Cox, Jacob Dolson. *Military Reminiscences of the Civil War.* 2 vols. New York: Charles Scribner's Sons, 1900.

Crary, Catherine S., ed. *Dear Belle: Letters from a Cadet & Officer to his Sweetheart, 1858–1865.* Middletown, CT: Wesleyan University Press, 1965.

Crist, Lynda Lasswell, ed. *The Papers of Jefferson Davis.* 17 vols. Baton Rouge: Louisiana State University Press, 1971–2008.

Crumb, Herb S., ed. *The Eleventh Corps Artillery at Gettysburg: The Papers of Major Thomas Ward Osborn, Chief of Artillery.* Hamilton, NY: Edmonston, 1991.

Crumb, Herb S., and Katherine Dhalle, eds. *No Middle Ground: Thomas Ward Osborn's Letters from the Field (1862–1864).* Hamilton, NY: Edmonston, 1993.

Cutler, Cyrus Morton. *Letters from the Front from October, 1861, to September, 1864.* [San Francisco, 1892].

Cutrer, Thomas W., ed. *Longstreet's Aide: The Civil War Letters of Major Thomas J. Goree.* Charlottesville: University Press of Virginia, 1995.

Dame, William Meade. *From the Rapidan to Richmond and the Spottsylvania Campaign: A Sketch in Personal Narrative of the Scenes a Soldier Saw.* Baltimore: Green-Lucas, 1920.

[Daniel, Frederick S.]. *Richmond Howitzers in the War: Four Years Campaigning with the Army of Northern Virginia.* Richmond, 1891.

Daniel, Larry J. *Battle of Stones River: The Forgotten Conflict between the Confederate Army of Tennessee and the Union Army of the Cumberland.* Baton Rouge: Louisiana State University Press, 2012.

———. *Cannoneers in Gray: The Field Artillery of the Army of Tennessee, 1861–1865.* Tuscaloosa: University of Alabama Press, 1984.

Dastrup, Boyd L. *The Field Artillery: History and Sourcebook.* Westport, CT: Greenwood, 1994.

[Davidson, Henry Martin]. *History of Battery A, First Regiment of Ohio Vol. Light Artillery.* Milwaukee: Daily Wisconsin Steam Printing, 1865.

Deane, Frank Putnam, II, ed. *"My Dear Wife . . .": The Civil War Letters of David Brett, 9th Massachusetts Battery, Union Cannoneer.* Little Rock: Pioneer, 1964.

"Diary of Jacob Adams, Private in Company F, 21st O.V.V.I." *Ohio Archaeological and Historical Society Publications* 38 (1929): 627–721.

Donnelly, Ralph W. "Rocket Batteries of the Civil War." *Military Affairs* 25, no. 2 (Summer 1961): 69–93.

Doubler, Michael D. *Closing with the Enemy: How GIs Fought the War in Europe, 1944–1945.* Lawrence: University Press of Kansas, 1994.

Douglas, Lucia Rutherford, ed. *Douglas's Texas Battery, CSA.* Tyler, TX: Smith County Historical Society, 1966.

Dozier, Graham T., ed. *A Gunner in Lee's Army: The Civil War Letters of Thomas Henry Carter.* Chapel Hill: University of North Carolina Press, 2014.

Dudley, Henry Walbridge. *Autobiography.* Menasha, WI: George Banta, [1914].

Duffy, Christopher. *Austerlitz, 1805.* Hamden, CT: Archon Books, 1977.

——. *The Military Experience in the Age of Reason.* London: Routledge & Kegan Paul, 1987.

Duménil, Anne. "Soldiers' Suffering and Military Justice in the German Army of the Great War." *Uncovered Fields: Perspectives in First World War Studies.* Edited by Jenny MacLeod and Pierre Purseigle, 43–60. Leiden, Netherlands: Brill, 2004.

Eby, Henry H. *Observations of an Illinois Boy in Battle, Camp, and Prisons, 1861 to 1865.* [Mendota, IL], 1910.

Echevarria, Antulio J., II. *After Clausewitz: German Military Thinkers before the Great War.* Lawrence: University Press of Kansas, 2000.

Ehlen, Judy, and Robert J. Abrahart. "Terrain and Its Affect on the Use of Artillery in the American Civil War: The Battle of Perryville, 8 October 1862." In *Studies in Military Geography and Geology,* edited by Douglas R. Caldwell, Judy Ehlen, Russell S. Harmon, 155–72. Dordrecht, Netherlands: Kluwer Academic, 2004.

The 1864 Field Artillery Tactics. Reprint. Mechanicsville, PA: Stackpole, 2005.

Ellison, Janet Correll, ed. *On to Atlanta: The Civil War Diaries of John Hill Ferguson, Illinois Tenth Regiment of Volunteers.* Lincoln: University of Nebraska Press, 2001.

Epstein, Robert M. "Patterns of Change and Continuity in Nineteenth-Century Warfare." *Journal of Military History* 56, no. 3 (July 1992): 375–88.

Erickson, Edgar L., ed. "With Grant at Vicksburg: From the Civil War Diary of Captain Charles E. Wilcox." *Journal of the Illinois State Historical Society* 30, no. 4 (January 1938): 441–503.

Eskildson, R. E. "Grape and Canister." *National Tribune,* September 12, 1907.

Farr, George A. "Grape in Field Artillery." *National Tribune,* June 6, 1907.

Fenner, Earl. *The History of Battery H First Regiment Rhode Island Light Artillery in the War to Preserve the Union, 1861–1865.* Providence, RI: Snow & Farnham, 1894.

Fitch, John. *Annals of the Army of the Cumberland.* 5th ed. Philadelphia: J. B. Lippincott, 1864.

Fitzhugh, Lester Newton, ed. *Cannon Smoke: The Letters of Captain John J. Good, Good-Douglas Texas Battery, CSA.* Hillsboro, TX: Hill Junior College Press, 1971.

Flanner, Henry G. "Flanner's Battery at the Crater, 30 July, 1864." In *Histories of the Several Regiments and Battalions from North Carolina in the Great War, 1861–'65,* 5 vols., edited by Walter Clark, 5:617–18. Goldsboro, NC: Nash Brothers, 1901.

Fout, Frederick W. *The Dark Days of the Civil War, 1816 to 1865.* N.p.: F. A. Wagenfuehr, 1904.

Furney, L. A., ed. *Reminiscences of the War of the Rebellion, 1861–1865, by Bvt.-Maj. Jacob Roemer.* Flushing, NY: Flushing Journal, 1897.

Gallagher, Gary W., ed. *Fighting for the Confederacy: The Personal Recollections of General Edward Porter Alexander.* Chapel Hill: University of North Carolina Press, 1989.

Gardner, Theodore. "The First Kansas Battery." *Collections of the Kansas State Historical Society* 14 (1915–18): 235–82.

Gibbon, John. *The Artillerist's Manual, Compiled from Various Sources and Adapted to the Service of the United States.* 2nd ed. New York: D. Van Nostrand, 1863.

Gibson, Charles Dana. "Hay: The Linchpin of Mobility." *North & South* 2, no. 2 (January 1999): 51–53.

Glatthaar, Joseph T. *Soldiering in the Army of Northern Virginia: A Statistical Portrait of the Troops Who Served under Robert E. Lee.* Chapel Hill: University of North Carolina Press, 2011.

Gordon, E. C. "The Battle of Big Bethel." In *Contributions to a History of the Richmond Howitzer Battalion,* pamphlet 1, 14–41. Richmond: Carlton McCarthy, 1883.

Gorgas, Josiah. "Contributions to the History of the Confederate Ordnance Department." *Southern Historical Society Papers* 12 (1884): 66–94.

Gould, David, and James B. Kennedy, eds. *Memoirs of a Dutch Mudsill: The "War Memories" of John Henry Otto, Captain, Company D, 21st Regiment Wisconsin Volunteer Infantry.* Kent, OH: Kent State University Press, 2004.

Govan, Gilbert E., and James W. Livingood, eds. *The Haskell Memoirs.* New York: G. P. Putnam's Sons, 1960.

Grandchamp, Robert. *The Boys of Adams' Battery G: The Civil War through the Eyes of a Union Light Artillery Unit.* Jefferson, NC: McFarland, 2009.

Green, Ann N. *Horses at Work: Harnessing Power in Industrial America.* Cambridge, MA: Harvard University Press, 2008.

Griffin, Richard N., ed. *Three Years a Soldier: The Diary and Newspaper Correspondence of Private George Perkins, Sixth New York Independent Battery, 1861–1864.* Knoxville: University of Tennessee Press, 2006.

Griffith, Paddy. *Battle Tactics of the Civil War.* New Haven, CT: Yale University Press, 1989.

———. *Battle Tactics of the Western Front: The British Army's Art of Attack, 1916–18.* New Haven, CT: Yale University Press, 1994.

Gudmundsson, Bruce I. *On Artillery.* Westport, CT: Praeger, 1993.

———. *Stormtroop Tactics: Innovation in the German Army, 1914–1918.* New York: Praeger, 1989.

Hackemer, Kurt H., ed. *To Rescue My Native Land: The Civil War Letters of William T. Shepherd, First Illinois Light Artillery.* Knoxville: University of Tennessee Press, 2005.

Halleck, H. Wager. *Elements of Military Art and Science.* New York: D. Appleton, 1862.

Hamilton, J. G. De Roulhac, ed. *The Papers of Thomas Ruffin.* 4 vols. Raleigh: Edwards and Broughton, 1920.

Hamilton-Williams, David. *Waterloo: New Perspectives.* London: Arms and Armour, 1993.

Harwell, Richard Barksdale, and Philip N. Racine, eds. *The Fiery Trail: A Union Officer's Account of Sherman's Last Campaigns.* Knoxville: University of Tennessee Press, 1986.

Hasegawa, Guy R. "Proposals for Chemical Weapons during the American Civil War." *Military Medicine* 173, no. 5 (May 2008): 499–506.

Haupt Herman. *Military Bridges: With Suggestions of New Expedients and Constructions for Crossing Streams and Chasms.* New York: D. Van Nostrand, 1864.

Hazlett, James C. "The 3-Inch Ordnance Rifle." *Civil War Times Illustrated* 7, no. 8 (December 1968): 30–36.

Hazlett, James C., Edwin Olmstead, and M. Hume Parks. *Field Artillery Weapons of the Civil War.* Rev. ed. Urbana: University of Illinois Press, 2004.

Heiss, Walter R. *Veterinary Service during the American Civil War: A Compilation.* Baltimore: Publish America, 2005.

Hess, Earl J. *Civil War Infantry Tactics: Training, Combat, and Small-Unit Effectiveness.* Baton Rouge: Louisiana State University Press, 2015.

———. *Civil War Logistics: A Study of Military Transportation.* Baton Rouge: Louisiana State University Press, 2017.

———. *Field Armies and Fortifications in the Civil War: The Eastern Campaigns, 1861–1864.* Chapel Hill: University of North Carolina Press, 2005.

———. *Fighting for Atlanta: Tactics, Terrain, and Trenches in the Civil War.* Chapel Hill: University of North Carolina Press, 2018.

———. *In the Trenches at Petersburg: Field Fortifications and Confederate Defeat.* Chapel Hill: University of North Carolina Press, 2009.

———. *Into the Crater: The Mine Attack at Petersburg.* Columbia: University of South Carolina Press, 2010.

———. *The Knoxville Campaign: Burnside and Longstreet in East Tennessee.* Knoxville: University of Tennessee Press, 2012.

———. "The Material Culture of Weapons in the Civil War." In *War Matters: Material Culture in the Civil War Era,* edited by Joan E. Cashin, 99–122. Chapel Hill: University of North Carolina Press, 2018.

———. *Pickett's Charge: The Last Attack at Gettysburg.* Chapel Hill: University of North Carolina Press, 2001.

———. *The Rifle Musket in Civil War Combat: Reality and Myth.* Lawrence: University Press of Kansas, 2008.

———. *Trench Warfare under Grant & Lee: Field Fortifications in the Overland Campaign.* Chapel Hill: University of North Carolina Press, 2007.

————. "The Twelfth Missouri Infantry: A Socio-Military Profile of a Union Regiment." In *A Rough Business: Fighting the Civil War in Missouri,* edited by William Garrett Piston, 145–65. Columbia: State Historical Society of Missouri, 2012.

Hewitt, Lawrence Lee, Thomas E. Schott, and Marc Kunis, eds. *To Succeed or Perish: The Diaries of Sergeant Edmund Trent Eggleston, 1st Mississippi Light Artillery Regiment, CSA.* Knoxville: University of Tennessee Press, 2015.

Hight, John J. *History of the Fifty-Eighth Regiment of Indiana Volunteer Infantry.* Princeton, IN: Clarion, 1895.

Hinman, Wilbur F. *The Story of the Sherman Brigade.* [Alliance, OH: Daily Review Press], 1897.

Historical Sketch of the Chicago Board of Trade Battery Horse Artillery, Illinois Volunteers. Chicago: Henneberry, 1902.

History of the Eleventh Pennsylvania Volunteer Cavalry Together with a Complete Roster of the Regiment and Regimental Officers. Philadelphia: Franklin, 1902.

History of the Fifth Massachusetts Battery. Boston: Luther E. Cowles, 1902.

History of the Fourth Maine Battery Light Artillery in the Civil War, 1861–65. Augusta, ME: Burleigh and Flynt, 1905.

History of the Organization, Marches, Campings, General Services, and Final Muster Out of Battery M, First Regiment Illinois Light Artillery. Princeton, IL: Mercer and Dean, 1892.

Hogan, Sally Coplen, ed. *General Reub Williams's Memories of Civil War Times.* Westminster, MD: Heritage Books, 2004.

Hogg, O. F. G. *Artillery: Its Origin, Heyday, and Decline.* Hamden, CT: Archon Books, 1970.

Holzhueter, John O., ed. "William Wallace's Civil War Letters: The Atlanta Campaign." *Wisconsin Magazine of History* 57, no. 2 (Winter 1973–74): 90–116.

Howard, Oliver Otis. *Autobiography.* 2 vols. New York: Baker and Taylor, 1907.

Howe, Daniel Wait. *Civil War Times, 1861–1865.* Indianapolis: Bowen-Merrill, 1902.

Hoy, P. C. *A Brief History of Bradford's Battery, Confederate Guards Artillery.* Petersburg, VA, 1903.

Hsieh, Wayne Wei-siang. *West Pointers and the Civil War: The Old Army in War and Peace.* Chapel Hill: University of North Carolina Press, 2009.

Hughes, Nathaniel Cheairs, Jr., ed. *The Civil War Memoir of Philip Daingerfield Stephenson, D.D.: Private, Company K, 13th Arkansas Volunteer Infantry and Loader, Piece No. 4, 5th Company, Washington Artillery, Army of Tennessee, CSA.* Conway: University of Central Arkansas Press, 1995.

————. *The Pride of the Confederate Artillery: The Washington Artillery in the Army of Tennessee.* Baton Rouge: Louisiana State University Press, 1997.

Hunt, Henry J. "The First Day at Gettysburg." In *Battles and Leaders of the Civil War*, 4 vols., edited by Robert Underwood Johnson and Clarence Clough Buel, 3:255–84. Reprint. New York: Thomas Yoseloff, 1956.

———. "Our Experience in Artillery Administration." *Journal of the Military Service Institution of the United States* 12, no. 49 (March 1891): 197–224.

———. "The Third Day at Gettysburg." In *Battles and Leaders of the Civil War*, 4 vols., edited by Robert Underwood Johnson and Clarence Clough Buel, 3:369–85. Reprint. New York: Thomas Yoseloff, 1956.

Imboden, John D. "Incidents of the First Bull Run." In *Battles and Leaders of the Civil War*, 4 vols., edited by Robert Underwood Johnson and Clarence Clough Buel, 1:229–39. Reprint. New York: Thomas Yoseloff, 1956.

Instruction for Field Artillery. Philadelphia: J. B. Lippincott, 1860.

Instruction for Field Artillery. New York: Greenwood, 1968.

Instruction for Field Artillery. Mechanicsburg, PA: Stackpole Books, 2005.

Jackson, Joseph Orville, ed. *"Some of the Boys…": The Civil War Letters of Isaac Jackson, 1862–1865*. Carbondale: Southern Illinois University Press, 1960.

Johnson, Curt, and Richard C. Anderson Jr. *Artillery Hell: The Employment of Artillery at Antietam*. College Station: Texas A&M University Press, 1995.

Johnson, R. W. *A Soldier's Reminiscences in Peace and War*. Philadelphia: J. B. Lippincott, 1886.

[Jones, Benjamin W.] *Under the Stars and Bars: A History of the Surry Light Artillery*. Richmond: Everett Waddey, 1909.

Jones, Charles H. *Artillery Fuses of the Civil War*. Alexandria, VA: O'Donnell, 2001.

Jones, J. H. "The Rank and File at Vicksburg." *Publications of the Mississippi Historical Society* 7 (1903): 17–31.

Jones, Jenkin Lloyd. *An Artilleryman's Diary*. [Madison, WI]: Democrat Printing, 1914.

Jones, Spencer. "The Influence of Horse Supply upon Field Artillery in the American Civil War." *Journal of Military History* 74, no. 2 (April 2010): 357–77.

Kaplan, Lawrence M., ed. *The Artillery Service in the War of the Rebellion, 1861–65*. Yardley, PA: Westholme, 2011.

Kerksis, Sydney C., and Thomas S. Dickey. *Heavy Artillery Projectiles of the Civil War, 1861–1865*. Kennesaw, GA: Phoenix, 1972.

Kimbell, Charles B. *History of Battery "A" First Illinois Light Artillery Volunteers*. Chicago: Cushing, 1899.

Krause, Jonathan. "The French Battle for Vimy Ridge, Spring 1915." *Journal of Military History* 77, no. 1 (January 2013): 91–113.

Krick, Robert K. *Parker's Virginia Battery, C.S.A.* Wilmington, NC: Broadfoot, 1989.

Kross, Gary M. "'I Do Not Believe That Pickett's Division Would Have Reached Our Line.' Henry J. Hunt and the Union Artillery on July 3, 1863." In *Three Days at Get-*

tysburg: Essays on Confederate and Union Leadership, edited by Gary W. Gallagher, 284–305. Kent, OH: Kent State University Press, 1999.

Laboda, Lawrence R. *From Selma to Appomattox: The History of the Jeff Davis Artillery.* New York: Oxford University Press, 1996.

Ladd, David L., and Audrey J. Ladd, eds. *The Bachelder Papers: Gettysburg in Their Own Words.* 3 vols. Dayton, OH: Morningside, 1994–95.

Landry, R. Prosper. "The Donaldsonville Artillery at the Battle of Fredericksburg." *Southern Historical Society Papers* 23 (1895): 198–202.

Lapham, William B. *My Recollections of the War of the Rebellion.* Augusta, ME: Burleigh and Flynt, 1892.

Lathrop, Barnes F. "A Confederate Artilleryman at Shiloh." *Civil War History* 8, no. 4 (December 1962): 373–85.

Lee, Susan P. *Memoirs of William Nelson Pendleton, D.D.* Philadelphia: J. B. Lippincott, 1893.

Lewis, George. *The History of Battery E, First Regiment Rhode Island Light Artillery, in the War of 1861 and 1865, to Preserve the Union.* Providence, RI: Snow & Farnham, 1892.

Lippitt, Francis J. *A Treatise on the Tactical Use of the Three Arms: Infantry, Artillery, and Cavalry.* Harrah, OK: Brandy Station Bookshelf, 1994.

Little, George, and James R. Maxwell. *A History of Lumsden's Battery, C.S.A.* Tuscaloosa, AL: R. E. Rhodes Chapter United Daughters of the Confederacy, [1905].

Longacre, Edward G. *The Man behind the Guns: A Biography of General Henry Jackson Hunt, Chief of Artillery, Army of the Potomac.* South Brunswick, NJ: A. S. Barnes, 1977.

Lord, Francis A. "Army and Navy Textbooks and Manuals Used by the North during the Civil War—Part II." *Military Collector and Historian* 9 (1957): 95–102.

———. "The Coehorn Mortar." *Civil War Times Illustrated* 5, no. 5 (August 1966): 18–19.

Lynn, John A. *The Bayonets of the Republic: Motivation and Tactics in the Army of Revolutionary France, 1791–94.* Urbana: University of Illinois Press, 1984.

———. "Forging the Western Army in Seventeenth Century France." In *The Dynamics of Military Revolution, 1300–2050,* edited by MacGregor Knox and Williamson Murray, 45–66. Cambridge, UK: Cambridge University Press, 2001.

———. *Giant of the Grand Siècle: The French Army, 1610–1715.* New York: Cambridge University Press, 1997.

Mahan, D. H. *An Elementary Treatise of Advanced-Guard, Out-Post, and Detachment Service of Troops, and the Manner of Posting and Handling Them in Presence of an Enemy.* New Orleans: Bloomfield and Steel, 1861.

Mallet, J. W. "Work of the Ordnance Bureau." *Southern Historical Society Papers* 37 (1909): 1–20.

Malone, Thomas H. *Memoir.* Nashville: Baird-Ward, 1928.

Maxwell, James Robert. *Autobiography of James Robert Maxwell of Tuskaloosa, Alabama.* New York: Greenberg, 1926.

Maxwell, Jerry. *The Perfect Lion: The Life and Death of Confederate Artillerist John Pelham.* Tuscaloosa: University of Alabama Press, 2011.

McCaul, Edward B., Jr. *The Mechanical Fuze and the Advance of Artillery in the Civil War.* Jefferson, NC: McFarland, 2010.

McCrae, Tully. "Light Artillery: Its Use and Misuse." *Journal of the Military Service Institution of the United States* 22, no. 93 (May 1898): 519–33.

McGreevy, Paul, and Andrew McLean. "Behavioural Problems with the Ridden Horse." In *The Domestic Horse: The Origins, Development and Management of its Behaviour,* edited by D. S. Mills and S. M. McDonnell, 196–211. Cambridge, UK: Cambridge University Press, 2005.

McKee, W. Reid, and M. E. Mason Jr. *Civil War Projectiles: Small Arms and Field Artillery.* N.p., 1971.

McWhiney, Grady, and Perry D. Jamieson. *Attack and Die: Civil War Military Tactics and the Southern Heritage.* Tuscaloosa: University of Alabama Press, 1982.

The Medical and Surgical History of the Civil War. 12 vols. Wilmington, NC: Broadfoot, 1991.

Melton, Jack W., and Lawrence E. Pawl. *Guide to Civil War Artillery Projectiles.* N.p.: Kennesaw Mountain, 1996.

Merrill, J. W., comp. *Records of the 24th Independent Battery, N.Y. Light Artillery, U.S.V.* Perry, NY: Ladies' Cemetery Association, 1870.

Military History and Reminiscences of the Thirteenth Regiment of Illinois Volunteer Infantry in the Civil War in the United States, 1861–1865. Chicago: Woman's Temperance, 1892.

A Military Record of Battery D First Ohio Veteran Volunteers Light Artillery. Oil City, PA: Derrick, 1908.

Moore, Edward A. *The Story of a Cannoneer under Stonewall Jackson.* Lynchburg, VA: J. P. Bell, 1910.

Morse, Charles F. *Letters Written during the War, 1861–1865.* Boston: T. R. Marvin, 1898.

Morton, John Watson. *The Artillery of Nathan Bedford Forrest's Cavalry.* Nashville: M. E. Church, South, Publishing, 1909.

Muir, Rory. *Tactics and the Experience of Battle in the Age of Napoleon.* New Haven, CT: Yale University Press, 1998.

Murphy, Douglas A. *Two Armies on the Rio Grande: The First Campaign of the US–Mexican War.* College Station: Texas A&M University Press, 2015.

Naisawald, L. Van Loan. *Grape and Canister: The Story of the Field Artillery of the Army of the Potomac, 1861–1865.* New York: Oxford University Press, 1960.

Neil, Henry M. *A Battery at Close Quarters: Paper Read before the Ohio Commandery of the Loyal Legion, October 6, 1909.* Columbus, OH: Champlin, 1909.

Nenninger, Timothy K. "American Military Effectiveness in the First World War." In *The First World War, vol. 1 of Military Effectiveness, edited by* Allan R. Millett and Williamson Murray, 116–56. Boston: Allen & Unwin, 1988.

Nesmith, V. E. "Stagnation and Change in Military Thought: The Evolution of American Field Artillery Doctrine, 1861–1905—An Example." Master's thesis, US Army Command and General Staff College, 1976.

Nevins, Allan, ed. *A Diary of Battle: The Personal Journals of Colonel Charles S. Wainwright, 1861–1865.* New York: Harcourt, Brace, and World, 1962.

[Newsome, Edmund]. *Experience in the War of the Great Rebellion.* Carbondale, IL: E. Newsome, 1879.

Nosworthy, Brent. *The Anatomy of Victory: Battle Tactics, 1689–1763.* New York: Hippocrene Books, 1992.

——. *The Bloody Crucible of Courage: Fighting Methods and Combat Experience of the Civil War.* New York: Carroll and Graf, 2003.

——. *With Musket, Cannon, and Sword: Battle Tactics of Napoleon and His Enemies.* New York: Sarpedon, 1996.

O'Brien, J. Emmet. "Telegraphing in Battle." In *Battles and Leaders of the Civil War,* vol. 6, ed. Peter Cozzens, 476–91. Urbana: University of Illinois Press, 2004.

The Ordnance Manual for the Use of the Officers of the Confederate States Army: Prepared under the Direction of Col. J. Gorgas, Chief of Ordnance, and Approved by the Secretary of War. Dayton, OH: Morningside Bookshop, 1976.

The Ordnance Manual for the Use of the Officers of the United States Army. 3rd ed. Philadelphia: J. B. Lippincott, 1862.

Otto, John. *History of the 11th Indiana Battery Connected with an Outline History of the Army of the Cumberland during the War of the Rebellion, 1861–1865.* Fort Wayne, IN: W. D. Page, 1894.

Owen, William Miller. "A Hot Day on Marye's Heights." In *Battles and Leaders of the Civil War,* 4 vols., edited by Robert Underwood Johnson and Clarence Clough Buel, 3:97–99. Reprint. New York: Thomas Yoseloff, 1956.

Perkins, John D. *Daniel's Battery: The 9th Texas Field Battery.* Hillsboro, TX: Hill College Press, 1998.

Pierson, Stephen. "From Chattanooga to Atlanta in 1864: A Personal Reminiscence." *Proceedings of the New Jersey Historical Society* 16, no. 3 (July 1931): 324–56.

Poe, Orlando M. *Personal Recollections of the Occupation of East Tennessee and the Defense of Knoxville.* Detroit: Ostler Printing, 1889.

Pooley-Ebert, Andria. "Species Agency: A Comparative Study of Horse-Human Relationships in Chicago and Rural Illinois." In *The Historical Animal,* edited by Susan Nance, 148–65. Syracuse, NY: Syracuse University Press, 2015.

Popchock, Barry, ed. *Soldier Boy: The Civil War Letters of Charles O. Musser, 29th Iowa.* Iowa City: University of Iowa Press, 1995.

Portrait Biographical Album of Oakland County, Michigan. Chicago: Chapman Brothers, 1891.

Prince, Justin G. *Million-Dollar Barrage: American Field Artillery in the Great War.* Norman: University of Oklahoma Press, 2021.

Proceedings of the Eighth Annual Session of the Survivors of the Battle of Stone's River. N.p.: Survivors of the Battle of Stones River, [1908].

"The Purcell Battery." *Southern Historical Society Papers* 21 (1893): 362–65.

Quimby, Robert S. *The Background of Napoleonic Warfare: The Theory of Military Tactics in Eighteenth-Century France.* New York: Columbia University Press, 1957.

Ramsay, John A. "Light Batteries A, D, F and I." In *Histories of the Several Regiments and Battalions from North Carolina in the Great War, 1861–'65,* 5 vols., edited by Walter Clark, 1:551–82. Raleigh: E. M. Uzzell, 1901.

"A Rebel Bull Session on Guns." *Civil War Times Illustrated* 6, no. 5 (August 1967): 26–29.

Reeves, Matthew B. *Dropped and Fired: Archeological Patterns of Militaria from Two Civil War Battles, Manassas National Battlefield Park, Manassas, Virginia.* Regional Archeology Program Occasional Report 15. US Department of the Interior, 2001.

Reichardt, Theodore. *Diary of Battery A, First Regiment Rhode Island Light Artillery.* Providence, RI: N. Bangs Williams, 1865.

Reminiscences of the Cleveland Light Artillery. Cleveland, OH: Cleveland Print, 1906.

Report of the Joint Committee on the Conduct of the War. 8 vols. Wilmington, NC: Broadfoot, 1998.

Revised United States Army Regulations of 1861. Washington, DC: Government Printing Office, 1863.

Rhodes, John H. *The Gettysburg Gun: Personal Narratives of Events in the War of the Rebellion, Being Papers Read before the Rhode Island Soldiers' and Sailors' Historical Society, Fourth Series, No. 19.* Providence, RI: Snow and Farnham, 1892.

———. *The History of Battery B, First Regiment Rhode Island Light Artillery in the War to Preserve the Union, 1861–1865.* Providence, RI: Snow and Farnham, 1894.

Ritter, William L. "Sketch of Third Battery Maryland Artillery." Pt. 4. *Southern Historical Society Papers* 11 (1883): 113–18.

———. "Sketch of Third Battery Maryland Artillery." Pt. 5. *Southern Historical Society Papers* 11 (1883): 186–93.

——. "Sketches of the Third Maryland Artillery." *Southern Historical Society Papers* 11 (1883): 433–42.

Roberts, Joseph. *The Hand-Book of Artillery, for the Service of the United States (Army and Militia).* 5th ed. New York: D. Van Nostrand, 1863.

Robertson, James I., Jr., ed. "'The Boy Artillerist': Letters of Colonel William Pegram, C.S.A." *Virginia Magazine of History and Biography* 98, no. 2 (April 1990): 221–60.

——. *The Civil War Letters of General Robert McAllister.* New Brunswick, NJ: Rutgers University Press, 1965.

Rogers, H. C. B. *A History of Artillery.* Secaucus, NJ: Citadel, 1975.

[Rood, Hosea]. *Story of the Service of Company E, and of the Twelfth Wisconsin Regiment, Veteran Volunteer Infantry, in the War of the Rebellion.* Milwaukee: Swain and Tate, 1893.

Rowell, John W. *Yankee Artillerymen: Through the Civil War with Eli Lilly's Indiana Battery.* Knoxville: University of Tennessee Press, 1975.

Rowland, Dunbar, ed. *Jefferson Davis, Constitutionalist: His Letters, Papers and Speeches.* 10 vols. New York: J. J. Little & Ives, 1923.

Runge, William H., ed. *Four Years in the Confederate Artillery: The Diary of Private Henry Robinson Berkeley.* Chapel Hill: University of North Carolina Press, 1961.

Saunders, Anthony. *Trench Warfare, 1850–1950.* Barnsley, South Yorkshire, UK: Pen & Sword, 2010.

Scott, Douglas D. "Civil War Archaeology in the Trans-Mississippi West." In *From These Honored Dead: Historical Archaeology of the American Civil War,* edited by Clarence R. Geier, Douglas D. Scott, and Lawrence E. Babits, 7–25. Gainesville: University Press of Florida, 2014.

Scott, H. L. *Military Dictionary.* New York: D. Van Nostrand, 1861.

Scott, Shelly R. "The Racehorse as Protagonist: Agency, Independence, and Improvisation." In *Animals and Agency: An Interdisciplinary Exploration,* edited by Sarah E. McFarland and Ryan Hediger, 45–65. Leiden, Netherlands: Brill, 2009.

Sears, Cyrus. "The 11th Ohio Battery at Iuka." *National Tribune,* November 6, 1884.

Sears, Stephen W. *To the Gates of Richmond: The Peninsula Campaign.* New York: Ticknor & Fields, 1992.

Sharrer, G. Terry. "The Great Glanders Epizootic, 1861–1866." *Agricultural History* 69, pt. 1 (Winter 1995): 79–97.

Shea, William L., and Earl J. Hess. *Pea Ridge: Civil War Campaign in the West.* Chapel Hill: University of North Carolina Press, 1992.

Sherman, William T. *Memoirs.* 2 vols. New York: D. Appleton, 1875.

Showalter, Dennis E. *Railroads and Rifles: Soldiers, Technology, and the Unification of Germany.* Hamden, CT: Archon Books, 1975.

———. *The Wars of Frederick the Great.* London: Longman, 1996.

Shultz, David. *"Double Canister at Ten Yards": The Federal Artillery and the Repulse of Pickett's Charge.* Redondo Beach, CA: Rank and File, 1995.

Smith, H. I. *History of the Seventh Iowa Veteran Volunteer Infantry during the Civil War.* Mason City, IA: E. Hitchcock, 1903.

Smith, Hampton, [ed.]. *Brother of Mine: The Civil War Letters of Thomas and William Christie.* St. Paul: Minnesota Historical Society, 2011.

Smith, Tunstall, ed. *Richard Snowden Andrews, Lieutenant-Colonel Commanding the First Maryland Artillery (Andrews' Battalion) Confederate States Army.* [Baltimore]: Sun Job, 1910.

Spring, Matthew H. *With Zeal and with Bayonets Only: The British Army on Campaign in North America, 1775–1783.* Norman: University of Oklahoma Press, 2008.

Squires, Charles W. "The 'Boy Officer' of the Washington Artillery." *Civil War Times Illustrated* 14, no. 2 (May 1975): 10–17, 19–23.

———. "My Artillery Fire Was Very Destructive." *Civil War Times Illustrated* 14, no. 3 (June 1975): 18–28.

Stevenson, Robert. *To Win the Battle: The 1st Australian Division in the Great War, 1914–18.* Cambridge, UK: Cambridge University Press, 2013.

Stewart, James. "Battery B Fourth United States Artillery at Gettysburg." In *Sketches of War History, 1861–1865: Papers Prepared for the Ohio Commandery of the Military Order of the Loyal Legion of the United States, 1890–1896,* 4:180–93. Wilmington, NC: Broadfoot, 1991.

Stiles, Robert. *Four Years under Marse Robert.* New York: Neale, 1903.

Straith, Hector. *Treatise on Fortification and Artillery.* 7th Edition. London: William H. Allen, 1858.

Sumner, George C. *Battery D, First Rhode Island Light Artillery in the Civil War, 1861–1865.* Providence: Rhode Island Printing, 1897.

Supplement to the Official Records of the Union and Confederate Armies. 100 vols. Wilmington: Broadfoot, 1995–99.

Sykes, E. T. *Walthall's Brigade.* [Columbus, MS, 1905].

Tapert, Annette, ed. *The Brothers' War: Civil War Letters to Their Loved Ones from the Blue and Gray.* New York: Vintage, 1988.

Tate, Thomas K., ed. *Col. Frank Huger, C.S.A.: The Civil War Letters of a Confederate Artillery Officer.* Jefferson, NC: McFarland, 2011.

Thomas, Dean S. *Cannons: An Introduction to Civil War Artillery.* Arendtsville, PA: Thomas, 1985.

Tourgée, Albion W. *The Story of a Thousand: Being a History of the Service of the 105th Ohio Volunteer Infantry, in the War for the Union from August 21, 1862, to June 6, 1865.* Buffalo, NY: S. McGerald & Son, 1896.

Tower, R. Lockwood, ed. *A Carolinian Goes to War: The Civil War Narrative of Arthur Middleton Manigault, Brigadier General, C.S.A.* Columbia: University of South Carolina Press, 1983.

Tracie, Theodore C. *Annals of the Nineteenth Ohio Battery Volunteer Artillery.* Cleveland: J. B. Savage, 1878.

Trepal, Dan. "The Gun Foundry Recast." *IA: Journal of the Society for Industrial Archeology* 35, no. 1–2 (2009): 73–90.

Trout, Robert J., ed. *Memoirs of the Stuart Horse Artillery Battalion: Moorman's and Hart's Batteries.* [Vol. 1]. Knoxville: University of Tennessee Press, 2008.

Tuthill, Richard S. "An Artilleryman's Recollections of the Battle of Atlanta." In *Military Essays and Recollections: Papers Read before the Commandery of the State of Illinois, Military Order of the Loyal Legion of the United States,* 1:293–309. Chicago: A. C. McClurg, 1891.

Twitchell, A. S. *History of the Seventh Maine Light Battery, Volunteers in the Great Rebellion.* Boston: E. B. Stillings, 1892.

Vance, Robert B. "Twenty-Ninth Regiment." In *Histories of the Several Regiments and Battalions from North Carolina in the Great War, 1861–'65,* 5 vols., edited by Walter Clark, 2:485–94. Goldsboro, NC: Nash Brothers, 1901.

Walton, Clyde C., ed. *Behind the Guns: The History of Battery I, 2nd Regiment, Illinois Light Artillery.* Carbondale: Southern Illinois University Press, 1965.

Waran, Natalie K., and Rachel Casey. "Horse Training." In *The Domestic Horse: The Origins, Development and Management of its Behaviour,* edited by D. S. Mills and S. M. McDonnell, 184–95. Cambridge, UK: Cambridge University Press, 2005.

Warner, Ezra J. *Generals in Blue: Lives of the Union Commanders.* Baton Rouge: Louisiana State University Press, 1964.

——. *Generals in Gray: Lives of the Confederate Commanders.* Baton Rouge: Louisiana State University Press, 1959.

The War of the Rebellion: A Compilation of the Official Records of the Union and Confederate Armies. 70 vols. in 128 pts. Washington, DC: Government Printing Office, 1880–1901.

Wawro, Geoffrey. *The Austro-Prussian War: Austria's War with Prussia and Italy in 1866.* New York: Cambridge University Press, 1996.

——. *The Franco-Prussian War: The German Conquest of France in 1870–1871.* New York: Cambridge University Press, 2003.

Way, Virgil G. *History of the Thirty-Third Regiment Illinois Veteran Volunteer Infantry.* Gibson City, IL: Gibson Courier, 1902.

Webster, Dan, and Don C. Cameron. *History of the First Wisconsin Battery Light Artillery.* N.p., 1907.

Wellons, Dave. "Direct Fire to Indirect Fire: Changing Artillery for the Future?" School of Advanced Military Studies, US Army Command and General Staff College, Fort Leavenworth, KS, 2000.

Wheeler, William. *Letters of William Wheeler of the Class of 1855, Y.C.* Cambridge, MA: H. O. Houghton, 1875.

White, William S. "A Diary of the War; or, What I Saw of It." In *Contributions to a History of the Richmond Howitzer Battalion,* pamphlet 2, 89–286. Richmond: Carlton McCarthy, 1883.

Wild, Frederick W. *Memoirs and History of Capt. F. W. Alexander's Baltimore Battery of Light Artillery, U.S.V.* Loch Raven, MD: Maryland School for Boys, 1912.

Wiley, Bell Irvin, ed. *Confederate Letters of John W. Hagan.* Athens: University of Georgia Press, 1954.

———, ed. *Reminiscences of Confederate Service, 1861–1865.* Baton Rouge: Louisiana State University Press, 1980.

Wiley, Kenneth, ed. *Norfolk Blues: The Civil War Diary of the Norfolk Light Artillery Blues.* Shippensburg, PA: Burd Street, 1997.

Wilkeson, Frank. *Turned Inside Out: Recollections of a Private Soldier in the Army of the Potomac.* Lincoln: University of Nebraska Press, 1997.

Williams, A. B. "Company C—Light Battery." In *Histories of the Several Regiments and Battalions from North Carolina in the Great War, 1861–'65,* 5 vols., edited by Walter Clark, 1:537–50. Raleigh: E. M. Uzzell, 1901.

Williams, Robert W., Jr., and Ralph A. Wooster, eds. "With Terry's Texas Rangers: The Letters of Dunbar Affleck." *Civil War History* 9, no. 3 (September 1963): 299–319.

Wise, Jennings Cropper. *The Long Arm of Lee; or, The History of the Artillery of the Army of Northern Virginia.* 2 vols. Lynchburg, VA: J. P. Bell, 1915.

Woodruff, George H. *Fifteen Years Ago; or, The Patriotism of Will County.* Joliet, IL: Joliet Republican, 1876.

INDEX